USES OF HERIT

Utilizing the latest research, including that from the UK, Australia and the United States, this book re-theorizes the idea of heritage. Smith challenges traditional Western definitions of heritage that focus on material and monumental forms of 'old', or aesthetically pleasing, tangible heritage, which are all too often used to promote an unchallenging consensual view of both the past and the present. An alternative conception of heritage is developed which establishes and develops themes of memory, performance, identity, intangibility, dissonance and place.

Using this theoretical framework the book explores a number of detailed case studies, which document both the ways in which heritage is used in a socially conservative fashion, and cases where heritage is used to actively question received ideas about identity. In these case studies the links between material culture and identity are identified and explored, based on extensive qualitative and ethnographic research. A picture emerges that suggests people are more active and mindful in their use of 'heritage' than has previously been assumed.

Examples include the English country house, industrial social history museums, working class community heritage, international heritage Charters and Conventions, Australian landscapes and Indigenous communities' use of heritage. This challenging and thought-provoking work confronts the assumptions often found in the study and use of heritage and will be a valuable resource for students and heritage practitioners.

Laurajane Smith is a Senior Lecturer in Cultural Heritage Studies and Archaeology at the University of York. She previously taught Indigenous Studies at the University of New South Wales, Sydney, and worked as a cultural heritage consultant for many years.

USES OF HERITAGE

Laurajane Smith

Routledge
Taylor & Francis Group

LONDON AND NEW YORK

First published 2006
by Routledge
2 Park Square, Milton Park, Abingdon, Oxon OX14 4RN

Simultaneously published in the USA and Canada
by Routledge
711 Third Avenue, New York, NY 10017

Routledge is an imprint of the Taylor & Francis Group, an informa business

© 2006 Laurajane Smith

Typeset in Garamond 3 by
RefineCatch Limited, Bungay, Suffolk
Printed and bound in Great Britain by
CPI Antony Rowe, Chippenham, Wiltshire

British Library Cataloguing in Publication Data
A catalogue record for this book is available
from the British Library

Library of Congress Cataloging in Publication Data

ISBN10: 0–415–31830–0 (hbk)
ISBN10: 0–415–31831–9 (pbk)
ISBN10: 0–203–60226–9 (ebk)

ISBN13: 978–0–415–31830–3 (hbk)
ISBN13: 978–0–415–31831–0 (pbk)
ISBN13: 978–0–203–60226–3 (ebk)

FOR GARY, HAMISH AND MAHALIA

CONTENTS

CONTENTS

FIGURES

TABLES

ACKNOWLEDGEMENTS

The British Academy funded the research discussed in Chapters 4, 6 and 7. An Australian Research Council Small Grant gained through the University of New South Wales funded the research discussed in Chapter 5.

I would like to thank the following people and institutions for graciously giving me and my survey team permission to conduct survey work on their grounds: May Redfern, Harewood House; Emma Carver, English Heritage; Bobbie Robinson, National Trust, Nostell Priory; Pippa Shirley, National Trust, Waddesdon Manor; Richard Saward, National Coal Mining Museum for England (NCMM); Trish Hall, North of England Open Air Museum, Beamish; Janet Pickering, Tolpuddle Martyrs Museum. I also want to thank Rhiannon Hiles (Beamish) and Rosemary Preece, (NCMM) for allowing me to interview them. Any misinterpretation of interview materials I acknowledge to be my own.

The following people helped administer the questionnaire surveys on which Chapters 4 and 6 are based: Gary Campbell, Dr Peter Gouldsborough, Sally Huxtable, Cath Neal, Lila Rakoczy, Emma Waterton, Rob Webley and Kate Wescombe. Anita van der Meer helped administer the questionnaires discussed in Chapter 5.

I am very grateful to the Castleford Heritage Trust (CHT), especially its executive committee, for allowing me to interview them, attend meetings and generally pester them with questions. Not only did they put up with me, but they also made me feel very welcome indeed. In particular, I want to very warmly thank: Alison Drake, Derek Catherall, Erick Crossland, Reg Lavine, Winifred McLoughlin, Harry Malkin, Hazel Parks, Shirley Schofield, Roy Sivorn, Greta Sharkey, David Wilders. Lorna Hay, Heritage Development Office, CHT, very kindly gave me her time and patience, helped organize interviews, and greatly facilitated my research. I want to thank all those people in Castleford, both members of the CHT and other residents who allowed me to interview them – I am unable to list everyone here, but thank you for giving me your time and patience, and allowing me into your homes and sharing your memories and recollections with me. Any errors in fact or in the interpretation of interview data are entirely my own. Thank you also to Keith Emerick and Neil Redfern, English Heritage, for introducing me to Castleford.

For the work undertaken in the Riversleigh region of Queensland, Australia, I particularly want to thank Anita van der Meer for all her help, friendship and effort. I also want to thank Anna Morgan, Del Burgan and Eunice O'Keefe for their help, all the people from Mount Isa, Riversleigh and surrounds who gave me their time and allowed me to interview them. I note, however, that any errors in fact and interpretation of interview data are all my own. Thanks also to Professor Michael Archer for introducing me to the region. Thank you to the Queensland National Parks and Wildlife Service for supporting the research undertaken in the Riversleigh region.

A number of people kindly read and commented on various drafts of chapters and I want to thank Emma Carver, Alison Drake, Keith Emerick, Jon Finch, Lorna Hay, Patricia Reynolds, Lynette Russell, Paul Shackel, Anita van der Meer, Kevin Walsh, Emma Waterton, David Wilders and Linda Young for giving their time and making constructive and useful comments. In particular, I want to thank Emma Waterton for all her time.

Most of all I want to thank my partner, Gary Campbell – without his active help, encouragement and support this book would most certainly not have been written. Gary, as always, edited and proofed this work, offered professional advice and help on the design and analysis of the questionnaires used in the research and discussed, debated and commented on all aspects of the work. I am more grateful than I can express. Yet again, I need to thank him, Hamish and Mahalia for putting up with the long hours that went into the writing of this book.

INTRODUCTION

What has sitting on the banks of the Gregory River in far northern Queensland fishing to do with heritage? I was watching a group of senior Aboriginal women from the Waanyi community fish as I tried to get my twelve-week-old daughter to sleep. We were about five hours' drive from the nearest major town, on a field trip with two of my colleagues, to record sites of heritage importance to Waanyi women in the Boodjamulla National Park and Riversleigh World Heritage area. Most of the women we were working with had travelled great distances to get here, some having flown in by light aircraft, and all had been eager to come and do some 'heritage work'.

Although we had done some recordings of archaeological sites and oral histories, fishing quickly became the order of our days in the region. Fishing was a leisure activity that filled the time between periods in which my colleagues and I pestered people with maps, site recording forms and tape recorders. But as my colleagues and I began to realize, fishing was a multi-layered activity. It was a leisure activity and a chance to catch dinner, it was also an activity to get away from us annoying archaeologists and heritage managers, and it was an opportunity that the women were using to savour simply being in a place that was important to them. It was in fact 'heritage work', being in place, renewing memories and associations, sharing experiences with kinswomen to cement present and future social and familial relationships. Heritage wasn't only about the past – though it was that too – it also wasn't just about material things – though it was that as well – heritage was a process of engagement, an act of communication and an act of making meaning in and for the present.

Listening to the senior women telling stories to younger women about the place we were in, or events that were associated with that place, I thought of the stories that members of my own family had told me, and that I would now pass on to my own children. I realized, too, that the meanings I drew out of those stories, and the uses I had made of them, would of course be different to the meanings, and uses, the generations both before and after me had and would construct. These family stories, shared memories, could sometimes be attached to material objects or family heirlooms, and while these

1

'things' were useful for making those stories tangible – they were not in and of themselves 'heritage'. For instance, I would still tell the stories associated with my grandmother's necklace, should I be unfortunate enough to lose it before I passed it on to my daughter. The real sense of heritage, the real moment of heritage when our emotions and sense of self are truly engaged, is not so much in the possession of the necklace, but in the act of passing on and receiving memories and knowledge. It also occurs in the way that we then use, reshape and recreate those memories and knowledge to help us make sense of and understand not only who we 'are', but also who we want to be. This is not to say that I would not be distressed if the necklace was lost or destroyed. However, I would grieve not for the loss of any monetary or inherent value it may have, but for the loss of the opportunity to pass it on, and the role it plays as both prop and prompt in the stories about my mother's family.

Can these observations about fishing and intimate moments of family memories tell us anything about why people visit World Heritage sites, national monuments, local and regional heritage sites and museums, or other places of heritage? Can they offer any insight into the sort of cultural and identity work that people do at these sites? Is heritage visiting simply a middle class leisure or touristic pursuit, as some sections of the heritage literature assert, or are there more varied and nuanced social and cultural processes at work? The idea of heritage as an act of communication and meaning making – indeed as an experience – is not something, however, that finds much synergy with the professional or expert view of heritage. My colleagues and I were required to map sites and places, to put dots on maps, identify conservation and management needs and so forth. How do you map, conserve and manage an experience? But then, of course, that is what we do as heritage managers, in managing and conserving places identified as 'heritage', we are also engaged in the management and conservation, or as I have argued elsewhere (Smith 2004) the 'governing', of the cultural and social values, meanings and associations they have. In effect, we are managing and defining people's 'heritage experiences' through the management and conservation process. By going fishing, the Waanyi women were taking themselves out of the technical processes of site recording and management, and both recreating and redefining their own sense of being in place and experiencing the moment of 'heritage'.

This book explores the idea of heritage not so much as a 'thing', but as a cultural and social process, which engages with acts of remembering that work to create ways to understand and engage with the present. In doing so, I draw on a range of ideas about the nature of heritage that have begun to emerge in the diverse interdisciplinary field of 'Heritage Studies'. Within this relatively new area of academic study a range of disciplines have come together to use the idea of 'heritage' to ask some interesting questions about modern practices of conservation, tourism and museums and site visitation.

This book, while making no claims to offer a fully rounded or synthetic statement, is an attempt to bring together disparate strands of thought and stimulate debate about the nature and use of heritage. For the purposes of structuring this book, I have developed themes of intangibility, identity, memory and remembering, performance, place, and dissonance, and used these ideas in various combinations to explore different aspects of the uses of heritage.

Indeed, the work starts from the premise that all heritage is intangible. In stressing the intangibility of heritage, however, I am not dismissing the tangible or pre-discursive, but simply deprivileging and denaturalizing it as the self-evident form and essence of heritage. While places, sites, objects and localities may exist as identifiable sites of heritage – we may, for instance, be able to point to such things as Stonehenge, the Sydney Opera House, Colonial Williamsburg, the Roman Coliseum, Angkor Watt, Robben Island, and so forth – these places are not *inherently* valuable, nor do they carry a freight of innate meaning. Stonehenge, for instance, is basically a collection of rocks in a field. What makes these things valuable and meaningful – what makes them 'heritage', or what makes the collection of rocks in a field 'Stonehenge' – are the present-day cultural processes and activities that are undertaken at and around them, and of which they become a part. It is these processes that identify them as physically symbolic of particular cultural and social events, and thus give them value and meaning. The traditional Western account of 'heritage' tends to emphasize the material basis of heritage, and attributes an inherent cultural value or significance to these things. Furthermore, the sense of gravitas given to these values is also often directly linked to the age, monumentality and/or aesthetics of a place. The physicality of the Western idea of heritage means that 'heritage' can be mapped, studied, managed, preserved and/or conserved, and its protection may be the subject of national legislation and international agreements, conventions and charters. However, heritage is heritage *because* it is subjected to the management and preservation/conservation process, not because it simply '*is*'. This process does not just 'find' sites and places to manage and protect. It is itself a constitutive cultural process that identifies those things and places that can be given meaning and value as 'heritage', reflecting contemporary cultural and social values, debates and aspirations.

In short, this book is about how the idea of heritage is used to construct, reconstruct and negotiate a range of identities and social and cultural values and meanings in the present. Heritage is a multilayered performance – be this a performance of visiting, managing, interpretation or conservation – that embodies acts of remembrance and commemoration while negotiating and constructing a sense of place, belonging and understanding in the present. Simultaneously the heritage performance will also constitute and validate the very idea of 'heritage' that frames and defines these performances in the first place. Although often self-regulating and self-referential, heritage is also inherently dissonant and contested. However, the traditional and authorized conceptions of heritage ensure that all conflict is reduced to case-specific issues, and the cultural process of identity formation that is basic to heritage is obscured. At one level heritage is about the promotion of a consensus version of history by state-sanctioned cultural institutions and elites to regulate cultural and social tensions in the present. On the other hand, heritage may also be a resource that is used to challenge and redefine received values and identities by a range of subaltern groups. Heritage is not necessarily about the stasis of cultural values and meanings, but may equally be about cultural change. It may, for instance, be about reworking the meanings of the past as the cultural, social and political needs of the present change and develop, or it may be about challenging the ways in which groups and communities are perceived and classified by others. Heritage is about negotiation – about using the past, and collective or individual memories, to negotiate new ways of being and expressing identity. In this process heritage objects, sites, places or institutions like museums become cultural tools or props to facilitate this process – but do not themselves stand in for this process or act.

Heritage is also a discourse. The idea of discourse does not simply refer to the use of words or language, but rather the idea of discourse used in this work refers to a form of social practice. Social meanings, forms of knowledge and expertise, power relations and ideologies are embedded and reproduced via language. The discourses through which we frame certain concepts, issues or debates have an affect in so far as they constitute, construct, mediate and regulate understanding and debate. Discourse not only organizes the way concepts like heritage are understood, but the way we act, the social and technical practices we act out, and the way knowledge is constructed and reproduced. One of the arguments developed in this book is that there is a dominant Western discourse about heritage, which I term the 'authorized heritage discourse', that works to naturalize a range of assumptions about the nature and meaning of heritage. Although this discourse is inevitably changing and developing, and varies in different cultural contexts and over time, there is nonetheless a particular focus and emphasis – primarily the attention it gives to 'things'. This often self-referential discourse simultaneously draws on and naturalizes certain narratives and cultural and social experiences – often linked to ideas of nation and nationhood. Embedded in this discourse are a range of assumptions about the innate and immutable cultural values of heritage that are linked to and defined by the concepts of monumentality and aesthetics.

The authorized discourse is also a professional discourse that privileges expert values and knowledge about the past and its material manifestations, and dominates and regulates professional heritage practices. However, alongside this professional and authorized discourse is also a range of popular discourses and practices. Some of these may take their cue from or be influenced by the professional discourse, but they will not necessarily be reducible to it (Purvis and Hunt 1993). Some discourses may also challenge, either actively or simply through their existence, the dominant discourse. This book also charts the work that the various discourses about heritage 'do', and the way they structure and frame different heritage experiences and acts of remembering and commemoration. From this, the book develops the argument that heritage may also be understood as a discourse concerned with the negotiation and regulation of social meanings and practices associated with the creation and recreation of 'identity'. Heritage is shown to have become a highly active discourse in the latter part of the twentieth century, having been raised as a particular environmental and social concern during the 1960s and 1970s, a period that also witnessed the consolidation of national and international technical processes of management and conservation. The reworking of the discourse of heritage at this time marks the development of an explicit and active way of negotiating cultural and social change. This is not to say that heritage as a process did not exist prior to this – certainly as Harvey (2001) notes, the processes that we today define as heritage are an integral part of human culture (see also Diaz-Andreu under review). However, the development of quite explicit professional discourses, and the burgeoning array of popular and community discourses on heritage that have developed over the last few decades, marks an explicit and sometimes self-conscious way of negotiating social and cultural identity, value and meaning.

The debates and arguments explored in this book draw on, and attempt to contribute to, the rise in ethnographic approaches that aim to understand the nature of heritage and how the past is constituted and utilized in the present. Since the 1990s there has been increasing multidisciplinary interest in the way diverse communities forge, maintain and negotiate their identities. Alongside this, a range of communities, defined either geographically or by cultural, social, ethnic, economic and/or other experiences, have increasingly asserted the legitimacy of their collective identities and social, political and cultural experiences. Consensual heritage narratives about the nation and national identity were challenged by the diversity of community experience and identity claims. Consequently, heritage debate and practice began to recognize and critically engage with issues of dissonance and the use of memory in the formation of heritage and identity. Increasing sophistication in writing about tourism has also lead to the realization that heritage tourists and other heritage visitors are far more active and critical – or 'mindful' – than they have previously been portrayed. Tourism may have more deeply layered or nuanced cultural and social meaning and consequence than its characterization as a leisure activity and economic industry often allows. These events have also coincided with increasing Indigenous and non-Western questioning of dominant Western perceptions of heritage, and the consequences that the dominance of these perceptions have had on the expression of their own identities. This critique has drawn attention to the issue of intangibility, and challenged the emphasis placed on the idea of material authenticity, and the preservationist desire to freeze the moment of heritage and to conserve heritage as an unchanging monument to the past. Arising out of the confluence of all these issues and moments is a new interdisciplinary subfield that offers the opportunity to redefine the idea of 'heritage' through an analysis of the consequence this idea has in people's lives.

The first section of this book outlines its theoretical basis. Informed by concepts of discourse analysis, the first chapter identifies and examines the orders of discourse that surround heritage, and considers how and when they developed, and who engages in this dialogue. An 'authorized heritage discourse' is identified, which works, it is argued, to construct a sense of what heritage is – and is not. How the discourse works to naturalize certain ideas about the immutable and inherent nature of the value and meaning of heritage within the practices of heritage conservation, preservation and management is also explored. Drawing on a range of interdisciplinary theoretical innovations, in particular ideas of place, remembering, and performance, Chapter 2 offers an alternative way of conceiving heritage that will be explored throughout the rest of the book. More specifically, it is argued that what heritage does is intersect with a range of social and cultural debates about the legitimacy of a range of values and identities, and subsequently plays a part in their validation, negotiation and regulation. By recognizing that the management of heritage has consequences beyond the preservation of historic fabric, it will be possible to explore the uses that heritage is put to outside of the management and conservation field.

The following two sections of the book examine a range of themes, all of which draw on original research work in England, Australia and the United States. Part II of the book (Chapters 3–5) examines the consequences of 'authorized' heritage, and explores how authorized discourses of heritage influence expert and professional heritage practices and are themselves perpetuated (Chapter 3), how such discourses influence the construction and expression of certain social and cultural identities (Chapters 4 and 5), and how it is used to regulate and arbitrate dissonance (Chapter 5). Chapter 3 offers a critical examination of the discourse of ICOMOS and UNESCO Charters and Conventions and the practices these documents influence. Chapters 4 and 5, respectively, are based on the results of survey and interview work with visitors to English country houses and with a range of stakeholders concerned with the use and management of Australia's Riversleigh World Heritage palaeontological site. In this section of the book it is argued that practices of management and conservation are themselves constitutive performances of heritage, and that the authenticity of heritage lies ultimately in the meanings people construct for it in their daily lives. Chapters 4 and 5 illustrate the ways in which the performative experience of heritage engages with the creation, recreation and legitimization of social and cultural bonds and identity in the present. In particular, they illustrate the way heritage may be used to regulate, legitimize and justify the maintenance of national narratives and social hierarchies. While heritage is shown to be an affirmation of identity and a sense of belonging, that identity may also nonetheless be one that is governed or regulated by wider social forces and narratives.

Part III (Chapters 6–8) examines subaltern uses of heritage, and explores the various ways authorized and received notions of heritage and the values they represent are contested. Chapter 6 explores the role of remembering and commemoration in the construction of social and family identities, and is based on survey and interview work undertaken with visitors to industrial museums in England. Chapter 7 is based on ethnographic, interview and survey work with residents of the town of Castleford, located in the coalfield of West Yorkshire, England. In this chapter, heritage is shown as a process that is actively and critically used to negotiate and facilitate social and cultural change within the community. Commemoration and remembrance are used as platforms from which the community is continually redefining and remaking both itself and the social networks that bind the people of the community together. Chapter 8 explores the ways in which Indigenous peoples, drawing on work in the United States and Australia, use heritage as a political and cultural resource. All three chapters demonstrate why control is an important issue in heritage.

Ultimately, the process or moment of heritage is shown to be potentially critically active and self-conscious, through which people can negotiate identity and the values and meanings that underlie that, but through which they also challenge and attempt to redefine their position or 'place' in the world around them. Heritage is not only a social and cultural resource or process, but also a political one through which a range of struggles are negotiated. The implications and consequences of the theorization of heritage as a cultural practice concerned with negotiating the tensions between received and contested identity has consequences for both academic analysis and heritage practice and policy.

Part I

THE IDEA OF HERITAGE

1

THE DISCOURSE OF HERITAGE

There is, really, no such thing as heritage. I say this advisedly, and it is a statement that I will qualify, but it needs to be said to highlight the common sense assumption that 'heritage' can unproblematically be identified as 'old', grand, monumental and aesthetically pleasing sites, buildings, places and artefacts. What I argue in this book is that there is rather a hegemonic discourse about heritage, which acts to constitute the way we think, talk and write about heritage. The 'heritage' discourse therefore naturalizes the practice of rounding up the usual suspects to conserve and 'pass on' to future generations, and in so doing promotes a certain set of Western elite cultural values as being universally applicable. Consequently, this discourse validates a set of practices and performances, which populates both popular and expert constructions of 'heritage' and undermines alternative and subaltern ideas about 'heritage'. At the same time, the 'work' that 'heritage' 'does' as a social and cultural practice is obscured, as a result of the naturalizing effects of what I call the 'authorized heritage discourse'.

The aim of this chapter is to demonstrate the discursive nature of heritage and to unpack this discourse to illustrate that the subject of our heritage 'gaze', to borrow from Urry (1990), is not so much a 'thing' as a set of values and meanings. 'Heritage' is therefore ultimately a cultural practice, involved in the construction and regulation of a range of values and understandings. How these observations are then dealt with is then the subject of Chapter 2. The argument advanced in this chapter is that there is a hegemonic 'authorized heritage discourse', which is reliant on the power/ knowledge claims of technical and aesthetic experts, and institutionalized in state cultural agencies and amenity societies. This discourse takes its cue from the grand narratives of nation and class on the one hand, and technical expertise and aesthetic judgement on the other. The 'authorized heritage discourse' privileges monumentality and grand scale, innate artefact/site significance tied to time depth, scientific/aesthetic expert judgement, social consensus and nation building. It is a self-referential discourse, which has a particular set of consequences.

The first consequence is the need to construct a material reality for itself – to establish claims about itself that make it real. In this process a number of boundaries are drawn. One boundary disconnects the idea of heritage from the present and present-day values and aspirations so that it becomes something confined to 'the past' (Urry 1996). Another ensures that heritage becomes the proper subject of analyses and responsibilities for a range of forms of expertise and associated 'experts'. The power relations underlying the discourse identify those people who have the ability or authority to 'speak' about or 'for' heritage . . . and those who do not. The establishment of this boundary is facilitated by assumptions about the innate value of heritage, which works to obscure the multi-vocality of many heritage values and meanings. Discourse works to identify particular forms of expertise that may be called upon to make pronouncements about the meaning and nature of heritage, and to mediate and adjudicate over any competing heritage discourses. This is not to say that expert pronouncements and judgements are not contested – they are – but in this process the boundaries of any negotiations over heritage values and meanings become very tightly drawn indeed, as they become specific contests over the management or interpretation of specific heritage sites. This process works to limit broader debate about, and any subsequent challenges to, established social and cultural values and meanings.

The discourse also constructs two important sets of heritage practices, those focused on management and conservation of heritage sites, places and objects, and those tied to the visitation of sites and institutions within tourism and leisure activities. However, the broader cultural work that these practices do is often obscured by the way the discourse of heritage constructs not only the idea of heritage, but also its practices. However, what these practices are involved in are the negotiation and regulation of a range of cultural and social values and meanings. Cultural heritage management and the acts of visiting heritage sites as a tourist or other visitor become acts directly implicated in the occasional construction or reconstruction, but most certainly the maintenance, or more precisely *conservation* and *preservation*, of social and cultural meanings.

To explore these ideas a bit further, this chapter does a number of things. Firstly, it briefly reviews theories of discourses and defines the concept as used in this work. The first section of this chapter thus presents a theoretical and methodological underpinning for the rest of this chapter and the book. The second section asks 'when was heritage' and examines when, why and where the dominant discourse of heritage emerged and how and why it became dominant. The chapter then briefly examines the consequences of the existence of this discourse and finally reviews the range of competing heritage discourses. These themes are examined in more detail throughout Parts II and III of the book.

There is no such thing as 'heritage'

The discursive construction of heritage is itself part of the cultural and social processes that are heritage. The practice of heritage may be defined as the management and conservation protocols, techniques and procedures that heritage managers, archaeologists, architects, museum curators and other experts undertake. It may also be an economic and/or leisure practice, and/or a social and cultural practice, as I am arguing, of meaning and identity making. These practices, as well as the meaning of the material 'things' of heritage, are constituted by the discourses that simultaneously reflect these practices while also constructing them.

I also want to use this section to carefully set out some parameters to my use of the term 'discourse'. In discussing how people talk and write about 'heritage', I don't want to get tangled up in debates on the relevance of post-modern arguments that discourse is all that matters. The position that I adopt epistemologically draws on critical realism and, though I acknowledge the usefulness of Foucauldian approaches to discourse, I anchor my analysis firmly in an understanding that social relations are material and have material consequences, in a way informed by *critical discourse analysis*. This is an important distinction, as I do not want to lose sight of the materiality of heritage at the same time as I am problematizing it.

The analysis I am constructing explicitly deals with the 'work' that the practices and performances of heritage 'do' culturally and socially. As such, I am also concerned with what Lorimer (2005: 84), drawing on the work of Thrift, calls the non, pre or more than representational aspects of social life, which are prior to or not dependent on discourse: 'focus falls on how life takes shape and gains expression in shared experiences, everyday routines, fleeting encounters, embodied movements, precognitive triggers, practical skills, affective intensities, enduring urges, unexceptional interactions and sensuous dispositions.'

This analysis offers insights into the political consequences of space, performance and affect. As Thrift argues (2003: 2022–3):

> Spaces can be stabilised in such a way that they act like political utterances, guiding subjects to particular conclusions. But, as a counterpoint, the fabric of space is so multifarious that there are always holes and tears in which new forms of expression can come into being. Space is therefore constitutive in the strongest possible sense and it is not a misuse of the term to call it performative, as its many components continually act back, drawing on a range of different aesthetics as they do so.

Thinking about discourse

At its most simplistic, as Wetherell (2001: 3) observes, discourse is the 'study of language use', it is an analysis of how language is used 'to do things', but is not reducible to language (see also Taylor 2001: 5). It is about the inter-relationship between language and practice (Hall 2001: 72). Discourse is a social action, and this idea of discourse acknowledges that the way people talk about, discuss and understand things, such as 'heritage', have a material consequence that matters. In addition, not only is discourse 'used' to do things by actors, but discourses also do things to actors and are productive independently of actors (Bourdieu and Wacquant 2000; Fischer 2003). A useful starting point is the idea of discourse 'as a specific ensemble of ideas, concepts, and categorisations that are produced, reproduced, and transformed in a particular set of practices and through which meaning is given to physical and social realities' (Hajer 1996: 44). As such, discourses are 'inherently positioned', and so the collection of ideas, concepts, and categorizations regarding heritage give rise to different ways of 'seeing' the social practice of managing 'heritage' according to the positions of social actors (Fairclough 2001: 235).

Foucault (1991), one of the more influential writers on discourse, argues that discourses are forms of expertise, collected into different disciplines, which deal with the construction and representation of knowledge. Discourse not only reflects social meanings, relations and entities, it also constitutes and governs them. The focus of much of Foucault's work was concerned with the epistemological issues of knowledge construction and practice, in particular the power–knowledge relations underlying forms of expertise and the relations of power underpinning dominant discourses. Although his work was concerned with the contestation of and challenges to the dominant discourse, focus tended to be on the dominant discourse itself and competing and/or everyday or 'popular' discourses tend to be overlooked, as are the ways in which they contest and challenge bodies of expertise or dominant discourses (Purvis and Hunt 1993; van Dijk 1998). This is because Foucault was concerned not so much with general political struggles but with identifying techniques of power (Rouse 1987, 1994). For Foucault, the relationship between power and knowledge – power/knowledge – was vital, and he identified knowledge as a particular technique of power (1991). As Hall notes (2001: 78), a major critique of Foucault's work on discourse is that he attempts to 'absorb too much' into the idea of discourse, and in particular to neglect the material, economic and structural factors in the way power and knowledge are deployed. Other critiques of Foucault have been concerned that his focus is 'not about whether things exist but about where meaning comes from' and that this focus leaves studies of discourse open to the charge of relativism (Hall 2001: 73), while others express concern that all social action may be perceived as reducible only to discourse (Fairclough

2000: 145). In addition, Foucault's ideas about discourse have been criticized for not offering a clear methodological approach, particularly in relation to the links between knowledge and practice and social change (Sayer 1992; Fairclough 1993).

As a remedy to these issues, Critical Discourse Analysis (CDA) offers a theoretical platform and methodological approach that aims to illuminate the links between discourse and practice, and the light this can shed on human relationships and social actions and issues. CDA is a well-established inter-disciplinary methodology for analysing discourse and discursive practice and is located within critical social scientific theory and analysis (Chouliaraki and Fairclough 1999). In particular, the philosophy of critical realism underlies CDA, which acknowledges that things exist independently of our knowledge of them, or indeed discourses about them, but that 'we can only know them under particular descriptions' (Bhaskar 1978: 250). Critical realism recognizes the power of discourses, but stresses the concrete social relations that underlie and generate discourses (Bhaskar 1989; Sayer 1992; Chouliaraki and Fairclough 1999; Fairclough et al. 2003).

A central concern of CDA is identifying and understanding how people organize themselves and act through particular discourses (Fairclough et al. 2004: 2). It is also important to understand the relationships between different discourses, as discourses are elements that constrain and constitute the various relationships between people. As such, discourses may be deployed to help regulate, maintain or challenge social relations. This is not to say that discourse represents the totality of social practice, but is one of the interlinked elements of that practice. However, if we accept that discourse is an irreducible part of social life, then one route to analysing what is going on socially can be achieved through the analysis of what is going on interdiscursively (Fairclough 2001: 240). Particular practices, sections of society, such as bodies of expertise, areas of policy development, public employees, community groups and so forth have particular discourses internalized within them that help them to shape social life and particular behaviour and practices (Fairclough 2000: 144–5). Discourse may also work to bind collectives to particular internalized ideologies, assumptions and practices. The important point here, however, is the recognition of the existence of competing and inter-relating discourses that are understood to have an impact on the way people think about and interact with the social and physical world.

Integral to CDA is not simply an analysis of discourse but also an analysis of the social and political context of that discourse and an analysis of the social effects that a discourse has – that one of its elements is 'looking closely at what happens when people talk or write' (Fairclough 2003: 3). Of particular concern is an examination of the way discourses become intertwined with the legitimation and maintenance of power (Marston 2004). In legitimizing and naturalizing the ideologies and range of cultural and social assumptions

15

about the way the social world works, discourses can have a persuasive power in maintaining and legitimating hierarchies of social relations (Fairclough 2003).

For Fairclough (2003: 124), the point of analysis is not only how those using a particular discourse see the world, but also a consideration of how discourses are also projective given that they may 'represent possible worlds which are different from the actual world [but are] tied in to projects to change the world in particular directions'. An important issue here is the idea that discourses are not just about sustaining and legitimizing certain practices and social relations, but may also simultaneously be engaged with social change (Fairclough et al. 2004: 2). While CDA may privilege the study of language and how it is used, it also sees language as a tool to reveal and reflect social projects and relations, and changes within these. The micro-analysis of discourse provides a macro-analysis of social contexts (Marston 2004: 38). CDA is, in sum, concerned with developing accounts of the inter-relation of discourse with power and domination, social hierarchies, gender relations, the work of ideologies, negotiations between different social identities and the acts of production and resistance within political spheres (Fairclough 2003; Waterton et al. 2006).

The idea of discourse used in the rest of this volume incorporates the notion of discourse as advanced by CDA; in short, that discourse is both reflective of and constitutive of social practices. The following section of this chapter identifies a particular discourse and area of discursive practice centred on ideas of 'heritage' and its management and conservation. This is a historically situated discourse; it is also a discourse, as I will argue, situated within certain Western social experiences and social hierarchies. Due to the limits of space, and for the sake of the arguments I develop in this volume, it is a generalized characterization of a discourse. Subsequently I recognize that some nuances of this discourse will be glossed over, and that this discourse is far more mutable across both time and space than I am characterizing it. Indeed, there are elements within it that recognize and pursue agendas for social change, although these are often obscured by the self-referential tendencies of the discourse. However, my task is to identify the general characteristics of the dominant discourse in heritage, and the way it both reflects and constitutes a range of social practices − not least the way it organizes social relations and identities around nation, class, culture and ethnicity.

When was heritage?

David Harvey (2001: 320) notes that a concern with 'heritage', or at least a concern with 'the past' and material items from that past, has a much deeper history than most contemporary debates around the idea of heritage usually allow. He notes that the use of the past to construct ideas of individual and group identities is part of the human condition, and that throughout human history people have actively managed and treasured material aspects of the past for this purpose (2001: 333; see also Diaz-Andreu et al. 2005). Certainly, the use of material culture in bolstering national ideology is well documented in the literature (see, for instance, Trigger 1989; Diaz-Andreu and Champion 1996; Boswell and Evans 1999; Carrier 2005; Diaz-Andreu under review). Harvey cautions that the tendency to see heritage as largely a modern phenomena works to reduce debates about heritage to specific technical issues over contemporary management and conservation practices, and subsequently any real engagement with debates about how heritage is involved in the production of identity, power and authority are obscured (2001: 320). However, my task here is to examine what Harvey (2001: 323) himself identifies as a particular 'strand', but which is more usefully discussed as a particular discourse, of heritage that emerged in late nineteenth-century Europe and has achieved dominance as a 'universalizing' discourse in the twenty-first century. One of the consequences of this discourse is to actively obscure the power relations that give rise to it and to make opaque the cultural and social work that 'heritage' does. While there is a general interest in the past, there is a discourse of heritage that creates a particular set of cultural and social practices that have certain consequences in the context of late modernity. Although some commentators today see heritage as having a particular post-modern expression tied to economic commodification and hyper-relativism, this is simply not the case. The origins of the dominant heritage discourse are linked to the development of nineteenth-century nationalism and liberal modernity, and while competing discourses do occur, the dominant discourse is intrinsically embedded with a sense of the pastoral care of the material past.

As has been well rehearsed in the heritage literature, the current concept of heritage emerged in Europe, particularly Britain, France and Germany, within the context of nineteenth-century modernity (for overviews see, for instance, King et al. 1977; Walsh 1992; Bennett 1995; Barthel 1996; Pearce 1998; Jokilehto 1999). Enlightenment rationality and claims about the possibility of objective truth had overturned medieval religious ideas about the nature of knowledge. The idea of progress took on particular force at this time and both legitimized and reinforced European colonial and imperial expansions and acquisitions in the modern era. Through colonial expansion new dialogues about race developed, and ethnic and cultural identity became firmly linked with concepts of biology or 'blood', and Europeans believed themselves to be representative of the highest achievements of human technical, cultural and intellectual progress. Debates over Darwinian evolution had also cemented the social utility and rationality of science, and social Darwinism had further helped to naturalize the conceptual link between identity and race, and the inevitability of European cultural and technical advancement and achievement (Trigger 1989).

The industrial revolution and associated urbanization of the nineteenth century dislocated many people from a sense of social and geographical security. The French Revolution had also altered the European sense of historical consciousness (Anderson 1991; Jokilehto 1999), and undermined previous ideas of territorial sovereignty, already challenged by the treaty of Westphalia. Nation states had emerged and nationalism developed as a new meta-narrative to bind populations to a shifting sense of territorial identity and to legitimize state formation (Graham et al. 2000: 12). The emergence of a mercantile middle class as feudalism gave way to capitalism had also destabilized the political and economic role of the aristocracy. All in all, the nineteenth century may be characterized as a period that called for 'new devices to ensure or express social cohesion and identity and to structure social relations' (Hobsbawm 1983b: 263). National and racial discourses coalesced and naturalized a link between concepts of identity, history, and territory to establish a doctrine of 'blood and land' (Olsen 2001: 53). It is within this context of the developing narrative of nationalism and of a universalizing modernity that a new, more pointed, concern for what we now identify as 'heritage' emerged. The sense of the new Modern Europe was to be expressed in the monuments that were to be protected and managed for the edification of the public, and as physical representations of national identity and European taste and achievement. As Graham et al. (2000: 17) note, 'to be modern was to be European, and that to be European or to espouse European values (even in the United States) was to be the pinnacle of cultural achievement and social evolution.'

The desire to propagate these values found synergy with the liberal education movement, whose sense of pastoral care identified a moral responsibility to educate the public about their civic and national duties, and to promote social stability by fostering a sense of national community and social responsibility. As Walsh (1992: 30) argues, museums developed as a consequence of the modern condition and narratives of progress, rationality and national and cultural identity became embedded in exhibition and collection practices. Museums took on a regulatory role in helping to establish and govern both social and national identity, and the existence of national collections demonstrated the achievements and superiority of the nation that possessed them (Bennet 1995; Macdonald 2003; Diaz-Andreu under review).

Along side of the institutionalization of museums as repositories and manifestations of national identity and cultural achievement, many European nations also turned their attention to the conservation and management of non-portable antiquities and historic buildings. Legislation to protect what was often defined as 'monuments' ushered in a particular practice of 'conservation'. Although the first legal decree to protect national antiquities dates to the seventeenth century in Sweden, the second half of the nineteenth century saw a surge in the development of legislation to protect ancient monuments or religious or other architecturally and historically significant buildings (Jokilehto 1999; Choay 2001). These acts, and other legal instruments and public agencies, included the English *Ancient Monuments Protection Act* of 1882; the 1807 chancellery recommendations in Denmark; the establishment in the 1830s of the Comité historique in France, amongst others (Kristiansen 1984; Schnapp 1984; Murray 1989; Choay 2001; Poirrier 2003). Explicitly following the European example, the United States also attempted to get similar legislation enacted during the late nineteenth century, although this was not successful until 1906 with the passing of the *Antiquities Act* (McManamon 1996; Murtagh 1997). Professional architects and the newly emergent discipline of archaeology were significant in the history of the development of these acts. Archaeology, particularly in England and the United States, pressed its case for status as an intellectual endeavour through its claims of stewardship over prehistoric sites and monuments in public debates around the development of these acts (Carman 1996; Smith 2004). Both architecture and archaeology, due to their ability to claim professional expertise over material culture, took on a pastoral role in identifying the appropriate monuments to be protected under these acts, and in caring for and protecting these places. Educating the public about the value and meaning of historic buildings and monuments also became embedded in a sense of a 'conservation ethic' that to disseminate these values was to ensure greater conservation awareness and appreciation of a nation's cultural heritage. This sense of a conservation ethic became institutionalized in organizations like the Society for the Protection of Ancient Buildings (SPAB) established in 1877, one function of which was to lobby and educate government and society at large about 'proper' conservation principles and about the value and aesthetic significance of ancient buildings.

The use of the term monument is particularly important in the European context. As Choay (2001) documents, the word took on particular registers of power, greatness, and beauty during the seventeenth century and came to affirm a sense of grand public schemes and aesthetic sensibilities. The monument became 'a witness to history and a work of art' that took on a commemorative role in triggering certain public memories and values, and is a concept that has come to embody a particular European vision of the world (Choay 2001: 15; Carrier 2005). The French idea of *patrimoine* – specifically the concept of inheritance – also underwrites the sense of aesthetic grandness (Choay 2001). This sense of inheritance promotes the idea that the present has a particular 'duty' to the past and its monuments. The duty of the present is to receive and revere what has been passed on and in turn pass this inheritance, untouched, to future generations. The French sense of patrimony found synergy in the English conservation ethos of 'conserve as found', heavily influenced by John Ruskin and his treatise *The Seven Lamps of Architecture* ([1849] 1899). In this work, Ruskin argued against the dominant nineteenth-century practice of restoration, where historic buildings would be 'restored' to 'original' conditions by removing later additions or adaptations.

For Ruskin, the fabric of a building was inherently valuable and needed to be protected for the artisanal and aesthetic values it contained:

> It is again no question of expediency or feeling whether we shall preserve the buildings of past time or not. We have no right what-ever to touch them. They are not ours. They belong partly to those who built them, and partly to all generations of mankind who are to follow us.
>
> (Ruskin [1849] 1899: 358)

As Burman (1995) notes, this sense of 'trusteeship' over the past was taken up by the SPAB and, as Emerick (2003) shows, became embedded and propa-gated in English legislation, policy and conservation principles and practices throughout the twentieth century. For the SPAB 'conservation repair' was advocated, so that there would be little intervention in the fabric of a build-ing, and repair work would principally be done to prevent decay. William Morris, one of the principal founders of the SPAB and heavily influenced by Ruskin, wrote in his 1877 manifesto for the Society that:

> To put Protection in the place of Restoration, to stave off decay by daily care, to prop a perilous wall or mend a leaky roof by such means as are obviously meant for support or covering, and show no pretence of other art, and otherwise to resist all tampering with either the fabric or ornament of the building as it stands . . . in fine to treat our ancient buildings as monuments of a bygone art, created by bygone manners, that modern art cannot meddle with without destroying.
>
> (Morris 1877)

This sense of protection or conservation is explicitly incorporated into English planning policy, notably within the document 'Public Planning Guidance 15' (PPG15), which oversees the conservation and use of historic buildings. Further, members of the public today seeking information about conservation principles in their local borough may download from the Internet documents from local government websites that recommend conservation procedures and practices that heavily quote William Morris and the SPAB (see, for instance, East Hertfordshire 2005).

The particular aesthetic championed by Morris and Ruskin owed much to nineteenth-century Romanticism, and many of the buildings they sought to save were essentially those built before the seventeenth century. Buildings to be protected were 'anything which can be looked on as artistic, pictur-esque, historical, antique, or substantial: any work, in short, over which educated, artistic people would think it worth while to argue' (Morris 1877). Romanticism, as a reaction to urbanization and industrialization, harkened back to a time of the 'rural idyll' and it was thus no accident that many of the buildings that most concerned the SPAB were churches and homes of the rural elite. The idea that architectural monuments were also something that could principally be appreciated by the educated is also embedded in this conservation philosophy – as it was the professional whose responsibility it was to care for and pass on the aesthetic values that lie at the heart of what it meant to be a 'Modern European'. More specifically, it was only the well-educated who had the necessary cultural literacy to understand grand social and national narratives that were inherent in the fabric of such monuments.

The European conservation principles spread to other parts of the world; actively so in places like the United States, where European conservation found synergy with the 'secular pietism' that characterized the nineteenth-century American preservation movement (Murtagh 1997: 11). In other countries like India, these principles were imposed as part of colonial rule, with the British colonial government legislating in 1863 for the conservation of buildings for their historical and architectural value (Thapar 1984; Menon 2002). These principles have also became embedded in the *Athens Charter for the Restoration of Historic Monuments* of 1931, and the *International Charter for the Conservation and Restoration of Monuments and Sites* (Venice Charter) of 1964, the first of a range of ICOMOS charters that continue to frame and define the debates about conservation and heritage management practices. European ideas about conservation, and the nature and meaning of monu-ments, have become internationally naturalized, so that these principles have become global 'common sense'. Denis Byrne (1991) has argued, more critic-ally, that they have become hegemonic and that the 'conservation ethic' has been imposed on non-Western nations.

The Romantic Movement also found expression in the conservation of 'natural' heritage. The idea of a 'pristine wilderness', and the nature/culture divide facilitated by Enlightenment philosophy, led to the concept of a nat-ural landscape that needed to be protected from the depredations of human activities (Head 2000b; Waterton 2005a). This idea of landscape was insti-tutionalized in the late nineteenth century with the creation of Yellowstone National Park in 1872, the world's first national park. In England, the National Trust for Places of Historic Interest or Natural Beauty was founded in 1895 to address threats to the landscape of the Lake District (Jenkins 1994). The socialist founders of the Trust were concerned to preserve com-mon land for recreational use as a reaction to the *General Enclosures Act* of 1845 (Weideger 1994). In particular, the initial founders of the Trust were concerned to ensure urban populations had access to rural lands and land-scapes for their cultural and physical health and well-being (Crouch 1963: 18). In 1907, an Act of Parliament established the National Trust, and gave the organization the right to declare any properties it possessed as inalien-able, so that they could be held in 'trust' for the nation (Crouch 1963: 7). Although initially concerned with areas of natural beauty, the Trust began to acquire buildings in the early twentieth century. In 1934, Philip Kerr, the eleventh Marquess of Lothian, lobbied a new generation of National Trust officials to consider the 'plight' of the country house (Mandler 1997: 295–6). By this time, death duties, other taxes and the impact of the First World War had had a debilitating impact on the ability of the landed gentry and aristocracy to maintain these buildings. Kerr (aka Lord Lothian) argued in 1934 that the Trust should be enabled to acquire houses, repair and modernize them and then let them to tenants, some of whom may be their old owners, 'who would respect and preserve, so far as they could, the tradition of beauty they enshrined' (quoted in Mandler 1997: 296). In 1937 and 1939, new legislation allowed owners of houses to gift or bequeath their properties, along with an endowment for their upkeep, to the Trust; in return, the Trust would maintain the property and generous tax concessions would be granted on the transfer of the property to the Trust (Cannadine 1995: 20). Subsequently, the Trust has become primarily associated in England with the country house and other properties of the English elite. Rather than the original sense of holding public lands in trust for the public, the National Trust adopted, at this time, a 'Ruskinian' sense of trusteeship over the types of buildings that inherently appealed to Romantics and organizations like the SPAB. In addition, the conservation ideas and the ideologies embedded in the European conservation movement helped to legitimate the Trust's almost seamless adoption of Kerr's 'Country House Scheme', and to become subsequently a major and natural advocate for the preservation of elite heritage as 'national' heritage.

Indeed this was no accident, as the discourse of monumentality and heritage as developed from the nineteenth century is not only driven by certain narratives about nationalism and Romantic ideals, but also a specific theme about the legitimacy and dominant place in national cultures of the European social and political elite. In Britain, for instance, the upper classes have dominated the conservation movement, by not only founding organizations like the SPAB and in hijacking the National Trust, but also in championing legislation. For instance, Lord Lubbock, early archaeologist and liberal politician, was the primary champion of the Ancient Monuments Act, which he saw as part of a wider social improvement scheme, in which the public would be made aware of the antiquity of their national and cultural character through the preservation of ancient antiquities and other monuments (Carman 1993, 1996). In the United States, the early leaders of what in that country is called the 'preservation movement' were drawn from the upper middle and upper classes (Barthel 1996: 6). Early campaigns in America concentrated on the preservation of the stately homes of historically significant men, such as George Washington's 'Mt Vernon' and Andrew Jackson's 'The Hermitage' (Murtah 1997). The motive behind this movement was, as Barthel (1996: 19) observes, to specifically engender and bolster American patriotism in the general public. Individuals like Lubbock and organizations like the SPAB in England, and early US preservationist organizations like the

Mt Vernon Ladies Association and Daughters of the American Revolution, were driven by a sense of liberal duty for social improvement, wherein their messages about patriotism, nationalism and the desirability of inheriting and passing on certain aesthetic tastes was seen as occurring for the general good and edification of the public.

The idea of 'preservation' is interesting here, as the nineteenth century was a significant period of social change. The European conservation movement and the American preservation movement developed in the context of this change, and what is revealing is what it was that early conservationists and preservations sought to 'save' in this context. Almost inevitably it is the grand and great and 'good' that were chosen, to 'remind' the public about the values and sensibilities that should be saved or preserved as representative of patriotic American and European national identities. Even when it is the 'bad' that is being preserved, it is very often the exceptionally 'tragic' event that is commemorated, rather than unpleasantness that is more mundane or reflective of the general inequalities of human experiences. The very idea of monumentality – drawing on a sense of the inevitability and desirability of inheritance, of grand scale and of aesthetic taste – derives ultimately from ruling and upper middle class experience. That these ideals came to dominate was not simply a function of the degree to which the upper classes were involved in early preservation and conservation movements. It was also the degree to which their own experiences and understanding of the importance of material culture in demonstrating lineage, cultural and social achievement and power became embedded in these movements and the conceptual frameworks in use today. This was also facilitated by a certain desire to maintain the legitimacy of those experiences on the social and cultural register.

In Australia, where the conservation movement developed relatively late, we can see the degree to which these concepts have become naturalized as common sense in the wider international discourse on heritage. Australia faithfully imported the basic philosophy of Ruskinian conservation as witnessed in the development of the first version of The Australian ICOMOS *Charter for the Conservation of Places of Cultural Significance (Burra Charter)* in 1979. This charter was an attempt to rework the Venice Charter for an Australian context, which by the late 1970s included self-conscious public debate about multiculturalism and Indigenous heritage. However, the 1979 Burra Charter focused attention entirely on the fabric of a place or building, a focus derived from the basic premises underlying the Charter that significance is deemed to be inherent in the fabric of a building. The Charter incorporates the basic conservation ethic that requires that as little as possible be done to damage or alter a building's fabric and thus its historic or other values. Although the Burra Charter was rewritten in 1999, the basic focus on fabric, and the underlying ethic and assumptions of innate value has not changed (Waterton et al. 2006). Indeed, as argued in detail in Chapter 3, the new version of the Charter, which attempts to incorporate greater community participation in conservation and heritage management matters, effectively works to compromise that participation (see also Waterton et al. 2006). It does so as it has not altered the dominant sense of the trusteeship of expert authority over the material fabric. Nor has it challenged the degree to which experts are perceived as having not only the ability, but also the *responsibility* for identifying the value and meanings that are still perceived to be locked within the fabric of a place. The degree to which the Burra Charter incorporates the common sense views about conservation and heritage are revealed in the extent to which this document, written *specifically* for the Australian context, is lauded and adopted internationally as a standard of good principles and practice. A number of countries in Europe, and in particular the United Kingdom, have now adopted and actively use the Burra Charter in conservation and heritage management.

In the 1940s, both America and Australia imported the English model of the National Trust. As various commentators have noted, the majority of houses and other properties preserved in Australia during the post-war period tended to be drawn from the Australian Squattocracy (rural upper class) and other elements of the ruling classes (Bickford 1981, 1985; Lake 1991; Pennay 1996). However, a significant moment in the history of the conservation movement in Australia was the activities of the Builders Labourers Federation (BLF), a now disbanded trade union, which in the 1970s, under the leadership of Jack Mundy, imposed 'green bans' (work bans) on areas in Sydney deemed by the union leadership and community groups as constituting both natural and cultural heritage. The first area thus successfully protected was a piece of bushland, 'Kelly's Bush', in the affluent Sydney suburb of Hunters Hill (Burgman and Burgman 1998). Another area that became the focus of Mundy's green bans was Victoria Street in the red-light and one time bohemian inner city suburb of Kings Cross. A large section of Victoria Street was due for redevelopment by a private landowner, and a significant number of Victorian terraced houses were due for demolition. Although these terraced houses had once been built for middle class occupation, they had by the 1970s largely been subdivided into boarding houses and were occupied by protected tenants, workers from the nearby dockyards and other low-income tenants. For many of the residents of Kings Cross, my own family included, the agenda for protecting these houses was not simply the aesthetic amenity of the streetscape, although that was important, but appreciably the agenda was also driven by the need to save not only low-income accommodation, but low-incoming housing that had an aesthetic amenity.

Victoria Street became a significant and very public community and trade union protest, which at times became very violent and was nationally broadcast on news programmes. This protest occurred at a time when there was wider agitation from organizations like the National Trust to develop legislation in the State of New South Wales, where these events were occurring, to protect heritage sites. The *NSW Heritage Act 1977* was duly enacted. The Victoria Street development did proceed, but in a modified form, and public pressure saw the preservation of some of the Victoria Street housing stock. However, the agenda for *why* these houses were saved was lost. Tenants were removed and the houses modified and 'restored' to their pre-boarding house days, and re-tenanted with, or sold to, the mobile middle classes that were, at this time, gentrifying the inner city. The actions of the BLF in Sydney were significant in that they helped raise public consciousness about environmental and cultural heritage issues, and the public protests they sparked helped to put pressure on the government to develop heritage policies and legislation. However, the dominant sense of heritage prevailed in this case, as the houses were saved for their aesthetic values, not their community values or as affordable homes. Perhaps these latter issues would never have gained political credence given the degree of economic pressure to redevelop the inner city; however, it is revealing nonetheless that it was the aesthetic argument that was seen as plausible and of enough political influence to protect these buildings. In short, it was the *houses* that were saved, and saved ultimately for middle class use, and not the sense of community that drove the protest for many local residents. The other point this example reveals about the nature of authorized heritage and monumentality is that it is inherently *material*, and that Victoria Street could be seen as a conservation victory rather than the local community defeat that it was, because the building stock, and not the community, had been saved.

The public concern with environmental and heritage issues that Mundy and the BLF, and indeed the National Trust of Australia, drew on in lobbying for heritage legislation during the 1970s was part of a growing wider Western concern with what were becoming identifiable as 'heritage issues' during the 1960s. Some commentators have seen this increased public debate as a consequence of the political and social changes of the 1960s (Chase and Shaw 1989; Lowenthal 1985; McCrone et al. 1995), while others suggest that it was a result of increased leisure time, and thus a greater public interaction with their built and cultural environments (Hunter 1981; Mandler 1997; Tinniswood 1998). Certainly, by the late 1960s and 1970s, there was an increasing momentum in two areas of heritage practice. One was the marked increase in heritage tourism. Prentice argues that mass consumption of heritage tourism became a significant economic and cultural phenomenon by the mid-1970s as public interest in heritage and history increased (1993, 2005; see also Urry 1990; Hollinshead 1997). Another was the degree to which national public heritage policy and legislation was being introduced and/or amended in the Western world. For instance, the Ancient Monuments Act in Great Britain was replaced with the *Ancient Monuments and Archaeological Areas Act 1979*, and other acts were put in place to protect portable antiquities, underwater sites and historic buildings (Hunter and Ralston 1993; Cookson 2000), and similar legislative activity was going on in other

European countries (see Cleere 1984). Australia also developed its first acts at this time to protect both Indigenous, archaeological and built heritage (Smith 2004). The United States, fearing in this period that it was lagging behind Europe in the area of buildings preservation, established a committee under Albert Rains, with the patronage of the American First Lady, Lady Bird Johnson, to review the European laws and procedures and introduce them into legislation in the United States (see Rains [1966] 1983). The US federal government in the 1970s also introduced a number of other acts designed to protect a range of archaeological resources (King 1998). International Charters and Conventions identifying and nominating procedures for protecting buildings and archaeological sites in a variety of different contexts or situations were also adopted.

By the 1970s, at least, it became possible to talk about and recognize a set of procedures and techniques, guided by national legislation and national and international charters, conventions and agreements, concerned with the preservation and management of a range of heritage sites and places. In the United States, this process is called Cultural Resource Management (King 2002), in Europe it tends to be referred to as Archaeological Heritage Management (Willems 2001; Carman 2002) and in Australia, where Indigenous criticism has challenged the idea of heritage both as a 'resource' and as the privileged purview of archaeologists, Cultural Heritage Management is increasingly used. Archaeologists and conservation architects inevitably dominate these processes. This is because, on a practical level, it is members of these disciplines that have lobbied for the legislation, worked within government heritage bureaucracies and amenity societies, and had a significant presence in UNESCO and ICOMOS. On a philosophical level, it is the ability of both disciplines to claim expert authority over material culture (whether as artefacts, sites or structures). Further, and as various historians of archaeology and architecture have identified, the conservation ethic developed in the nineteenth century was both constituted by and continually reinforced within the epistemological frameworks of both disciplines (see, for instance, Murray 1989; Trigger 1989; Byrne 1991; Smith 2004 for archaeology; and Lowenthal 1985; Jokilehto 1999; Earl 2003 for conservation architecture).

The Venice Charter of 1964 is, as Starn (2002: 2) correctly identifies: 'the canonical text of modern' heritage practices. This document reinforces the conservation ethic and stresses one of the key principles of heritage management: that the cultural significance of a site, building, artefact or place must determine its use and management (see Chapter 3). Inevitably, it is those holding expert knowledge that must identify the innate value and significance, which are often defined in terms of historical, scientific, educational or more generally 'cultural' significance. There have been extensive debates about the nature and need for self-conscious significance assessments in Western heritage management, particularly in North America (see, for instance, McGimsey 1972; Lipe 1977, King 2000, Mathers et al. 2005),

Australasia (Sullivan and Bowdler 1984; Fung and Allen 1984; Johnston 1992; Pearson and Sullivan 1995; Byrne et al. 2001) and Europe (Darvill et al. 1987; Darvill 1995, 2005; Carman 1996, 1998; Clark 1999, 2005; Deeben and Groenewoudt 2005). Although extensive, these debates have historically focused on the technical issues of assessment and 'best practice'. Ironically, however, it is in England, the source of many of the justificatory texts of conservation, where the debate about the nature of heritage significance and assessment processes have been less developed relative to other countries such as the United States or Australia. In England (this is less the case in the rest of the UK), value appears to be largely, and often unproblematically, assumed. This may be an expression of the degree to which the cultural values of heritage are part of the cultural common sense of the nation. In the post-colonial contexts of the United States and Australia significance values, as discussed below, have been one of the first areas contested by competing heritage discourses.

The year 1972 is another noteworthy milestone in the development and institutionalization of the heritage discourse. In that year, UNESCO adopted the *Convention Concerning the Protection of the World Cultural and Natural Heritage*, which established an international agenda for the protection and conservation of sites of universal significance, and importantly confirmed the presence of 'heritage' as an international issue. In addition, the World Heritage Convention further institutionalized the nineteenth-century conservation ethic and the 'conserve as found' ethos. As Choay (2001: 140) has argued, the European sense of the historical monument as universally significant underwrites this Convention, which inevitably universalizes Western values and systems of thought (see also Byrne 1991). A glance at the World Heritage List today demonstrates the degree to which the sense of the monumental underwrites the convention, with cathedrals and grand buildings of state dominating the listing process (Cleere 2001). Under this convention, heritage *is* not only monumental, it *is* universally significant with universal meaning, and it *is*, ultimately, physically tangible and imposing. The idea of 'authenticity' is also significant in this convention, and in many ICOMOS charters. Starn (2002) argues that the degree of attention given to the idea of authenticity in heritage management and conservation is a relatively new issue and was not one that exercised nineteenth-century European conservationists, and suggests that it was not until the writing of the Venice Charter that authenticity becomes a notable problem. He sees the concern with 'authenticity' in this document as deriving largely from a reaction to the devastation caused to cityscapes during the Second World War and the runaway urban development of the 1960s. He suggests the use of the word was a call for continuity in the rapid post-war changes to urban centres (2002: 8). Certainly the concept has taken on added force and authority in the post-war period, and has found a certain synergy with the conservation ethic. As Colin Graham (2001: 63) notes: 'authenticity tends to a monologic unquestioning discourse concurrent with the idea of the "nation", it arises also out of contexts in which the nation becomes an active arbiter between the past and a "people" . . . [it] combines the prioritisation of "origins" with the "pathos of incessant change".'

This section has demonstrated that there is a self-referential 'authorized heritage discourse', whose authority rests in part on its ability to 'speak to' and make sense of the aesthetic experiences of its practitioners and policy makers, and by the fact of its institutionalization within a range of national and international organizations and codes of practice. The *when* of heritage stretches back to nineteenth-century values and cultural concerns, the *where* of this discourse may be found not only in Western Europe, but also more specifically in the authorial voices of the upper middle and ruling classes of European educated professionals and elites. It is as much a discourse of nationalism and patriotism as it is of certain class experiences and social and aesthetic value. However, this discourse has not been unchallenged. Internationally, the World Heritage Convention has been criticized, in particular by non-Western nations and commentators, for universalizing Western concepts of heritage and the values inherent within that (see, for instance, Blake 2001; Cleere 2001). In response to this, UNESCO adopted the 2003 *Convention for the Safeguarding of the Intangible Cultural Heritage*. This convention attempts to recognize new and non-Western ways of understanding heritage – how successful this is in challenging the dominant discourse is discussed in Chapter 3.

In addition, community groups from within many Western countries have also challenged the dominant discourse and advocated greater community participation; demanding that practitioners recognize not only locally geographically defined communities, but also communities bound together by common social, cultural, economic and/or political experiences. Also Indigenous criticism in post-colonial countries about the inequities inherent in the ways in which museums, archaeologists and other heritage practitioners have dealt with human remains and other items of cultural value and significance have been increasingly influential. A second prong of attack has centred on the economic commodification and 'Disneyfication' of mass heritage tourism (Handler and Saxton 1988; McCrone et al. 1995; Brett 1996; Waitt and McGuirk 1996; Handler and Gable 1997; Waitt 2000; Choay 2001; Greenspan 2002). In the United Kingdom, this criticism has been particularly vociferous, marshalled as a critique of the so-called 'heritage industry' led by historians Robert Hewison (1981, 1987) and Patrick Wright (1985, 1991), which has also criticized the self-referential and elitist nature of the discourse. The next section of this chapter will examine in more detail the consequences of the authorized heritage discourse and then return to consider these competing discourses in more detail.

The authorized heritage discourse and its use

The authorized heritage discourse (AHD) focuses attention on aesthetically pleasing material objects, sites, places and/or landscapes that current generations 'must' care for, protect and revere so that they may be passed to nebulous future generations for their 'education', and to forge a sense of common identity based on the past. This section briefly outlines some of the key consequences of this discourse in constituting and legitimizing what heritage *is*, and in defining who has the ability to speak for and about the nature and meaning of heritage.

One of the consequences of the AHD is that it defines who the legitimate spokespersons for the past are. One of the ways the AHD does this is through he rhetorical device of 'the past', which is used as a shorthand or an alternative to 'heritage'. 'The past' is vague, though the use of the definite article also identifies something both singular and concrete. The vagueness of 'the past', its mystery and 'hard to pin downness', immediately works to render it subject to the judgements of experts such as archaeologists and historians. It is part of the discourse that maps out what it is archaeologists and other areas of expertise may have domain over – the vagueness being particularly useful here. Yet, the definite article also identifies that there is *a* past that will be looked after by expert analysis and study. The important point here is that terms like 'the past', when used to discuss and define heritage, disengage us from the very real emotional and cultural work that the past does as heritage for individuals and communities. The past is not abstract; it has material reality as heritage, which in turn has material consequences for community identity and belonging. The past cannot simply be reduced to archaeological data or historical texts – it is someone's heritage.

One of the other ways the AHD maps out the authority of expertise is through the idea of 'inheritance' and patrimony. The current generation, best represented by 'experts', are seen as stewards or caretakers of the past, thus working to disengage the present (or at least certain social actors in the present) from an active use of heritage. Heritage, according to the AHD, is inevitably saved 'for future generations' a rhetoric that undermines the ability of the present, unless under the professional guidance of heritage professionals, to alter or change the meaning and value of heritage sites or places. In disempowering the present from actively rewriting the meaning of the past, the use of the past to challenge and rewrite cultural and social meaning in the present becomes more difficult.

Another crucial theme of this discourse is the idea that 'heritage' is innately valuable. This is because 'heritage' is seen to represent all that is good and important about the past, which has contributed to the development of the cultural character of the present. Moreover, embedded within this discourse is the idea that the proper care of heritage, and its associated values, lies with the experts, as it is only they who have the abilities, knowledge and understanding to identify the innate value and knowledge contained at and within historically important sites and places. This is an embedded assumption within the discourse that has a legacy in antiquarian understandings of knowledge and material culture. Principally, it is architects, historians and archaeologists who act as stewards for the past, so that present and future publics may be properly educated and informed about its significance.

The heritage literature maintains that heritage is a symbolic representation of identity. Material or tangible heritage provides a physical representation of those things from 'the past' that speak to a sense of place, a sense of self, of belonging and community. The emergence of the heritage discourse within the context of nineteenth-century nationalism has meant that the primary form of identity often associated with heritage is that of the nation (see Macdonald 2003; Graham et al. 2005). This is reinforced by the nationalizing discourses that underlie the discipline of archaeology and history (Meskell 2001, 2002, 2003; Kane 2003; Diaz-Andreu under review) and the emphasis on the universality of heritage values and principles embedded in documents such as the World Heritage Convention (Byrne 1991). Such an emphasis means that other forms of identity are often obscured or devalued. The literature on globalization has made strong claims about the localizing affects of this process, whereby the local has become a greater focus in terms of identity work (Chang et al. 1996; Escobar 2001; Berking 2003; Castells 2004). However, this shift in focus is not accommodated easily by a discourse that is ultimately assimilationist in nature, drawing as it does on the narrative of nation and universality of world heritage. The heritage discourse, in providing a sense of national community, must, by definition, ignore a diversity of sub-national cultural and social experiences. Ultimately, the discourse draws on too narrow a sense of experience of what heritage is and what it may mean to readily incorporate sub-national identities.

Within the narrative of nation, the heritage discourse also explicitly promotes the experience and values of elite social classes. This works to alienate a range of other social and cultural experiences and it has been no accident that the heritage phenomena has been criticized for absenting women (Johnston 1993; Smith 1993; Dubrow 2003), a range of ethnic and other community groups (Leone et al. 1995; Hayden 1997; Ling Wong 1999, 2000; Shackel 2001), Indigenous communities (Langford 1983; Fourmile 1989b; Deloria 1992; Ah Kit 1995; Watkins 2003) and working class and labour history (Johnston 1993; Hayden 1997; Dicks 1997, 2000a). While the AHD may work to exclude the historical, cultural and social experiences of a range of groups, it also works to constrain and limit their critique. It does this on a broad level by privileging the expert and their values over those of the non-expert, and by the self-referential nature of the discourse, which continually legitimizes itself and the values and ideologies on which it is based. However, the emphasis on materialism in this discourse also helps constrain critique.

Linked to the idea of the materiality of heritage is the idea of its 'bounded-ness'. Heritage has traditionally been conceived within the AHD as a discrete 'site', 'object', building or other structure with identifiable boundaries that can be mapped, surveyed, recorded, and placed on national or international site registers. This ability to reduce the concept of heritage to 'manageable' and discrete locales helps to reduce the social, cultural or historical conflicts about the meaning, value or nature of heritage, or more broadly the past, into discrete and specific conflicts over individual sites and/or technical issues of site management. Over the last decade, however, and as disciplines such as geography start to consider heritage issues, greater attention has focused on the idea of cultural landscapes and their heritage values (see, for instance, Titchen 1996; Jones and Rotherham 1998; Fairclough 1999; Cotter et al. 2001; Fairclough and Rippon 2002). As Head (2000b) has demonstrated, the philosophical separation of concepts of 'nature' and 'culture' during the Enlightenment has lead to an assumption that landscape is inherently a nat-ural rather than a cultural phenomena. Waterton (2005a) and Titchen (1996) have argued that this has affected the ability of heritage organizations to embrace the idea of cultural landscape as heritage. However, this ability is also hindered by the discursive construction of heritage that naturalizes it as a discrete 'spot' or locale within a landscape. This conceptualization helps to obfuscate wider cultural and historical debates about the meaning of the past, and works to draw tight conceptual and knowledge boundaries around the meanings and values given to these locales. The idea of a cultural land-scape as heritage makes both conceptual and physical space for a wider range and layering of competing values and meanings than does the idea of 'site'. The consequence of this will be explored in Chapter 5.

However, another aspect of the AHD's obfuscation of, and attempts to exclude, competing discourses is the way it constructs heritage as something that is engaged with passively – while it may be the subject of popular 'gaze', that gaze is a passive one in which the audience will uncritically consume the message of heritage constructed by heritage experts. Heritage is not defined in the AHD as an active process or experience, but rather it is something visitors are led to, are instructed about, but are then not invited to engage with more actively. The 'glass case' display mentality Merriman (1991) iden-tified for museum exhibitions is equally present in traditional interpretation and presentations of heritage sites and places (see also Hall and McArthur 1996).

This mentality helps to exclude non-traditional conceptions of heritage as it is assumed that heritage visitors will not value sites and places that do not fit into the dominant aesthetic. An example is Diane Barthel's (1996: 68–9) discussion of the possibility of interpreting an industrial site in such a way that it recalls the inequities, aggression and unpleasantness of industrial life. She states that: 'the raw masculinity . . . [of the industrial workplace] is not the usual subject for tours of schoolchildren and senior citizens or for family

31

outings. Layers of dirt and grime violate tourist expectations, and serious questioning of industrialism's costs runs counter to the ideology of many political and economic interests involved in preservation.' Despite the critical acuity of her latter point, she does assume that visitors to such sites have uncritically accepted the dominant discourse, and that they tend only to be interested in the traditional aesthetics of heritage and nothing else. Not only is she assuming that dominant perceptions of heritage *are* indeed universally shared, she also assumes that heritage visitors are inherently uncritical and passive.

'The public', and more specifically visitors to heritage sites and museums, are too often conceptualized as 'empty vessels' or passive consumers of the heritage message (Mason 2004, 2005). The idea of the passivity of the gaze of heritage visitors or consumers derives from three factors. Firstly, it has a legacy in the values and ideologies of the liberal educational movement that influenced early museum development and the conservation movement. Secondly, it lies in the 'conserve as found' ethos that identifies sites as something to be looked upon and passed unchanged on to the future. Work by Emma Waterton (2005b) on the visual imagery of England's heritage agency, English Heritage, demonstrates the degree to which this ethos permeates the perception of heritage and management practices in that country. In her critique, she identifies the systemic absence of people in the visual imagery used to attract visitors and represent its heritage properties more widely. She also notes that although many properties are ruins, they are neatly – almost ostentatiously – maintained. Keith Emerick (2003) also argues that the on-site manicured presentation of most heritage properties managed by English Heritage is a direct reflection of the Ruskinian conservation ethic, citing policy documents from throughout the twentieth century instilling the need for site managers to keep sites neat and tidy. This sense of tidy control is brutally represented by the immaculate lawns that characteristically surround most ruins, buildings and other English Heritage properties and which help facilitate the management aim of:

> conserving the beauty and the stability of the old buildings in its charge without involving the removal or alteration of a single old stone or the addition of a single new one, except upon obvious structural necessity. The monuments are allowed to tell their own story without the intrusion of modern architectural design, whether good or bad, affecting the question.
>
> (William Harvey, architect in the Office of Works – the then body responsible for heritage – 1922, cited in Emerick 2003: 112)

Thirdly, it owes something to the recent developments in mass tourism. During the 1980s a strong critique of heritage emerged that focused on the development of mass consumption and tourist marketing of heritage attractions. A focus of this critique was the idea that tourism reduced heritage to simple entertainment, with the derogative motif of 'theme park' becoming central to this critique. Patrick Wright (1985), for instance, warned that Britain had itself become one gigantic heritage theme park, which Hewison (1987) thought was integral to the cultural decline of Britain. This critique has been echoed in other countries, where heritage has been accused of stifling creativity and sanitizing or simplifying the historical messages of the past (McCrone et al. 1995; Brett 1996; Choay 2001: 4–5; Burton 2003). For instance, Colonial Williamsburg, one of the American Flagship heritage sites often associated with American patriotism, cultural achievement and aesthetics, has been a particular focus of this critique. The need to attract more visitors has resulted in what Greenspan identifies as 'low brow' advertising, and he reports the unease felt by heritage professionals that the 'fun' side of the site has been promoted over its educational role (2002: 175). While the Disneyfication of tourism marketing and interpretation is a feature of real concern (Smith et al. 1992; Hollinshead 1997; Waitt 2000), this critique has been extended to heritage interpretation more generally. Hewison (1987) scornfully identifies a 'heritage industry', which commodifies, sanitizes and creates a false past and stifles cultural development and creativity.

While Rafael Samuel (1994) has demonstrated that it is inappropriate to lump all heritage under this label, and that heritage does much more than offer a sanitized version of the past, nonetheless it is a critique that has had some force both in Britain and internationally. Although it appears to stand in opposition to the AHD, the heritage industry critique, as discussed below in more detail, reproduces some of the work the AHD does in constructing heritage visitors or users as passive consumers. Within this critique visitors are redefined as 'tourists', which further distances heritage users from an active sense of engagement with heritage sites – as tourists they are by definition culturally foreign to the heritage site in question and may be conceived as 'simply passing through'. The idea that most visitors or users of heritage sites are 'tourists' has now become a pervasive motif in the AHD; the consequence of this will be discussed more fully in following chapters (particularly 2, 4 and 6).

The advent of mass heritage tourism, together with the economic rationalist discourse of the market that took hold in the 1980s and 1990s (Dicks 2003: 33), has also brought the lexicon of 'consumption' into heritage debates. Jane Malcom-Davies, in her critique of the history of heritage interpretation, identifies its conservation and preservation origins, which she then claims as overlain by a more recent 'heritage phase' and states that: 'The "heritage" phase is the one in which the resource is transformed into a product for consumption in the marketplace' (2004: 279). In this construction, 'heritage' is conflated with mass tourism and the processes of engagement with heritage are reduced to simple consumption. This is not to say that heritage is not an economic resource, rather that the reduction of heritage as only or largely a product of the marketplace helps to reinforce the idea that heritage is a 'thing' that is passively and uncritically consumed. Embedded in 'common sense' views of consumption is the perception that it is a passive process in which mass consumers are manipulated by the narcotic effect of the media (Abercrombie and Longhurst 1998: 5) or, in this case, tourism marketing.

Subsequently, what is absent in the AHD is a sense of 'action' or critical engagement on the part of non-expert users of heritage, as heritage is about receiving the wisdom and knowledge of historians, archaeologists and other experts. This obscures the sense of memory work, performativity and acts of remembrance that commentators such as Nora (1989), Urry (1996) and Bagnall (2003) identify as occurring at heritage sites (these ideas are discussed in more detail in Chapter 2). However, the point to be made here is that the AHD establishes and sanctions a top-down relationship between expert, heritage site and 'visitor', in which the expert 'translates', using Bauman's (1987) sense of the word, the site and its meanings to the visitor. The very use of the term 'visitor' also facilitates the construction of passivity and disconnection. When 'visitors', or heritage users, step outside of this legitimized relationship the critique from heritage professionals can be swift and uncompromising. Witness the degree of condemnation of heritage re-enactments and re-enactors within the heritage and museum literature, which condemns such activities as being amateurish, unauthentic, sanitized, escapist and so forth (see, for instance, Hewison 1987: 83; Dening 1994: 4–5; Kammen 1991: 605–6; Beidler 1999; see exchanges in Sutton 2001; see also Handler and Saxton 1988; Uzzell 1989; Abroe 1998 for extended critical commentary). Mike Crang (1996) argues, on the other hand, that re-enactors are often concerned with actively engaging and negotiating the meaning of the events they re-enact and the sites at which these events occurred, and that it is part of a personal strategy of negotiating heritage meaning. As he notes, re-enactors are often patronized by academics, although, as he illustrates, many re-enactors carry out extensive research into the events they reconstruct and the roles they play as actors within the reconstructed events. The point is that regardless of whether we agree or disagree with the interpretations produced, what is produced is perceived as an authentic and legitimate way of understanding and using heritage sites for those involved. For some of us, the activities of re-enactors may be viewed as an eccentric or irrelevant hobby. However, it is a process that nonetheless challenges the roles established for non-expert users of heritage, and the strength of reactions it engenders in the traditional heritage literature, highlights the degree to which the AHD decrees that heritage is to be viewed from afar as an unchanging vista rather than actively *used*, remade and negotiated.

Subaltern and dissenting heritage discourses

As Graham et al. observe (2000: 258), 'heritage may represent the dominant ideological discourse, but that also ensures that it can become the focus of alternative meaning for those who dissent'. There are a number of dissenting discourses and critiques about the nature, meaning and use of heritage. Two broad strands of debate are identified here. The first concerns the expression of subaltern discourses of community participation in heritage management and conservation processes. These are 'subaltern' in that they stand outside of the dominant discourse, and this section outlines the development of this broad area of dissent and examines the responses of both heritage institutions and the heritage literature to it. It is argued that in large part the official responses, although often well meaning in their attempts to deal with this critique, are constrained in their attempts because of the conceptual problems of extending debate and practices outside of the frameworks established by the AHD. The second strand of dissent outlined is that developed around the critique of the British 'heritage industry' and heritage tourism more broadly. This strand of critique cannot be identified as part of a 'subaltern' discourse, nor, as it is argued, does it offer a concrete challenge to the AHD, as the heritage industry critique shares all too much discursive space with the AHD.

There is a growing literature in heritage studies that expresses a strong desire to identify and engage with community participation in heritage management, interpretation and conservation work, which is often expressed as community outreach or social and cultural inclusion (see, for instance, Hayden 1997; Newman and McLean 1998; Hodges and Watson 2000; Byrne et al. 2001; Smardz Frost 2004; Gard'ner 2004; amongst many others). Specific disciplines that engage directly with the heritage management process have also participated in extensive debates about community involvement in research and heritage practices, although these are often relegated to marginalized subfields, for instance in archaeological and historical debates about 'public archaeology'/'public history' (Carman 2002; Hodgkin and Radstone 2003b). The need, and in some cases even the desire, to identify and work with community groups has arisen as a consequence of the agitation by these groups for greater inclusion and consideration of their own needs, aspirations and values in the way the past is used in present society.

The greatest challenge has arisen from agitation by Indigenous or First Nations peoples from around the world. Although often focusing on issues surrounding the reclamation and reburial of Indigenous human remains, the claims by Indigenous communities to control their past is more profound than simple conflicts over the possession or 'ownership' of particular relics, remains or artefacts. The issues revolve around the cultural politics of identity – who has the legitimacy and power to define who a particular group or community *are* and who they are not (see Chapter 8 for more details). The ability to control your own identity, to define who you are and to establish a sense of community belonging is emotionally and politically a powerful act. A sense of identity must inevitably draw on a sense of history and memory – who and what we are as individuals, communities or nations is indelibly formed by our sense of history and the way individual and collective memory is understood, commemorated and propagated.

The primary targets for Indigenous criticism were those with the intellectual authority and power to define how the past is used to legitimize (or not) certain forms of identity within Western societies – so criticism was particularly targeted at archaeologists, anthropologists, museum curators and historians. Although these criticisms were particularly pointed in post-colonial contexts, they nonetheless have pointed correspondences for post-imperial nations within Europe. The universalizing tendencies of the World Heritage Convention have also been singled out for criticism by Indigenous peoples and other non-Western cultures for failing to incorporate culturally relevant concepts of heritage (Cleere 2001; Munjeri 2004; see also Chapter 3).

The issue of community participation is often, at least in the archaeologically informed heritage literature, defined as 'indigenous issues'. However, these criticisms have been echoed by many other culturally- and socially-defined community groups in many Western and non-Western countries. In the United Kingdom, for instance, organizations such as the Black Environmental Network (BEN) have lobbied for greater involvement of ethnic communities in government heritage polices (Ling Wong 1999, 2000) and various local community groups and interests apply pressure on heritage practitioners and government agencies alike (Hall 1999; Littler and Naidoo 2004). Throughout the world a range of interests are also highly active in challenging traditional heritage practices or reworking new understandings of heritage (Hayden 1997; Shackel 2001). A number of issues are raised in these critiques; of particular note is the issue that traditional and authorized definitions of heritage tell nationalizing stories that simply do not reflect the cultural or social experiences of subaltern groups. This is problematic as it discounts the historical legitimacy of the experiences of these communities and thus the social, cultural and/or political roles they play in the present are ignored or trivialized. It also helps to obfuscate continuing social inequities and perpetuates social and political marginalization (see, for instance, Langford 1983; Fourmile 1989a, 1989b; Ling Wong 1999; Deloria 1992; Watkins 2001, 2003; Littler and Naidoo 2004). In addition, definitions of heritage that stress its materiality also fail to acknowledge non-material or intangible forms of heritage, and thus the resources or processes used in sub-national group identity work are denied or marginalized (Teather and Chow 2003: 115). Yet another issue is that the 'conserve as found' mentality means that more active interactions and engagements with heritage become problematic as community groups attempt to step out of the passive role of the heritage 'visitor' defined within the AHD. This issue is often raised in tensions over the use of sites like Stonehenge by alternative religious groups (Chippindale 1985, 1986; Bender 1992, 1998; Skeates 2000) or in the use of historic battlefields by re-enactment groups (Hewison 1987: 83; Beidler 1999; Sutton 2001) or the repainting of Aboriginal rock art sites in Australia by their Indigenous cultural owners (see Mowljarlai and Peck 1987; Bowdler 1988), amongst other examples.

The so-called 'post-modern' concern with multi-vocality has also facilitated the acknowledgement of divergent and multiple conceptualizations of history and heritage within academic and public policy contexts. For instance, research by historians Rosenzweig and Thelen (1998) in the United States reveals a significant difference in the ways Euro-Americans and African-Americans and Indigenous-Americans understand and use history. Their research demonstrates that Euro-Americans tend to see the past within the context of a national and authorized narrative, while for many of the African- and Indigenous-Americans surveyed a more community and family orientated sense of history was expressed, which, unsurprisingly, often stood in opposition to the national narrative. A similar survey in Australia has also found that many people engage with history at a far more personal and engaged level than previously understood (Ashton 2005). In England, a MORI (2000) poll commissioned by English Heritage surveyed public attitudes to heritage, which also revealed that many Black and Asian British people saw traditional definitions of heritage and its association with national narratives as irrelevant to them. The response to both agitation by community organizations and other interest groups, and the increasing realization of competing conceptualizations of heritage, have seen many government heritage agencies and amenity societies initiate policies for greater community participation in the ways the past is understood and used. One such response is the 'social inclusion/exclusion' policies of the current British Labour government, responses that are expressed in similar terms or as 'outreach programmes' in other European countries and the United States (Newman and McLean 1998, 2004; Newman 2005) and as community participation in Australia.

However, what I want to suggest here is that these policies too often tend to be assimilationist and top-down in nature rather than bottom-up substantive challenges to the AHD. In the first instance, these policies and debates are often framed in terms of how excluded groups may be recruited into existing practices, and how may non-traditional visitors be attracted or encouraged to visit existing heritage sites. Laudable, as far as they go – but this creates a conceptual framework that heritage practitioners must simply add the excluded and assimilate them into the fold rather than challenge underlying preconceptions. As Pendlebury et al. (2004: 23) observe, 'merely enabling more people to enjoy heritage, or extending how it is defined to recognize the diversity of society, does not in itself challenge power relations and control over the process by which heritage is defined and managed.' Community consultation undertaken without an active sense of negotiation between community understandings and values and those of practitioners can simply become gestural politics. As I have argued elsewhere (2004), a critical and engaged understanding of the power and authority of competing heritage discourses, and the relative power and authority that underpins them, is necessary before negotiation can commence. However, this is not easy as the AHD naturalizes a sense of the legitimacy of traditional definitions of heritage, which are institutionalized in heritage legislation, and national and international government and amenity policy documents. Heritage practitioners who may wish to challenge the AHD must walk a perilous tightrope between those community groups they may wish to support or concede knowledge and experience to, and those that, for a range of political and cultural reasons, they may wish to challenge and exclude.

Heritage practitioners are required to adopt an overt political agenda in defining which groups and interests they seek to support and those they challenge (Schadla-Hall 2004). For instance, some practitioners may wish to support the aspirations of locally geographically defined communities, or support issues that address such things as ethnic, gender and/or class inequality. However, they may also wish to actively challenge creationist view points, or those who may wish to exclude view points that ignore the role of class, gender and other contentious issues in the history and experiences of the past, or may wish to challenge the value of some heritage to local communities. The overt political nature of supporting (or otherwise) community and other interests is viewed as particularly problematic within the bureaucratic processes of heritage management and conservation, based as they are on the ideologies of the impartiality of expertise. Subsequently, the issue of community participation in framing and implementing heritage practices teeters between a desire to include and a hesitancy to surrender or reduce the authority of both the AHD and the heritage practitioners to wield it, and to recognize the inherently political and discordant nature of heritage.

The other strand of critique examined here is that centred on the advent of mass tourism, which in Britain has been led by historians Wright (1985, 1991) and Hewison (1981, 1987, 1991). Both saw increasing mass interest in heritage as a symptom of a backward-looking country, in which a nostalgic yearning for better times had stifled cultural innovation and development, and was itself an expression of a loss in cultural confidence and overall cultural decline. Hewison (1987) identified what he called a 'heritage industry', which he argued offered sanitized, false and inauthentic history to a gullible audience of heritage tourists.

For Wright (1985, 1991: 45f.), in particular, the elitist nature of heritage was particularly alarming. One symptom of the retarding gaze of heritage he identified was the post-war increase in the mobilization of public interest in country houses, alongside the growth of country house visiting. This phenomenon was an expression of the degree to which certain versions of the past were being reinforced and propagated. He noted (1985: 22) that, 'in a world where the social hierarchy has lost its settled nature, it is not so surprising that old forms of security become alluring', while going on to note that in the traditional mode of 'upstairs/downstairs' life the distinct divisions between servants and 'family' offered a certain comforting authority for modern life. In this process, the social values of the elites were argued as actively being preserved as part of a politically conservative backlash to prevent cultural and social change in the present and future (see also Lowenthal 1985; Hewison 1987: 53; Walsh 1992). Heritage was thus identified as part of a conservative backlash against post-war social and economic change.

Visitor surveys, as Prentice (2005: 249) reports, have continually demonstrated a disproportionately middle class profile of participants in heritage tourism (see also Merriman 1991), further fuelling the sense that heritage is an elite concern presenting social messages only of relevance to the socially and economically comfortable. It was also these classes that were leading the gentrification of deindustrialized urban areas and the reinforcement of various aesthetic values through conspicuous heritage consumption added to the sense of self-referential and self-congratulatory social politics of the time (Urry 1995). In Britain, heritage became synonymous with rightwing politics and entrepreneurialism, with some commentators associating it with Thatcherite cultural and social control and free market enterprise (Shanks and Tilley 1987; Corner and Harvey 1991; Dicks 2000a: 33). Samuel noted that heritage had been characterized as 'Thatcherism in period dress' (1994: 290). Certainly, Urry (1996: 52) is correct in observing that the dominant trend in British heritage is to make history 'safe, sterile and shorn of danger, subversion and seduction'. As Wright (1985, 1991) observed, these tendencies were not confined to Britain, but became more pervasive during the cultural, economic, and political climates of Britain during the 1980s. Three social trends may be associated with this. Firstly, it may be a symptom of the insecurity of England's sense of national identity, tied as it is to the collective 'Britain' and the imperial history and loss of imperial identity that Union now represents (Daniels 1993: 3; Colley 1999; Lumley 2005: 15).

Secondly, this national angst is coupled with a greater hesitation in recognizing post-imperial multiculturalism, and there has been greater public tensions and debates about multicultural issues in post-colonial countries than has occurred in England (see also Barthel 1996). Thirdly, England takes a certain pride in the degree to which it perceives itself to have greater continuity in cultural traditions, institutions and expressions than other European nations, which have more frequently and directly been subject to wars and revolutions. This sense of cultural pride in social and cultural continuity is well demonstrated by the Duke of Norfolk in his foreword to *The Cambridge Illustrated Dictionary of British Heritage*:

I have often pointed out that, although we are part of Christendom and have taken part in so many of the activities of our European neighbours, such as the Crusades and the Renaissance, our heritage of buildings (castles, palaces, country houses, cathedrals and, indeed, whole towns) has not suffered to the same extent from the destruction that took place across the English Channel owing to the wars and revolutions that have ravaged their lands. Many of our political, legal, educational, and economic institutions too, have survived many centuries with little change. We can indeed be proud of our continuity, which is well illustrated by the fact that our Queen can provide direct descent from the Saxon King, Cerdic, who died in 534 AD.

(Norfolk 1987: vii; see Pearce 1989: 124, for similar sentiments)

Whatever the cause, Hewison, Wright and others hit a chord in English public and academic debate, and the idea of 'heritage' in England took on an uncomfortable and problematic edge in public policy debate thereafter, with English Heritage in recent years reinventing 'heritage' as the 'historic environment'. What Lowenthal (1998: 100) defines as the 'antiheritage animus' is not confined to debates amongst British historians, but is internationally pervasive in the heritage critical literature. The concern that 'heritage', and/or its commodification as an economic and cultural resource, inherently stifles cultural creativity, encourages reactionary nostalgia and a consensual view of history while focusing public cultural attention backward is conspicuous in the international literature (see, for instance, Bickford 1981, 1983; Beckman 1993, cited in Hjemdahl 2002: 106; McCrone et al. 1995; Schouten 1995; Brett 1996; Lowenthal 1998; Choay 2001; Knecht and Niedermüller 2002; Gable and Handler 2003; Debary 2004). Likewise, critiques about the sanitization of history for the sake of tourism revenue and the emphasis on historical titillation as a form of tourism experience are prevalent (Smith et al. 1992; Hollinshead 1997; Waitt 2000; Rowan and Baram 2004).

Authenticity has become a central issue, and the rising interest in reconstructions and on-site dramatizations further fuels concern over the degree to which heritage may move away from the authority of historical texts and archaeological fact, and spill into the so-called 'heritage theme park'. Although the search for cultural 'authenticity' is understood to paradoxically drive the tourist experience while also constructing cultural experiences that must undermine it (MacCannell 1973, 1999; Harkin 1995), the tourism literature has begun to question the nature of traditional accounts of 'authenticity' and authentic experiences. Commentators within tourism studies have suggested that tourists may understand authenticity entirely differently than it is traditionally defined and understood within the AHD, with its emphasis on inherent material qualities. Instead, they have begun to stress the idea of emotional and experiential authenticity (Prentice 1998, 2001; McIntosh and Prentice 1999, 2004). This is discussed more fully in Chapter 2; however, a particular problem here is that the tourism literature invariably frames all discussions of this thorny issue in terms of marketing and consumption, which many researchers of the humanities and social science disciplines that intersect with heritage issues often see as intellectually simplistic, and thus of little intellectual utility. It is worth noting that, as Tribe (1997) observes, not all tourism studies are so simplistic, though they are nonetheless often seen as such.

While the heritage industry critique warns against some cultural and socially stultifying and reactionary uses of heritage, its critical utility in advancing debates about the nature and use of heritage is limited. This is because it tends to assume that all 'heritage' innately invokes a sense of nostalgia. 'Nostalgia' is commonly assumed to be intrinsically conservative, and is seen as synonymous with a plea for social continuity, often in the face of change or in response to a sense of social loss (Grainge 1999: 623). There is, however, nothing inherently reactionary nor right wing or indeed progressive and left wing in the idea of heritage. It may be inherently conservative, but not necessarily with a capital C. Its sense of conservation can resonate with ideologies of 'it was better back then', but equally may engage with more critical and challenging social values and experiences. Rafael Samuel (1994), in response to the heritage critique, demonstrates that heritage does far more, and is employed in far more progressive and socially diverse ways, than has been generally admitted to in the British heritage literature. Indeed he argued that 'so far from heritage being the medium through which a Conservative vision of the national past becomes hegemonic, one could see its advent as part of a sea-change in view of the national past – liberal, radical or Conservative in tatters' (1994: 281). Some of the diverse ways heritage is used and expressed are explored more fully in later chapters; however, it is important to note here that the totalizing critique offered by the 'heritage industry' literature is itself problematic. By identifying all heritage as either elitist and/or commercially inspired pastiche, little conceptual room is made for alternative uses of heritage, or for identifying the roles that disciplines like history and archaeology play in the constitution and legitimization of heritage. Lowenthal (1998: 104) has quite correctly argued that heritage and history (and for which we could also add archaeology) 'serve quite different purposes' and thus are not the same. However, this does not mean that disciplines such as history and archaeology can identify themselves as bystanders in the development of heritage narratives. As Hollinshead (1997: 179) points out: 'sanctioned history remains tilted to the story-lines of the privileged: in practice, that is perhaps history, by definition.'

The reaction to the development of mass visitation or heritage tourism in the 1970s also hints at disciplinary boundary marking. There is a sense that emerges in this literature that mass interest in the past is *inherently* negative.

As people engage with 'heritage' (however we define it), a conceptual 'intermediary' enters the equation and the public become 'once removed' from the pronouncements about history and the past made by the disciplines of history and archaeology. In this critique, heritage audiences are, as in the AHD, defined as passive, if not dupes, of the heritage industry (Samuel 1994: 267). The public are unknowingly manipulated by tourism marketing, as they are not under the direct supervision of historical or other intellectually-sanctioned expertise. This is not to say that the Wright and Hewison critique does not have some application to various heritage scenarios as demonstrated in Chapter 4; however, it is simply not the full story. Further, the concern with authenticity and commodification, and the identification of 'heritage' with social and political reaction, share all too much conceptual ground with the AHD, which leaves the significance of 'heritage' at an intellectual impasse between the AHD and the heritage industry critique.

Conclusion

This chapter has attempted to map out the discursive field of heritage, and has identified the authorized or dominant discourse against which a range of dissenting and subaltern discourses interact. The authorized discourse of heritage creates a particular set of cultural and social practices that have certain legacies in the context of late modernity. It is now the task of the rest of the book to examine the consequences of the existence of the authorized discourse and to illuminate the social relations it both reflects and constructs and the ways in which it is challenged and subverted. For the purpose of the arguments developed in this volume, the characterization of the authorized discourse as reflecting the grand narratives of nation and aesthetics, and as bolstering and privileging expert and professional judgements and steward-ship over 'the past', has tended to stress overarching themes and skated over more nuanced aspects of the discourse. Certainly, the authorized discourse as I have characterized it will vary over time and will reflect and give particular emphasis to differing elements in different cultural contexts in the West (see, for instance, Chapter 5). However, the identification of a historically, insti-tutionally and politically situated discourse is useful for identifying the ways in which certain understandings about the nature and meaning of heritage have been excluded in heritage practices, and the consequences this exclusion has had for the expression of cultural and social identity. Its identification also helps to understand the nature of 'heritage' itself as a social process concerned with the creation and maintenance of certain social and cultural values.

As this chapter illustrates, the discourse of heritage not only establishes who has the power or 'responsibilities' to define and 'speak for' the past, but is also a process that continually creates and recreates a range of social rela-tions, values and meanings about both the past and present. The authorized discourse is itself a form of 'heritage' in that it legitimizes and defines the identities of a range of social actors and mediates the social relations between them, while also defining and legitimizing values that underpin those relations. Understanding the discursive element of heritage – the way ideas about 'heritage' are constructed and legitimated – also facilitates the identification of the philosophical and conceptual barriers that may exist in either recognizing or in engaging with competing or excluded forms of 'heritage'. Chapter 2 takes up the challenge offered by the analysis of the authorized heritage discourse and attempts to develop an idea of 'heritage' that takes us beyond the conceptual field provided by both the authorized discourse and the heritage industry critique.

2

HERITAGE AS A CULTURAL PROCESS

The aim of this chapter is to explore new ways of understanding the nature of 'heritage' and the 'work' that this concept does. The last chapter identified the dominant discourse of heritage, and argued that this discourse constitutes the idea of heritage in such a way as to exclude certain social actors and interests from actively engaging with heritage. Not only does this discourse frame heritage audiences as passive receptors of the authorized meaning of heritage, it also creates significant barriers for active public negotiation about the meaning and nature of heritage, and the social and cultural roles that it may play. Consequently, most attempts at public or community inclusion into heritage programmes are inevitably expressed in assimilatory terms, in that excluded community groups become 'invited' to 'learn', 'share' or become 'educated' about authorized heritage values and meanings. Although there has been significant criticism about the nature of heritage, centred on the critique of economic commodification, this criticism shares all too much conceptual space with the authorized discourse. Although this critique does significantly contribute to the account of what the AHD does, it does not tell the whole story (Urry 1990: 112; Samuel 1994). Subsequently, we are left at a theoretical impasse – how might a sense of heritage be constructed that is both more inclusive of alternate discourses, and provides a framework for analysing the use of heritage beyond that already identified within the heritage industry critique?

To explore this issue, this chapter commences from the premise that 'heritage' is not a 'thing', it is not a 'site', building or other material object. While these things are often important, they are not in themselves heritage. Rather, heritage is what goes on at these sites, and while this does not mean that a sense of physical place is not important for these activities or plays some role in them, the physical place or 'site' is not the full story of what heritage may be. Heritage, I want to suggest, is a cultural process that engages with acts of remembering that work to create ways to understand and engage with the present, and the sites themselves are cultural tools that can facilitate, but are not necessarily vital for, this process. Harvey (2001: 327) defines heritage as a verb related to human action and agency, and

44

suggests that it is a process concerned with the legitimization of the power of national and other cultural/social identities. Indeed, the idea that heritage is a cultural process is not new in the literature; Bella Dicks, for instance, has suggested heritage may be understood as a culturally-defined communicative practice (2000a, 2000b), and David Lowenthal (1985) has argued that heritage is a way of acquiring or engaging with a sense of history. However, what exactly people 'do' – subjectively and culturally – at heritage sites or with the concept of heritage itself, is as yet an under-theorized issue in the literature. Subsequently, the aim of this chapter is to explore a range of insights and concepts that may, when taken together, have a useful synergy when applied to understanding 'heritage'. These concepts will then be used in later chapters to frame and analyse the various and diverse ways that heritage is used. This framework is important as, by moving us beyond the AHD, it aims to open up conceptual space to not only recognize competing heritage discourses, but also to engage with the new and different ways they constitute 'heritage', and the significance that these may have for developing a more holistic understanding of the uses and nature of heritage in contemporary societies.

Heritage as experience

Before the conceptual heritage suitcase is repacked, however, I want to unpack it a little bit more and outline a particular experience that led me, as someone trained originally in archaeology, to reconsider my adherence to the dominant and framing concept that heritage *is* a material object or site. In 1999, while undertaking research work (reported in Chapter 5; see also Figure 2.1) in northern Queensland, Australia, senior Indigenous women from the Waanyi community approached two colleagues and myself to be involved in a project they were developing. The Waanyi Women's History Project aimed to get Waanyi women's concerns about their heritage, and the sites that they had cultural custodianship over, onto the local land management agendas. The women considered that, as women, their concerns had not been given adequate attention or legitimacy by governmental land management agencies. Many of their cultural heritage sites fell within the boundaries of Boodjamulla National Park, which was at this time moving to joint management between the Waanyi community and the Queensland Parks and Wildlife Service. It had become vital to the women for them to secure a strong voice in these negotiations. As has been detailed elsewhere (Smith et al. 2003a, 2003b), our invitation to participate as heritage archaeologists was, in part, a move to grant authority to the project: if experts were involved, then government agencies would more likely pay attention. However, it was the Waanyi women who determined the nature, specific aims and outcomes of the project. Two field seasons were undertaken during 2000, ostensibly, at least as the archaeologists involved in the project understood,

45

Figure 2.1 Waanyi Women's History Project (A. Morgan).

to record women's heritage sites. However, as the project unfolded we spent much of our time recording oral histories and these, rather than the site recordings, became a central feature of the project.

What was interesting for us was that for the Waanyi women these oral histories were perceived to be as much their heritage as the sites we had intended to record. More significantly, however, it became obvious that it was important for the women to recite and record these histories, not at home over a table, but in their cultural territory or 'country'[1] and, where relevant, at the appropriate cultural site. Passing on the oral histories and traditions was, for the women, an act of heritage management, as this heritage was being recorded and preserved as recordings. However, in also passing on histories and traditions to the younger Waanyi women who were present, the project became itself an act of heritage. Heritage was not the site itself, but the act of passing on knowledge in the culturally correct or appropriate contexts and times. The sites and the 'country' we were in were more than *aide-mémoire*, but rather, following Samuel (1994), were 'theatres of memory'. That is, while the sites, and indeed the whole Boodjamulla landscape or country, did play a mnemonic role, they also provided background, setting, gravitas and, most importantly, a sense of occasion for those both passing on and receiving cultural meaning, knowledge and memories. While the sites were intrinsically important to the women, it was the *use* of these sites that made them heritage, not the mere fact of their existence.

In addition to oral history recordings, a significant amount of time was spent fishing during the project. At first, this was difficult for archaeologists trained in a certain work ethic to accept. However, for the women, simply being in their cultural landscape, being 'in country', was to experience a sense of heritage. For many of the women involved, the project offered a rare chance to visit their country or cultural territory. Almost all of the women lived some distance from Boodjamulla, and had to be flown to the park by light aircraft due to the hazards and time involved in driving long distances in far northern Queensland. In addition, although many of the elderly women taking part in the project were related, or had known each other since they were girls, many had not seen each other for lengthy periods due to the difficulties and costs involved in travelling in the region. Just being in country and having the time to enjoy 'just being there' was significant. It allowed women to not only affirm a sense of their historical and cultural identities, but also to network, meet and renew old friendships and pass on news about mutual friends and relatives. This socializing was also knitting together a sense of community, sometimes frayed by geographical separation, in a place that symbolized certain cultural values and meanings and at a time that was politically important to them.

What emerged from this project was a sense that heritage had to be experienced for it to be heritage and that, moreover, it *was* the experience (Smith et al. 2003a: 75). What also becomes apparent is a sense of the importance of memory, remembering and of performance. While women were affirming a sense of their gendered cultural identity at Boodjamulla, it was both culturally and politically important to reinforce its value by locating it in a particular place of performance. The Waanyi women undertook a range of heritage acts or actions that in themselves conveyed and carried meaning, but took on particular force because of the context in which they occurred. These acts, or performances, not only concerned keeping cultural heritage and knowledge alive by passing on their meanings and values to younger women, but also involved asserting a sense of their identity as Waanyi women both for themselves and the audience in the Queensland Parks and Wildlife Service.

Heritage also involved acts or performances of remembering, not just performances of remembering in terms of recounting oral histories, but also in embodying that remembering. Taking time to fish was, in part, a needed break during the project from oral history recording, but it also allowed time to reflect and to experience and re-embody those memories and acts of remembering in the cultural landscape of Boodjamulla. New memories were also being created, which was especially significant for the younger women who were gaining new collective memories passed on from the elder women, but everyone was also gaining new memories through the process of being at Boodjamulla whilst also negotiating new meanings about what it meant to 'be' at Boodjamulla. In this sense, then, heritage as experience meant that heritage was not static or 'frozen in time', as the conservation ethic tends to demand, but rather was a process that while it passed on established values and meanings was also creating new meanings and values. Ultimately, this project also illustrates the degree to which different conceptualizations of heritage stand outside of the dominant discourse. Although we had little conceptual role to play in the development of the project, it was the presence of archaeological 'experts' that facilitated an awareness of this project within government agencies – that helped make at least one of the audiences pay attention. Our expertise was used as a commodity to broker the legitimacy of the project, precisely because the project stood outside of the dominant, and to a certain extent androcentric, concepts and values embedded in the AHD.

This example identifies a range of concepts such as 'identity', 'power', 'memory', 'place' and 'performance', amongst others, which need elaboration and consideration. The following sections explore a reworking of the idea of heritage around these themes.

Heritage as identity

The association between heritage and identity is well established in the heritage literature – material culture as heritage is assumed to provide a physical representation and reality to the ephemeral and slippery concept of 'identity'. Like history, it fosters the feelings of belonging and continuity (Lowenthal 1985: 214), while its physicality gives these feelings an added sense of material reality. As Graham et al. (2000: 41) state: 'heritage provides meaning to human existence by conveying the ideas of timeless values and unbroken lineages that underpin identity.' How the links between identity and heritage are developed and maintained, however, is an area that has not had much scrutiny in the heritage literature. The sorts of 'identity work' that people actually do at heritage sites, and how these links are constructed and maintained, are often assumed and unproblematized in the literature (Urry 1996; Bagnall 2003; McLean 2006).

Certainly, the representational and symbolic value of heritage in constructing and giving material reality to 'identity' is well recognized, although analysis of the way heritage is thus used is often articulated in terms of national identity. A great deal of critical attention has been paid to the ways in which the ideologies of nationalism and national identities have been consciously and unconsciously articulated and legitimized in terms of heritage (Diaz-Andreu and Champion 1996; Meskell 2002, 2003; Crouch and Parker 2003; Carrier 2005). This focus is a consequence of the way the AHD both constructs the idea of heritage and the official practices of heritage, both of which stress the significance of material culture in playing a vital representational role in defining national identity. Indeed, as identified in Chapter 1, the AHD was itself both constituted by, and is a constitutive discourse of, the ideology of nationalism. In identifying 'national heritage', the 'nation' is symbolically and imaginatively constituted as a real entity (Brett 1996: 156). In heritage literature and practice the monumental, the grand, rare or aesthetically impressive is most often identified as being quintessentially representative of national identity. However, Billig (1995) draws our attention to the banal and the vernacular, arguing that it is often the commonplace symbols and everyday activities and habits that work to continually 'flag' or remind people of their national identity. While his argument draws on a range of practices and habits, he also shows that it is the banality and frequency of various symbols, the flag on the government building being the most obvious, that work to unconsciously remind and identify. To some degree the pervasiveness of the nationalizing discourse of heritage has itself become banal in the sense that Billig uses the term. The everyday ubiquities, and thus banalities, of nationalizing heritage through increasing leisure and heritage tourism activities, even at its most monumental, has perhaps facilitated and helped drive the heritage industry critique.

The process that Billig (1995) identifies may also work on a sub-national level in helping members of particular social, ethnic, cultural or geographically regional or local groups to define their sense of identity. Specific communities also use the same symbolic elements to define and constitute who they are – and who they are not – and to adhere to particular sets of group values and habits. Brett (1996: 8–9) uses Bourdieu's idea of 'habitus' – the ideational environment that reflects durable dispositions and values that defines individual and group conduct, taste and expectations and helps to ensure regularity in new situations – to develop this link between identity and heritage. As modernization erodes customs and expectations, Brett argues, individuals and communities are forced to re-articulate and recover a sense of the past and to affirm or renegotiate a sense of habitus. It is important at this point, however, to draw a distinction between authorized or received and subversive expressions of identity. The heritage industry critique has stressed the degree to which heritage often propagates received notions of identity, both at a national and class level. Bourdieu's idea of cultural capital is an influential one in the heritage literature, and one that facilitates a sense that received identity dominates the heritage process. Heritage is identified as part of the cultural capital that may be invested in to help identify a person's membership to a particular social group or class, but may also require a particular attainment of cultural literacy to ensure that the meanings and 'messages' believed to be contained within or represented by various heritage forms may be read and understood. However, heritage may also be actively used to reject or contest received notions of identity, and the dominance of the cultural capital thesis tends to obscure the possibility of subversive uses of heritage (Graham 2002: 1004).

As much of the globalization literature proclaims, however erroneously, the end of the nation state, critical attention has begun to focus more assiduously on expressions of sub-national, and particularly 'local', constructions of identity and the role of heritage (Inglehard and Baker 2000; Berking 2003). Greater critical analysis of how specific class identities are articulated and communicated through heritage has emerged from this (Bruno 1999; Dicks 2000a; DeBlasio 2001; Linkon and Russo 2002; Macdonald 1997; Kirshenblatt-Gimblett 1998), how ethnic and cultural identities are defined in multicultural contexts (Hayden 1997; Knecht and Niedermüller 2002; Littler and Naidoo 2004, 2005), how gender and sexuality is identified (Butler 1993; Holcomb 1998; Dubrow 2003) and how regional and local communities, amongst others, articulate a sense of identity (Derry and Malloy 2003; Jones 2005). What emerges from this literature is a much greater sense of conscious agency in the expression of identity than is found in the literature that has focused on the nationalizing uses of heritage. This may in part be an expression of the way in which the AHD focuses and frames research in this area, or a real element associated with these types of identity formations (see chapters in Part III). However, the articulations of identities, which often stand in opposition to nationalizing and other received identities, and to the AHD itself, must require an active sense of construction and expression.

The issue of agency and heritage audiences will be discussed in more detail below; however, it is useful to consider here the active way in which heritage is used in 'identity politics'. As Crouch and Parker (2003: 405) show, heritage is used as a legitimizing discourse in constructing and maintaining a range of 'identities'. Heritage can give temporal and material authority to the construction of identities, especially if the heritage in question has been recognized as 'legitimate' through state-sanctioned heritage management and conservation practices, and/or through the research attentions of experts such as archaeologists, historians, historical architects and so on. The interplay between authorized and subversive identities is quite revealing about the work that the AHD does in helping to de-legitimize and legitimize certain forms of identity. In earlier work, drawing on a critical reading of the Foucaldian thesis of 'governmentality', I documented how certain archaeological conceptualizations of 'heritage' became embedded within heritage or 'cultural resource' legislation and the state-sanctioned heritage management process in both the United States and Australia (Smith 2004). I argued that in governing or regulating the political and cultural legitimacy of Indigenous cultural identity, policy makers and state bureaucracies used specific archaeological knowledge about the nature and meaning of Indigenous heritage. In this way, those things that archaeologists objectified as 'material culture', and those things that Indigenous people were identified as treating subjectively as 'heritage', became resources of power in struggles over the legitimacy of certain claims to sovereignty, land and other economic and social resources that Indigenous people made in wider political negotiations with the state. They became resources of power because claims to cultural identity often framed the political legitimacy with which policy makers viewed wider claims to sovereignty and economic and social justice. Although this work focused on quite specific and explicit conflicts over identity claims, and was concerned with the power/knowledge consequences of archaeological expertise and the specific use this is put to in state agencies, it offers some insights for the current project of understanding how heritage is used in much more diffused ways.

There are three points I want to draw on from this previous work. The first is that expert knowledge and experts are not simply another interest or stakeholder group in the use of heritage. Expert values and knowledge, such as those embedded in archaeology, history and architecture amongst others, often set the agendas or provide the epistemological frameworks that define debates about the meaning and nature of the past and its heritage. One of the ways this is actively done is through the whole process of cultural heritage management, wherein wider social debates about the meaning of the past, and its utility for the present, are relegated to bite-sized and manageable chunks by reducing them to specific debates over the meaning, 'ownership' and/or management of specific sites, places or artefacts. A second, and related, point is that experts often have a vested interest in maintaining the privileged position of their knowledge claims within both state apparatuses and wider social debates about the meaning of the past. The position of privilege ensures that they are not treated as just another stakeholder but as stewards for, and arbitrators of, debates over the past. In turn, this helps to facilitate access to sites, artefacts, places and other resources that are part of the database of these disciplines. The ability to possess, control and give meaning to the past and/or heritage sites is a re-occurring and reinforcing statement of disciplinary authority and identity.

The third point relates to the governmentality thesis itself and the idea of a heritage 'mentality'. The governmentality thesis argues that expert knowledge in the social sciences can and has been mobilized by bureaucracies to govern the 'conduct of conduct' of populations (Foucault 1991). Intellectual knowledge becomes incorporated into the act of governing populations and social problems by 'rendering the world thinkable, taming its intractable reality by subjecting it to the disciplined analyses of thought' (Rose and Miller 1992: 182; see also Dean and Hindess 1998; Dean 1999). Subsequently, particular social problems become 'amenable to interventions by administrators, politicians, authorities and experts' (Rose 1993: 289). This process is based on liberal modernity and its emphasis on rationality and the universality of knowledge. In this process, expert knowledge about the meaning and nature of the past, and the heritage objects that represent that authorized and universalized past became useful in defining populations. These may be Indigenous populations as I have already documented (2004), or they may be national or a range of sub-national populations. The application of 'rational' expert knowledge renders any social problems or debates over the legitimacy of certain identities it may govern as 'non-political'.

Specifically, identity debates are reduced to debates over 'ownership' issues – 'who owns the past', a recursive theme in the heritage literature, is a discursive devise that hides the more politically significant and charged issue of 'control'. Who controls the past, or who controls the meaning and value of heritage, is a much more unambiguous question for examining the identity politics of heritage, and as such it is often made more tractable and open to regulation by reducing it to technical issues of owning and possessing. What the governmentality thesis does here, however, is highlight the degree to which we can conceptualize heritage as a 'mentality', or in Graham's (2002) terms 'a knowledge', for regulating and governing identity claims and making sense of the present.

The AHD constructs not only a particular definition of heritage, but also an authorized mentality, which is deployed to understand and deal with certain social problems centred on claims to identity. Heritage is, in a sense, a gaze or way of seeing. Urry (1990) identifies the institutionalization of the 'tourist gaze' and the way this gaze constructs reality and normalizes a range of touristic experiences. As Hollinshead (1999: 10–11) points out, the idea of the gaze has an intellectual debt to Foucault, and refers to the ways different professions learn to see and how this may be used to govern others. For Hollinshead, as for Wright, Hewison and others, authorized heritage becomes a form of social control (1997: 186). However, what happens when, as Coleman and Crang (2002b) point out, those gazed upon gaze back?

As I identified in terms of Indigenous identity politics those gazed upon, or subjected to the governance of certain 'mentalities', are not passive, and can and do use heritage in subversive and oppositional ways. Although the Foucaldian idea of governmentality only theorizes the process in which bodies of expertise and knowledge deploy power, it is often those very resources of power that are then utilized to contest received knowledge and, in this case, identity. Heritage thus becomes not only a tool of governance, but also a tool of opposition and subversion. Heritage can therefore be understood as an important political and cultural tool in defining and legitimizing the identity, experiences and social/cultural standing of a range of subnational groups as well as those of the authorizing discourse. However, it may also be an important resource in challenging received identity and cultural/social values. This latter use of heritage is often undervalued, but is as important and significant as is its use in constructing and validating identity. How this is undervalued is evident in the often strident criticism of the phrase 'identity politics'. This criticism becomes particularly disparaging when minority groups overtly and self-consciously engage in identity politics. However, this criticism is simply revealing of the extent to which the identity politics played out as authorized heritage is so naturalized and taken for granted. It is also indicative of the political power of the politics of recognition. As Nancy Fraser (2000) argues, recognition or misrecognition of identity and cultural values is politically powerful and harmful. In the so-called 'culture wars' in North America and other post-colonial countries, the ability to validate identity is as important as the ability to challenge and overthrow misidentification. This ability is no less significant for other subaltern groups whose self-perception may be at odds with, or sits entirely outside of, received ideas of their heritage and identity.

In summary, the theoretical task then is to construct a sense of the links between heritage and identity that recognizes the various nuanced ways identity is constructed, reconstructed and contested. As I am suggesting here, the links between heritage and identity can be expressed in any number of ways: actively or passively within the AHD (Chapters 4 and 5), or in active and self-conscious opposition to the AHD (see Chapter 8), or in ways that are less self-conscious and are constructed without reference to or outside of the AHD (see Chapters 6 and 7). In complicating the issue further, no community, group or individual aligns themselves to a single identity. Individuals have layered identities and may belong to any number of 'communities', further any community may within itself have layers or a range of sub-community identities (Corsane 2005: 9). It is also suggested that these identities need not necessarily be constituted or symbolized by the monumental, and that even the grand narratives of identity such as those of nation and class may be built upon the commonplace or banal. Further, it is argued that these constructions are by their nature political, in that they often involve the deployment of resources of power and prestige.

Heritage, it is argued above, has power as a legitimizing or de-legitimizing discourse. However, there is another dimension to the political power of heritage. This power rests within the naturalization of heritage as material object. Material heritage objects are symbolic not only of identities but also of certain values. Heritage may be embodied as objects of desire and prestige in and of themselves, not because of any inherent value, but in so far as the symbolic ability to control desired, fetishized and prized objects reinforces not only the identity, but the power of the identity of the nation, group or individual in possession (Weiner 1992; Lahn 1996). The materiality of heritage is itself a brutally physical statement, at least within the confines of the AHD, of the power, universality, objectivity and cultural attainment of the possessors of that heritage. The physicality of heritage also works to mask the ways in which the heritage gaze constructs, regulates and authorizes a range of identities and values by filtering that gaze onto the inanimate material heritage. In this gaze, the proper subject of which *is* the material, a material objective reality is constructed and subjectivities that exist outside or in opposition to that are rendered invisible or marginal, or simply less 'real'.

The intangibility of heritage

In recognizing the subjectivities of heritage, it becomes necessary to destabilize the idea of the 'objectivity' of heritage. This needs to be done both in terms of questioning the assumed objectivity of the constituting and author-ized discourse and narratives about heritage as was done in Chapter 1, but also in terms of redirecting the heritage gaze from its obsessions with physic-ality. In destabilizing the idea of objective heritage there is, however, no need to embrace extreme relativism. Accepting the philosophical position of critical realism (Bhaskar 1978, 1989), it may be understood that while there may be a physical reality or aspect to heritage, any knowledge of it can only ever be understood within the discourses we construct about it. More-over, the consequences of heritage are real, and have real power in many people's lives, but how the heritage process is conceived and understood cannot be assumed to necessarily have universal validity or reality. In short, understanding what heritage *is* and *does* may be defined by the discourses that we work within and the 'discourse' constructed in this chapter argues that heritage is not an 'object'.

If heritage is a mentality, a way of knowing and seeing, then all heritage becomes, in a sense, 'intangible'. The issue of intangibility has been a signifi-cant one in Western heritage literature and debate in recent years. Some commentators assert that the increasing debate in the West about intangible heritage is due to a late twentieth-century re-evaluation of modernity, and an increasing concern with the local in response to fears of globalization (Deacon et al. 2004: 10; see also Berking 2003; Castells 2004). Non-Western conceptualizations of heritage have begun to question the hegemonic domi-nance of the idea of the materiality of heritage, and have come to play an important role in questioning received ideas about it. Challenges to Western traditional conceptualizations have occurred in response to specific events, such as the controversy and debate sparked by the 're-painting' of rock art sites in Western Australia during the 1980s. In this case, Aboriginal cus-todians were accused of re-painting sites in 'non-traditional' ways and thus 'destroying' ancient rock art. The custodians countered that what was important, in terms of Aboriginal perspectives, was the maintenance of cul-tural practice and meaning. The act of re-painting was vital in keeping alive certain values and meaning in a way that the simple existence of the sites could not. The point here was that it was the practice and not the types of material used in that practice, or the site itself, that maintained meanings and cultural knowledge (see Mowljarlai and Peck 1987; Bowdler 1988; Mowljarlai et al. 1988, for details of this debate).

This event directly contradicts the 'conserve as found' ethos and questions the universality of the assumption that it is fabric that is important as heri-tage. However, challenges to these assumptions have also occurred through a general increased awareness in the West that other cultures, particularly from Africa and Asia, perceive heritage differently. For instance, invoking a sense of heritage similar to that in the re-painting debate, some Japanese historic buildings may be regularly and entirely rebuilt with modern materials and techniques without compromising their heritage values or sense of authenticity to the Japanese (Graham 2002; Munjeri 2004; Yoshida 2004). The awareness of a competing sense of heritage has arisen, in part, due to the lobbying of organizations such as ICOMOS and UNESCO by countries from these regions. Dinu Bumbaru, General Secretary Executive Committee Member of ICOMOS (1993–2002), noted that it was working with colleagues in Africa that facilitated the recognition of intangible heritage by that organization (2003). Awareness has also been raised due to the weight of scholarship by non-Western heritage commentators and heritage practitioners on the nature and meaning of heritage. In this literature, heritage values are identified as occurring within the maintenance of social networks (Teather and Chow 2003; Munjeri 2004); in such things as music, dance, food, language, theatre and other performances (Amselle 2004; Deacon et al. 2004); and in oral history, traditions and knowledge or, what some refer to as, 'folklore' (Fourmile 1989b; Hufford 1994; Ah Kit 1995; Echo-Hawk 2000); and, amongst other elements, in the skills and knowledge held by individual craftspersons, musicians, dancers and others (Nas 2002). In response to this, UNESCO's *Convention for the Safeguarding of the Intangible Cultural Heritage* was adopted in 2003 (see Chapter 3).

While the literature and sense of heritage practice embedded in the AHD has began to acknowledge intangible heritage, this does not mean that it is easy with it. The unease of the AHD with this concept, however, is evident in the identities of the state parties who have ratified this convention at time of publication. Notable absences in the state parties to the convention are European countries (with the exception of Belgium, Bulgaria, Romania, Hungary, Belarus, Latvia, Lithuania, Iceland and Croatia), Canada, The United States, Australia and New Zealand. Certainly, in post-colonial contexts ratification of this convention would have significant consequences for the political legitimacy granted to Indigenous concepts of heritage, and in Western contexts where tensions occur over the legitimacy of multiculturalism any challenges to concepts of identity validated by the AHD and sanctioned through state heritage programmes would certainly be problematic.

The debate over the 2001 UNESCO Proclamation of Masterpieces of the Oral and Intangible Heritage of Humanity is instructive. The first Proclamation saw 19 'traditional cultural expressions' identified as 'masterpieces', only one of which was from a Western country (Fog Olwig 2002: 146; Nas 2002). This inscription, characterized by Nas as benefiting scholarship in cultural anthropology (2002: 143), was greeted with some concern about what it would mean in terms of the potential fossilization of cultural practices. While the issue of fossilization has certainly been raised in terms of tangible heritage, what is revealing here is the way debate in response to Nas' discussion of the event expressed real concern that it would mean cultural practices could become frozen in time and thus meaningless. For many of the commentators on this event, cultural expression was dynamic, and that as such a real problem was presented by inscribing cultural practices and traditions on a 'heritage register'. Although not stated as such, there emerges a sense that, by definition, the registration of these events as 'heritage' would instigate management practices laden with the burden of preservation and thus cultural expression would be stifled (see, in particular, Claessen 2002; Fog Olwig 2002; Kurin 2002; Sears 2002). What is revealed here is a tension between the idea of 'heritage' and the idea of current and mutable cultural practices.

Despite this tension, and in response to the events described above, the definition of heritage has started to broaden itself to include cultural elements like memory, music, language, dialects, oral history, traditions, dance, craft skills and so forth. However, within the international classification of heritage, there is a decided tendency to define 'heritage', and then 'intangible heritage', as two separate things. It is my task here to not only marry these two concepts of heritage together, so that 'intangible heritage' becomes simply 'heritage', but also to redefine all heritage as inherently intangible in the first place. That is, what is actually the subject of management and conservation/preservation practices, and what visitors and tourists engage with at heritage places, are the values and meanings that are symbolized or represented at and by these heritage sites or cultural practices. Whether we are dealing with traditional definitions of 'tangible' or 'intangible' representations of heritage, we are actually engaging with a set of values and meanings, including such elements as emotion, memory and cultural knowledge and experiences. It is value and meaning that is the real subject of heritage preservation and management processes, and as such all heritage is 'intangible' whether these values or meanings are symbolized by a physical site, place, landscape or other physical representation, or are represented within the performances of languages, dance, oral histories or other forms of 'intangible heritage'.

In defining all heritage as intangible, the heritage gaze is directed to the affect of heritage rather than to the cultural 'object' or 'event' itself. This sense of 'affect' draws on the work of Nigel Thrift (2004), who argues that urban space, and the way it is configured and used, engenders certain emotional, political and cultural affects. Thrift (2004: 60) defines affect as a form of thinking, although this may be indirect and non-reflective, which may be embodied thinking both in terms of space/place and in action. This effect may be regulated and governed within the context of certain discourses such as the AHD, or, as Thrift notes, designed into spaces, but it can also be, as Dolores Hayden's (1997) work demonstrates, redirected in subversive and oppositional ways. Hayden has used and redesigned urban spaces in Los Angeles to actively engender affects that challenge the historical and present-day social and cultural invisibility of African-American, Latina and Japanese communities. Hayden argues that the ordinary and mundane forms of the city can be remapped through research and community involvement to nurture collective memory and to actively illicit senses of belonging and identity. The various case studies she presents demonstrate the 'power of place' to invoke emotion, memory and belonging that become ways of rethinking about the past and the present. Although both Hayden and Thrift emphasize a sense of physical place and space, the idea of affect can also be understood as an *embodiment* of thought and emotion. This concept helps to link the physical sense of heritage, as symbolically embodied with particular values and meanings or affects, with traditional ideas of intangible heritage as performances or acts of embodied meaning and affects. However, traditional or common sense ideas of 'place' and 'performance' need reconsideration in developing this sense of heritage, and these concepts are examined and discussed in further detail below. However, by focusing the heritage gaze on affect, the idea that all heritage is intangible also offers greater conceptual space for the idea of memory and the activity of remembering.

Memory and remembering

Critical interest in the idea of 'memory' has substantially increased within the social sciences and humanities since the 1980s, so much so that some have identified and criticized the development of a 'memory industry' (Klein 2000). However, this increase in critical interest in memory also coincides with increasing social interest in commemoration and remembering in Western societies. Barbara Misztal (2003: 2) identifies a 'commemorative fever', which she sees as also having taken force from the 1980s. The increasing concern with social memory is, she notes, associated with the number and frequency of civic anniversaries that began to be marked in this period in connection with events such as The Second World War, a process that may also have been further helped along by the change of the millennium. In addition, the 1980s also marked increasing social debate brought about by the assertions of memories that challenged received or authorized ideas of history by a range of ethnic and cultural minorities. These challenges occurred in a range of contexts, including the commemoration of bicentenaries in post-colonial nations like the United States and Australia, with the end of the Cold War, and in the context of debates about the meaning of the Holocaust, the role of the Vichy regime in France and so forth.

A particular driving force behind the interest in memory that must be emphasized is the work that comes from Jewish scholars and communities over memory and the Holocaust. This is important to emphasize, as unlike traditional work on heritage issues, work on memory has often explicitly emphasized subaltern and not necessarily nationalizing narratives. Misztal (2003) also cites the increasing importance of sites of commemoration and remembrance in the tourism and heritage movements as being significant in the growth in attempts to talk about and theorize memory. Despite the increase in memory studies, however, there has only been a passing concern with memory issues in the traditional heritage literature (Hall 2001; Shackel

2001, being some of the exceptions). Although it is often recognized, for instance, that memory and identity are linked, and that heritage places may invoke individual and/or collective memories, this observation is often simply nodded at rather than given close critical attention. This, in part, may lie in the tensions that inevitably exist between the idea of memory, which must always invoke a sense of the possibility of forgetting, and the idea of heritage as constructed in the AHD. Heritage in this context is almost inevitably about the 'good' things, events and cultural expressions that lend credence to a sense of cultural and communal pride in identity. Although the existence of such things as 'dissonant' heritage is acknowledged, as is discussed below, a sense of dissonance is often marginal to the authorized sense of what heritage is about (see also Graham et al. 2000: 24f.). Subsequently, a sense of forgetting acknowledges that there may be some memories or pasts that are not necessarily 'good', and thus the idea of memory creates certain tensions within traditional and authorized accounts of heritage. These tensions are exacerbated by the way the relationship between memory and history is often treated as oppositional (Nora 1989; Samuel 1994). Memory may be seen as subjective and not always reliable, whereas history is about the accumulation of fact within an authorized narrative. Thus, while heritage sites may help societies to remember, it is the legitimacy or facts of that remembrance or commemoration that is privileged and given critical attention, and not the emotional or subjective activity itself that is acknowledged, nor the possibility of meanings that this activity may have outside of the AHD.

As with heritage, memory is not an object to possess, memories are not 'like books in a library that we can pull down, open up, and read' (Conway 1997: 4). Rather, memory is an active cultural process of remembering and of forgetting that is fundamental to our ability to conceive the world (Misztal 2003: 1). Remembering, as James Wertsch (2002) argues, is an active process in which the past both collectively or individually is continually negotiated and reinterpreted, through not only the experiences of the present but also the *needs* of the present. The past can never be understood solely within its own terms; the present continually rewrites the meaning of the past and the memories and histories we construct about it within the context of the present. Urry argues that time is an abstract concept, and the sense of linear construction and measurement of it is simply a cultural construction (see also Bender 2002; Figlio 2003; Schwarz 2003). Thus, Urry argues, 'there is no past out there or back there. There is only the present, in the context of which the past is being continually re-created' (1996: 48). This remaking and recreating occurs through the activities of remembering and reminiscing, which take place in the context of interactions between people and their environments, including heritage sites and museums (Urry 1996; Davison 2005).

This does not mean to say that the past does not exhibit its own influences on the present, but rather those influences will entirely be understood and remade through the dominant discourses of the present day. Language is important in this process, as studies in social psychology reveal how we talk about our individual and collective memories – the discourse we use to understand them and give them meaning – also shape and form our memories and frame the process of remembering and forgetting (Pennebaker and Banasik 1997). This is also true in terms of the way memory is discussed and defined within the memory literature itself. The dominant construction of 'memory' as, Wertsch points out, often objectifies memory in so far as memories are things that we 'have' rather than 'something we do' (2002: 17). For Wertsch, memory is the mediated action of remembering, which itself is a process engaged with the working out and creation of meaning.

This objectifying of memory is reflected in the different 'types' of memory that may be identified in the literature. These include procedural memory – the memory of fact – autobiographical, cognitive memory, flashbulb memory – the memory of important or emotionally-charged events – habitual memory and collective or social memory (see Casey 2000; Misztal 2003). These different forms of memory, or more usefully forms of remembering, are done for different reasons and in different contexts. The forms of memory work most often associated with heritage are collective or social memory and habitual memory. The idea of collective memory commences with the work of Maurice Halbwachs ([1926] 1992), who argued that every group constructs an identity for itself through shared memories. However, as Wertsch (2002: 5) notes, the idea of collective memory has many meanings and, as Klein (2000: 135) warns, can often be used as a stand in for the 'bad old Romantic notions of the "spirit" or the "inner character" of a race or nation' (see also Olick 1999: 334). This is where we need to be careful of how the idea of collective memory is defined, as this sense easily finds synergy with authorized views of heritage. For Halbwachs, however, shared or collective memories are socially constructed in the present, and are collectively legitimized in that they make meaningful common interests and perceptions of collective identity. They work to bind the collective and give it stability and continuity. Collective memory is passed on and shaped in the present by commemorative events, and is reshaped daily through transmission between members of the collective social or cultural group and the language they employ to frame and define those memories. He observes that 'recollections are . . . located . . . with the help of landmarks that we always carry within ourselves, for it suffices to look around ourselves, to think about others, and to locate ourselves within the social framework in order to retrieve them' (1992: 175).

Halbwachs draws a distinction between collective memory and history. History, defined as a universalizing and objective narrative that clearly differentiates the past from the present, is separated from collective memory and its subjective and unselfconscious workings (see Wertsch 2002: 40f., for more detail). As Wertsch (2002: 66) usefully notes, 'in contrast to history, collective memory reflects a committed perspective, and belongs to one group, and not others'. Memory, unlike history, has an intimate relation to the present through the personal and collective actions of remembering. History, on the other hand, chronologically separates past 'periods' as units of expert scrutiny and analysis. Further, as Nora points out:

> there are as many memories as there are groups, that memory is by nature multiple and yet specific; collective, plural, and yet individual. History, on the other hand, belongs to everyone and to no one, whence its claim to universal authority. Memory takes root in the concrete, in spaces, gestures, images, and objects; history binds itself strictly to temporal continuities, to progressions and to relations between things. Memory is absolute, while history can only conceive the relative.
>
> (Nora 1989: 9)

The useful point here is that memory is an important constitutive element of identity formation, unlike professional historical narratives, it is personal and thus collective memory has a particular emotive power. This sense of memory becomes particularly powerful as it 'takes root' in the concrete, which must work to give this sense of memory further emotive power through the tangibility of its representation. This materialization or embodiment of memory in Nora's *lieux de mémoire*, sites of memory, has occurred, he argues, due to dilation of the social *milieux* that previously framed and contained it. Although Nora is envisaging more than traditional definitions of tangible heritage in his characterization of 'sites of memory', the nationalizing tendencies of heritage do reinforce a sense of collective memory that ignores the subaltern and other sub-national forms of memory and remembering, and works to draw on and define the 'inner character' of race and nation. Although Klein is warning against the simplicity of Halbwachs theorization of collective memory, the point here is that, through heritage at least, these totalizing narratives do have real force, and there is a tendency for the 'many groups' to become ignored. Nor is this process necessarily entirely random. Drawing on ideas of collective memory work, the authors in Hobsbawm and Ranger's (1983) *The Invention of Tradition* examine the way the state and the ruling classes used 'invented' traditions as a means of shaping collective memory and socializing individuals into the established social order. They examine a range of contexts in which invented traditions, by which they mean those consciously constructed or developed in a 'brief and datable period' (Hobsbawm 1983a: 1), were used to define and control various subaltern populations, both in colonial and European contexts, while masking relations of power they help to establish and maintain (see also Philp and Mercer 2002). For Hobsbawm (1983a: 1), 'invented tradition' equates to 'a set of practices, normally governed by overtly or tacitly accepted rules and of a ritual or symbolic nature, which seek to inculcate certain values and norms of behaviour by repetition, which automatically implies continuity with the past'. The issue of continuity is stressed as it both establishes the authority of the tradition and the work that it does in socializing populations.

As Misztal (2003: 60) notes, the 'invented tradition' thesis does not necessarily account for why some traditions are privileged over others and enjoy social support, nor does it necessarily account for oppositional accounts of the past. However, the embodiment of memory into sites of memory, or at least those that are given particular authority as aids to memory as 'heritage', provides some clue as to why some traditions, either 'invented' or not, are privileged over others and why some are actively 'forgotten'. This embodiment of memory and tradition as 'heritage' renders these intangible processes as 'manageable' and open to regulation. As Figlio (2003: 152) observes, linking memories to objects, or giving them a tangible reality through heritage, means that they can be collected, preserved, lost, destroyed or restored. Further, the simple aspect of their materiality makes them more convincing and powerful. This materiality also privileges a certain sense, as with heritage, of historical experience, but as Denis Byrne (2001, 2003) points out, there are experiences and 'memory traces' that leave no material remnant, and thus are subsequently and inevitably seen to lack authority and 'substance'. The materiality of tradition, and its legitimizing power, can be witnessed by the degree of national and international debate sparked by the repainting of Aboriginal rock art mentioned above. One of the issues in this debate was the perception that the tradition of repainting had been 'broken' because the Aboriginal artists in undertaking the repainting had not used 'traditional' materials. Another example are the debates over the rights of Indigenous Australians to exercise their traditions of fishing either in areas not open to the wider population (such as National Parks[2]), or their legal ability to fish some protected species. These traditional rights are often criticized publicly and forcefully for being non-traditional because the fishing is undertaken in 'non-traditional' ways, for instance with aluminium dinghies rather than bark canoes. The ability to equate tradition and memory to material items provides powerful authenticating 'common sense' legitimacy. Here, the sense that tradition and memory is material is a powerful controlling and regulating mechanism, and any breaks in the material tradition of an activity or ritual renders the memories it represents as separate from the present and thus relegated to history – and no longer part of collective or 'living' memory.

The above examples illustrate that those groups or individuals who may stand in opposition to the collective sense of legitimate cultural expression of social and cultural memory can be forgotten or marginalized socially or culturally, which in turn may have implications over the power these groups exercise in wider society. Another concern about most accounts of collective memory is thus the conceptual ability to identify subaltern or other oppositional groups who may challenge the collective consensus. Here, the work of Raphael Samuel is important. Samuel (1994) directs critical attention to the variety of ways the past is understood, represented and negotiated in British society. He argues that history should engage with memory and abandon the 'fetishization of archives' and manuscripts and reconsider the nature and scope of the history discipline (1994: 269). Hodgkin and Radstone (2003b: 3) assert that Samuel's challenge has not been fully taken up within the discipline of history, noting that any attempts to deal with memory tend to be relegated to the subfield of 'public history'. This tendency also occurs in the discipline of archaeology, where work on 'archaeological data' that may also be perceived as someone else's 'heritage' is relegated to 'public archaeology' or 'cultural resource management' (Smith 1993, 2004; Carman 2002). However, what is important in Samuel's work is that he not only directs critical attention to memory, but demonstrates that this is often negotiated and not static. He notes that people do not mindlessly engage with heritage or other material objects or the visual, and that while this negotiation may take place in specific realms, spaces or with particular material props such as in heritage enactments, house renovations or use of period photographs and so on, it does occur. This observation is also reflected in the increasing amount of ethnographic work on heritage, particularly from North America, Africa and Australasia, that emphasizes its dissonant nature, particularly in terms of challenging received forms of identity (see, for instance, Leone et al. 1995; Ashworth and Tunbridge 1996; Hall 2001; Shackel 2001; Derry and Malloy 2003; Mellor and Stephenson 2005; Smith and Wobst 2005; Stanton 2005; amongst others).

McCrone et al. (1995) note that a range of post-modern cultural shifts have occurred that question the stability of British cultural and social narratives, and give rise to new uses of heritage. While the increasing awareness of subaltern understandings and memories may have been facilitated, both in Britain and the rest of the Western world, by post-modernist shifts in intellectual theorizations, their existence is not a reflection of this. Certainly, the use of heritage to contest received history and collective memory is particularly pronounced in post-colonial nations, but has perhaps been rendered invisible in Britain due to the existence of what Urry (1996: 58) identifies as the pervasive and powerful anglocentric masculinist, Home Counties vision of British history. However, as social milieus expand, as Nora (1989) observes, and social boundaries change, new social groups and communities are established. The de-traditionalization literature argues that as society becomes less 'stable' new groups or 'new sociations' (Hetherinton, cited in Urry 1996) are formed, and individuals may drift between these as they attempt to find associations that satisfy their sense of common experiences or social/cultural aspirations (see also Heelas et al. 1996). As Heelas (1996: 8) points out, no 'tradition' is static, they are always open to human agency, and are 'never simply received as pre-given verities'. Thus, de-traditionalization tendencies may have also occurred in the past and are not simply a response to growing multi-vocality in the present.

However, the important point arising from this literature is that in the present, we are now aware that there is a greater sense of active negotiation occurring over the values, meanings and ideologies represented in the links individuals and groups establish with the past, and the sense of continuity and identity that is drawn from those links. Urry (1996: 59) argues that a specific realm of these 'sociations' is heritage, and that membership of groups such as amenity societies like the National Trust, or preservation societies, or local action groups to save particular historic buildings or other sites, is an expression of the negotiation of new social identities and meanings. Although Urry (1996: 60) sees these groups of 'collective enthusiasts' as operating to challenge the speed of social and cultural change, it is likely that other, less conservative, forms of social, cultural and memory work are at play (see Chapter 7). As Connerton states, the 'struggle of citizens against state power is the struggle of their memory against forced forgetting' (1991: 15). However, the ability of groups to use memory to subvert authorized narratives is problematic, unless it is directly experienced memory, as the subjective and representational nature of memory can, and often is, subsumed by the authority of history and its totalizing narrative (Hodgkin and Radstone 2003b: 2). As Heelas (1996: 11) also notes, certain peoples have more opportunities to exercise choice in the de-traditionalization process, and thus in the renegotiation of the meanings of the links between memory, tradition and the past, than others.

Certainly, the point that both the de-traditionalization thesis and Samuel's work emphasizes is that collective memories do not necessarily have to reside at national level, and that a sense of shared memory and value works to bind a range of social groups. As Misztal (2003: 15) puts it, there are a range of mnemonic communities (these may be families, regional or national collectives, or social or ethnic groups) which socialize their members into accepting those things that should be remembered and those that should be forgotten, and this in turn socializes and binds together community identity and values. However, what is also apparent is that this sense of 'binding' and 'memory' is not static. Further, that while a sense of collective memory may provide individuals and the collective with feelings of continuity and thus belonging and emotional security, it does not necessarily follow that there *is* historical continuity. Rather, there may be an emotional affect that the rehearsal and sharing of collective memories, whether these memories are individually or collectively experienced first-hand or retold and passed on, can engender which then facilitates a sense of community continuity. In Benedict Anderson's (1991: 6) terms, this continuity may be 'imagined'. Anderson's important work on nationalism and nation argues that a nation is an imagined political community or cultural artefact. It is imagined simply because members of a nation will never meet or know each other, but that 'in the minds of each lives the image of their communion' (1991: 6). The sense of continuity or belonging engendered by the sharing of memory becomes 'imagined' in that it may not have the common sense associations of deep time depth associated with ideas of 'continuity', but that it nonetheless works to provide a sense of connection and communion. This does not mean that either the memory or the sense of continuity it may provide is somehow false or not real – but rather that it has an important emotional affect in creating a sense of belonging.

Wertsch (2002: 60) addresses this affect when he observes that collective memory 'tends to be impatient with ambiguity and to represent itself as representing an unchanging reality'. In doing so, collective memory is understood as a way to socialize members of a group into privileging and agreeing upon a particular view and understanding of the past. Wertsch argues that in socializing members of a collective the actions of remembering, as much as the memories themselves, are important aspects of the socializing process. He identifies textual resources around which communities may define themselves or be defined. He notes that the definitions and creations of some communities may be almost effortless, while others may require an active effort to sustain them. The textual resources he identifies are the narratives that are developed around specific cultural tools that are used in acts of remembering. These cultural tools may be many and varied – for instance, he recounts the use of Amazon.com to help him remember the title of a book he required (2002). Heritage sites, places, museums and so forth may certainly be identified as textual resources around which specific narratives are written and negotiated and thus become cultural tools in the processes of remembering. In privileging the process of remembering over memory, Young's (1989: 90) observation that memory is not merely passed down from generation to generation is pertinent. Young argues that memory is recast in the minds of each generation and each ceremony of commemoration or act of communication or remembering adds one more 'patina of meaning' (1989: 90). Not only are new meanings created and negotiated for the memories commemorated and told, but this process has a consequence for those who accept, celebrate or otherwise engage in that remembering:

> Memory, then . . . is not tied to the individual who experienced a given event, but dispersed and transmitted to subsequent generations. But the process of transmission changes the rememberers too: the parents who share their memories find their memories changing.
> (Hodgkin and Radstone 2003a: 27)

This does not make either individual or collective memories untrue or false, but rather highlights that memories and remembering, as indeed is forgetting, are cultural processes of meaning making. As Casey (2000) argues, collective remembering is inherently social. Either if we accept that heritage as defined traditionally as tangible or intangible cultural expressions or, as I am defining it, as a process itself of meaning making, it must then be understood as playing a part in remembering. Heritage becomes both cultural tool and part of the wider process of creating and recreating meaning through reminiscing and remembering. Here, a tension is identified between the material realities of heritage as 'things to have' and 'as something that is done'; however, both work to foster social memory. As 'a thing to have', it offers itself up as a specific cultural tool in rehearsing the authority of certain narratives. As 'something that is done', it offers the possibility of the negotiation of change and reworking of meaning. How heritage in this latter sense does this may be illuminated by considering the idea of habitual memory.

Paul Connerton (1991), working from the premise that collective social memory exists, focuses on how collective remembering is achieved through non-textual sources, specifically commemorative ceremonies and in bodily practices. The emphasis here is on performance: commemorative ceremonies rehearse master narratives that represent collective autobiography, sustained and remembered through ritual performance. He also argues that our bodies remember through their ability to perform certain skills and actions. For instance, he notes that we may not remember how we first learnt to swim, but that the memory of swimming lies in the act of swimming, which may be achieved without any help from representational clues, although a mental picture may be summoned should we feel insecure in our ability. He goes on to state: 'Many forms of habitual skilled remembering illustrate a keeping of the past in mind that, without ever reverting to its historical origin, nevertheless re-enacts the past in our present conduct' (1991: 72). The past is thus embodied. What he defines as incorporating practices impart messages and meaning through gestures and actions, while inscribing practice is a way of recording and storing social memory and meaning (1991: 72–3).

Urry's (1996: 49) difficulty with this idea of remembering is that it ignores many other aspects of the social nature of memory. While these ideas do not necessarily have to be taken as representing the *only* way that memory work is done, they do have a particular explanatory power for understanding the uses of heritage. If heritage is something that is done, and part of what is done is remembering, then a sense of embodied memory is useful:

> In the doing, moments of memory are recalled, reactivated in what is done, and thus, may be drawn upon in new combinations of signification. It is less that memory is practiced in repetition than it is in doing. It is in embodied practical encounters that it is made sense of. . . . Memory is worked again and again, differently, and embodied thereby, grasped and wound up in body-performance and interaction with place.
>
> (Crouch and Parker 2003: 396)

Thus, visiting and engaging with heritage sites becomes a cultural and political statement and an act of remembering. This remembering may simply be a rehearsal or a performance of legitimating memory and meaning, it may involve taking up or 'learning' established collective memories, or it may involve active and politicized reworking of meanings. As Crouch and Parker (2003: 406) observe, 'redoing or consciously reenacting can be but a step away from doing', and thus the 'doing' or performance of heritage becomes an active cultural performance of both memory making and of remembering.

By explicitly acknowledging the links between memory and remembering, and linking them with the idea of heritage, we can get a more nuanced understanding of the emotional quality and power of the cultural process of heritage. Further, it reinforces the idea that heritage is not a passive subject of management and conservation or tourist visitation – but rather an active process engaged with the construction and negotiation of meaning through remembering. Ideas about collective and habitual memory allow us to acknowledge that sharing memories, and perhaps more importantly engaging collectively in the act or performances of remembering, helps to bind groups or populations together. This may occur not only at national but also at sub-national levels. These processes do not create static meanings and values, but rather these are negotiated and continually reworked by the processes of remembering and commemoration. These processes may be authorized by the state and used to regulate and govern a sense of collective or received identity or they may, indeed, be contested or created and enacted in more discreetly defined populations and groups. In recent times, the process of meaning making and negotiation has become more urgent or overt, and within this some people or groups have a greater ability to negotiate meaning than others. Overall, acknowledging that heritage engages with remembering forces us to acknowledge that heritage is a culturally directed personal and social act of making sense and understanding. This may help us bind ourselves, or may see us become bound to, national or a range of sub-national collectives or communities, but it remains a process of intense emotional power.

Heritage as performance

The idea of performativity arises forcefully out of the literature on remembering and this concept requires closer examination. Work by Gaynor Bagnall (2003) emphasizes the idea that visiting heritage sites is a physical experience of performance and reminiscing. Bagnall undertook qualitative interviews with visitors to the Museum of Science and Industry at Manchester and the heritage site Wigan Pier at Wigan, both in England. She argues (2003: 90) that a form of reminiscence is practised at these sites, in which personal and family memories and biographies are used to help visitors to emotionally engage with the site and the interpretive material presented there. It is

66

explicitly through this emotional engagement that visitors make the history they are viewing more meaningful to their lives and experiences. Reminiscence is a performance of remembering that Casey (2000) defines as explicitly social and framed by the exchange of meaning and memory. Bagnall (2003: 88–91) goes on to argue that meaning, and a sense of authenticity, is engendered through constructing a plausible experience and emotional response which is used either to affirm or reject the version of history that is offered to the visitor by the museum in question. Bagnall challenges the idea of passivity in heritage visitors – the issue of agency is a vital one, and needs to be considered in terms of both those responsible for presenting 'heritage' and heritage audiences themselves. In considering the idea of performativity it becomes important to challenge traditional accounts of how heritage messages and meanings are transmitted to and from heritage visitors or users.

Traditional accounts inevitably see the process of communication as occurring in one direction, and that heritage visitors passively take in the messages intended by heritage professionals at museums and state-managed sites, or those intended by tourist operators at commercial venues. Abercrombie and Longhurst (1998) offer 'spectacle/performance' as a new paradigm for understanding the changing relationship between performance and audience, which allows new insights into the nature of heritage audiences. They argue that audiences can no longer be conceived of as passive or neutral, a clear distinction between consumption and production cannot be maintained, and that the performances audiences engage with diffuse out into everyday life to inform ideas of individual and group identity. Three types of audience are identified: the simple, mass and diffused. The simple audience is one that gives focused attention to a specific event or performance – such as a theatre production or sporting event, and is associated with specific rituals. These rituals become less pronounced in mass audiences, and these audiences often exist in private rather than public spaces, for instance in the home in the case of television viewing. However, for the purposes here, their identification of the 'diffused audience' is important. This new form of audience they see as developing due to increasing spectacularization and the social constitution of individuals as narcissistic. The diffused audience cannot be isolated from day-to-day life as the divisions between private and public have become blurred, while being a member of an audience can no longer be seen as an exceptional event. Further, they argue that the experiences of being an audience are themselves constitutive of everyday life (1998: 68–9). These experiences diffuse, or leak out, from the performance events that had previously contained them into the wider realms of everyday life, and in doing so interact with identity formation (1998: 36). Or as Crouch observes, 'there is fertile ground for considering how far performance in the mundane can extend and leak into and across other values, relations, and significations through which individuals may act, feel, think and adjust' (2003: 1958–9).

It is also difficult to maintain a clear distinction between consumption and production (Abercrombie and Longhurst 1998: 165). The roles between performer, or message producer, are intermeshed with those of audience, or message receiver, as the mediating institutions and social distances which separated them are eroded. This does not mean to say that the other forms of audience experience do not co-exist, but that in identifying a diffused audience Abercrombie and Longhurst point out that performers and audiences *can be the same*. In short, participation in heritage events or the simple act of visiting sites is an embodiment or active statement of identity in which visitors become embroiled in a performance for which they are also audience.

Longhurst et al. (2004) applied the strategy of the spectacle/performance paradigm to a qualitative study of museum audiences. They found that the idea of cultural capital, which has dominated assumptions about the motivations of museum visiting (Merriman 1991; Walsh 1992), while occurring, did not find expression in all visitors' discussions of what it meant to visit museums. For some of the people they interviewed, museum visiting was seen as part of the identity of their parents, and that being a 'good parent' was defined through the activity of museum visiting and that 'consideration and imagination of a visit to the museum performs a desired state' (2004: 121). Although this does invoke a sense of attainment of cultural capital, in that the ability to go to a museum confirmed a sense of desired identity, they further note that museum visits, although valued this way, were 'rarely explicitly narrated in these terms' (2004: 121). What is important in this account is that it was the *act* of visiting, and what it represented, that was significant and held meaning for visitors.

Subsequently, both visitors to heritage sites and those concerned with their management and interpretation may be usefully understood as engaging in a cultural performance. The very act of possessing, managing and conserving heritage sites and museum collections is 'itself a performative utterance of having an identity' (Macdonald 2003: 3). The whole processes of cultural heritage management and museum curation are sustained cultural performances in which certain cultural values and identities are continually rehearsed and thus preserved. Moreover, the performance of preservation and curation is itself a performative statement which constructs the objects or 'props' utilized in this performance as 'heritage'. Schwyzer, in discussing the scouring, or weeding, of the 3,000-year-old Uffington white horse, cut into the chalky subsoil of Oxfordshire, England, notes that the continual performance of scouring, which appears to have occurred for millennia, makes this site significant to 'English' identity, even though its moment of origin predates the formation of 'England'. What makes the horse 'English' is not the date of its making, but the performative act of its preservation. Schwyzer (1999: 58) notes that preservation is an activity so deeply English that it transforms such ancient sites into a feature of the national heritage. Alternatively, the *idea* that preservation is 'inherently' English, or perhaps British (whether it is true or not) suggests the enabling role the AHD plays in national discourses of identity formation.

However, the most obvious sense of heritage performance is that of commemoration, ranging, for instance, from the national rituals associated with events like Armistice Day, to the more personal rituals associated with familial anniversaries. As various commentators have noted, the doing of commemorative events or performances engenders strong emotions as collective memories and identities are either maintained and transmitted to younger generations or contested and remade (Young 1989; Frijda 1997; Pickering and Tyrrell 2004) and through which traditional values and relations of power may be rehearsed and retained (Cannadine 1983; Philp and Mercer 2002). Another obvious sense of 'performance' is that of battle or other historical events re-enactments. These, as Crang (1996) argues, are performances in which participants engage in overt negotiations about the meaning of the past and present. Another sense of performance is that of the use of costumed actors or interpreters at sites – or 'live interpretation'. This form of interpretation has traditionally received some strident criticism, not only for blurring the lines between education and entertainment, but for being explicitly entertainment focused (Lowenthal 1985: 301; Hewison 1987; Reas and Cosgrove 1993). Live costumed interpretation is often perceived as inherently 'fake' simply because of its theatrical overtones (Malcom-Davies 2004: 281). However, this form of interpretation has become particularly popular and commonplace in many Western countries (Evans 1991). Practitioners of this genre of interpretation are often quite critically and self-reflexively explicit about their educational aims and argue that education and entertainment are not mutually exclusive, while education is actually facilitated through actively engaging audiences (see, for instance, Evans 1991; Malcom-Davies 2004). The discourse of 'inauthenticity' that often dogs such interpretive performances is inevitably entered into as a means to maintain the authority and gravity of expert knowledge.

The expertise of archaeologists, historians and architects traditionally associated with heritage sites and museums is inevitably challenged by the popular appeal of live interpretation. This form of interpretation is particularly challenging as it requires active participation or interactions between the audience and the interpreters, and any sense of active agency on the part of heritage audiences challenges the assumptions and ideologies that underpin the AHD. While the idea of 'performativity' has been metaphorically used in archaeological theory to describe the act of excavation and other research (see Tilley 1989; Shanks 1992, 2004; Pearson and Shanks 2001), there is nonetheless a view here, and in terms of the critique of live interpretation more generally, that the audiences to these performances are 'simple'. Simple not only in the sense that Abercrombie and Longhurst use the term to describe audiences of a defined and self-contained event, but also in terms of their lack of perspicacity and critical facilities. It is the experts who must drive the performance, whether that be the interpretive process overall or the excavation or other research on which the interpretation is based, so that the audience is educated correctly. However, audiences at heritage sites are not simple and may be more adequately described as 'diffused' – as inevitably interactions with heritage sites and museum objects and exhibitions do 'leak out' into everyday lives, where they influence and inform personal and community identity.

There is, however, a far less overt form of heritage performance that is useful to consider. Although the day-to-day visitation of heritage sites and museums may be self-perceived as activities of leisure or tourism, the act of visiting is also a subtle performance in which the visitor, and indeed site manager, engages with a range of what Bagnall (2003: 87) defines as 'emotional, cognitive and imaginative' issues. Visiting a heritage site or museum is a performative statement about identity in which the performer is also audience to the management and interpretive performances of the heritage site/museum management and interpretive staff. This does not necessarily mean that the act of visiting requires that the visitor, as both heritage performer and audience, uncritically accepts the messages they are invited to take away – they may, but they may also engage in their own performances of equivocation or rejection in which the authorized meanings are adjusted, negated and/or new meanings and identities created. If meaning at heritage sites and museums is mediated through constructing and engaging with a plausible experience, rather than simply through presenting and reading the facts on interpretive panels, the heritage visitor becomes intimately concerned with decoding the meaning of those experiences. The plausibility of that experience may in part be determined by the social literacy that particular visitors may have with the site or museum exhibition in question (Bagnall 2003: 87), but equally may be influenced by their own wider social experiences and political and social values which are tied up in the processes of 'doing' and remembering.

A key issue in considering the performativity of heritage is that of emotion. As Fridja (1997) observes, the performances of commemoration are drenched in a range of both positive and negative emotion. This emotion is often explicitly engendered by the ritual commemorative performance itself, as well as in the acts of remembering and memory making that are framed and directed by the commemorative performance. The engagement of emotion and the sharing of this emotive experience or performance, together with sharing of acts of remembering and memory making, are vital elements of the glue that creates and binds collective identities. While the emotions encountered in commemorative events may be quite raw, emotion is also significant in other forms of heritage performance. Certainly, Bagnall found that 'emotional realism' was a key issue for visitors at the museums she surveyed and that 'visitors required that the sites generate emotionally authentic responses' (2003: 88). This idea of emotional realism, or emotional authenticity in which visitors can validate or measure the legitimacy of their own social and cultural experiences outside of the heritage sites they are visiting, adds another layer of consequence to the idea of performativity. Thus, heritage performances are not only physical experiences of 'doing', but also emotional experiences of 'being'. The emotional content of performance is a significant aspect of the 'heritage experience', which itself not only makes, transmits and maintains social values and meanings, but does so in a manner that invokes, and indeed requires, self-conscious emotional acts of remembering and memory making. As Tuan observes, 'experience is compounded of feeling and thought' (2003: 10), and one of the things that this emotional content ensures is a sense of reflection or mindfulness on the part of the 'heritage performer'. The emotional content of these performances is significant in ensuring that the meanings and values they rehearse or create are infused with realism or given reality or 'authenticity' in and for the performer's daily life.

The idea that cultural meaning is both fluid and created through 'doing' has also been used to understand the practices of tourism (Coleman and Crang 2002a). Crouch argues that tourism is not so much a product or destination, but an embodied practice, in which our bodies encounter space in its materiality, and that materiality is itself constructed and understood through our engagement and encounters with it; subsequently: 'tourism is a practice of ontological knowledge, an encounter with space that is both social and incorporates an embodied "feeling of doing" ' (2002: 211). The idea of 'experience', particularly the search for the 'authentic experience', has been traditionally important as a marketing strategy in heritage and museum cultural tourism (Prentice 1993, 2001). Although this sense of 'experience' tapped into by tourism marketing has not been given wide critical examination as a cultural and social agency in the tourism literature, the fact of its significance however has not been missed or dismissed as it has in much of the heritage literature. While the sense of experience often created in tourism has been criticized for its tendency to commodify or Disneyfy the past, or for its tendency to transform identities 'through pernicious vogue storylines' (Hollinshead 1999: 19), it nonetheless demonstrates the importance of 'doing' and 'being' at a 'place'.

While the performance literature within tourism stresses the idea that performances by both tourists and the cultures visited can be conceived as a process in which place, meaning and identity is actively created and recreated by both the visited and the visitor (Coleman and Crange 2002b; Fairweather 2003) is useful, there are some cautionary observations that need to be made. Turnbull notes that, 'we create space in the process of travelling through it and in creating narratives of journeys we construct knowledge' (2002: 133) and thus in the performance of travel 'knowledge and space are coproduced in memory and movement' (2002: 137). This sense of travelling or 'passing through' is a metaphor employed by the archaeologist Ian Hodder at the

9,000-year-old Turkish site of Çatal Hüyük. Hodder (2003: 142) defines all those, including the Turkish, who interact with or have an interest in the site as time travellers as they may be viewed, at least in the context of the long history of the site, as 'passing through'. This concept of passing through, intended or not, reduces both locals and global visitors alike to the status of 'tourists'. This conceptualization is not confined to ancient sites like Çatal Hüyük, but rather is a common consequence of the AHD and the degree to which it relegates visitors to the status of passive audiences.

Visitors to heritage sites are frequently defined or classified as 'tourists' within the heritage literature, particularly with respect to non-museums based heritage (see Chapter 4). This classification of visitors is especially pronounced where heritage sites are primarily defined as 'archaeological sites' or as 'historic buildings'. This tendency is a reflection of the degree to which these sites are often, following the dictates of cultural heritage management practices, under the direct custodianship or stewardship of a body of expertise, usually archaeology, architecture or history. Enshrined within both the literature and practices of cultural heritage management is the assumption that the meanings of such sites, particularly ancient archaeological sites, but no less sites valued by the state for their architectural features, are only really accessible by expert research and knowledge (Smith 2004). As such, non-expert visitors to these places are inevitably identified as disconnected passers by – as tourists. The point here is that this sense of 'passing through', of being simply a 'tourist', in turn invokes a sense of personal, cultural, historic or emotional disconnection with the site or place in question, or suggests that the meanings constructed by the performance of travel may be so fluid that they lack any solidity or consequence for the traveller.

Perhaps this is indeed the case when the visitors to heritage sites are culturally and emotionally quite distant from the place being visited. International visitors to sites like Çatal Hüyük, Stonehenge, English country houses, Colonial Williamsburg and so on, may have an emotionally different response to these sites than either local communities or visitors who see these sites as symbolic of their own nation. Certainly, a dominant assumption in the heritage literature is that geographical proximity to a heritage site equates with close cultural links, while geographical distance is perceived to reduce cultural affiliation. Thus, the idea of 'local' communities tends to be privileged in heritage inclusion or outreach policies and activities. This is not to say that local communities are not important by any means; however, 'local' itself may not necessarily be only defined by geography. The diasporas of peoples through Europe and the geographical displacement of Indigenous communities in many post-colonial countries illustrate that people with close cultural, social or historical ties to sites may not be geographically close to those sites. Thus, 'local' may not simply include a geographically-defined community, but may include displaced communities, also dispersed communities that share cultural, social or historical experiences – the local here being a measure of the intensity of attachment rather than necessarily geo-graphical proximity. Coleman and Crang (2002b: 3) identify 'glocalization', a concern for the local, as a reaction to globalization where the local has to be recovered and packaged and sold as 'heritage' as a unifying strategy in parts of the West. Whether this concern drives this process or not, there is cer-tainly a preoccupation in Western heritage policy and practice with geo-graphically-defined 'local' communities. However, such communities, while certainly important, are not the full story with regards to the diversity of links and associations that are made with heritage sites.

Work by Poria et al. (2003) surveying tourists in Israel, noted that people behave differently at heritage sites depending on how closely they feel them-selves to be culturally or emotionally linked to the site being visited. The nature of the links self-identified by visitors can be many and varied, and can exist both within and outside of the AHD. International travellers, for instance, may perceive themselves linked to a heritage site for any range of reasons. These reasons may be part of an authorized discourse about the universality of heritage values and may be emotionally very real to the person expressing these values. Or, at one extreme, these links may exist well out-side the dominant discourse as with the 'goddess groups' that tour Çatal Hüyük and see themselves as religiously and emotionally linked to this site (Hodder 2003). For domestic or local travellers links to sites may exist for a range of reasons, and with varying degrees of emotional and cultural inten-sity, or indeed, may not be valued at all. The intricacy of the web of associations and values that can overlay any heritage site, object or place is often obscured not only by the nature of the AHD, but also specifically by the dismissal of heritage performativity and 'experience' as a touristic commodity.

There are three useful points that can be drawn out of this discussion of travel and tourism. Firstly, that the tendency to classify visitors to sites as 'tourists' is an integral element of the AHD, and renders the emotional and physical experiences of heritage performances as culturally illegitimate or inauthentic. This is despite the observation, or indeed perhaps because of it, that the pragmatics of tourism marketing demonstrate the importance of both emotional and physical experience, and the emotional authenticity of that experience (MacCannell 1999), as an integral element of 'heritage'.

Secondly, the embodiment of travelling and the interaction of individuals with space and place reinforce the sense of 'occasion' that distinguishes an event in which individuals singularly or collectively engage with, construct and negotiate heritage meanings. The act of visiting can be an integral part of the performance of heritage, and is not necessarily an indication that the visitor or traveller is somehow culturally, socially or historically distant from a site. The act of travelling or of visiting can be many layered and complex. It may indeed be an expression of cultural distance – for instance, the American visiting an English country house may have a very different cultural experience at such a site than an English visitor – conversely the act of travelling (whether a few miles or many hundred) can be part of a performance which denotes those places or spaces in which it is appropriate to engage with certain memories, values or meanings. This is not to say that travelling *has* to be a part of a heritage performance, but that it does not necessarily render that performance as invalid or emotionally less real.

Thirdly, the emotional and cultural links to heritage that people may hold are not *necessarily* or only determined by geographical proximity, and can be expressed in many and varied ways. There are many layers or complexities of performance that will be influenced by the links people understand themselves to have with the heritage sites or spaces they encounter. In short, any heritage site or place will have a range of different meanings for different groups or interests, and any one group or individual may see a site as having many layers of meaning for them. A simple observation, perhaps, but it is one that has profound consequences for understanding the nature of heritage and what it does and how it is used.

The idea of the performativity of heritage helps to challenge the idea of the passivity of heritage audiences, and allows a theorization of those audiences as active agents in the mediation of the meanings of heritage. In turn, this must make conceptual space for the recognition of the multiplicity of meaning that any aspect of tangible or intangible heritage inevitably must have. It also must make problematic the idea of space and place, particularly with respect to how these are physically and emotionally encountered. The ideas of place and then dissonance are considered next. Neither of these concepts are new within the heritage literature but require reconsideration in light of the foregoing.

Place

In the discussion so far, links between heritage and identity have been emphasized, alongside the role heritage plays as a cultural tool in the acts and performances of remembering. In this discussion, I have been surfing a tension between the idea of the intangibility of heritage – the idea that heritage *is* the cultural processes of meaning and memory making and remaking rather than a thing – and the critical reality that there *are* physical things or 'places' we call and define as heritage. In exploring the idea of 'place', rather than resolving this tension, I want to tease it out a little more by considering both the physicality of place, and the conceptualization of identity or social place, and the inevitable interlinking of these ideas. As Escobar (2001: 140) argues, place is both 'a category of thought' and 'a constructed reality', and I am suggesting that this tension is a central aspect of 'heritage'. While heritage is representational or symbolic both in its physicality and in the intangible acts of doing or performing heritage, it is also a process and a performance where the values and meanings that are represented are negotiated and worked out. Although the physicality of heritage provides a sense of the immutability of value and meaning, these are never fixed, but always subject to negotiation and change.

Thus, heritage does more than simply construct or represent a range of identities or memories. The values that inform any sense of identity or underlie memory are also used to construct ways of understanding and making the present meaningful. Heritage is about a sense of *place*. Not simply in constructing a sense of abstract identity, but also in helping us position ourselves as a nation, community or individual and our 'place' in our cultural, social and physical world. Heritage, particularly in its material representations, provides not only a physical anchor or geographical sense of belonging, but also allows us to negotiate a sense of social 'place' or class/community identity, and a cultural place or sense of belonging. I am using the term place in both of Escobar's meanings here – as a sense of geographical space, as 'a constructed reality', but also in a sense of social position and value production as 'a category of thought' (2001: 140). In a very real sense heritage becomes a cultural tool that nations, societies, communities and individuals use to express, facilitate and construct a sense of identity, self and belonging in which the 'power of place' is invoked in its representational sense to give physical reality to these expressions and experiences.

The relation between identity and place, however, is not simply representational; there is also a pre-representational affect that place has on the expression of identity and social value. However, the term is also used to identify and negotiate those values and meanings that help define both a sense of place and a cultural and social framework for dealing with the present. The ability 'to know one's place', to construct a sense of one's position in the intangible, yet real, network of social relations within which we live and act is another meaning that I want to explore in this section.

Critical attention to the idea of place has increased in recent years, particularly in response to debates about globalization, but also as scholars 'working at the intersection of environment, culture and development . . . [are] confronted with social movements that commonly maintain a strong reference to place and territory' (Escobar 2001: 141). Although critical debates about the nature and role of 'place' exist, particularly, within geography and anthropology (see, for instance, Keith and Pile 1993; Low and Lawrence-Zúñiga 2003a), similar discussions are infrequent in heritage studies (although, see Graham et al. 2000). Despite the general lack of focused critique, the term 'place' is becoming increasingly used within the heritage literature and management and conservation policies and practices. Traditionally, it is the term 'site' that has dominated heritage discourses, a legacy of the dominance of both archaeology and architecture in the management of material culture. However, there has been a gradual, but increasing shift to the word 'place' as demonstrated in its use in the Australian Burra Charter (Australia ICOMOS 1999) and in major policy documents such as the English *Power of Place* policy manifesto (English Heritage 2000). This shift is a recognition that 'site' is a relatively restrictive term and tends to invoke a sense of well-defined archaeologically- or architecturally-mapped locations and locales, primarily of archaeological/architectural or other scientific/aesthetic value. Conversely, the idea of 'place' allows for a more fluid sense of physical boundaries, while, more importantly, also incorporates a sense that heritage has direct linkage to the construction of identity in a way that 'site', with its often implied preceding 'archaeological' or 'architectural' descriptor, does not. As Crang (2001: 102) notes, the idea of place invokes a sense of belonging; it represents a set of cultural characteristics and says something about where you live, come from and who you are — it provides an anchor of shared experiences between people and a physical demonstration of continuity over time.

Places are socially constructed — they are not, as Margaret Rodman (2003: 204–5) argues, simply locations where people 'do things', they are 'not inert containers'. Rather they are 'politicized, culturally relative, historically specific, local and multiple constructions' (Rodman 2003: 205). For many commentators, place may be understood as the way space is meaningfully organized (Low and Lawrence-Zúñiga 2003b). Place or the 'local' is not inevitably subsumed by the national or global, rather the national or regional are made up of innumerable places (Lefebvre, quoted in Richardson and Jenson 2003: 11). However, for Edward Casey 'place is prior to space'; a concern with space was simply a preoccupation of modernity that has tended to de-emphasize the significance of place (1996: 16, see also 1997; and Tuan 2003). Place, he believes, is universally significant and 'there is no knowing or sensing a place except by being in that place, and to be in a place is to be in a position to perceive it' (Casey 1996: 18). Place is part of lived experience, and for Tuan place is an embodiment or material representation of feelings, images and thoughts so that not only specific locales but also whole landscapes and cityscapes become sculptured and meaningful spaces (2003: 17). However, this does not mean that place is simply an expression of past human experiences; it also has an affect — at this point we return to Thrift's idea of affect discussed above. Urban studies have demonstrated how cityscapes both represent cultural meaning, but also affect that meaning. The geographer David Harvey views social relations as spatial and that these relations exist within places embedded in social meanings (1996: 122). This sense of affect structures human encounters with place so that 'bodies are disposed for action in a particular way' and emotions, ideas and relations are structured and framed by those experiences (Thrift 2004: 62). Thrift argues that this affect is not accidental, but can be, and is, mobilized knowingly and deployed politically (2004: 58). This sense of affect finds synergy with Casey's observation that 'to live is to live locally, and to know is first of all to know the places one is in' (1996: 18). Further, for Casey place is more than a thing, it is also an event — thus it *is* a place where things happen, but importantly this 'doing' has particular meaning *because* of the place of its doing.

This idea of place is vital for understanding heritage. Heritage as place, or 'heritage places', may not only be conceived as representational of past human experiences, but also as creating an affect on current experiences and perceptions of the world. Thus, a heritage place may represent or stand in for a sense of identity and belonging for particular individuals or groups. However, it may also structure an individual's response and the experiences an individual may have at that place, while also framing and defining the social meanings these encounters engender. This is not to return, however, to the precepts that underlie, and are continually remade within, the AHD and the 'heritage industry' critique, that visitors to sites mindlessly accept social meanings that are somehow inherently 'fixed' within a heritage site. Rather, it simply acknowledges that the brute physicality of heritage places elicits an emotional response in people. Not simply the visual, but the full range of bodily senses engenders emotional responses (Bender 2002). This response may become the raw material that is knowingly or inadvertently shaped or moulded through the interpretation process at heritage sites, and/or under-writes the sense of passion that individuals or groups may hold for particular places. Basically, there is a 'dialectical relation between material practices and the symbolic meanings that social agents attach to their environment' (Richardson and Jensen 2003: 8). The significant point here is that a sense of place demands recognition that the act of *being* at a heritage place and experiencing that place – whether site managers or tour operators regulate that experience or not – is fundamentally significant. Those experiences of being in place will have an affect that will help to define the meanings and ideas an individual constructs. This will be done not only in terms of the past represented at the heritage place, but also the meanings it has for and in the present, and in terms of the sense of social and cultural constructs of 'place' or identity that an individual takes away. The meanings and memories of past human experiences are thus remembered through contemporary interactions with physical places and landscapes, and through the performances enacted within them – and with each new encounter with place, with each new experience of place, meanings and memories may subtly, or otherwise, be rewritten or remade. These experiences help to bind groups and communities not only through shared memories and identities, but also through shared experiences:

> places, like voices, are local and multiple. For each inhabitant, a place has a unique reality, one in which meaning is shared with other people and places. The links in these chains of experienced places are forged of culture and history.
>
> (Rodman 2003: 208)

Landscapes are also places of symbolic importance. Landscapes are not only shaped by cultural practices, but are symbolic of cultural and social beliefs (Crang 2001), and in turn also shape and structure social encounters and relations (Bender 2002; Byrne 2003). The idea of cultural or even 'heritage' landscapes has been a recent concern in heritage studies and management practices (see, for instance, Fairclough et al. 1999; Grenville 1999; Cotter et al. 2001; Fairclough and Rippon 2002). However, I am flagging landscape as a particular issue in my discussion of place because it currently represents two important policy and philosophical debates in heritage management that have a consequence for any definition of 'heritage place'. The first concerns the issue of the nature/culture divide over the meaning of landscape and thus place, and the second is the issue of 'multi-vocality'.

The idea of landscape has become important in heritage studies as heritage managers have attempted to move from a management approach that emphasized 'dots on a map', whereby individual heritage 'sites' were viewed as representing specific points in time (Boyd et al. 1996). The idea that 'sites' existed in a landscape initially opened the conceptual boundaries in heritage management to allow a sense that sites may represent histories over multiple time 'periods' and may exist, not in isolation from each other, but inter-related with other points or sites in the landscape, if not the landscape as a whole. The concern for heritage landscape studies and landscape categorization has been facilitated by recent archaeological landscape research, and has been used to not only predict 'site' occurrence for planning purposes, but also in developing more holistic approaches for understanding the past of particular regions or localities (Fairclough 1999). The idea of landscape used here is that of a palimpsest, where the landscape is understood to have been continually written over by human physical and cultural interactions with it (Boyer 1994; Crang 2001; Huyssen 2003). However, following the legacy of Enlightenment rationality, 'landscape' has traditionally been viewed in heritage agencies such as UNESCO as inherently 'natural' (Titchen 1996; Waterton 2005a). With increasing recognition that there is no landscape on the planet that has not had some form of human interaction with it, however, the idea that we can differentiate between 'natural' and 'cultural' landscapes has been challenged (Head 2000a, 2000b). Not only are landscapes inevitably physically shaped or altered by human cultural practices – and in that sense 'cultural', but they are also 'cultural' in the sense that the way they are conceived and understood dictates how they are managed and used.

As Lowenthal (2005) demonstrates, the concept that landscapes, and heritage more generally, are either inherently 'natural' or 'cultural' will determine what types of management strategies and practices are deployed for their conservation or preservation. Thus, the way a landscape or place is defined determines its management and use – a choice that is not only culturally driven but consequently physically and conceptually shapes the landscape being managed. Landscapes are also 'cultural', in that they are symbolic of the social and political ideologies that people use to understand and conceptualize them, which are in turn embodied within the landscape through human action. As Graham et al. state, 'landscape interconnects with a series of interacting and constantly mutating aspects of identity', which they note as including 'nationalism, gender, sexuality, "race", class, and colonialism/postcolonialism' (2000: 32).

UNESCO now lists cultural landscapes and landscapes with combined 'natural' and 'cultural' features as being of World Heritage status. However, as Lowenthal (2005: 89) observes, there is a marked sense that nature is superior to culture, and that within UNESCO policy documents, even though the idea of the possibility of 'pristine wilderness' is understood to be non-existent, there still exists the implication that 'nature is perfect and culture a nuisance'. The point of stressing the facility of the nature/culture divide is to note that there is a tendency within the heritage management and conservation process to extract 'place' from its physical and wider cultural contexts and manage it in much the same way as the 'site' of traditional management conceptualizations and practices. In some way the built, or otherwise human-shaped aspects of landscape, are perceived as still separate or divorceable from wider contexts, which are after all 'natural', and narrowed down to manageable locales. Thus, any sense of place becomes inevitably constrained by the boundaries defined for it by management practices and classification, listing or scheduling systems that require well-definable boundaries. In the legislative and planning processes that drive most cultural heritage management systems, this need is unavoidable – but what it does is to limit the possibility of the fluidity and mutability of meaning by constraining and framing the physical experiences and interactions people may have with place. The ability to map and define boundaries is a political act of naming and defining which has implications for knowledge/power of and about place (Harley 1988). Thus, the experiences of heritage landscape/place are inevitably themselves managed, and heritage performances become 'staged', and meanings and memories become scripted or regulated by the way a place or landscape has itself been defined, mapped and thus managed – in effect heritage experiences/performances become regulated by the management process itself.

This issue is particularly problematic if we accept the multi-vocality of place. If place is both an expression of, and has a consequence for, human experience and inter-relations then, as Massey notes, plurality of meaning must be accepted in any definition of place (1994). Place as a collage of intersecting and overlapping meanings is not only a space where meaningful experiences occur, but is also where meanings are contested and negotiated. However, as discussed in Chapter 1, the naturalization of the AHD tends to not only restrict the ability of competing heritage discourses to be heard and dealt with equitability within heritage management processes, but also requires the maintenance of a consensual view of the past and its meanings for the present. A sense of place, as Hayden (1997) observes, is inherently about not only the commonalities, but also the differences of lived experiences. As social movements use reconfigurations of place and space to challenge accepted narratives of capital and modernity (Escobar 2001: 165), and as heritage places increasingly play important roles in the representational politics of cultural, class and ethnic identities (Graham et al. 2000; Meskell 2001; Smith 2004), there has been an increasing awareness of the need to understand and theorize these tensions. It is at this point that the idea of 'dissonance' becomes useful.

Dissonance

An important contribution to heritage studies is the work by Ashworth and Tunbridge on 'dissonant heritage' (1996). They acknowledge the contested nature of heritage and argue that the tensions that underlie heritage can be encapsulated and understood, and subsequently managed and mitigated, through the concept of dissonant heritage. The root cause of the dissonant nature of heritage lies in their observation that heritage is created by interpretation. Not only what is interpreted, but how it is interpreted and by whom, will create quite specific messages about the value and meaning of specific heritage places and the past it represents (1996: 27). These messages do not always find consensus and thus cause dissonance. This has a particular emotive, cultural and political consequence because:

> all heritage is someone's heritage and therefore logically not someone else's: the original meaning of an inheritance [from which 'heritage' derives] implies the existence of disinheritance and by extension any creation of heritage from the past disinherits someone completely or partially, actively or potentially. This disinheritance may be unintentional, temporary, of trivial importance, limited in its effects and concealed; or it may be long-term, widespread, intentional, important and obvious.
>
> (Ashworth and Tunbridge 1996: 21)

In effect, the past is valued and understood differently by different peoples, groups or communities and how that past is understood validates or not a sense of place. In particular contexts this can be disabling for those groups or communities whose sense of history and place exist outside of the dominant heritage message or discourse, though it can be enabling for those groups whose sense of the past either sits within or finds synergy with authorized views. For Ashworth and Tunbridge, dissonance is most evident in the economic uses of heritage, as the creation of 'heritage products endows those products with the tensions and dilemmas inherent in all commodification for contemporary markets' (1996: 21). This dissonance is particularly marked, as debates about the so-called heritage industry discussed in Chapter 1 reveal, when heritage and the messages subsequently constructed about that heritage become a touristic product. This process, in which the past is *seen* (even if it is not) to become divergent from the direct objective and pastoral care and control of 'history', renders any interpretation subject to observations and criticisms of 'sanitization', 'trivialization', lack of authenticity and so forth.

Although Ashworth and Tunbridge tend to focus on the touristic uses of heritage and the consequent dissonant tensions that arise, they also draw our attention to negative heritage places, such as sites of human atrocity or natural disaster. Such sites may include German concentration camps, massacre sites, war memorials, prisons and so forth. The discomfort, as they identify, that is felt by many at the idea of commemorating sites of human trauma as 'heritage' reveals the extent to which heritage is almost inevitably associated with comfortable, harmonious and consensual views about the meaning of the past. However, all heritage is uncomfortable to someone, not only because any meaning or message about a heritage place may 'disinherit' someone else, but because heritage has a particular power to legitimize – or not – someone's sense of place and thus their social and cultural experiences and memories. The traditional interpretation of the grand country houses of the rural elites in Europe and North America may provide, for instance, a comfortable and even a comforting view of the past, as is revealed in Chapter 4. However, for those whose collective social experiences and memories are disinherited by this view, for instance the descendents of servants, slaves or estate/grounds workers and so forth, such heritage is at best problematic, if not intrinsically uncomfortable.

The point that Ashworth and Tunbridge (1996) make, that dissonance is inherently created when something takes on the status of 'heritage', is a vital one. This is because it not only draws our attention to the multi-vocality that must underlie the meanings given to and acquired through performance and remembering, it also locates this observation within a political context. Dissonance acknowledges the inevitability that the meaning of these values will be contested and challenged, and that this in turn will have a consequence for the legitimization – or not – of a sense of place. Ashworth and Tunbridge note that heritage may be a political resource, and while they tend to identify this in terms of nationalism, it is important to point out that a sense of 'politics' is also inherent in all – including sub-national – constructions of heritage. By politics, I simply mean that some groups, individuals or communities will have a greater ability to have their values and meanings taken up and legitimized than others, and power both moulds and is moulded by this process. As Graham et al. (2000: 25) note, the view of heritage in any given society will inevitably reflect that of the dominant social, religious or ethnic groups. This is a reflection not only of the political, economic and social power of these groups but also, in some measure, of the power of heritage itself as a legitimizing discourse to not only validate but also reproduce certain social and cultural values, experiences and memories.

While Ashworth and Tunbridge argue that a sense of dissonance is an intrinsic quality of heritage (1996; see also Tunbridge 1998; Graham et al. 2000, 2005), there is a significant hesitancy in the heritage literature to actively incorporate this into a definition of the term. Rather, there is a tendency to identify 'heritage' and 'dissonant heritage', as if the contested nature of heritage were something that can be separated from a more comfortable and unproblematic sense of the term. Most importantly, there is a very real sense that there is this thing we can call heritage, and then there are *specific* conflicts or dissonant events that will arise in the management of heritage from time to time. Ashworth and Tunbridge themselves fall into this trap as they suggest that dissonance can and should be actively managed to promote a 'sustainable cultural heritage' for both 'socio-political stability and economic success' (1996: 268). They go on to note that management strategies need to be developed to ensure that problems may be anticipated and where possible diffused, while still acknowledging the diversity of the heritage resource (1996: 270). Pearson and Sullivan (1995) and King (2000) make similar pleas, and note the importance of recognizing the potential for conflict and mitigating its occurrence in the management process. While the idea of 'sustainability' is never clearly defined, what this call for 'management' does is to inadvertently resurrect the AHD and the consensual idea of heritage.

An understanding of the dissonant nature of heritage cannot be incorporated into definitions of heritage if the contested nature of heritage is reduced to site-specific management 'problems' that are simply about differences of opinion that need to be 'managed'. I am not saying here that conflicts should not be arbitrated; however, what this site-specific idea of dissonance does is obscure the wider cultural and political contexts within which heritage both sits and serves. What is actually being done within the management process is the 'management', or rather the regulation and governance, of memory, identity and sense of place, a process which is obscured by reducing it to a site-specific problem of dissonance. Rather than viewing these conflicts as case specific, the cultural process and performance that is heritage is *about* the negotiation of these conflicts. Heritage *is* dissonant – it is a constitutive social process that on the one hand is about regulating and legitimizing, and on the other hand is about working out, contesting and challenging a range of cultural and social identities, sense of place, collective memories, values and meanings that prevail in the present and can be passed to the future.

Conclusion

With the discussions of 'place' and 'dissonance', we return to the point of departure for this discussion of heritage, and return inevitably to issues of 'identity' and power. The various themes and concepts discussed above have been, to some extent, somewhat artificially separated from each other for the purposes of argument – however, these concepts are all inter-related and interlocking, and it is now necessary to integrate them. So what does the conceptual repacking of the heritage suitcase reveal?

What emerges foremost in the above discussion is a sense of action, power and agency. Heritage is something vital and alive. It is a moment of action, not something frozen in material form. It incorporates a range of actions that often occur at places or in certain spaces. Although heritage is something that is done at places, these places become places of heritage both because of the events of meaning making and remembering that occur at them, but also because they lend a sense of occasion and reality to the activities occurring at them. There is an interlinked relationship between the activities that occur at places and the places themselves – but it is this tension between action and material representation that is an important element of heritage. The tension may at once be about creating and maintaining historical and social consensus, but simultaneously it can also be a process of dissent and contestation.

If heritage is something that is 'done', what then is done? There is no one defining action or moment of heritage, but rather a range of activities that include remembering, commemoration, communicating and passing on knowledge and memories, asserting and expressing identity and social and cultural values and meanings. As an experience, and as a social and cultural performance, it is something with which people actively, often self-consciously, and critically engage in. What then does heritage do; what are the consequences of these moments that identify them as 'heritage'? The product or the consequences of heritage activities are the emotions and experiences and the memories of them that they create, and while these then work to facilitate a sense of identity and belonging it is not all they do. What are also created, and continually recreated (rather than simply 'maintained'), are social networks and relations that themselves bind and create a sense of belonging and identity. These networks and relations are facilitated through an activity in which social and cultural values, meanings and understandings both about the past and present are sometimes explicitly, and sometimes implicitly, worked out, inspected, considered, rejected, embraced or trans-formed. Identity is not simply something 'produced' or represented by heri-tage places or heritage moments, but is something actively and continually recreated and negotiated as people, communities and institutions reinterpret, remember and reassess the meaning of the past in terms of the social, cultural and political needs of the present. It is thus simultaneously about change and continuity; it is a mentality or discourse in which certain realities and ideas of 'being' are constituted, rehearsed, contested and negotiated and ultimately remade. Cultural meanings are fluid and ultimately created through doing, and through the aspirations and desires of the present, but are validated and legitimized through the creation and recreation of a sense of linkage to the past. Heritage provides a mentality and discourse in which these linkages are forged and recast. What makes certain activities 'heritage' are those activities that actively engage with thinking about and acting out not only 'where we have come from' in terms of the past, but also 'where we are going' in terms of the present and future. It is a social and cultural process that mediates a sense of cultural, social and political change.

Part II

AUTHORIZED HERITAGE

3

AUTHORIZING INSTITUTIONS
OF HERITAGE

Chapter 1 established the existence of the Authorized Heritage Discourse (AHD). It is the task of this chapter to examine how the AHD is institutionalized and embedded within some of the primary documents and processes of heritage, management and conservation. The conventions and charters enacted by UNESCO and ICOMOS may be understood as authorizing institutions of heritage, as they define what heritage is, how and why it is significant, and how it should be managed and used. This authority comes in part from the influence these organizations have within the policy process at both national and international levels. However, it also derives from the persuasive power of the AHD, which frames the charters and conventions that influence national and international heritage conservation and preservation policies and practices. In turn, the AHD, and the assumptions, values and ideologies embedded within this discourse, is itself reinforced and perpetuated through the policy and technical processes that are driven or underlined by the various charters and conventions.

The argument to be advanced in this chapter develops three interrelated central points. The first is that the AHD, in privileging the innate aesthetic and scientific value and physicality of heritage, masks the real cultural and political work that the heritage process does. Chapter 2 attempted to identify and define this 'work' by arguing that heritage is most usefully perceived as a cultural process about meaning making – it is a discourse that individuals, groups, communities, nations and a range of institutions use to create and define identity and social and cultural meaning in and about the present. The past, it was argued, is drawn on in this process to give explanatory weight to the experiences of the present, but heritage itself is the moment of experience, remembering and meaning making that may occur at physical places. The places of heritage may give added meaning and authority to the act of heritage – but the idea or substance of 'heritage' is not itself innately embedded in a physical relic or place. In sum, then, the cultural and political work or consequence of heritage is to negotiate and define cultural and social meaning in the present. However, the very masking of this process by the AHD has its own consequences. One of these relates to the second point developed in this chapter, which is to acknowledge that the technical process of management and conservation established and framed by the AHD is itself a cultural process that creates value and meaning. Heritage management, conservation, preservation and restoration are not just objective technical procedures, they are themselves part of the subjective heritage performance in which meaning is re/created and maintained. The meanings subsequently created speak to the cultural and social needs of the present, but these meanings will be linked to the past so that they in turn are given authority and validity. Some of the central values re/created and rehearsed in this process relate to narratives of nation, national identity and the social and historical identities of Western elites.

The third point to be developed is that the heritage management and conservation process is not only about the management of fabric. Rather, it engages in the regulation or 'management' of cultural and social value and meaning. Not only are certain values embedded in the AHD perpetuated, but dissonance is itself regulated and arbitrated by the values and ideologies embedded in the AHD. This is once again obscured by the AHD, which draws our attention continually to the tangible and material fabric of heritage places. These three points are developed in the context of exploring the way the AHD is promulgated within some of the key heritage conventions and charters, and the consequence this has for authorizing certain values and definitions of 'heritage'.

Venice Charter

The non-governmental organization ICOMOS, based in Paris, is an international network of heritage and conservation practitioners and specialists concerned with the protection and conservation of historically important sites and places. It is, at both national and international levels, a highly successful and powerful lobby group, which influences the development of management and conservation polices and legal frameworks in many countries. One of the primary avenues of this influence is through the adoption of national and international charters, which act to guide and inform the conduct of its members – many of whom are employed within a range of governmental and non-governmental heritage organizations, or who work as heritage consultants or academics. The charters themselves may be viewed partly as lobby documents, and are used by national and local governments to inform policy and practice. The lobbying power of ICOMOS in part lies in its international scope, while the international committee is also supported by national chapters across the world. Its members are drawn from a range of professions who deal with conservation, preservation and management issues, and as such the weight of expertise represented by ICOMOS carries considerable political legitimacy.

Prior to the inception of ICOMOS, the First International Congress of

Architects and Technicians of Historic Monuments, under the patronage of the League of Nations, adopted the Athens Charter in 1931. This charter established international awareness about conservation issues, laid down a guideline to frame conservation philosophy and practice, and helped to influence the development of Western national practices and legislation. The Athens Charter was reassessed at the Second International Congress of Architects and Technicians of Historic Monuments in 1964, which thereby produced the *International Charter for the Conservation and Restoration of Monuments and Sites*, otherwise knows as the Venice Charter. An international committee comprised largely of Europeans, but also of representatives from Mexico, Peru and Tunisia, drafted this charter, and ICOMOS was created shortly after in 1965 to support and propagate it (Grieve 2005). Subsequently, this charter has become one of the primary and foundational texts of conservation philosophy and practice (Starn 2002).

The charters and conventions that frame conservation and heritage management are a product of *modernity*, and the expertise that underlines and underwrites these chapters is highly significant in the authorization of these documents. The ability of intellectuals and professionals to make binding statements and pronouncements of authority is well documented in Western contexts (Bauman 1987). This authority, however, is both reproduced in, and is continually reproduced through, the enactment and use of the charters – so much so that the authority of expertise, and subsequently the principles they espouse, become so naturalized as to be understood as 'common sense' or 'good sense'. The Venice Charter establishes and defines the nature of historic monuments and provides guiding principles on how they should be cared for and managed. These principles are based on, as one commentator notes, 'enormous scholarly good sense' (Grieve 2005).

The narratives of *nationhood* interwoven in the AHD drive the very definition of 'heritage' offered by the Venice Charter. In defining the subject of conservation and management, the Charter states that:

> The concept of an historic monument embraces not only the single architectural work but also the urban or rural setting in which is found the evidence of a particular civilisation, a significant development or an historic event. This applies not only to great works of art but also to more modest works of the past which have acquired cultural significance with the passing of time.
>
> (Article 1)

The use of the term 'civilization' is interesting here. In post-Enlightenment Western Europe, the developing nations saw themselves as having reached a pinnacle of cultural evolutionary achievement – a perception that both underwrote the development of national sentiments and underpinned a range of colonial and imperial projects. As Waterton (2005a) argues, it was in this intellectual context that Ruskin's and Morris's philosophies on authenticity, aesthetics and the sense of inherent value of monuments and buildings arose. The 'conserve as found' ethos is embedded with the idea of immutable inherent value, while the sense of monumentality and aesthetics speaks to the achievements of the 'highly civilized nation' (Waterton 2005a: 313). In the structuring of this definition, the cultural value of great works of architecture and art are taken for granted. Their value is constructed here as part of what Fairclough identifies as the 'common ground' of shared or taken for granted meanings that underpin a sense of fellowship – in this case, a professional fellowship of concern over the preservation and conservation of the past (2003: 55). The first sentence of this definition both expresses the existential assumptions about the nature of 'heritage' and also shapes and defines the common ground of conservation philosophy by reproducing those assumptions as authoritative text. Existential assumptions – assumptions about what exist – are one of the discursive devices that both mark and shape 'common ground' principles and beliefs (Fairclough 2003: 56). In the first sentence of Article 1, items from a 'civilized' context are defined as inherently valuable – in as much by what is said as by what is not said. There is no attempt to explain and justify – monuments from grand backgrounds are valuable, full stop. This is visible in the semantic relations of the text, the 'not only' applied to 'great works of art' implies that we already know these things are valuable and important – an evaluation is here being put across as a statement of fact because they are assured values. However, a concession is made to 'more modest works' which may *acquire* significance, not through innate value necessarily, but once they become old enough. The value judgement of what constitutes 'modest' is not explained – it is known by the writers and readers of this document. Further, the value of 'modest works' is assumed to lie in their status as antiquarian curiosity rather than because they may represent an historical or significant event. Subsequently, those monuments or sites from grand Western contexts are perceived to be inherently valuable, while those things from more modest contexts, presumably non-Western cultural contexts or less grand Western social contexts can, in certain circumstances, acquire or be acknowledged as valuable. Here, the narrative of Western *nationalism* that underpins the AHD is given expression. Moreover, colonial and imperial perspectives are also given voice and credence in this document. As will be illustrated below, this legacy continues to have consequences for the enactment of, and practices guided by, the World Heritage Convention.

The idea of the inherent nature of the value and significance of a monument identified in Chapter 1 as a feature of the AHD is rehearsed throughout the Venice Charter. Not only are monuments 'imbued with a message from the past' (preamble), but a monument is also 'inseparable from the history to which it bears witness and from the setting in which it occurs' (Article 7). Monuments are thus also 'living witnesses of their age-old traditions' (preamble). The idea here that a monument is a 'witness' to history and tradition anthropomorphizes material culture and creates a sense that memory is somehow locked within or embedded in the fabric of the monument or site. The anthropomorphizing of monuments and buildings is a common form of legitimization in the conservation movement, and is a discursive device that helps naturalize the authority of the values and meanings a place may represent by helping to cement them as inherent (one of the consequences of this will be discussed in Chapter 4). A sense of place is also inherently fixed within the fabric; for instance, in Article 7 a 'sense of place' is made inherent within the fabric of the monument when it becomes 'inseparable' from its setting. The idea of the inherent value of the fabric of a monument is embedded in the guidance the Charter gives to conservation and restoration processes. Article 5 notes that monuments should be used for 'socially useful' purposes, but that any use 'must not change the lay-out or decoration of the building'. This is not because 'unity of style' is to be preserved (Article 11), but because the 'intention of conserving and restoring monuments is to safeguard them no less as works of art than as historical evidence' (Article 3). These statements reveal the existential assumption about the inherent value of a monument that underlies the heritage management process. The idea of 'safeguarding' and the phrase 'no less' trigger the assumptions that 'works of art' and 'historical evidence' are the values most desired about monuments, and that it is their aesthetic and historic qualities that are fundamentally important. The Charter makes these value assumptions appear as unquestioned 'common sense' and as such, the Charter is doing important ideological work in legitimizing and universalizing these values.

The authority and 'common sense' of these values, and their inherent immutable nature, is continually legitimized throughout the Charter by appeals to morality. In Critical Discourse Analysis, a number of strategies have been identified that are used to legitimize the ideology underlying the discourse (van Leeuwen 1999; Fairclough 2003). One of these strategies is to make a moral appeal about what 'must' be done; however, this may also take the form of a narrative cautionary or morality tale (Fairclough 2003: 99). Both of these devices are used in this charter. While the Charter does not construct a clear morality tale in a traditional sense, it makes allusions to and special moral pleas to a sense of duty and morality. Article 15 notes that care must 'be taken to facilitate the understanding of the monument and to *reveal it without ever distorting its meaning*' (my emphasis). The wording of this statement is very strong, demanding total commitment to the values underlying it. It is the work of experts, and the Charter is very stern in its assertion that professional experts are those best suited to care for and protect monuments and sites, that must reveal and expose the meaning of the monument in an objective manner so that its meaning is not distorted. This 'exposure' must be done carefully, not only to avoid 'distortion', but also because 'monuments must be the object of special care in order to safeguard their integrity and ensure that they are cleared and presented in a seemly manner' (Article 14). 'Must' linked to the idea of 'special care' (experts) is not only illustrative of a strong or total commitment to the idea of experts, but more importantly this is played out along side it in order to safeguard 'integrity' (value assumptions) – as to not employ the special care of experts is to compromise the integrity of monuments. Like a Victorian middle class woman, their virtue must be the subject of special treatment and care, so that the artistic or historic evidence is not falsified and their cultural 'virtue' not challenged or altered. The aim is to 'preserve' the aesthetic and historic value (Article 9), but this preservation is 'based on respect for original material and authentic documents'. Here again, value is assumed as being innate to the fabric of the monument, but the use of the word 'respect' is important. A moral appeal is made with this term and it is suggested that only those with such a 'respect' have the ability to care for monuments and their values in a 'seemly' way. It is also a call for respect for the aesthetic and historic values inherent in fabric that experts also have a duty of care to 'safeguard' (Article 3). Throughout the Charter there is an appeal to a sense of fellowship based on an appeal to respect the legitimacy of certain values and meanings and to make these values and meanings universal. The preamble notes that, 'people are becoming more and more conscious of the unity of human values and regard ancient monuments as a common heritage'. Thus, it becomes the duty of those upholding the Charter to ensure these universal values are revealed, understood and propagated as consensual history and heritage: 'It is our duty,' the preamble continues, 'to hand them on [to future generations] in the full richness of their authenticity'.

This charter establishes and reinforces a sense of the innate aesthetic and historic values of the grand and 'good'. It further maintains that experts must ensure that these values are not altered and distorted, but rather are safeguarded in the way that monuments are protected and maintained. What emerges here is one of the key underlying principles of heritage management and conservation, which is that the value or significance of a site or place should determine how that site or place is conserved and managed (Kerr 1990; Pearson and Sullivan 1995; King 2000; Mathers et al. 2005).

The Venice Charter is, as noted above, one of the foundational texts for the conservation and preservation movements that developed in the 1960s. It also underlines and gives a philosophical basis for the technical processes of heritage management that began to emerge in many Western countries as a formal legal and policy process during the 1960s and 1970s. The Charter, and the processes of conservation, restoration and management that it underpins, is a document that is shaped by the AHD and continually reinforces and authorizes that discourse, by its very nature as a canonical text actively supported and propagated by ICOMOS. One of the more subtle ways that it continually reauthorizes itself is the way it positions readers of the Charter as adherents to the particular set of commonsense assumptions, values and meanings it shapes and communicates. Readers are addressed or 'hailed as particular kinds of individuals or subjects' and are subsequently drawn into the philosophical or ideological position of the discourse (Edley 2001: 210). This is done through appeals to our 'duty' to, and 'respect' for, monuments and appeals to the safeguarding of monuments for 'future generations' (preamble). The legitimization of the Charter's principles is achieved through these appeals, but readers of the document are also invited to become members of the fellowship of 'good' practitioners as well. Consequently, one of the things the Charter also establishes is a sense of professional and community identity for heritage practitioners and conservationists. This process of identity construction is as powerful as the construction of national or sub-national community identities through the cultural processes played out at, or in association with, monuments and other places of 'heritage'. Subsequently this and other charters and conventions are also a monument of heritage in so far as they represent a discourse, laden with cultural and social meaning, that is continually reproduced and performed through a range of practices, and which also constructs and reinforces collective identity, cultural meaning and memory – in this case, the collective is heritage practitioners/experts. This process is masked or obscured, however, because of the extent to which the discourse is naturalized internationally by its users and understood to simply represent 'good sense'.

This process is of course a reinforcing circle. The AHD constructs and frames a charter or convention of influence and authority – in part because of the authority of the discourse of expertise used. However, the sense of the authority of both discourse and its users is continually reinforced and remade through not only the authority and status of the document in guiding policy and practice, but also in the way it establishes and maintains a community of expertise through a sense of fellowship and commitment to a set of principles. This, of course, in turn reinforces the AHD and its explanatory power as good sense. However, in this way the embedded Western narratives of national and elite historical and cultural experiences and values are propagated as authorized heritage. The practices of heritage management and conservation, which the AHD informs and frames, continually rehearse and disseminate the social and cultural values that are assumed inherent and embedded in the fabric of monuments and sites. By managing and conserving places to maintain the cultural significance and historical character, certain assumed values and historical meanings are maintained and preserved. As will be illustrated throughout the rest of this book, the way sites, monuments, landscapes and other places identified as 'heritage' are used influences the types of social or cultural meanings and experiences that are constructed, legitimized and circulated. The processes of 'management', 'conservation', 'restoration' and/or 'preservation' are particular uses of heritage places that create, legitimize and disseminate their own particular cultural and social meanings, and are thus themselves part of, and not separate from, the 'heritage process' of meaning making. As heritage sites are managed, the performance of what is chosen to be remembered and forgotten about the past is enacted, and its conservation and presentation to the public will affect 'sense of place' and other experiences. However, this process is obscured and redefined as external to the process of heritage because of the way value is assumed as immutable and innate – management and conservation become things that are *done to* sites and places, but are not seen as organically part of the meaning-making process of heritage itself.

The above arguments may appear to rest somewhat shakily on a single, albeit canonical, text. However, the Venice Charter itself is in dialogue with other authorized and authorizing texts. Following the Venice Charter, both ICOMOS and the inter-governmental agency UNESCO have produced a plethora of charters, recommendations, guidelines and conventions, which aim to safeguard, protect, conserve or manage various aspects of the world's heritage. These texts may seek to make specific recommendations about the management of archaeological sites (ICOMOS 1990), underwater heritage (ICOMOS 1996; UNESCO 2001a), buildings, urban areas and landscapes (ICOMOS 1982, 1987, 1999a) and portable material culture (UNESCO 1970). Or they may seek to redefine or propagate specific principles, such as that of authenticity (UNESCO 1954; ICOMOS 1994) or appropriate conduct in certain circumstances (ICOMOS 1999b). The intertextuality of these texts is itself important. As Fairclough (2001: 233) note, 'any text is a link in a chain of texts, reacting to, drawing in, and transforming other texts'. The charters, conventions and similar texts from part of a genre chain, or chain of texts, that collectively reinforce and bind the authority of the AHD. Individually and collectively, they create a text of consensus – the very structure of each individual text, as with the Venice Charter, is styled around simple straightforward statements in which a number of assumptions about the nature and value of heritage are made. The content of these assumptions is transformed across the chain of texts even though each charter or convention may move between different networks of social practices. As the chain of texts interlink and propagate, their assumptions and values are given an international 'presence' and the sense of self-referential authority of conservation and management philosophy and practice is achieved. While there is insufficient space here to examine all the individual texts to illustrate the ways in which they are shaped by and reshape various aspects of the AHD as defined in Chapter 1 – the point here is that their intertextuality *is* the AHD. Individually and collectively, they represent the authorizing texts of heritage discourses. To get a deeper sense of what they do and the AHD that they espouse, I wish to turn to an examination of the practices associated with UNESCO's World Heritage Convention. This convention is a leading text in terms of influencing management practices and perceptions of heritage across the globe. It is defined as UNESCO's most successful Convention in the cultural heritage field (Blake 2001: 72). However, it is also in the practices and strategies it establishes, in association with the development and maintenance of the World Heritage List, that we can see how the Western AHD as defined in Chapter 1 and illustrated by the Venice Charter, is played out, and the consequences it has for shaping and defining authorized 'heritage'. It is also useful to examine the World Heritage Convention because it has become a target of non-Western critiques about the nature of heritage. This critique has highlighted both the Convention's ethnocentrism and its tendency to favour elite notions of heritage values. In response, the *Convention for the Safeguarding of the Intangible Cultural Heritage* was ratified in 2003, and the dialogue between these texts will also be examined later in the chapter to analyse the extent to which the Western narratives identified in Chapter 1 as underlying the AHD have – or have not – shifted or changed.

World Heritage Convention

The UNESCO General Conference in Paris, 1972, adopted the *Convention Concerning the Protection of the World Cultural and Natural Heritage*, or, as it is otherwise known, the World Heritage Convention. As UNESCO's website records, this convention, drafted with advice from ICOMOS, was influenced by the American practices of jointly managing and conserving natural and cultural sites. The construction of the Aswan High Dam in Egypt, and the subsequent international campaign to salvage and save a range of cultural material from inundation and destruction, demonstrated 'the importance of solidarity and nations' shared responsibility in conserving outstanding cultural sites' and thus the potential for such a convention (UNESCO 2005).

However, the preamble also suggests that the Convention's inception originates in concerns caused by 'changing social and economic conditions' that threatened the destruction of cultural sites and that the deterioration or loss of items of 'cultural or natural heritage constitutes a harmful impoverishment of the heritage of all the nations of the world'. As Henry Cleere, formally ICOMOS World Heritage Coordinator, observes, the document is characteristic of the spirit that reigned in the 1960s (2001: 22). Certainly, a growing concern about the perceived rapid cultural and social changes represented by European post-war reconstruction, and post-war economic developments in the Western world generally, were of growing public concern during this time. That the Convention was responding in part to perceived rapidly changing social conditions, which were seen to 'aggravate the situation' of threat to cultural sites, is an important one, and will be returned to below. The World Heritage Convention, however, establishes the World Heritage List on which cultural and natural sites of 'universal' importance are listed, the first inscriptions onto the list occurring in 1978. As part of the listing process, management plans for the listed properties must be developed. Sites for listing may be nominated by State Parties to the

Convention and the World Heritage Committee assesses and determines their suitability for listing. The Committee is elected from the State Parties to the Convention, and representatives from organizations such as ICOMOS, and the International Centre for the Study of the Preservation and Restoration of Cultural Property (ICCROM) offer advice to the Committee.

Like the Venice Charter before it, the World Heritage Convention makes a range of existential assumptions about the nature of heritage, and again like the Venice Charter, the Convention unintentionally identifies a hierarchy of monuments. Although it defines three types of 'cultural heritage', they are ranked in two groups or tiers. The first tier is represented by the first two types, 'monuments' and 'groups of buildings', the second by 'sites':

> monuments: architectural works, works of monumental sculpture and painting, elements or structures of an archaeological nature, inscriptions, cave dwellings and combinations of features, which are of outstanding universal value from the point of view of history, art or science;

> groups of buildings: groups of separate or connected buildings which, because of their architecture, their homogeneity or their place in the landscape, are of outstanding universal value from the point of view of history, art or science;

> sites: works of man or the combined works of nature and man, and areas including archaeological sites which are of outstanding universal value from the historical, aesthetic, ethnological or anthropological point of view.

> (Article 1)

The first two definitions represent the 'grand' and unproblematic aspects of authorized cultural heritage. Once again, these things are perceived to have universal values and these values are assumed to lie in 'history, art or science'. Sites, on the other hand, are defined as the 'works of man [sic] or the combined works of nature and man [sic]' that may also have ethnological or anthropological value. The phrase 'works of man' is somewhat odd, as presumably monuments, buildings and so forth are all works of human beings. Why this phrase is used is revealing about the relative value placed on 'sites' as opposed to 'monuments' and 'buildings' – as sites here have to be identified as cultural through their creation by 'men'. Monuments and buildings need no explanation, they are obviously universally important and quintessentially 'cultural'. In the practice of World Heritage Listing, 'sites' tend to be those places that do not fit into the grand narratives of Western nationalism. They tend to be places of importance to communities such as Indigenous populations in post-colonial contexts where the division between 'nature and culture' is, from the point of view of post-Enlightenment Europe, less pronounced. Or they come from the European 'deep past', prior to the development of the cultural diversity that is popularly perceived to mark the culture histories that led to the formation of nation states (see Cleere 1996). Here we see a slight shift in the discourse from the Venice Charter with the inclusion of material not naturalized by the European AHD, and this inclusion needs to be explained by their explicit identification as 'man made'.

What Cleere (2001: 23) defines as the 'fundamental touchstone' of outstanding universal value is not defined in the Convention, as it is the World Heritage Committee's task to define criteria. The current criteria are:

i. represent a masterpiece of human creative genius; or
ii. exhibit an important interchange of human values, over a span of time or within a cultural area of the world, on developments in architecture or technology, monumental arts, town-planning or landscape design; or
iii. bear a unique or at least exceptional testimony to a cultural tradition or to a civilization which is living or which has disappeared; or
iv. be an outstanding example of a type of building or architectural or technological ensemble or landscape which illustrates (a) significant stage(s) in human history; or
v. be an outstanding example of a traditional human settlement or land-use which is representative of a culture (or cultures), especially when it has become vulnerable under the impact of irreversible change; or
vi. be directly or tangibly associated with events or living traditions, with ideas, or with beliefs, with artistic and literary works of outstanding universal significance (the Committee considers that this criterion should justify inclusion in the List only in exceptional circumstances and in conjunction with other criteria cultural or natural);

(UNESCO 1997)

However, like the Convention itself, these criteria make a number of existential assumptions about, for instance, what constitutes a 'masterpiece', a 'human value' or a significant development in human history. They are necessarily vague so as to be flexible and inclusive. However, the vagueness of both these criteria and the general vagueness of the Convention, especially with regard to defining 'universal value' and 'heritage', work to create a sense that the reader assumes that they know what is meant. This both invites the reader into fellowship with the document, while the simple statements of what is of value and principle creates once again a text of consensus and authority (Fairclough 2003). The vagueness, as Cleere (2001) reminds us, is an attempt at inclusiveness; however, the AHD and the assumptions it frames nonetheless will fill in the gaps left by any ambiguity or lack of specificity. Most of the Convention is given over to procedural matters such as the formations of committees, their powers and roles and so forth. However, what is most revealing about the AHD, and the way it functions with respect to this document, is the way the value assumptions of the AHD are applied through the listing process, as what is listed is revealing of the influence of the AHD.

In 2000, Cleere (2001: 25) analysed the distribution of the 630 sites then listed on the World Heritage List and revealed that 55 per cent of those listed were located in European countries. Asia represented 14 per cent of the listing, with most of the listed sites occurring in China and India. The Latin America/Caribbean region represented 12 per cent of the list, with Arab states representing 11 per cent, North America 5 per cent, Africa 4 per cent and Australia and Oceania 1 per cent. Five years later, this statistic has altered slightly, with European properties now representing 49 per cent of the 812 currently listed, although properties in Western countries in total represent 56 per cent of the list. Cleere (2001: 25) notes that the European imbalance is maintained by the frequency with which European countries put their heritage places forward. While Lowenthal (1998: 239) observes that Europeans 'rate their own national heritage as so superior it *ought* to be global'. However, the eurocentrisim of the listing reflects the dominance of the AHD, which frame and underpin the listing criteria. This affects the ability of certain cultures to have their sites perceived as heritage. For instance, the listing of some culturally important areas in Australia to Indigenous communities has only been able to occur due to their joint listing as natural properties. Several of the sites listed in Africa, for instance, belong to the European colonial period and are themselves colonial creations (Cleere 2001: 26). Further, the sites listed themselves tend to speak to grand narratives and European notions of aesthetic and national identity, with elitist architecture, including cathedrals, castles and palaces, being over-represented on the List (Munjeri 2004: 16). As Cleere (2001: 26) himself observes, the definition of cultural heritage employed in the World Heritage Convention was meant to be all-embracing, however:

> The process of compiling the World Heritage List has proceeded within a more restricted perception, deriving from largely European aesthetic notions relating to monumental cultures. Although most of the world's landscapes are to a considerable extent human artefacts, representing countless generations of human activity and creativity, these have for the most part been ignored, since they lack the monumental elements inseparable in the European mind from the traditional 'cultural heritage'.

This imbalance is not simply caused by disproportionate nominations by European countries, but by the AHD that frames and legitimizes the assumptions made in the listing criteria. The World Heritage List itself is a process of meaning making – it is a list that not only identifies, but also *defines*, which heritage places are globally important. The listing process creates or recreates sites as universally important and meaningful. Once again, the process of listing is an act of heritage management that is itself an act of heritage in which, on this occasion, a sense of universal 'human identity' is created. That the human identity that is performed through the List tends to be European is expressive of the degree to which the listing process is informed by, and reinforces, the European AHD.

Cleere (2001: 24) also draws our attention to criticisms levelled at the idea of 'universality', and argues that such ideas can only really be applied to the very earliest phases of human cultural development, or to the global culture of the late twentieth century. The cultural diversity of human experience, he goes on to observe, means that not only different histories will perceive different things as significant, but that cultural differences mean that not all cultures will share the same concepts of what constitutes heritage and heritage values, and that on occasion these cultural differences may be insurmountable. This concept of universality is, as Cleere (2001: 24) observes, 'deeply rooted in the European cultural tradition, combining historical and aesthetic parameters that derive from classical philosophy'. It is also deeply rooted in the processes of colonization and imperial expansion and assumptions about the cultural and technological evolutionary achievements of the West. Part of the authority of the European AHD, subsequently, lies in its own legitimizing assumptions that it *is* universally applicable and that there is, or must be, universal cultural values and expressions. The whole discourse of universality is itself a legitimizing strategy for the values and nature of heritage that underline the AHD. The discourse of universality makes a moral plea to a sense of 'brotherhood' of 'mankind' (and in this discourse the masculinity of identity is inevitably reproduced). This sort of appeal is one of the less obvious strategies of legitimization identified within Critical Discourse Analysis, but its subtlety can add to its persuasive power (van Leeuwen and Wodak 1999: 108). Although the claims to universality within the text of the World Heritage Convention and associated guidelines, practices and debates appear to offer a straightforward description of a value that simply *is*, it is nevertheless an explicit argument about the legitimacy of European cultural narratives and values. It also becomes only natural and legitimate that both this convention and other international heritage documents 'demonstrate the importance, for all the peoples of the world' (preamble) of these cultural narratives and values.

The work the World Heritage Convention effectively (but unintentionally) does is to not only recreate heritage as universally significant, and in doing so authorize and legitimize the Western AHD within an international context, but also create a cultural and discursive climate in which certain values and ideologies become dominant in defining cultural development and change. The opening paragraph of the preamble to the Convention states:

> *Noting* that the cultural heritage and the natural heritage are increasingly threatened with destruction not only by the traditional causes of decay, but also by changing social and economic conditions which aggravate the situation with even more formidable phenomena of damage or destruction

This may read as a straightforward concern about how social and economic changes experienced in the post-war period were accelerating the physical destruction of the historic environment. However, as 'heritage', the physical manifestations of the past are valued in the Convention, and by the AHD generally, because of the values they are regarded as possessing. Here is a concern to not only save a sense of aesthetic, but implicitly also save the social and cultural values this represents. It is, as noted above, no accident that the very discourses of 'heritage' and concerns about its loss arose in a period perceived to mark major social and cultural changes, and as public debate, facilitated by increasing public access to a range of media resources, increased about environmental, political and social issues. These debates and perceived changes needed to be made sense of, understood and negotiated. Heritage as a 'mentality' (see Chapter 2) provides a point of focus through which the present and its relationship to the past can be mediated. It is a way of thinking about, acting and managing this relationship and the cultural values and meanings that flow from it. In short, heritage is an attempt to deal with, negotiate and regulate change. It is thus no accident that the World Heritage List is heavily represented by European 'universally significant places', as Europeans attempt to come to terms with the changing place of their nations in a world where the European colonial and imperial pasts (and present) are increasingly being reconsidered, and as European states redefine themselves as part of a unified Europe. The perception of a European cultural legacy to 'world civilization' is asserted and recreated through the World Heritage List as part of the renegotiation of both individual and collective European identities. Countries like Italy, Spain, Germany and France (each with 40, 38, 31 and 30 listings, respectively, as of late 2005) vie with each other to top the list of countries with most listed sites, because listing is a process in which certain national narratives and values become authorized. The competition to get places of heritage listed is part of cultural negotiations and assertions of the cultural and historical authority and legacy of these countries in a reformulated and unified Europe.

All of the above are also dissonant practices, as these negotiations both react against and respond to competing discourses, but also because it is a process in which competing discourses become themselves regulated, if not marginalized. The discourses and narratives that may compete with each other may do so at many levels; for instance, inter-regionally between Western and Eastern discourses about the very nature of heritage and human identity, or between and within European and other Western states about the legitimacy of their historical legacy to Western or European 'civilization' and so forth. The regulation of dissonance is achieved through the listing process as nominations for inclusion on the list are moulded and framed in terms that will attempt to ensure that the places being nominated are indeed listed. That means that heritage places may be defined or redefined, and at some level recreated, in ways that will find synergy with, and meet the expectations and assumptions of, the Committee's perceptions of 'universal significance'. Subsequently in this process cultural value, memory and meaning become themselves managed, and the speed and direction of social and cultural change and dissonance become subject to management.

The sense that places of heritage are recreated through the listing process and given new and universal layers of meaning is also revealed in the use of the term 'property'. The idea of heritage 'property' is a term particularly associated with the World Heritage Convention, which uses it to define cultural heritage that has met the criteria of Article 1 (reproduced above). As heritage places move through the listing process they become World Heritage 'properties' and, as Carman (2005) argues, the idea of property assumes a right of possession – in this case it becomes possessed by the 'World'. The values become 'owned' by the world community and are subsequently further legitimized with this discourse. The term 'property' also reinforces the sense in which the cultural values associated with a place or object can be captured and frozen (Handler 2003: 363).

The above discussion has identified a range of strategies of legitimization and processes where by cultural values and narratives become the subject of management and regulation. These are established by the Convention and played out in the listing and management process; however, it is important to note that these strategies are not always successful. Certainly, UNESCO and the World Heritage Convention have been criticized for their Eurocentrism, and the emphasis that is placed on the tangibility of heritage, but the fact of this criticism means the processes identified above are resisted and contested. Importantly, UNESCO has also responded to these concerns with a range of programmes and strategies to acknowledge and deal with the concept of intangible heritage. Koïchiro Matsuura, Director General of UNESCO, states:

> While UNESCO, in accordance with its mission concerning culture and the preservation of cultural diversity, has effectively developed a powerful instrument, the 1972 World Heritage Convention, the World Heritage List nevertheless reveals a growing imbalance. The

Tangible and monumental heritage of countries of the 'North' is more widely represented. This situation reflects a weakness in the organization's historic focus on the protection of tangible heritage, rather than intangible heritage, thereby marginalizing a vast range of cultural expressions which often belong to the countries of the 'South' and which are crucial for the map of cultural diversity. In order to truly fulfil its mission to foster cultural diversity, UNESCO is determined to safeguard both tangible and intangible heritage.

(Preface to UNESCO 2001b: 2)

These UNESCO initiatives, developed to be more inclusive in the way it deals with heritage, are important for mapping the changes to the AHD identified in Chapter 1. However, before examining the UNESCO strategies to safeguard intangible heritage, I want to turn to another document that has been explicitly modified and rewritten to become more inclusive of dissonant interests. Australia ICOMOS originally wrote the *Charter for the Conservation of Places of Cultural Significance* (Burra Charter) in 1979, basing it firmly on the Venice Charter, and it aimed to make its principles relevant to the Australian context. As I have suggested elsewhere (Smith 1996), this document incorporates many of the Western assumptions about the inherent value and meaning of the material or 'fabric' of heritage. However, this charter was extensively rewritten in 1999, in response to increasing pressures from Indigenous and non-Indigenous Australian communities for more active participation and consultation in the heritage management and conservation process. A detailed discourse analysis has been undertaken of this document by Waterton, myself and Campbell (2006), which I will not rehearse here. However, it is useful to summarize our arguments in the context of the current discussion as the Burra Charter, although a national document, has been both widely adopted for use in a range of European countries, but is also internationally hailed as a progressive and useful attempt at integrating community concerns and values into the management and conservation processes. While the Burra Charter is not a response to the critiques levelled at the World Heritage process, it is nonetheless a response to very similar critiques about cultural and social inclusiveness and representation. The point of reviewing the reworked Burra Charter here is to not only examine the ways in which the Western AHD has shifted, but to reveal also the problematics of that shift. The analysis will then return to the international programmes dealing with intangible heritage, and identify the light that they shed on the nature and consequences of the AHD.

Burra Charter

Like the Venice Charter, the Burra Charter has also been identified as based on 'good sense' (Domicelj 1992: 5) and is a text of consensus whereby readers are invited or hailed as members of a community whose sense of cohesion focuses on shared principles and philosophies. As Waterton et al. (2006) argue, this text, like many other charters, once again employs a straight-forward form of address around a sequence of simple authoritative state-ments, against which readers form a sense of fellowship or ownership with the documents underlying assumptions, principles and philosophy. The 1999 Burra Charter explicitly attempts to deal with plurality and multi-vocality. Australia ICOMOS, in commenting on the new charter, note on their website that it 'recognises the need to involve people in the decision-making process, particularly those that have strong associations with a place' (2005). However, the text is dialogically closed, thus reducing the ability of community perceptions of heritage and its conservation to fully engage in dialogue with the underlying philosophy of the Charter. Utilizing language which does not invite dialogue, the text becomes authoritative and reduces difference, or dialogue, between 'author' of the text and other voices com-pletely. This is at odds with the desire of the 1999 version of the Charter to involve a range of stakeholders in the management and conservation process. The authority and philosophy of the AHD, and subsequently the practices it informs, are never really challenged by the new version of the Charter. The discourse of the new Charter does not abandon its authority, while implicitly reducing the authority of non-experts, and thus rendering values external to the AHD marginal to or reliant on expert arbitration and regulation.

Once again, this charter constructs a sense that the value and meaning of heritage is inherently physically manifested by a heritage place. A key aspect of the Charter is the concept of 'cultural significance', which is inclusively defined as 'aesthetic, historic, scientific, social or spiritual value for past, present or future generations' (Article 1.2). The idea that the cultural signifi-cance of a place must determine how the place is used or managed is a defining theme of the Burra Charter. The term 'place' is one specifically adopted by the Burra Charter (both in 1999 and earlier versions) as a more inclusive term rather than 'monument', 'site' and so forth, as it implicitly recognizes the social value that heritage 'places' may have. However, the fabric defined as 'all the physical material of the place' (Article 1.3) is also all important in the Charter. How the fabric of a place is used, restored, man-aged and conserved is the primary focus of the document – as is indeed reasonable in a document that attempts to define 'good' management and conservation practices for tangible heritage places. However, this becomes problematic for the inclusiveness of the document as the idea of fabric assumes that cultural significance is inherently fixed within it. As Article 1.2 asserts, cultural significance is 'embodied in the place itself, its fabric, setting . . .'. As Waterton et al. (2006) argue, this works to naturalize cultural significance as a material concern, and something that becomes unproblem-atically the appropriate, if not sole, concern of experts in the material sciences. In addition, the Burra Charter rehearses the same legitimizing techniques identified above in the Venice Charter. It again appeals to the moral authority of expertise through a continual appeal to not only 'respect' fabric, and the cultural significance embedded within it, but to also apply 'caution', and to 'safeguard' and 'protect' while eschewing 'distortion' and 'conjecture' in favour of objective 'evidence'. For instance:

> *Conservation* is based on a respect for the existing *fabric, use, associations* and *meanings*. It requires a cautious approach of changing as much as necessary but as little as possible.
>
> (Article 3.1, original emphasis)

> Changes to a *place* should not distort the physical or other evidence it provides, nor be based on conjecture.
>
> (Article 3.2, original emphasis)

While Article 3.1 makes explicit reference to associated meanings and respect for the current use of a place, the apparent inclusiveness of this is overshadowed by the appeals to authority and validity of professionals to prevent 'distortion' or to allow 'conjecture'. Who determines what is or is not of cultural significance, or is or is not 'conjecture', and what is or is not 'evidence' is never addressed in the Charter and is left to the judgement of the 'good sense' on which the Charter is based. This is difficult in cross-cultural situations, particularly in dealing with Indigenous Australians, where a sense of 'evidence', and indeed 'cultural significance', is entirely different and non-complementary.

Although the Charter asserts the need for community participation in conservation, interpretation and management (Article 5.1), and that 'Co-existence of cultural values should be recognised, respected and encouraged' (Article 13), this inclusiveness is problematic. As Waterton et al. (2006) point out, as there is no active sense of what community participation actually means, the Charter does not explain to what extent, or how, expertise should give ground or engage with non-expert participation. However, the relative 'place' of non-expert interests is clearly defined in the following:

> Groups and individuals with *associations* with a place as well as those involved in its management should be provided with opportunities to contribute to and participate in understanding the *cultural significance* of the place. Where appropriate they should also have opportunities to participate in its *conservation* and management.
>
> (Article 26.3, original emphasis)

Groups and individuals here are relegated to the position of passive audience. They must be given opportunities to 'understand' the cultural significance of a place, that is, they are being required to assimilate expert values. There is simply no sense that such communication may be two-way or that the authority of expertise to make binding judgements about cultural significance is challenged. Inclusion is also to occur 'where appropriate' and, as Article 30 states, all work done at places must be undertaken under:

> Competent direction and supervision should be maintained at all stages, and any changes should be implemented by people with appropriate knowledge and skills.

The status of expertise and the consensual values established by the AHD are maintained as external to the whole heritage process of meaning making. Waterton et al. (2006) draw our attention to the observation that conservation values and responsibilities are of course another set of 'cultural values' as much as community values are. However, this point is entirely missed, not only in the Burra Charter, but in all documents of this sort. Subsequently, expertise is recreated as a technical process that does things to heritage (for its own good), and that community groups and individuals become part of the elements to be managed and dealt with in the processes of management and conservation. There is no inclusive 'partnership', but rather another set of issues, alongside issues of physical threats and economic opportunities, which must also be managed so that fabric and cultural significance is maintained. This relegation of non-expert or community values is also established by the continuous discursive use of the phrase 'the cultural significance', which reduces the plurality of cultural values and meanings to the singular and thus leaves little conceptual room for challenging the nature of significance (Waterton et al. 2006). Although the existence of community values and meaning are acknowledged throughout the Charter, they are never actually linked or associated with the all-important term 'cultural significance' – the assessment of which drives the whole management and conservation process. In addition, throughout the document central terms like cultural significance, fabric, expert practices and so forth are defined, as Waterton et al. (2006) note, unambiguously, for instance, 'cultural significance *is* . . .' while non-expert issues are described far more passively with terms such as 'may' or 'might'. The authors of the Charter are totally committed to cultural significance, but express doubt about non-expert issues. Their commitment is revealed by the modal verb 'is' – the assertion of a knowledge claim – while their doubt is revealed by 'may' and 'might', which mark a modalized statement of truth. The level of commitment expressed by both translates as a difference between 'certainty' and 'possibility'.

The authority of expertise never comes close to being challenged in the new Burra Charter. However, the philosophies and assumptions underpinning the AHD are not only uncontested and unchanged, they are actively remade and reauthorized against the concerns of community inclusion. Although it is not intended by the authors of the Charter to downplay community participation and values, the Charter nonetheless does this simply because the AHD in which it is framed was never really identified, examined or challenged in the 1999 rewriting. Subsequently, the appeals to authority made within the AHD inevitably mean that those values and meanings that are situated outside the dominant discourse are sidelined. The discourse itself compromises inclusion, as it continually recreates and validates the dominant philosophies and assumptions. This does not mean to say that individual practitioners cannot, through their own practices, participate in equitable dialogue with community groups – but it does mean that to do so requires an *active* decision to work outside of the AHD as defined in the Charter. The very authority of the Charter as a policy and professional document makes this difficult, when the weight of professional opinion and legal practice sees this, and other similar documents, as having binding professional authority.

Effectively, what the Burra Charter does is re-establish the authority both of expertise and of the AHD itself, while defining non-expertise as an object of the technical process of management and conservation. Although attempting to deal with community issues, the document explicitly ignores the dissonant nature of heritage (Waterton et al. 2006). This is telling, as it is dissonance that is nonetheless an implicit focus of the document. Non-experts are invited to assimilate expert values on cultural significance, and thus reach accord with conservation philosophy. The regulation of non-expert value effectively becomes part of the heritage management process. Community groups and their values are 'managed' in such a way so that the social values and historical narratives – the cultural significance – attributed to heritage by the AHD is preserved and disseminated. The maintenance of these values is assured due to the prominence given in the document to fabric, and the need to 'respect' it, combined with the underlying assumption that cultural significance is innate and embodied in the fabric itself, and thus immutable.

Intangible heritage

UNESCO, despite its historical emphasis on tangible heritage, has had a long-term concern for intangible heritage. Concerns for 'folklore' have been expressed in terms of copyright concerns since the 1950s (Blake 2001: 32; Aikawa 2004). Following issues raised by a range of non-Western delegates at UNESCO sponsored meetings, and a questionnaire sent out to Member States in 1979, UNESCO initiated a sequence of measures to address the safeguarding of intangible heritage (see, for instance, Moyo and Sumaili 1985; Blake 2001: 32). However, as Aikawa (2004: 138) reports, this was often not an easy process, with various initiatives during the 1980s identified as 'premature'. In 1989, however, a General Conference adopted the Recommendation on the Safeguarding of Traditional Culture and

Folklore unanimously. Janet Blake (2001: 33), in her report to UNESCO, which evaluated its provisions on intangible heritage, observes that this Recommendation offers a very narrow definition of folklore, while van Zanten (2004: 36) observes that it is a term that carries considerable colonial baggage. Blake notes that the Recommendation has been criticized because the view of 'safeguarding' developed in the Recommendation had been 'designed with the needs of scientific research and government officials in mind', while expertise had been privileged in the identification, dissemination and conservation process. She warns that this does not meet the aspirations of Indigenous peoples, and other producers of intangible heritage, to control their heritage, nor does it offer a process for informed consent and consultation with individuals and groups whose heritage was to be 'safeguarded' and 'revitalized' (see also van Zanten 2004).

In 1993 and 1998, respectively, UNESCO developed the Living Human Treasures Programme and the Proclamation of Masterpieces of the Oral and Intangible Heritage of Humanity. The former was proposed by the Republic of Korea and is a programme to identify, and to keep a list of, those bearers of intangible cultural skills, techniques and knowledge, and to provide opportunities for those bearers to practise their skills and knowledge and to transmit it to younger generations (UNESCO n.d.). This was the first time that skills and knowledge were placed as a focus point of preservation (Blake 2001: 45). In recognition that the World Heritage Convention was not applicable to intangible heritage, the programme of Proclaiming Masterpieces of Oral and Intangible Heritage was put in place. Since its inception, there have been three Proclamations – the first in 2001, followed by Proclamations in 2003 and 2005 – resulting in the listing of 90 Masterpieces. This programme, as Blake reports, has been criticized for the use of the term 'masterpiece', which it is argued tends to create a hierarchy of cultures (2001: 46). The Convention for the Safeguarding of the Intangible Cultural Heritage was adopted after the 'international community decided to shift to a high gear by moving from a non-binding 'soft-law' Recommendation to a 'hard law' Convention (adopted 2003), which is binding on those States which decide to become Parties to it' (UNESCO 2003a: 3). Guidelines for the implementation of this Convention were still being developed at the time of writing of this book. However, the definition of intangible heritage offered by the new Convention (UNESCO 2003b) is:

> The practices, representations, expressions, knowledge, skills – as well as the instruments, objects, artefacts and cultural spaces associated therewith – that communities, groups and, in some cases, individuals recognise as part of their cultural heritage. This intangible heritage, transmitted from generation to generation, is constantly recreated by communities and groups in response to their environment, their interaction with nature and their history, and provides

them with a sense of identity and continuity, thus promoting respect for cultural diversity and human creativity. For the purposes of this Convention, consideration will be given solely to such intangible cultural heritage as is compatible with exiting international human rights instruments, as well as with the requirements of mutual respect among communities, groups and individuals, and of sustainable development.

(Article 1)

This definition is similar to that adopted in the Proclamation Programme, which acknowledges the continuing changing nature of intangible heritage, its importance in underpinning cultural identity and the desirability of its preservation to recognize cultural diversity. Indeed, the preamble to the Convention stresses the importance of 'intangible cultural heritage as a mainspring of cultural diversity', which is under threat from the 'process of globalization and social transformation [and] the phenomenon of intolerance'. What is highly significant for the purposes of this discussion is the recognition of the possibility of cultural change and the issue of diversity. Both these mark a significant change in the discourse, as indeed does the whole issue of 'intangibility'. A significant indictor of this apparent change, and the widening of the discourse on and about heritage, is the statement in the preamble to the Convention that there is a 'deep-seated interdependence between the intangible cultural heritage and the tangible cultural and natural heritage'. This point was reinforced by the Deputy Permanent Delegate of Zimbabwe to UNESCO in 2004, Dawson Munjeri, when he observed that 'cultural heritage should speak through the values that people give it and not the other way round . . . the tangible can only be understood and interpreted through the intangible' (2004: 13). These statements suggest the possibility of extending the definition of heritage not only beyond the monumental, but also challenge the dominant assumptions about the inherent nature of the value and meaning of tangible heritage.

While these developments represent an apparent shift in the AHD, but this has not been accomplished without considerable opposition. The extent to which this shift has actually occurred is also hard to gauge, as the 2003 Convention has yet to become operational. However, the criticism and debate over the Proclamations of Masterpieces and the Convention itself reveal both the resistance of the AHD to change, but importantly some of the assumptions and cultural work that has done, and continues to be done, in preserving and disseminating certain perceptions, experiences and ideologies. This discussion will centre on three issues raised by the Convention and the Proclamation Programme.

The first issue is that of the applicability of Intangible heritage. While 120 Member States voted for the Convention, there were abstentions – notably Australia, Canada, the United Kingdom, Switzerland and the United

States (Kurin 2004: 66). Some Western countries have objected to the relevance of the document – one official in a leading government heritage organization in the United Kingdom having asserted the irrelevance of the Convention as the 'UK has no intangible heritage'.[1] Certainly, as noted in Chapter 2, the absence of most Western countries as State Parties to the Convention is telling. For the governments of countries where issues of multiculturalism and the rights of Indigenous inhabitants are contested, the possibility of drawing international attention and kudos to minority cultural achievements is certainly politically problematic. However, the issue also relates to the inability of intangible heritage to 'speak to' or find synergy with the dominant sense of historical and social experiences that underline the Western AHD. The emphasis on materiality, and the experiences it represents, is fundamentally different from a sense of heritage as oral tradition, skills and knowledge – simply because the sense of audience for these performances is so very different. Underlying the notion of monumentality is the idea of its universal applicability, that it has a universal audience. Embedded in the idea of the monumentality of heritage lies the ideology and perceptions of cultural evolution, wherein monuments are identified as representing, or more to the point as 'being', the pinnacle of cultural achievement. This, by its own logic, must be universally relevant and applicable, and is a performance of heritage that is intended to speak to and influence the cultural and social perspectives of a wide audience. Intangible heritage, such as oral histories and traditions, tend to address much smaller audiences as intimate performances of cultural continuity and identity creation.

The Convention and Proclamation Programme are dedicated to recognizing and celebrating cultural diversity. This is the second issue that requires examination, as this appears to represent a marked shift from the Venice Charter, World Heritage Convention and similar documents with their emphasis on universal values. Although the 1989 Recommendation stressed the idea that folklore is part of the 'universal heritage' (preamble), and the Masterpiece programme (UNESCO 2001c) also tends to underscore its identification of eligible material as universally applicable – the discourse of 'masterpiece' itself recalling the discourse of monumentality – this stress has shifted in the Convention which explicitly celebrates 'diversity'. As Blake (2001: 12) observes, there is a conceptual difficulty in valuing intangible heritage as 'universal heritage', and that this has underscored the conceptual problems faced by UNESCO in developing its various programmes for safeguarding intangible heritage. Blake notes that in keeping with UNESCO's universalist task any instrument that UNESCO develops to protect intangible heritage should employ the notion of universality (2001). She notes that:

> It is advisable to make reference to intangible heritage as a 'universal heritage of humanity' in the Preamble as a justification for protection

but to avoid its use within the definition itself. In this way the specific value that this heritage has for the community is safeguarded while the need for its international protection of the grounds of preserving cultural diversity is underlined.

(Blake 2001: 12)

Blake was concerned about avoiding legal contradictions in the way UNESCO's conventions are constructed, and goes on to explain that issues of universality should not occur within the actual convention definitions, as such a move may be seen by Indigenous groups as an attempt at cultural appropriation and colonization of their heritage (2001: 13). However, what is important is that the issue of universality is conceived as an important legal and moral ideology for protection. While it is interesting that this term does not subsequently appear in the preamble or anywhere else in the Convention, Blake's concerns identify the persuasive power of that discourse up, at least, to that point. The conceptual difficulty that Blake identifies, however, does not lie in how intangible heritage is conceived, but in the legacy of colonial and imperial experiences and cultural evolutionary assumptions that underly the Western AHD. The issue is not whether intangible heritage is universal, but where tangible heritage is. The assumption of universality denies the possibility of dissonance. There is no site on the World Heritage List that will be seen to be valuable to all cultures – or even to all people within the state in which the 'world heritage' site may exist. The ability, as Lowenthal (1998: 227) argues, for heritage to be all things to all people is simply absurd. Any item of heritage will represent different experiences to different individuals and groups. For instance, any World Heritage Listed cathedral may be valued for its architectural and aesthetic achievements by some, its religious values by others, disregarded for its religious values by others, seen as a site of historical and continuing social oppression by others – but it is not representative of universal experiences and beliefs. It, like intangible heritage, speaks to particular and limited audiences. This may seem an obvious point, but it is one that is glossed over in assumptions about universal values, that relegate dissonance to being an extraordinary event rather than an integral element of heritage. Moreover, although there appears to have been a shift in the discourse, it remains to be seen whether the lack of 'universal' applicability of intangible heritage will continue to result in its international marginalization. Certainly, there appears to be a differential power or sense of gravity applied to tangible as opposed to intangible heritage. This is illustrated in the discourse of Matsuura's announcement that:

Culture no longer solely inhabits the proud temple that European civilizations had raised up to it: theatres, operas, museums and libraries. Throughout the world, it has moved into cities and countryside, descending into the streets, pervading the forests and fields, endorsing traditions, customs and know-how, encompassing oral tradition as well as the written word in expression of the memory and of creativity, drawing together the functional object and the work of art, and relativizing the distances that used to lie between actual experience and creation.

(Director-General of UNESCO in UNESCO 2003a: 1)

This statement prefaces a document of cultural diversity that discusses both the World Heritage Convention and the new Convention dealing with intangible heritage. The image is arresting: 'culture', like some creeping fescue, can 'descend' from the high cultural achievements of Europe to the more modest achievements of 'the streets'. Europe has recognized the cultural achievements of the rest of the world and anointed them as 'legitimate'. Perhaps this is just an unfortunate turn of phrase from the Director General; however, the power relations of the Western AHD with other conceptualizations of heritage revealed by this statement cannot be ignored. UNESCO is, as Blake (2001) noted, a universalizing project. It is also a project of legitimization – of recognizing and giving authority to certain expressions of culture and heritage. How something is recognized can be as important as the very act of its recognition. In the above passage, Europe does clearly 'endorse' as the 'distances' between functionality and aesthetics are relativized, and the suggestion is that the power of the European AHD has not really been challenged.

The third issue that needs to be examined is that of cultural change. As argued in Chapter 2, the idea of cultural change and the mutability of cultural values and meanings are anathema in the AHD. However, the concept of change lies at the heart of definitions of intangible heritage. The term 'living culture' is often employed in UNESCO documents and in the debate more widely about intangible heritage. It has been observed that the term 'living culture has the advantage to refer immediately to the people practising it. Furthermore, it is to be distinguished from "dead" cultural artefacts' (van Zanten 2004: 28–9). The use of the concept living culture throws into sharp relief the idea of the immutability of value and meaning given to tangible – or dead – heritage. Several commentators have expressed concern about the logic of UNESCO's programme of Proclaiming Masterpieces. One of the criteria for listing Masterpieces on a list designed in part to 'protect' them is their vitality. This is contradictory, as Kirshenblatt-Gimblett (2004: 56) points out, as a thing of vitality hardly needs safeguarding (see also Nas 2002: 143; Kurin 2004). Others have noted that creating lists and measures to safeguard intangible heritage will inevitably result in the 'freezing' or fossilization of cultural change (Sears 2002: 147; Amselle 2004; van Zanten 2004: 41). These concerns highlight some of the underpinning assumptions of the AHD: firstly, that management and protection is indeed about, and should be about, fossilization; and, secondly, that the inherent values of tangible heritage are immutable. As with the issue of 'universality', the concern about fossilization needs to be reversed and the question asked, is tangible heritage really inert and static? Of course it is not static. As Munjeri (2004) observes, heritage only becomes recognizable when it expresses the values of a society; the values associated with objects are intangible and it is only through these values that heritage can be both recognized and known. Subsequently, what the debate about intangible heritage as living culture also throws into relief is the idea that the listing process, either of tangible or intangible heritage, is itself a performance of meaning making. For any item or event of heritage to be listed as either a 'masterpiece' or as a 'world heritage' site its cultural values must, by definition, be pronounced and vital. While the list may be aimed at protection, what it does first and foremost is proclaim the cultural values and meanings that are given authority and legitimacy. Protection is then afforded through the authority given to those values — but what lies at the heart of the sense of 'protection' is the preservation of the legitimacy of certain cultural values, historical and social experiences and understandings about the world.

Several commentators have noted that the Proclamation Programme has tended to list the colourful and the exotic, those things that the West tends to romanticize, while there has also been a tendency to represent nationally-valued movements or events so that Indigenous and minority works are under-represented (Kurin 2002, 2004; Kirshenblatt-Gimblett 2004). Kirshenblatt-Gimblett (2004: 57) also makes the point that in creating a list separate from the World Heritage List both the Convention and the Proclamation Programme have created an intangible heritage programme that is equally as exclusive. She notes that neither the Bolshoi Ballet nor the Metropolitan Opera are likely to be nominated for the intangible list, but that Nôgaku, a Japanese theatre form already protected in Japan, is. She goes on to observe that:

> By admitting cultural forms associated with royal courts and state-sponsored temples, as long as they are not European, the intangible heritage list preserves the division between the West and the rest and produces a phantom list of intangible heritage, a list of that which is not indigenous, not minority, and not non-Western, though no less intangible.
>
> (2004: 57)

Of concern here, is the degree to which the AHD has been able to shift sufficiently enough to relinquish its role in creating and recreating the Western worldview of both itself and the 'other'. It is relatively early days in the implementation of international intangible heritage management programmes, and although there is some shift in the AHD there is nonetheless evidence that this shift has not substantially recast the gaze or mentality through which heritage is defined and understood. The power of the Western AHD does not appear to have been greatly affected, and indeed, if Kirshenblatt-Gimblett is correct, it has not been challenged at all, and the work that it does in asserting and preserving cultural meaning through institutions like UNESCO and ICOMOS seems assured, at least for the moment.

Conclusion

The various conventions, charters, recommendations and other texts enacted by UNESCO and ICOMOS, as authorizing institutions of heritage, play a role in the maintenance of the authority of heritage discourses. They represent a dominant form of discourse, and one that tends to privilege European, and more generally Western, assumptions about the meaning and nature of heritage. The persuasive power of the Western AHD, which frames and legitimizes the various programmes and texts discussed above, is continually reasserted and legitimized both in and by these documents and the practices they guide. A community of heritage practitioners and conservationists is created by these documents, their identity defined by their respect for and commitment to a set of principles and underlying philosophies. In short, these documents are part of the process of heritage in that they identify and create meaning and identity. This is done in terms of creating a community of practitioners and expertise, but also in terms of creating a sense of 'world' or 'national' identities.

The analysis of the Venice Charter drew attention to the ability of the AHD to create a sense of heritage conservation and management as something that is done *to* heritage and not part of the heritage performance itself. Heritage management and conservation is established as a technical process in which expertise and objectivity are valued and privileged. This then obscures the cultural and political work that the management and conservation process does in itself, creating and recreating heritage and the intangible meanings and values they may represent and legitimize. The World Heritage Convention is revealed as processes in which certain values and cultural meanings, which often speak to or represent European and Western narratives and experiences of nation and class, are authorized, safeguarded and broadcast. It is also a process in which dissonance and difference is regulated, arbitrated and managed.

In the analysis of both the Burra Charter and the international programmes for safeguarding and protecting intangible heritage, the power of the AHD and its resistance to change was identified. This resistance revealed integral aspects of the AHD, but also illustrated that changes to heritage management practices, when they do occur, are continually redefined and controlled with reference to the authority of the existing discourse. This does not mean that the AHD is static and unchanging, but that change when it does occur does not necessarily abandon the underlying philosophies and ideologies buried in the discourse, and that these can, and often do, retard or hinder the progress of change to heritage practices. What this means, however, is that for effective change to be initiated an explicit and critical recognition of the cultural and political nature and consequences of the AHD does need to be made. Only from such a point of recognition can effective changes to the discourse, its underlying ideology and the practices it frames and directs, be implemented.

4

THE 'MANORED' PAST
The banality of grandiloquence

It is a truth universally acknowledged that a country house not in possession of a good fortune must be in want of a heritage tourist. The English country house (see Figure 4.1) as 'heritage site' became, during the 1980s, a specific target for the heritage industry critique. In this critique, the ruling elites were identified as cynically encouraging the growth of the latter twentieth-century phenomena of the country house visit, turning it into a lucrative profit-making enterprise to maintain their crumbling properties and estates. Within this process, the elites were also identified as selling a self-justificatory view of their historical and contemporary importance to English national identity, which in turn helped to encourage the historical and

Figure 4.1 An example of the English country house: Audley End, Essex (reproduced with permission of English Heritage).

cultural validity of country house visiting and tourism as a contemporary and culturally-valid activity. Within the authorized heritage discourse it is also a truth universally acknowledged that heritage is intimately concerned with the expression, construction and representation of 'identity'. However, it is rarely actively considered how links between heritage and identity are made, maintained and articulated. This chapter explores two things. Firstly, it examines how the authorized heritage discourse is taken up, expressed within and frames the heritage narratives of visitors to one type of authorized heritage site. Secondly, it explores the meanings and nature of those visits to visitors, and examines the types and nature of the 'identity work' undertaken at these sites. In effect, the chapter asks: are the ideas of heritage actually as universal or uniform as the policy discourses adopted both nationally and internationally tend to assume? Does the process of identity work simply involve reading the cultural symbolism, or is there a more physically active sense of performance and place involved in this process? Are visitors to heritage places simply passive receptors of an intended message, or is something more active and mindful going on?

The chapter is based on the results of an in-depth qualitative questionnaire survey of 454 visitors to six English country house sites during the spring, summer and autumn of 2004. The country houses which are examined in this chapter are those associated with the English aristocracy. Although the landed gentry also own elite and stately homes in England, it is the houses of the aristocracy that tend to be emblematic of the idea of the 'country house', and it is at houses associated with the aristocracy that the surveys were undertaken. Although visitor surveys are quite common at such sites, they tend to be concerned with marketing issues and, as various commentators have noted, there has been a startling lack of attempts to understand why people visit country houses, and heritage places more generally, and what the visit actually means to them (Lowenthal 1999; Trentmann 1999; Newman 2005a). Although this chapter draws on a specific English example of the house museum, which country houses effectively are, the occurrence of house museums is internationally widespread. As a category of heritage, the house museum tends to be dominated by the houses of social elites. Although non-elite house museums are increasingly being identified and developed, the representational icon is still overwhelmingly that of the grand, monumental and architecturally aesthetic houses of the elites. This is not to claim that the observations of the English country house visits discussed in this chapter are universally applicable, but rather to note simply that the country houses examined in this chapter are a significant element of the pantheon of heritage as constructed by the AHD. Alongside cathedrals, walled cities, ancient archaeological structures and castles, the country house (or stately home, manor, château, etc.) is one of the iconic authorized images of Western heritage. Although it has a particular cultural resonance in England, the country house often being typically and uncritically portrayed as one of England's major contributions to Western culture (see, for instance, Gower 1950, quoted in Isaacs and Monk 1987: 121; Pearce 1989: 124; Mandler 1996: 105; Mandler 1997: 1), the homes of the social and economic elites are typically portrayed in the West as representational of national heritage and identity.

What this chapter reveals is that the creation of an elite, authorized heritage discourse has levels of complexity that have not generally been apparent in the heritage literature. While the warnings by Wright (1985) and Hewison (1987) and others about the propagandizing of the aristocracy through the commodification of the country house as a nationalizing heritage icon is alarmingly borne out – there is, however, embedded in this discourse a seam of ambivalence and resistance to the meanings and ideologies of the AHD, and those represented by the country house in particular. Subsequently, tied up in the heritage discourse about country houses are elements that indicate that the discourse and meanings constructed within and about the country house visit are not at all stable, and are in the processes of change and re-negotiation. Further, the chapter reveals that, while many visitors were not particularly 'mindful' about their visits, nonetheless visitors were somewhat paradoxically often undertaking quite an active sense of identity formation. The performance of the country house visit, that is the 'doing' of the country house, is revealed as being highly significant to the identities constructed and rehearsed at these sites. While a sense of national identity was pervasive at these sites, this was intimately interlinked with a very active construction and performance of what it meant to be not only 'English', but more specifically 'English middle class'.

The country house as authorized heritage

The history and symbolism of the country house as heritage

Peter Mandler, in his extensive study of the history of the English stately home, notes that they are 'the quintessence of Englishness: they epitomize the English love of domesticity, of the countryside, of hierarchy, continuity and tradition' and that they are, ultimately, the 'embodiment of the English character' that their aristocratic owners have 'bequeathed' to the future (1997: 1). They are an emblem of English 'civilization' and of 'modernity': it was with the Tudor period that castles tended to be replaced by non-fortified halls and other elite dwellings. As one commentator notes, it was at the end of the 'lawless' medieval times and in the Tudor age – the beginning of the modern period – 'that Englishmen learnt how to live' and started to build 'homes' rather than castles (Welldon Finn [1937] 1948: 193).

The country house is made up of more than grandiose architectural styles and monumentalism. Integral to the traditional conceptualization of the country house are also the ordered rural landscapes or parks within which they sit, the art collections, natural history and/or antiquarian collections, statuary, botanic collections, furniture, wall and floor coverings, ceiling decorations, stables and other outbuildings and, in some instances, associated estate villages and so forth. The country house is materially rich, both visually and in the extent of its elements, and brutally physical in its symbolism and presence in the wider English landscape. The rural landscapes or parklands within which the houses are located are often by themselves seen as an emblem of the nation (Daniels 1993: 8), while also expressing control over nature and a sense of social orderliness. These houses are often characterized as 'treasure houses' full of collections demonstrating a British aesthetic, and it is this aspect of them that is often used to justify the idea that they are a major contribution to Western 'civilization'. Collections, as one commentator explained (seemingly without any sense of irony or self-reflection), as having been acquired due to the 'penetration of European seamen to most parts of the globe' (Isaacs and Monk 1987: 121). As significant monuments to British imperialism, these collections, often only made possible due to British colonial acquisitiveness, are traditionally identified as England's 'major contribution to European art' (Pearce 1989: 124; see also Mandler 1996: 105).

A very significant motif in the symbolism of country houses is the idea of continuity. As Pearce (1989: 124) notes, the relative political stability of England has ensured that more complete examples of elite houses and their art collections have survived in England than in other European countries. This idea of continuity underscores the sense of the validity of country houses as nationalizing icons. Although Mandler questions the contemporary assumptions that country houses are 'triumphant symbols of aristocratic continuity' (1997: 317), there is nonetheless a very real sense that they are:

> used as a talisman for a conservative vision of organic rural values: a landscape of squires and reciprocal relations between classes that has been consistently mobilised as the opposite of state welfare, contrasting the personal attachment of people and places, the way people are known and know their place in these landscapes with the impersonal bureaucratic welfare state.
>
> (Crang 2001: 31)

Certainly, the country house embodies the inequities of the social relations between the different classes (West 1999). The history of the country house is far from elegant, not only for all that it means about the English class system, but also because much of the wealth through which some were built and subsequently maintained was drawn from the brutalities of acquisition and commercial exploitation of British colonies. In addition, although it is not clear how many, a number of elite families and their wealth owe much to the British slave trade (Walvin 2000; Tyrrell and Walvin 2004). The more traditional focus on the history of Britain's involvement in slavery tends to concentrate on the activities of the abolitionists, and thus moves historical focus off both the slaves themselves, and from the crucial fact that Britain was a leading nation in the slave trade (Tyrrell and Walvin 2004: 148). The understatement of the history of the slave trade in public historical debate and consciousness in England is, it must be emphasized, a long-term and significant phenomena that has implications about how these houses are understood and valued. As Gilroy (1987: 208) notes, the incomplete acknowledgement and understanding of slave history in Britain is an expression of, and underpins, ongoing racism.

During the last 400 years of the construction of country houses there has been a significant tension between their role as displays of power and wealth and their role as private homes (Stone 1991). However, above all else, these houses are about power; their architectural design is not about ensuring a sense of 'home', but is an explicit statement about the status and power of the family within. The parklands were also designed for show, and although often walled off to maintain the privacy of the household, they are nonetheless a statement of control and power (Williamson 1995). These walls themselves make bold statements about who were and who were not permitted to engage with the aesthetic delights within. The interiors of these houses and their collections were again amassed primarily for show; although as Stone (1991: 230) notes, these were originally displayed only to that select body of visitors and relations who were allowed entrance to the house. From the seventeenth century much of the political power in England was largely in the hands of the owners of the country house, and Stone argues that this is reflected in the use of space within these houses (1991: 231). From this period there is an increasing divide between private and public spaces inside the building, with the movement of visitors through the internal space carefully controlled to ensure that they understood their exclusion from the privileged spaces and inner sanctum of the house.

Although highly symbolic of elite privilege, these houses are also deeply emblematic of a sense of England's national heritage. Mandler (1996, 1997) argues, however, that the nationalizing of the country house is a relatively recent post-war phenomenon (see also Tinniswood 1989). Although there is a long history, as Mandler documents, of country house visiting it took on a particular tenor and fervour in the latter half of the twentieth century. In the eighteenth and nineteenth centuries, country house visiting was undertaken by the elites themselves, or by the upper middle classes, and was considered an educational activity in which visitors were acquiring taste and understanding about art and architecture, the visit replacing the Grand Tour during the Napoleonic Wars (Wilson 2001: 9). Mandler argues that during the nineteenth century the country house became caught up in a European drive to develop a sense of national history, and that by the mid-nineteenth century the country house was viewed as 'common property', belonging to all

'England' and, with this view in place, the first wave of mass country house visiting occurred (1997: 5). This consensus about national identity fragmented after the Second World War, when the populace became more critical about the aristocracy, and country house visiting rapidly and markedly declined (Tinniswood 1989; Mandler 1997). The process of twentieth-century nationalizing Mandler views as occurring due to the conjunction of a range of events and was not one necessarily driven by the aristocracy themselves. He observes that for many aristocrats their concern to preserve their artworks and houses was not due to a sense of obligation or stewardship for the nation, but rather a sense of stewardship for their own descendents (1997: 377). However, the ability to call on public money through the postwar refocusing of the National Trust onto stately homes, and increasing tax cuts during the post-war period for country house owners, helped to facilitate the preservation of the country house, and the need to justify this was not lost on the aristocracy. As Lord Montague of Beaulieu, quoted in Mandler (1997: 396), warned in 1967:

> We must remove the great prejudice against apparent wealth both at public and private level . . . Unless we can adapt ourselves to the times and conditions in which we live we shall suffer a fate as final, if less dramatic, as the French feudal aristocracy at the end of the eighteenth century. If this happens our great Country Houses will become as empty and lifeless as many of the Chateaux of the Loire.

Mandler (1997) argues that the twentieth-century trend to value the country house as a national heritage icon, begun in the pages of *Country Life* during the 1930s, was accelerated by the work of the National Trust and, more specifically, in the 1970s and early 1980s by organizations such as SAVE Britain's Heritage – who were concerned to preserve these houses as symbolic of a way of life (see, for instance, Cornforth 1974; Allen and Cantell 1978; Andreae and Binney 1978; Binney and Grenfell 1980; Andreae et al. 1981; Aslet 1982; Binney and Martin 1982; Binney and Milne 1982; SAVE 1984). A significant event in the preservation history of the country house was the 1974 exhibition at the Victoria and Albert Museum: *The Destruction of the Country House, 1875–1975*. Organized by members of SAVE, this exhibition, and the SAVE campaign itself, raised public interest over the fate of these buildings, and it was in this decade that the label 'heritage' was specifically applied to the country house (Binney 1984; Mandler 1997: 401; Cornforth 1998; Barker 1999: 203). As Littler and Naidoo (2004: 331) note, this exhibition made strong polemical arguments about the heritage values of the houses as part of a campaign against the wealth tax. The application of the 'heritage' label was consciously undertaken so as to align the fear of private loss with nationalist sentiments. Deckha (2004) demonstrates that this strategy worked, in so far as the country house became central to British conservation activism during the 1970s and 1980s, and the concern to save a 'lost' way of life spawned a nationalist cultural discourse with country houses as its symbolic centre. This perceived loss of lifestyle coincided with increasing public debate about the meaning of the loss of empire, and coalesced into a national cultural desire to maintain emotional linkages to past grandeur, and imperial and cultural achievements. On a more pragmatic level, the conservation movement of the 1970s and 1980s also found synergy with the gentrification process of many previously working class inner-city neighbourhoods and districts (Deckha 2004: 413). The conservation movement, with the country house as centrepiece, provided the gentrifying middle classes with an aesthetic framework to foster and legitimate their investments.

The growth of the 'cult of the country house', and the associated steady increase of visitors to these properties since the 1950s, is often characterized as resulting from a combination of increased leisure time coupled with greater mobility and disposable income (Mandler 1997: 380f.; Tinniswood 1998). Mandler notes that women played an important role from the 1960s onwards in planning leisure time and were drawn to 'domestic sites' such as the country house (1997: 386). Others have suggested a sense of voyeurism has always been an element of the visit, as is middle class aspiration for a more opulent lifestyle (Tinniswood 1998: 194). However, as Lowenthal (1999) and Trentmann (1999) note, there is yet little real understanding of *why* in particular the country house should have benefited from changing patterns in leisure time and mobility.

While Mandler (1997: 416) argues that the aristocracy does not have a tradition of preserving and cherishing their country houses as heritage, and thus tends to absolve the aristocracy of an active responsibility in the process, this argument does not sit comfortably with the observation that these places were primarily created for public display in the first place (Stone 1991). Nor does the invention of a tradition mean that the new values and meanings thus created are illegitimate or do not do real cultural and political work (Hobsbawm 1983a). Further, Mandler's argument downplays the consequences of the apparent messages the preservation of these houses as national heritage have for the political, economic and social legitimacy of the aristocracy. Hewison (1987: 53) argued that the reactionary nostalgia represented by the country house actively reinforces and legitimizes the social values of the aristocracy in the present. Although the country house is often targeted in the heritage industry critique, this critique identifies these reactionary messages as deriving ultimately from the commodification of heritage in which the nation became 'a nation of caretakers' (Goody 1998: 197). In this process, the entire nation is characterized as being overly concerned with gazing over its collective shoulder into a past reconstructed as more gentle and elegant than the present – a sense of elegance apparently personified by the country house.

This reactionary nostalgia is often presented in the literature as something that 'just happened', simply because of the nature of nominating things as heritage, and then commodifying them as a tourist resource – but how and why this happened is often not explained. Hewison (1987), however, did identify this process as symptomatic of British cultural decline and of a loss of cultural confidence. Brett (1996: 10) takes issue with the idea of 'decline' and sees the preservation of elite houses in other countries, such as the US and Ireland, as celebratory rather than heavily nostalgic. Tinniswood (1989: 2) also rejects the idea of decline and identifies the country house visit as a 'cultural process', part of a long tradition of visiting. The idea of cultural decline perhaps overstates or oversimplifies the issues, though certainly the nationalizing cult of the country house plays on contemporary tensions about English identity, such as the decline of the British Empire, the discomfort at the role of England in colonial history, and anxiety about the way that Britain fits into Europe. More specifically, English anxiety over devolution has identified the need to define an 'English' national identity always previously heavily reliant and interwoven with a sense of what it meant to be 'British' (Colley 1999; Burton 2003). With devolution, the tensions of what it means to be English have become more keenly felt and publicly uncertain. The continuity of the country house motif perhaps adds some cultural stability within this process – whatever the country house represents or means, however, it does currently reside within a web of tensions about what it means to be British and, more specifically, English.

The country house visit

The economic phenomenon that is the country house cannot be overstated. In the post-war period, more and more houses were opened to paying visitors during the summer months to help alleviate maintenance and other costs associated with running a country house; others were handed over or bequeathed to the National Trust, who managed the properties whilst many owners maintained residences within the house or grounds (Tinniswood 1989). To encourage public visitation, many houses in direct private ownership developed specific attractions; for example, the Marquess of Bath turned the grounds of Longleat into a leisure park in 1949, and then during the 1960s developed a lion park within the grounds (Mandler 1997). As Tinniswood notes, the aristocracy themselves became primary attractions; the Duke of Bedford, for instance, made tours of his house so he could be spotted by visitors (1998: 198). Ironically, the conservation game park suggested by Longleat becomes a metaphor for the continuing relations between the country house and their elite inhabitants: preservation of habitat and lifestyle through tourism revenue.

The development of mass country house visiting to help alleviate maintenance costs was facilitated by two specific discourses: that of 'nationalism' and 'education'. The idea that these houses were nationally iconic helped to facilitate and justify their marketing as places at which to spend leisure time and money. A sense that the visit was educational also permeates the literature on country house conservation and visiting; though as Cornforth (1998: 242) notes, the concept of 'public benefit' became quite explicit after 1953 as public money was increasingly granted for repair work. As Wilson (2001: 9) has observed, the visit continues to be understood as a means by which 'aristocratic culture percolate[s] down to an increasingly affluent and emulative "middle sort" '. However, what is significant in this discourse, despite its justificatory appeals to national identity and 'education', is that owners and the National Trust have always seen visitors as 'other' – that is, as a resource to be mined for running and upkeep costs. As Tinniswood (1998: 191) notes in his history of the National Trust, conservation will take precedence in the Trust over access. Very quickly in the historical literature on the country house, visitors were labelled as 'tourists'. This discourse works to distance the visitor from any sense of cultural 'ownership' of the country house. Traditionally, tourists visit the cultural 'other' – but if country house visiting is, as Tinniswood (1989) asserts, a British cultural practice with historical standing, is this really tourism? Although the modern mass version of the visit has taken on its own unique expressions, it *does* have historical linkages and specific cultural currency for English visitors, and if these visitors are engaged in a practice culturally close to themselves, can they really be defined as tourists in the traditional meaning of the term? The definition of 'tourist' used here, centred on the search for the 'authentic other' by a non-critical and passive tourist audience, is one that is being challenged in the tourism literature itself as too simplistic and narrow. Prentice and colleagues, for instance, demonstrate that tourists are far more critical, mindful and engaged than traditionally categorized, and that the search for the authentic does not necessarily only occur in encounters with the 'genuine' material article, but rather in experiences that have emotional resonance and significance for memory making and reminiscing (Prentice 1998, 2001; Prentice et al. 1998; McIntosh and Prentice 1999).

'Heritage tourism' is therefore not simply the convergence of heritage with tourism, as it is so often categorized (Apostolakis 2003), but rather part of the wider cultural process of heritage meaning making and identity work. However, the point here is that the 'tourist' discourse used in the country house literature and management policy and practices is essentially grounded in the traditional idea of 'tourist', and thus inevitably conjures up a sense of 'distance' and 'divide' between the viewer and the viewed (Urry 1990). The problem here, however, is that the construction of visitors to country houses as 'tourists' has inevitably meant that 'visiting' is understood as a marketing issue within both the critical literature and public policy debates surrounding country house conservation and management. Consequently, little conceptual room is made to consider the cultural processes of heritage that are actually going on by and within the visit. Visitors are constructed as passive receivers of the country house message (what ever that may be), and what they do at sites is only valued in terms of its economic, rather than cultural or social, consequences.

While the particularities of the modern mass country house visit may have a limited historical pedigree, as Mandler (1997) points out, this does not necessarily make the meanings that are made and remade by the act of visiting less socially or culturally 'real' or significant. Since MacCannell's (1973) identification of tourism as the search for the 'authentic', the literature on heritage tourism has been obsessed with discussions of how the authentic and inauthentic may be identified, defined, measured, understood and, above all, marketed. A central concern of this literature are critical examinations of the apparent authenticity, or lack of it, in the so-called heritage 'theme parks' or open air museums, such as Colonial Williamsburg (USA), Beamish and Ironbridge Gorge (UK), and Sovereign Hill (Australia), amongst many others, and the management and marketing of historical districts and precincts. Although both Wright (1985, 1991) and Hewison (1987) have critiqued the authenticity of the county house as national icon, more sustained examinations of its 'authenticity' have not been made. There is a difficult paradox at play in the way country or other elite houses in England and elsewhere are treated both as a cultural and tourist resource. On the one hand, they can be and are criticized for how their national historical significance tends to be marketed and over-emphasized, and the degree to which their presentation excludes social history and makes invisible servants, slaves and women. Yet outside of the writings of Wright and Hewison, their 'authenticity' is never really questioned.

Accusations of the sanitization of the past so frequently applied to open air museums of the everyday and less grand, although present, are less conspicuously applied to the grander heritage theme park that is the country house (however, see for instance, Bickford 1981; Dubrow and Goodman 2003, for this critique). In large part, the authenticity of elite houses is simply assumed: elite houses just 'are'. Heritage professionals, and architectural conservationists in particular, set a lot of store in the materially authentic – what Barthel-Bouchier (2001: 222) identifies as the near-sacred calling of heritage professionals towards authentic fabric. The houses of the elite have a long historical association in many Western countries with heritage conservation and preservation, as it was often fights to save the grand and aesthetically impressive that spearheaded the earliest conservation and preservation movements (see Barthel 1996; Murtagh 1997; Deckha 2004). This association, along with the imposing scale of elite houses, facilitates the common sense assumption of the material – and subsequently historical and cultural – authenticity of the country house. This assumption underlies the degree to which houses tend to be presented without social context and history, and are left to stand with minimal interpretation, to be 'read' as authentic statements with inherent meaning and value . . . at least to those who have the cultural capital to do the 'reading'. However, there is tension nonetheless about the apparent 'authenticity' of these places, as evidenced by the justificatory assertions of authors like Tinniswood (1989, 1998) about the long historical traditions of house visiting, in the face of criticism and acknowledgement of the relatively recent vintage of mass visiting (cf. Wright 1985; Hewison 1987; Mandler 1997; Lowenthal 1998).

These tensions over 'authenticity' and the historical lineage of the late twentieth- and early twenty-first century country house visit are, however, more interesting about what they say about how country houses are understood in the heritage literature than of any real value in and of themselves. This is because, firstly, 'authenticity' is a socially constructed value with a range of political and cultural reasons and consequences. Secondly, concerns over the historical lineage of the visit only obscure the contemporary meanings and consequences of the visit. Authenticity is one of those concepts that defies clear definition, but exists within the AHD as a device through which heritage professionals may authorize and legitimize the past and its material remains as universal heritage (Barthel-Bouchier 2001: 237). While authenticity can mean many things to many different people, the expert's ability to pronounce upon it is assured by the authority conferred by the AHD, and the iconic position of the elite aesthetic house in the history of historic conservation and preservation reinforces the authenticizing power of the country house. The nature of the twenty-first century country house visit is not made 'inauthentic' because it is a relatively recent phenomena or one that has converged with heritage tourism. As Barthel-Bouchier (2001) has argued in connection to visits to the Amanas religious community in the US, the visit and the inter-relation this has with the heritage 'attraction' is an ongoing cultural process whose authenticity lies in the meanings this has for the present, and not in some meaning that heritage professionals or historians consider it might have had in the past. In sum, although the nature of country house visiting in England may have changed significantly over the last 200 years or more, the historical 'authenticity' of the visit is an irrelevant issue, as what is significant about these visits are the meanings they construct in and for the present.

A conservative estimate suggests that there are collectively at least 550 houses in England open to paying visitors.[1] Some of these are managed by the National Trust or by the public body English Heritage, while others are in private ownership or trusteeship. The Historic Houses Association (the representative body for private owners) itself lists over 350 houses open to paying public visitors. Country house visiting represents a multi-million pound industry, with the National Trust reporting that 12 million people visited their pay-for-entry sites in 2004 (National Trust 2005). It also represents a significant cultural phenomenon, in which it is socially quite exclusionary, being primarily a middle class pastime. Although traditional wisdom in the heritage literature holds that visiting or otherwise engaging with not only country houses, but heritage sites and museums in general, is a predominantly middle class activity, this is not necessarily the case, as is explored in Part III of this book (see also Samuel 1994). Traditionally, the country house visit was confined to the elites and upper middle classes; however, in the post-war period it has been firmly established as a general middle class pastime (Tinniswood 1989: 1; Markwell et al. 1997). It is currently almost impossible to move through the rural English landscape without encountering brown signs pointing you to a country house attraction. The conspicuous presence of country house sites in the English landscape not only reinforces and validates the ideas of history represented by the country house, it also reinforces the authorized discourse of heritage management. Ideas about the materiality of heritage, its aesthetic qualities, its grand scale and so forth are materially reinforced and symbolized by a landscape peppered with brown signs that themselves give authority and a certain reality to the objects that they signify. The conspicuousness of these sites, not only in the landscape but also on numerous BBC television programmes, in film, English literature and a range of other media, work to publicly reinforce a heritage discourse that continually defines what may be identifiable as legitimate national heritage. So ubiquitous are country houses and their associated brown signs in the landscape that the country house has become banal.

Although Michael Billig's (1995) thesis on banal nationalism argues that it is everyday objects rather than the grand or monumental that most successfully symbolize and thus convey a sense of national identity, the country house has nonetheless become banal despite its monumentality. This banality is expressed in two ways. Firstly, their ubiquitous presence in the landscape renders them commonplace; secondly they are banal also in the frequency with which they are presented to visitors without context or explication. One of the significant and pervasive features of the country house genre of presentation is that interpretive material is generally minimal – visitors are invited to walk around the grounds and the house, drink in the atmosphere and engage with the artwork and craftspersonship of the house and its collections. Information will be given on the owners and their ancestors, but as a rule there will be little if any wider social history or commentary. This minimal interpretation is representative of the genre of elite house museums and not simply a reflection of budgetary or other logistical issues.[2] Minimal interpretation is the norm as visitors are meant to be able to 'read' the inherent meaning of the house and its collections. Visitors are often not allowed into the working areas of the house, such as kitchens, laundries, workshops and so forth or to the servants' and estate workers' sleeping quarters, or if access is given, as has recently started to occur, it tends to be limited with little active interpretation.

The lack of social commentary and the exclusion of working areas of houses on the visitors' tour are not confined to the English country house. As

West (2003: 84) notes, these absences are typical of house museums generally and work to make women, servants, slaves and estate workers invisible, which excludes the house from the wider historical and contemporary social contexts in which it resides (see also Donnelly 2002; Diethorn and Bacon 2003; Dubrow 2003). There are exceptions to this; for instance, Harewood House in West Yorkshire has instigated what is seen, at least in the industry, as a revolutionary 'below stairs' exhibition where visitors are encouraged to tour the kitchens and view collections of artefacts used by servants. The National Trust has also started to open some of the servants' work areas in some of their properties, but the majority of houses concentrate exclusively on 'upstairs' life. Harewood is also unique in acknowledging its past connections to slavery – with a small interpretive panel included in the below stairs exhibition about the Caribbean sugar plantations owned by the ancestors of the current Earl of Harewood. However, most country houses are presented as simply being there because they are there – they are 'conserved as found' and represent the embodiment of this philosophy in English conservation practices. Inherent in the interpretation policies for these places, and significant in the country house literature generally, is a sense that the country house 'speaks for itself'. Detailed interpretation is not necessary, as they are things that speak and that have their own power and agency in the landscape. The visitor will hear the message of the country house as they engage with its inherent and materially authentic and aesthetic wonders. The anthropomorphizing of the country house and the assumption that it speaks with a grandiloquence that needs no interpretation underpins both conservation and visitor management principles and strategies at these sites. As discussed below, however, there is also a sense that the performance of visiting country houses, of *doing* the country house visit, raises the complex disjuncture of a sense of grandiloquence of the country house architecture and landscape alongside a banal sense of engagement.

Methodological note

So what does the country house visit mean? What is the message and meaning that the country house so eloquently delivers? To explore this, 454 visitors were interviewed at six houses during 2004, using a questionnaire designed to elicit basic information about the visitor and reasons for their visit, with 13 open-ended questions designed to explore the types of 'identity work' that visitors undertook by and during their visits. The open-ended questions delved into such things as how visitors defined heritage, what messages, impressions or cultural or social meanings they obtained from coming to the site they were visiting, the feelings engendered, the experiences they sought and so on. It was administered one to one, with the interviewer taking verbatim notes. In analysing the open-ended questions, all responses were read through and themes identified. All questions were then

127

re-read and coded according to these themes. These codes were used to derive descriptive statistics after being entered into the Statistical Package for the Social Sciences 11 (SPSS). In the discussion below, extracts from interviews are referenced with an interview code alongside the gender, age and self-identified occupation of the respondent being quoted.

The questionnaires were quite extensive and many managers and owners of country houses approached for permission to undertake the research considered that the questionnaire was too complicated for visitors. As I was informed in an email by the management team from one house rejecting the request:

> Unfortunately the Proprietor [sic] feels that these sorts of questions are a little to indepth [sic] for our customers – we do not want them to leave [house name] feeling they have been harrassed! [sic]

In the event, however, many visitors we interviewed found the questionnaire unproblematic, and rejection rates were less than 10 per cent. Although many of those surveyed noted it made them think about things they had never thought about before or had taken for granted, respondents did not identify this as a problem, while many people also actively voiced interest and pleasure in being asked about what they thought about heritage sites.

   The locations at which the visitor interviews were undertaken were: Harewood House, Nostell Priory, Waddesdon Manor, Audley End, Brodsworth Hall and Belsay Hall. *Harewood House*, West Yorkshire, managed by an independent trust and owned by the Earl of Harewood, is one of the most visited country houses in England. It is classified as one of the ten 'treasure houses of England' and is still home to the Lascelles family. Built by Edwin Lascelles between 1759 and 1771, designed by John Carr, and with interiors designed by Robert Adam, it contains an extensive collection of Chippendale furniture and European art, and is set within parklands designed by Lancelot 'Capability' Brown. The National Trust manages *Nostell Priory,* West Yorkshire, while members of the family still reside in one wing of the house. Built on the site of a medieval priory, the house was completed in 1733, designed by James Paine, with interiors by Robert Adam. It also contains extensive collections of Chippendale furniture and European art. The National Trust also manages *Waddesdon Manor*, Buckinghamshire, commissioned by Baron Ferdinand de Rothschild, built in the Renaissance-style and completed in 1889, which has extensive collections of European art and of French eighteenth-century decorative arts in particular.

   English Heritage manages the remaining three houses. *Audley End* in Essex was completed in the 1660s, sits within grounds later designed by 'Capability' Brown, and contains an extensive natural history collection. *Brodsworth Hall*, South Yorkshire, was built between 1861 and 1863 in the

Italianate style and sits within extensive gardens (Allfrey 1999). *Belsay Hall* in Northumberland was built in the Greek Revival style in 1807 and sits within extensive grounds of exotic plantings, which also contain the ruins of a medieval tower house. Against normal practice, Belsay is managed without interior furniture and without extensive restoration work, while it is also used for modern art and fashion exhibitions.[3]

Knowing your place: Performing identities at the country house

The country house visit is a created event replete with extensive and multi-layered symbolism. It usually begins when the visitor enters the parklands of the great house, which normally requires passing through the walls that enclose the estate and driving or walking past the gatehouse, which immediately establishes the feelings of being 'allowed' through a boundary. In some instances, however, the visit will commence, as it does at Harewood, as you pass through the associated estate village, the historical core of which will architecturally, as well as historically and economically, be linked to the great house as part of its original or current estate. Entrance fees will be collected at some point – as Markwell et al. (1997) note, these fees will be relatively expensive as the country house industry attracts, and aims to attract in part through its pricing policies, a largely middle class clientele who are identified as being able to afford these fees. The landscape thus entered represents a mature vision of the plantings and landscaping that was originally designed to promote a vision of power, and which itself features heavily in the iconography of the nation. The house will sit within this carefully controlled and manicured landscape – a symbol of not only power and control but one that also identifies the house as 'heritage'. As Emerick (2003) has demonstrated, the management of heritage in England has long been dominated by the desire to present ruins, houses and other heritage places within the context of a neat and controlled setting – well-mown lawns being a favoured backdrop of both English Heritage and the Office of Works (who prior to the 1980s had care of England's heritage). Sir Charles Peers, active in the SPAB, established the conservation philosophy for the Office of Works, which, as Emerick argues, still underpins contemporary English Heritage practices. Peers, writing in 1933, states that any conservation work undertaken at heritage properties must remain unobtrusive and that the appeal of the architectural beauty of a structure can only be enhanced if 'set reverently in a simple setting of grass lawns' (quoted in Emerick 2003: 113). The manicured lawn is a reoccurring motif at heritage sites within England – it almost seems that something cannot be heritage unless it has closely-mown lawns, and nowhere can one find lawns as extensive as those around most country houses.

Visitors may be invited to view the façade of the house and wander through the gardens and terraces that surround the house and imbibe the bucolic panorama, and the delights of the botanical collections. They may enter the house, usually through a side, lower or trade entrance, which itself sends a message of social place and social exclusion from what is being viewed, and pass through the public spaces to view the internal architectural details of mouldings, architraves and ceilings and consider the treasures, furniture and art works contained within. Visitors will almost inevitably partake in the performance of taking tea in the ubiquitous tearooms – usually built in transformed stables, other outbuildings or servants' work areas, which again makes a statement about the social place of the visitors. Gift shops will offer a range of merchandise, which may include prints of art works seen in the house and even reproductions of objets d'art or furniture from the house; some shops may sell plants and seeds found on the estate, in addition to running simple nursery businesses. In some National Trust gift shops, reproductions of a specific piece of furniture or objets d'art may be ranked by price depending on the degree of 'authenticity' of materials used and the care undertaken to replicate the object. The most expensive version of a reproduced object will be very detailed and finely crafted, the middle-priced reproduction of the same object will be made with less detail and with lower-quality material, while the cheapest reproduction may be made with materials that simply simulate the original fabric. Here, visitors are invited to identify their social ranking by the type of reproduction that they purchase.

Visitors are both audience to and performers in the performance of the country house visit as described above. How the symbolism and messages of this performance are worked out, processed and then understood and accepted or rejected by visitors has not been something given much attention in the literature. Although the literature observes that this visit is something that largely attracts middle-class people, there is little understanding about why it should do so, and how a sense of place is developed and made mean-ingful (or not) to visitors. The 'performers' of the country house visit inter-viewed for this research tended to fit within the usual visitor profile, in that over half were women (62 per cent), over 70 per cent were over 40 years of age, and 75 per cent occupied managerial, professional or other occupations traditionally associated with the middle class, and almost half (47 per cent) had been educated to university level. Table 4.1 gives a breakdown of the occupational and educational profile of the people surveyed. The majority of people surveyed self-identified as English or British, with only a small hand-ful of overseas visitors included in the survey (7 per cent of people surveyed), and an even smaller handful of British visitors self-identified as coming from ethnic backgrounds other than 'White-British' (1 per cent). The sample of overseas visitors did not, as a group, significantly differ in their responses to the houses summarized below. Just under half of those surveyed, 48 per cent, were members of heritage organizations or amenity societies (either National

Table 4.1 Country houses: Profile of survey population

	Frequency	%
Occupation		
1.1 Senior managerial	30	6.6
1.2 Higher professional	97	21.4
2 Lower managerial/professional	154	33.9
3 Intermediate occupations	61	13.4
4 Small employers/own account	13	2.9
5 Lower supervisory/technical	8	1.8
6 Semi-routine	25	5.5
7 Routine	9	2.0
8 Unemployed/students	57	12.6
Total	454	100
Education		
No response	2	0.4
'O' levels/GCSE	73	16.1
'A' levels (Matriculation)	44	9.7
Undergraduate degree	110	24.4
Postgraduate degree	101	22.2
Technical qualifications	65	14.3
HND/HNC	16	3.5
No formal qualifications	43	9.5
Total	454	100

Note: For description of occupation categories, see Office of National Statistics (2004).

Trust, English Heritage[4] or similar society) and 42 per cent of those surveyed identified themselves as repeat visitors to the site at which they were surveyed. Individuals undertaking repeat visits to a particular heritage site are more likely to be emotionally engaged with the site in question, and are expressing a close association with the site as part of their personal heritage (Poria et al. 2003). Just over 67 per cent of those surveyed had travelled from a home address, while 39 per cent identified themselves as 'locals' to the house being visited. The age, gender and occupational and educational profiles of the visitors surveyed for this chapter are similar to the visitor profiles recorded previously at Harewood House – the only house where such statistics were available (Anon 2005). The results of the survey discussed in more detail below have been grouped together rather than examined house by house as no significant variation in the results cross-referenced to survey location.

What is heritage? Reproducing the AHD

For these visitors the idea of 'heritage' was, for the most part, expressive of the authorized heritage discourse. Table 4.2 summarizes the response to the

Table 4.2 Country houses: What does the word heritage mean to you?

Response	Frequency	%
No response	11	2.4
Educational	4	0.9
History in general	70	15.4
Identity – personal link	63	13.9
Material things from the past	55	12.1
Non-material/intangible past	67	14.8
Negative word/connotations	12	2.6
Patrimony/preservation	148	32.6
Royalty/aristocracy	8	1.8
Simply 'The past'	16	3.5
Total	454	100

question 'What does the word heritage mean to you'. A dominant theme was a clear acceptance that heritage was not only an inheritance, but also that there existed a duty by the current generation to engage in and support active preservation. Thus for many, the National Trust itself was identified as England's 'heritage', as was the *process* of conservation. In response to the question, What does the word heritage mean?, the following responses were given:

History, the National Trust.

(CH56, female, 30–39, musician)

History, tradition, the National Trust is its protector.

(CH48, male, 40–59, school inspector)

From the past, lives on – looked after and conserved.

(CH363, female, 40–59, teacher)

Preserving the good things of centuries gone by.

(CH134, male, 40–59, regional manager, retail)

Something we should look after from the past.

(CH268, 28, female, 40–59, government officer)

Maintaining cultural goods and property.

(CH295, male, secretary general of a professional association)

All the beautiful buildings and gardens – history being preserved.

(CH141, female, 40–59, specialist practitioner)

Preserving that which we value from our past and that of our forebears.

(CH237, male, over 60, retired RAF officer)

For some, the act of visiting a country house was a statement of not only supporting their conservation but also actively 'doing their bit' to contribute to the preservation of these buildings. This was achieved both in terms of paying the entrance fees to support the maintenance of the house, and also in the very act of the visit as a demonstration that country houses 'mattered':

It's a nice afternoon out and I feel I am supporting the [National] Trust by coming and using local facilities.

(CH238, male, 40–59, fire-fighter)

Everyone should see and understand it to be part of heritage, that is to see how valuable it is to continue the tradition of conserving.

(CH442, female, 30–39, teacher)

The links within the family are important – it's something in their blood that needs to be preserved, opening these places to the paying public preserves them – paying our entry fee means doing our duty to the past.

(CH123, female, over 60, telephonist)

[heritage is] Something we are likely to look after and pass on to the next generation. We are our heritage.

(CH329, male, over 60, company director)

The act of conservation is thus identified as a cultural tradition – not simply as a process in which heritage is seen to be identified and looked after, but the very act of conserving is itself a tradition – is itself 'heritage'. Thus, the act of visiting itself becomes an act of heritage – 'we are our heritage' – an act in which the visitor considers they are participating in a national process of maintaining values and historical meaning (if not the actual aristocratic blood as implied by CH123). Moreover, many also considered this a privilege, which is a pervasive theme in the narratives people constructed about their visit to country houses. An idea of privilege was often expressed in terms, for instance, that it was a 'privilege to be allowed in' (CH281, female, 40–59, managing director), or even '[I feel] proud and privileged to be able to see the place' (CH116, female, over 60, teacher). This sense of privilege not only includes the fact of the visit, but extends to include a sense that people felt privileged that these houses had been preserved, for instance: [I feel] 'Very privileged to live in a country of such interesting history and beautifully maintained fantastic landscape' (CH369, female, over 60, academic).

A significant theme in definitions of heritage was the usual authorized material suspects of 'stately homes and grand places' (CH66, female, 18–29, clerical) or 'Houses, churches [and] historical buildings' (CH78, female, 40–59, warehouse manager), or fit snugly with a dominant bucolic sense of an anglocentric Home Counties vision of England, so that heritage was 'lots of things – churches, the monarchy, battles, music, the village green, cricket, Elgar' (CH387, male, over 60, academic) or even 'all that's good in England – Royalty' (CH89, male, over 60). However, there is a sense of complexity in the way the AHD is used to narrate and define heritage. This complexity rests on the degree to which respondents saw it as an active process of identity making, and the degree to which the non-material or the intangible was incorporated into their definitions. Although many briefly summed up their idea of heritage as simply 'history' or 'the past', and a handful dismissed the idea of heritage as a negative idea, noting for instance that heritage was 'keeping that which aught to be alive dead. Heritage has become an industry and is stalling creativity' (CH251, male, 40–59, artist), or that heritage meant 'virtually nothing – bastard word – use "historic" instead or "cultural" ' (CH290, male, over 60, solicitor), a third of respondents offered ideas about heritage that while not significantly challenging the AHD did push its boundaries. In terms of the inclusion of ideas of intangible heritage, such things as 'traditions', 'ways of life', 'culture' and 'important things that we build up, important memories, a collection of important values from the past' (CH138, male, 40–59, professional consultant) or 'associations, preservations, tradition, class' (CH367, male, 18–29, musician) were identified. The inclusion of definitions of heritage that include intangible elements is significant, as the United Kingdom was one of the countries that actively opposed the development of the 2003 UNESCO charter on intangible heritage, and it is often stated and assumed within the English AHD that England does not have intangible heritage. In terms of identity formation, the boundary pushing was less clear, but no less significant, for instance:

> Somewhere we can explore our background.
> (CH244, female, 40–59, head teacher)

> Something that belongs to my country, which I feel very strongly about, and myself that we should take care of – it's very precious, because if it does go we can't get it back. It's your background, your whole ethos.
> (CH285, female, over 60, personal assistant)

> Historical cultural background, to be shared. Part of our nationality,

part of our past — hard to totally define. How people live and lived, here or abroad. Means more emotive, deeper.

(CH292, female, 40–59, engineer)

The past is the present who makes us who we are — cultural, history, background.

(CH299, female, 18–29, civil engineer)

Sense of belonging, but wider than immediate family, but not equal to patriotic feelings, not straightforward.

(CH357, female, 40–59, computer technician)

Here, heritage is expressive of identity, in most cases national identity and in some something far more personal and emotional. Certainly, it is a place where identity is 'explored', and not always passively received. What is significant, though, in many of these responses is the tension people had with the word 'heritage' — it was something about national identity, but actually something more than that as well. It was often very hard for people to define that 'something more', in large part because a sub-national sense of identity, or the something more for which they searched, was outside of the dominant discourse and thus the conceptual ability of the AHD to express what these respondents were searching to define. This as a point is particularly evident in the following:

I hate the word heritage, it seems so made up, but refers to the modern connotations of old things. History and culture is better — more depth, in terms of learning our future (it's necessary to understand our past to know our future). I really don't like the word [heritage], nor English Heritage's 'historic environment'. Heritage is too old, but the word is too new, but it's not confined to either.

(CH314, female, 40–59, arts co-ordinator)

Other researchers have observed this tension, or noted an inability to put into words the feelings and emotions engendered by 'heritage'. Cameron and Gatewood (2000, 2003) identify what they call a sense of the 'numinous' that they observed in interviews with people visiting heritage sites in Bethlehem, Pennsylvania, the United States. While the idea of numinous, which invokes a sense of the spirituality of the past, or the idea of 'numen-seeking' as a motivation for heritage visiting, does not necessarily need to be invoked to explain this tension, there is nonetheless an issue here of how to adequately express the emotional responses people have to heritage. There is a real feeling that emerges from the country house interviews that some people did not find within the authorized discourse the appropriate concepts or words to express the sense of engagement or meaning they had derived from visiting country houses. Time and again I, or other members of the survey team, encountered visitors who would quite proudly or matter-of-factly tell us they had visited over 100 country houses, some told us they went every summer weekend or spent their summers largely visiting country houses. As one person summarized: 'It's what we do – it's our hobby – visiting stately homes' (CH166, female, 40–59, teacher). We interviewed another person who had kept a list of 300 houses she had visited, and another who had been to six houses that week alone – and common to all these people was the fact that they could not tell us *why* they visited. The continual repetition of visiting country houses was simply something they did and enjoyed – but what drove them to do so was something they explicitly admitted they could not identify or express. As one person stated, 'I can't express [what being at a country house meant] in words' (CH181, female, 40–59, secretary) and another noted, 'I do feel content being here out in the gardens, although not sure exactly how' (CH373, male, 30–39, computer programmer). Or as one who had been to 100 houses noted, 'it's just an enjoyable day. I don't keep things in my head, so words are no good, it just is' (CH365, female, housewife, husband an electrical engineer).

Although tension about national identity did exist, an unproblematic sense of national identity was more commonly expressed. As one respondent noted, they felt part of the history of the country house: 'Because I'm English. Stately homes are important to being English' (CH79, female, 30–39, general manager). Interestingly, however, this sense of nationalism was often expressed in an oppositional way to other European countries and the United States in particular. Here the country house, and more specifically *its conservation*, was something that set England apart and defined its identity. Thus, the point often made in the critical literature that heritage conservation has become a part of English identity and nationalism rings a bell (see Hewison 1987; Goodey 1998; Schwyzer 1999; amongst others). For instance, the country house as heritage represented:

A continuum – a continuing history: America does not have a heritage.

(CH29, male, over 60, teacher)

English architecture – something the USA does not have. Something that belongs to us.

(CH21, female, over 60, retired RAF)

Now I know why so many Americans love it [country houses and royalty] – its history, heritage, belonging.

(CH89, male, over 60)

Unlike USA – we are keeping history – it's not Disneyland – it's

British – set out of buildings which will always be there unlike today's buildings.

> (CH135, male, 18–29, radio producer)

Englishness. I am proud of our rich history and see why foreign visitors are engaged by it.

> (CH384, female, 40–59, teacher)

I like it [the house]. Proud – that we are proud to be English, that we can see royalty and get into places like this. Proud to be British – the Americans envy us and what we have . . . Seeing what made Britain great – let's face it we have not much that is great these days – don't want to lose the Royals or go to Europe and become just a state in Europe.

> (CH147, female, over 60, housewife, husband a mechanic)

[They] haven't got this history in Germany – England is a historical land, Germans don't bother about history as much.

> (CH148, female, over 60, housewife, husband a banker)

Although the AHD is identified as being at work in defining people's perceptions of heritage, there were also points at which the AHD was being extended by the inclusion of intangible ideas of heritage. What is also important to note, however, is that 'education' is almost entirely absent in the discourse used by visitors to discuss heritage. One of the dominant ideas about the value of heritage is that it has a vital educational role to play in informing the public about the past. However, only four people out of 454 interviewed identified education as part of any definition of heritage. Nor did education feature significantly in answer to other questions where education was either an option or an expected answer – it was not a visible feature of these visitor's sense of heritage or the role of the country house. This lack of concern or acknowledgement of the educational values of sites has also been observed in other studies of visitors to heritage places (see Markwell et al. 1997: 97; Cameron and Gatewood 2003: 55; Prentice 2005: 250–1).

In terms of valuing the country house, respondents most frequently (38 per cent) saw the houses as representative of the history of the aristocracy, although significantly it was often not expressed in these terms (Table 4.3). The idea of 'the family' was highly significant in the discourse of the country house visit. The families associated with the houses were rarely referred to as the 'aristocracy' or 'ruling class', or talked about in terms of class and power, but instead were almost inevitably and somewhat cosily and comfortably referred to as 'the family'. This cosy and comfortable motif is a significant one and will be returned to below. However, what is important to note here is that in terms of representing the heritage of the 'nation', only 17 per cent

Table 4.3 Country houses: Whose history are you visiting here?

Response	Frequency	%
No response/don't know	106	23.3
Architectural history	13	2.9
Aristocracy/ruling class – 'The Family'	170	37.5
Industrial	0	0
Local/regional	26	5.7
My own – my family's/working people	22	4.8
National	75	16.5
No one's	9	2.0
Period specific	33	7.3
Trade Unions/Unionism	0	0
Working class	0	0
Total	454	100

of visitors saw the country house they were visiting as being representational of the nation's history. However, this lack of emphasis on 'nation' may simply represent the degree to which the ruling class stands in for both nation and empire. The majority (62 per cent) of visitors when asked felt that they were not represented in the history of the house, while 48 per cent also identified that the house did not 'speak' or invoke strong links or associations for their own personal identities (see Table 4.9, below). However, as will be seen below, country houses were seen by many respondents as having significant nationalistic meanings. If heritage is generally seen to invoke a sense of identity (as many respondents themselves defined), how then does the country house as heritage invoke a sense of place, particularly given that many respondents felt little personal connection with the house, or indeed identified country houses as being *not* representative of national history?

The country house sense of place

When given a list of reasons for visiting a country house, the two most frequently chosen were a touristic sense of leisure or recreation (26 per cent) and for 'the country house experience' (19 per cent); the latter option being most frequently chosen by people with a university education (Table 4.4). Only 5 per cent identified 'education' as a reason for visiting, 5 per cent nominated taking the children (but this was primarily to 'keep them occupied' rather than for their education – as a subset of this only 1 per cent were taken for their 'education'), and 10 per cent had come to see the gardens. Although recreation or 'a nice day out' were most frequently cited as the initial response to the question about why people were visiting, deeper

Table 4.4 Country houses: Reasons for visiting (chosen from a list supplied)

Response	Frequency	%
Recreation	116	25.6
Education	22	4.8
It's a pleasant pretty place	23	5.1
Architectural merits/interest	28	6.2
To see the collection in the house	46	10.1
To see the gardens	44	9.7
For the experience of going to a country house	88	19.4
Taking the children	24	5.3
To see a specific exhibition	57	12.6
Other	6	1.3
Total	454	100

interrogation through open-ended questions revealed a much more complex set of reasons associated with the sense of place engendered by the country house. This sense of place is encapsulated in the idea of 'the country house experience' as a reason for visiting – or simply 'doing' the country house visit and the experiences and emotions it engendered.

People were asked about the feelings elicited by their visit, what 'being' there at the country house meant to them, and the experiences they most enjoyed or hoped to have during the visit. What emerges here is a very strong sense that the country house is a safe, comfortable and secure place to be – people were made not only physically but also socially comfortable and 'safe' by their visit (Table 4.5). This sense of comfort was often inter-twined with a sense of deference – in which people took comfort in 'know-ing their place'. Also intertwined with a sense of social safety and comfort is a very strong, and often quite reactionary, sense of nostalgia – the past was 'better' and safer because people knew their place, because people had closer connection to place, which meant they knew who they were in terms of not only national identity, but more particularly in terms of class identity.

The country house visit was often seen as an 'authentic' experience for many visitors because it engendered emotions and feelings that helped vis-itors make sense of and legitimize their social experiences in the present – or those experiences were made more comfortable and thus acceptable. Quite explicitly, people nominated that the country house made them feel 'comfortable, proud and contented', for instance:

> Gives a sense of comfort – the history and stability and continuance
> of it. I like old houses – interested in how people lived, not what
> people lived – the servants and owners, the interdependence of their

Table 4.5 Country houses: How does it make you feel to visit this place?

Response	Frequency	%
No response	30	6.6
Aesthetically engaged	25	5.5
Comfortable/comforted	113	24.9
Creating/maintaining links	9	2.0
Cultural capital	21	4.6
Dissonance	22	4.8
Humbled – deferential sense	42	9.3
Humbled – positive sense, expressing empathy	16	3.5
Interested/education	50	11.0
Nationalistic	32	7.0
Nice day out	22	4.8
Nostalgic – reactionary	12	2.6
Nostalgic – social memory	4	0.9
Numinous	9	2.0
Privileged to be allowed to visit	46	10.1
Proud of workers' achievement	1	0.2
Total	454	100

lives . . . [it is also] comforting to know that it is still being preserved thanks to English Heritage and the National Trust.

> (CH286, female, over 60)

I like the house – it is warm and welcoming. I feel comfortable and at home here.

> (CH269, female, 30–39, computer systems operator)

Comfortable, pride as well.

> (CH328, female, over 60, housewife, husband a painter and decorator)

Proud and comfortable.

> (CH363, female, 40–59, teacher)

Exciting, and feel very comfortable being here.

> (CH343, female, 40–59, engineer)

Contented – wouldn't change my lot for this.

> (CH329, male, over 60, company director, and who identified that his mother had been 'in service')

Restful and reassured that things go on.

> (CH97, female, 30–39, solicitor)

Comfortable about visiting even though it was built on slavery, but nonetheless it's part of the country's history.

(CH122, male, 30–39, night shift team leader)

The sense of comfort is explicitly being linked here to not only a pleasurable leisure experience, but also a sense of identity. The relaxing, neat and controlled surroundings, the ambience of place (even though it may have negative historical associations) is *making* history and a sense of national identity comfortable and indeed comforting. There is an interlinked affect occurring in which place elicits an emotional response, which renders the symbolism of the place acceptable and non-problematic. The sense of place as 'event' that Casey (1996) identifies – the doing of an action within a specific place – structures the emotional responses. The comfortable and comforting identity subsequently created is illustrated by these respondents, who note that they feel:

Nostalgic. Whenever I am in these places, I feel a sense of calm and belonging.
(CH365, female, over 60, housewife, husband an electrical engineer)

Feeling of satisfaction, of solidity, of continuity in this modern restless world.

(CH267, male, 40–59, writer)

The comfort of place is also expressed through the physical security of the country house place – separated, as it is both physically and emotionally from the rest of social experience and life. This separation is achieved through the physical boundaries of the estate walls, by the act of passing through gatehouses and other grandiose estate entrances, and by the very *act* of undertaking the visit itself. This sense of separation facilitated a sense of a 'comfortable, pleasant, safe environment' (CH129, female, 30–39, police officer). Safety as a narrative motif emerges often, initially in terms of the environment – people felt that nothing bad could happen to either themselves or to their children as it was a 'safe place' to play. For instance:

Relaxed, safe – much more so than [in near by city].
(CH79, female, 30–39, general manager)

Cleanliness, litter free, safe.
(CH80, female, 40–59, company director)

Staff pleasant. Safe, clean, open.

(CH81, female, 30–39, GP)

Fun – nice, safe place.

> (CH130, female, 30–39, personnel)

Beautiful; it took my breath away. Peaceful and safe. Free from stress.

> (CH397, female, 40–59, catering assistant)

Quality time with the children in a safe environment.

> (CH119, female, 30–39, police officer)

However, this sense of safety, and indeed comfort, was more than about physical security, as it was also expressed quite explicitly in terms that people felt socially safe and secure. At the country house you would only meet people like yourself, and thus be made to feel secure and unchallenged; as one respondent noted, 'I feel safe here with the kids, as the same sort of people visit here – there is no danger – it's relaxing' (CH58, female, 30–39, lunchtime supervisor). The way in which the sense of place elicited a sense of comfort and safety that helped established a sense of identity is illustrated in the interview with CH118 (male, 30–39, police officer) detailed below. In this narrative the respondent moves backwards and forwards between feelings of safety and comfort to statements about the desired nature of British life, a sense of national identity and pride, regional identity and also personal family memory – all of which is made comfortable and unproblematic. The issue of class inequality is never far from the surface in this response and is clearly present in the man's own family experiences – however, these are themselves made unproblematic, if not 'comfortable and safe'. In response to the question, How does it make you *feel* to visit this place?, the following responses were given:

> CH118: Relaxed . . . Safe and pleasant environment to take the kids . . . The whole experience – it's safe and relaxed and pleasant . . . [the messages I take away are] a sense of permanence, cultural stability, it's safe and pleasant for everybody – what everywhere should be like . . .

> *Interviewer: What meaning does a place like this have in modern England?*

> CH118: Don't know that it has any meaning for modern England – what is modern England? [Stops and reconsiders] However . . . this place brings everyone together – opposite of how life is in the modern England . . . [This place and the people who own it are important] to us – it's a local family with links to the Queen so I get a sense of pride coming here as the family has local links. It stands for a lot of things this place . . . The place is spotless and safe and relaxing and

very well run, very professional . . . my family was in service in the past – the exhibition [of servants' artefacts and kitchen workspace] is interesting and makes me feel like I belong . . . Both grandmothers were in service – so it brings that to life. As a Yorkshireman it makes me proud that it is still here and so well run.

What adds another dimension to this narrative is that it was prefixed with the observation that 'heritage' not only meant 'historic identity, country houses and Englishness' but that it also meant 'coming here with my Mum and Dad when I was a kid' (CH118). The *act* of visiting is conceived and understood as heritage, and the visit may be understood as a family tradition he was maintaining with his own children in which national, regional and family identity are actively being created by both place and the act and experiences of visiting. Thus, a particular act of 'doing' is made meaningful and given meaning because of the place of its doing.

However, not everyone was made comfortable by the country house experience. Although only a relatively small number (5 per cent, Table 4.5 and a further 1 per cent, Table 4.6 below) reported either feelings or experiences of dissonance, this was often reported in terms of 'discomfort':

That there was a big gulf between those who had and those who didn't have. It's nice to be able to visit, but I am not very comfortable about the class structure.

(CH310, female, 40–59, print maker)

Uncomfortable – don't like the building.

(CH440, female, 40–59, health visitor)

I don't belong in a house like this.

(CH167, male, 30–39, chartered surveyor)

Sometimes it's a privilege to come around such a house. Sometimes I get a funny feeling going through someone else's house, like I am intruding in a class I don't belong to.

(CH204, male, 80, academic)

For the authors of the above, the country houses they were visiting were seen as sterile and offering no sense of place. For CH167 and CH204, for instance, the house was simply of bland architectural interest and/or a place that they could value for its educational values (some of the few who did). As an educational resource, they could 'learn something' but not have to emotionally engage with it, and in not emotionally engaging some critical observations could be made; for instance, CH204 goes on to say:

I value it for learning about the past centuries, the way people lived and learning about the upper and lower classes, and also seeing the architecture . . . It [the house] doesn't have much [importance] really other than its educational value. If they were all blown up we would be the poorer for it, but it doesn't affect modern life . . . [My impression of the place is] the opulence that they lived in, those few well-to-do families and the divisions between rich and poor, servants and masters in society.

This is not to say that all those who expressed dissonance or discomfort with the country house sense of place and symbolism were emotionally disengaged – we encountered a small handful of individuals who were quite passionate in their rejection of the symbolism – however, in identifying the resource as simply 'educational' the respondents above were removing themselves from 'place'. The country house was seen as something that could tell them how 'the other half lived', but that they did not have to engage beyond that. On the other hand, however, others who did emotionally engage with the houses occasionally did find them educational, although this was often expressed in terms of what factual information people could take away, or it was expressed in terms of what they hoped *other people* would learn, particularly with respect to social values. For instance, 'More people should visit to learn about heritage – they might have more respect' (CH274, female, over 60, Lloyds of London) and 'I learnt about Englishness' (CH414, female, 40–59, teacher).

Interwoven with the comfortable and comforting sense of place were three other persistent themes in people's responses: feelings of humility, nostalgia and nationalism, all often linked to an active sense of attaining cultural capital. Although a high frequency of people initially identified the reason of their visit as recreational, when asked about the experiences they valued on visiting only 9 per cent actually identified recreational experiences (Table 4.6).

Table 4.6 Country houses: What experiences do you value on visiting this place?

Response	Frequency	%
No response	48	10.6
Dissonant identity – memory work	5	1.1
Educational/informational	47	10.4
Empathy with people in the past – active	17	3.7
Gaining cultural capital	161	35.5
Passive connection with the past	29	6.4
Physical sense of being at, or visiting, country house	108	23.8
Touristic/recreational	39	8.6
Total	454	100

This suggests a more mindful reason for the visit than the initial reasons given for visiting would indicate, or simply that an act of recreation and leisure has cultural and social meaning beyond simply 'a nice day out'. For many respondents, the experiences most frequently nominated as being of value were tied to the gaining of cultural capital, which included experiencing the aesthetic qualities of the house and grounds, of enjoying 'reading' the aesthetic and cultural symbolism around them (Table 4.6). What was important was a combination of being at a particular place, being a participant in the public recognition of its aesthetic and social values, and the subsequent accumulation of cultural capital. For some, this was expressed in terms of 'soaking up the atmosphere' that fed feelings of connectedness and identity:

> One leaves much enriched and with a broader understanding of where we come from.
>
> (CH275, female, 40–59, project manager)

> Tranquillity, craftsmanship, lovely gardens, so much – soak up the atmosphere.
>
> (CH281, female, 40–59, managing director)

> Get out of the city – see something grand and epic, very proper and English.
>
> (CH67, male, 30–39, clerical)

> The peace and tranquillity and sense of history, and the feeling that it has been looked after for so long and the artefacts remain.
>
> (CH165, female, 40–59, solicitor)

> Came with friends – usually do an outing to lift our spirits and broaden minds.
>
> (CH362, male, 30–39, academic)

> Nice to share artistic experience with friends and family – it gives us common reference points.
>
> (CH414, female, 40–59, teacher)

For others, their acquisition of cultural capital was expressed more overtly, often in terms of valuing the experience of making physical links or showing their appreciation of the royalty and the upper classes through being in place:

> [Experiencing] connection with royalty.
>
> (CH219, male, 21, student)

Admiration of the acquisitiveness of the family.
(CH182, male, over 60, bank manager)

I like the tradition of it all – knowing my roots.
(CH221, female, 30–39, chef)

Very interesting, enjoyment of putting yourself in the position of those who lived here.
(CH373, male, 30–39, computer programmer)

Important that children come to these places as it's part of their nation's heritage. Even though the British Empire exploited people, we did so many good things with the money they [the aristocracy] got – improving the arts and so on.
(CH123, female, over 60, telephonist)

In this last response, uncomfortable history is once again made comfortable through a sense of place. Class difference and privilege and problematic national history are rendered acceptable through the good works the aristocrats did for 'the arts' – grandly represented in and by their own country homes. Many respondents noted feelings and experiences of being humbled by their visit to country houses, of being 'awed by the size and grandeur', while almost 50 per cent (Table 4.5) of respondents described their feelings on visiting a country house which, in various ways, acknowledged social deference and recognized the social authority of the ruling classes. This humility was not only made comfortable by place, but the social differences symbolized by the country house were also often rendered unproblematic. As one respondent illustrates:

[Being here I have] just pleasant, relaxed, contented feelings. Don't resent them [aristocracy] as they're working hard to keep the house and they are sharing it and they have kept it beautifully without cheapening it!
(CH101, female, over 60, librarian)

Not only is class difference made comfortable, it is also made desirable. This desirability was expressed in terms of cultural capital, but is also, as discussed in the next section, expressed in terms of the propriety, utility and security of knowing one's place as a member of the middle classes. However, before discussing how place is used in the construction and expression of middle class identity, it is first important to examine the messages and meanings these houses have for their audiences as these were also rendered unproblematic and acceptable by sense of place.

When visitors were asked about the sorts of messages they took away from country houses, the answer was unequivocal. For 34 per cent of visitors, the message was a socially conservative one of deference and 'knowing your place' (Table 4.7). However, for these respondents this message was not seen as problematic. A further 11 per cent saw these conservative messages but were either critical of them or rejected them outright. A further 11 per cent took away a message about the preservation and conservation values of the house – that is, that these houses were important and needed to be saved. The feelings and experiences expressed by many respondents worked – often in quite startling ways – to validate the symbolism of the country houses, for instance:

> Slave trade, class thing – not a negative thing – created places like this.
>
> (CH82, female, 30–39, civil servant)

> It's very different today. It sums up certain parameters of life as with upstairs downstairs life. There is a lack of structure now – you knew where you were then and whatever you did or wherever you lived you respected something.
>
> (CH436, female, 40–59, community supporter)

> The idea of going back in time and thinking about the past and bringing it back to life – grandeur, balls, gowns.
> (CH350, female, 40–59, housewife, husband an electronic engineer)

> Two societies in many ways, yet we needed them both to produce gold – keep the country going and move us on – no resentment for them.
>
> (CH315, female, over 60, teacher)

Table 4.7 Country houses: What messages do you take away from this place?

Response	Frequency	%
No response	52	11.5
Confirms aspects of personal identity	1	0.2
Conservative social message	155	34.2
Critical engagement/dissonance	51	11.3
Gratitude/historical debt	27	6.0
How society has changed	7	1.5
Nationalistic	22	4.9
No message	37	8.2
Preservation message	48	10.6
Sense of loss	3	0.7
Vague or specific historical information	51	11.3
Total	454	100

That they lived in a golden age of privileges – pride of England. Pride of everything.

> (CH325, female, over 60, farmer)

England is in decline – people are now unable to keep up the standards of a bygone age.

> (CH230, male, 40–59, academic)

And as Lord Montague of Beaulieu (see above) would perhaps be interested to hear:

Thankful – that it is still here as so many places have gone. Death duties are a bad thing for heritage. These big families hold our heritage in trust and they look after it well – we should not begrudge them their wealth.

> (CH144, female, over 60, housewife, husband a banker).

The role and significance of the aristocrats in forming the English way of life.

> (CH146, male, 18–29, accountant)

Another example of how class difference was made safe and nostalgically desirable is the interview with CH331 (female, 40–59, radiographer). She had come to the house to look at a temporary exhibition entitled 'maids and mistresses' because 'being a woman is part of the past and present history' and noted that country houses had a particular interest to her as 'I had a great/great grandmother who was a lady's maid in a hall less grand. She had a big influence within the family. The values she brought from service were passed on.' A clue to what these values were is illustrated here: 'What a beautiful place it must have been, and I hope that the people who worked here were able to appreciate the setting and house' and that she felt 'slightly sad that it is not used [the house] – sad that the family could not maintain the home as they were'.

For only a few respondents (5 per cent), the message was about nationalism or national identity, and that country houses represented 'the Great in Great Britain and hard work' (CH128, male, 40–59, teacher). Interestingly, however, when asked what *meaning* (Table 4.8) these houses had in modern England, respondents most frequently (31 per cent) considered that they were expressive and symbolic of English nationalism, for instance:

It should be kept as it is and we should not lose sight of our history, we are not just a nation of shopkeepers as Hitler [sic] said we were.

> (CH103, male, 30–39, foreman, builder)

148

Table 4.8 Country houses: What meaning does a place like this have in modern England?

Response	Frequency	%
No response	11	2.4
Aid to memory – personal identity	32	7.0
Circular heritage statements – 'it is heritage so it has meaning, its meaning is that is heritage'	59	13.0
Critical identity work	19	4.2
Educational resource	105	23.1
Nationalism/reactionary nostalgia	142	31.3
No value	6	1.3
'Should conserve' – vague statements	25	5.5
'Should not forget' – vague statements	33	7.3
Touristic	22	4.8
Total	454	100

Don't like the word 'modern' – this is old England and has to be old England. This is real England.

(CH148, female, over 60, housewife, husband a banker)

Proud to be British as these are a beautiful part of our country. Other countries don't have as much culture as us.

(CH60, male, 18–29, recruitment manager)

Without [places like this] we would lose English identity and history. Their family history is not important to me, but without them we would not have places like this.

(CH59, male, 40–59, commercial manager)

It is important – it is a benchmark for values in a time of cultural decay.

(CH75, male, over 60)

Tremendous importance – the past is important as we won't know who we are if we don't know our past. We are a small island and yet admired so much, this place shows that.

(CH123, female, over 60, telephonist)

It was only in discussing the meaning of these houses that the issue of education became very visible (Table 4.8). Houses were identified as important in teaching children about what it meant to be English, and of teaching people more generally about appropriate social values or, as one person put it, these houses could 'improve the manners of the tribe against a wave of vulgarity' (CH290, male, over 60, solicitor). While another noted, without any sense of irony, that country houses were 'incredibly important [in] stop-[ping] us going down the road of materialism and being superficial – they don't build them like this today' (CH275, female, 40–59, project manager). Another noted that their educational value was important for assimilating immigrants into English life:

> Very, very important, even in its present state, to keep for young people to study. I also don't think that enough is done to integrate and educate Asians and immigrants, they need to integrate, as we have a different culture to others which we need to maintain.
> (CH387, male, over 60, academic)

Country houses were viewed here as ethnically 'white', and thus of utility in assimilating immigrants into the hegemonic Anglo-British culture. The assumption of the 'white' ethnic ownership of the country house was also expressed by a group of five white-British women on a day trip to Harewood House from Hull, East Yorkshire. While talking to me, they broke off to observe a school group from Bradford, West Yorkshire, comprised of children largely from Pakistani-British and other Asian-British ethnic backgrounds. These women then expressed some contempt amongst themselves at the presence of this school group and turning to me one commented that such people 'had no right to be here, this place is not part of their history'.

Tightly interlinked with the nationalist meaning of these houses was again an uncritical acceptance of class difference, which was often expressed as a nostalgic yearning for a time when people knew their place. This recurring theme was perhaps most brutally and succinctly summed by this respondent:

> It's part of modern England as our history is part of being England. We would be still in the slums without places like this, *but it gives us something to tip our hats to* – it allows us to belong to both sides of history.
> (CH128, male, 40–59, teacher – emphasis added)

These responses about national identity may seem to contradict the observation that the vast majority of visitors did not see the country house as representing a history they considered themselves part of. What is happening here, however, is that although people recognize the iconic national meaning of the country house they do not feel personally represented by it in this mode. That is because the history of the country house is that of the ruling classes, even though that history is authorized and defined as the history of the nation. Where people seem to engage on a more personal or active level is in the messages they take away. The specific messages invoked and engaged with by the country house experience are most frequently ones about accepting and nostalgically rejoicing in class difference, rather than about national identity. This is because, at a personal level, the country house is about class identity. The messages and visitor experiences of the country house sense of place are about rendering certain difficult histories and social experiences of class difference and privilege conformable, safe and acceptable. Having made these historical and social issues 'safe', how then are they, if indeed they are, taken up and used to engender feelings and expressions of belonging and identity, and what identity if not national identity is constructed? The next section examines the country house performance, and identifies how the experiences of place do indeed construct and express feelings of belonging and community that speak directly to and about English middle class identity.

Remembering and performing the country house

As illustrated above, the act of 'doing' the country house visit helps to create a sense of place. But what specific, personal or deeper meanings does 'looking around the building and then going to the tea shop' (CH196, male, 40–59, police officer), as one visitor described their experience, have? When respondents were asked if the country house 'spoke' to any aspects of their personal identity, a frequent response (26 per cent) was that it 'spoke' to a sense of cultural and social aspiration (Table 4.9). Certainly, for some the performance was, as noted previously, a public statement and expression of their aspiration and the acquisition of cultural capital:

> There must be [a personal link] to come but can't identify it [respondent's friend chimed in stated the respondent was a 'social climber'].
>
> > (CH71, female, 40–59, senior manager)

> Yes – it's part of everyone's wish to be part of *Brideshead Revisited*, we all have an aristocrat deep down inside us.
>
> > (CH99, female, 30–39, teacher)

> Speaks to me as an individual and my interest in heritage. Speaks to the posher side of me – I'm not from a posh background, but it talks to the bit of me that would like to be.
>
> > (CH219, male, 21, student)

> I have a family history that goes back a long way – but we haven't any money so like to think what would have been.
>
> > (CH230, male, 40–59, academic)

151

Table 4.9 Country houses: Does this place speak to any aspect of your personal identity?

Response	Frequency	%
No response	21	4.6
Does *not* speak to them	191	42.1
This *is* my heritage	18	4.0
Aspiration/cultural capital	118	26.0
Active distancing or rejection of themselves from house	25	5.5
Conservation issue/statement raised	2	0.4
Critical reflection on past for commentary on the present	2	0.4
Elicited tourist response 'nice day out'	8	1.8
Empathy with people in the past	7	1.5
Find it educational	14	3.1
Numinous	4	0.9
Part of my English/British identity	26	5.7
Personal reminiscing/affirming nostalgia	11	2.4
Social memory – commemoration/remembrance	5	1.1
Trivial observation	2	0.4
Total	454	100

> Makes you wonder what you can achieve – gives you something to achieve, although no one will ever own houses like these again.
> (CH232, male, 30–39, train driver)

However, the performance is not simply about *acquiring* certain social values or knowledge, it is a statement of identity, it is a statement about the values you possess that make you 'belong' to a certain community. When respondents were asked if their views about the past had changed upon coming to the house, 85 per cent considered that they had not, and that their views, and by extension values and opinions, were simply reinforced. As one respondent noted, 'I like the house – it is warm and welcoming. I feel comfortable and at home here' (CH269, female, 30–39, computer systems operator). This sense of belonging is not necessarily aspirational or about joining the upper classes – visitors understood that they were 'visiting' and that they were not and never would be part of the social strata that owned or once owned these places. Rather, it was more often the visit rather than the place that specifically spelled out or flagged a person's identity – to visit was a middle class thing to do and marked you as a member of that class. When asked about the importance of the house, people most frequently identified the country houses as important to 'everyone', but a telling sub-theme emerged here – many identified the house as important to everyone, but particularly those who show an interest or who were visitors. That is, the house was constructed as important to visitors or 'the middle class, like most people here today'

(CH430, female, 30–39, IT management). This links back to the issue of safety wherein people expressed comfort and safety because 'like people' visited these houses. As another noted, these places are 'well looked after – people enjoy it. Very middle class here' (CH367, male, 18–29, musician). For some people, the place embodied these values – its neatness and tidiness, for instance:

> Structure – formal gardens. It is nice to see something formal and smart – it makes you feel special, and is an antidote to dressing down so prevalent nowadays.
>
> (CH11, female, 40–59, civil engineer)

Here, it may be argued that the structure of the garden, its control and formal setting, was being read as a metaphor for the English class structure and thus an apposite 'theatre' for their performance of their class identity. For others, their social values and identity were clearly embodied by the visit itself:

> As well as being in touch with heritage – it's a very important part of leisure time – very middle class thing to do. . . . Particularly import-ant to middle class – gives pleasure. But that's all right, different places appeal to different people.
>
> (CH369, female, over 60, academic)

> To the vast majority it doesn't mean a thing – people would rather go shopping. It seems to be a middle class thing [visiting country houses] due to education and how you are brought up to reflect, it reflects the direction of your education.
>
> (CH409, male, over 60)

Numerous commentators have noted that the country house visit is a middle class thing to do – and that is precisely the point, it is what a certain section of the middle class *do*, and it is a public and personal statement of middle class identity and value. As one respondent so neatly sums up:

> I like the National Trust, *it makes you feel part of a club*.
>
> (CH238, male, 40–59, fire fighter – emphasis added)

Nor was this person alone in this view; several respondents identified both the National Trust and English Heritage as 'middle class' and that by attend-ing sites like country houses they on the one hand supported these organiza-tions in their 'good work', but also identified themselves as part of 'this club'. What needs pointing out here is that, to be part of the middle class, or a certain section of it, you not only visit country houses to demonstrate the possession of certain social values and tastes by being able to read and understand their aesthetic and bucolic qualities and symbolism, but also to show that you appreciated their heritage values. Preserving 'heritage', the act of its preservation, which some respondents saw themselves participating in through either their membership of the National Trust/English Heritage or other amenity society (48 per cent surveyed were members), or simply through the act of their visiting, was also very much associated with *being* middle class: 'I don't know that Tom, Dick or Harry cares [about the house]. National Trust members are largely middle class [they care]' (CH29, male, over 60, teacher).

The performativity of the country house visit is also illustrated by the observation that some people had 'learnt' to visit from their parents and were continuing a 'tradition', as illustrated by this respondent: 'My father when I was a child used to take me to a cultural site every Sunday and that interest has always stayed with me – been to over 100 houses, [I] visit one a week' (CH328, female, over 60, housewife, husband a painter and decorator). Many others were taking children to visit country sites so that they could 'learn' their 'heritage', as the visit 'makes children aware of their heritage' (CH144, female, over 60, housewife, husband a banker). Although what is being learnt is far more than historical fact, but rather the performativity of the visit. As CH127 (female 18–29, teacher) notes, the visit is 'educational and fun for children so it will leave a good impression, taking kids to museums they get bored and don't learn, but here they will have a good experience' and through this experience these children are learning their sense of place.

The performativity of the visit is also about remembering – specifically about remembering your social place in English society. Only 11 visitors (2.4 per cent) were undertaking any act of personal remembering at these sites (see Table 4.9), which is of course not surprising as many people did not have personal connections to these houses. One, for instance, had been evacuated in 1943 to a house similar to the one he was visiting, and he was reminiscing in the kitchens about how he used to have to clean stoves and ranges like the ones he was viewing. Others were remembering family histories and stories about parents or grandparents who worked as servants or as estate workers in stately homes (see below). However, a strong sense of the country house performance can be identified as a collective remembering about the social values, taste and deference and preservationist values that constitutes a certain vision of being middle class. However, this is not just a collective remembering of the past, but importantly also a collective remembering of what the experience of the visit itself means in the present. Some respondents identified the country house visit as being about the creation of memory. Thus the country house becomes, in Samuel's term, a 'theatre of memory', in which the performance of remembering is not only about the past, but also specifically about the creation of new memories that may be returned to and remembered off site. When people talked about what it meant to be at the house, or what experiences were important, some revealingly identified that it was about 'creating memories' (CH151, male, over 60, chemist) or 'memory of places visited' (CH425, female, over 60, typist) or of obtaining 'happy memories' (CH81, female, 30–39, GP) and 'wanting to return [because of] happy memories' (CH80, female, 40–59, company director). Here the experiences and performance of the heritage visit and how it created and reinforced happy and comfortable feelings was what was being created to be remembered later. As respondent CH390 observed, the visit meant 'memories, different places give different impressions [memories]' (male, over 60, postman), different heritage sites create different impressions, experiences and emotional responses and subsequently different memories and meanings. Thus the country house visit was creating pleasant memories that would facilitate the remembrance of place and the comforting reassurance of 'knowing your place' and social identity in English society.

Dissonance and the country house

The sense of place and the performative meanings identified above were not universally expressed. A significant sub-theme of 'discomfort', already identified above, needs further elaboration. Although not many people were critical of what country houses meant in modern England, or expressed dissonant feelings or experiences at the country houses (see Tables 4.6 and 4.7), there was a critical element nonetheless. This was particularly evident when people talked about the messages they took away from the houses (11 per cent were critical of these; Table 4.7), and in their comments about the interpretive material available at the houses and the overall interpretation of the houses themselves. In respect to the latter, 21 per cent stated that they wanted either more information about the servants, estate workers or slaves, and/or they wanted more work areas and the living quarters of the servants and estate workers opened up for viewing (Table 4.10). Some people noted that it was all very well to open up the kitchens, but that it was where the servants slept that would really tell people about what their lives were like: '[We] don't get to see where the staff lived – it would be interesting to see how they lived and compare their level of comfort to those upstairs' (CH70, male, over 60, electrical engineer).

The dissonant messages that people took away were entirely about the inequities between the social classes, and that the country houses simply 'reinforce England as a class-ridden society' (CH184, male, 40–59, storeman). This discomfort was expressed occasionally in terms of empathy for the servants and other workers; for instance, one person mused: 'It's about the experiences people had: was it cold in winter? What were the dresses like to wear? Who lived here? Were the horses better cared for than the

Table 4.10 Country houses: Commentary on the interpretation and information provided to visitors

Response	Frequency	%
No response	47	10.4
A bit sanitized	0	0
Critical social commentary	6	1.3
Fine as is	190	41.9
Live re-enactments wanted	8	1.8
Mild presentational comment	15	3.3
More child-friendly interpretation	3	0.7
More historical detail	22	4.8
Less historical detail	2	0.4
More information on elites	61	13.4
More information on workers (servants, slaves, estate workers)	95	20.9
More personal information wanted	4	0.9
Not happy with it at all	1	0.2
Total	454	100

workers? What created the wealth here?' (CH400, female, 40–59, commercial manager). While others used their visit to critically reflect on their own lives and social experiences, for instance:

> I would have been a servant – I took more interest in this exhibition [downstairs, kitchens, etc.], but they have sanitized the servants' quarters.
>
> (CH149, female, 40–59, farmer)

> The unevenness of wealth in Britain over many centuries. Having said that, in modern society the same inequality exists.
>
> (CH417, female, 40–59, academic)

Others more pragmatically read the messages of the country house with critical disdain:

> Rich landowners – had wonderful houses – did they appreciate that this was due to the gap between them and the servants?
>
> (CH359, female, 80s, teacher)

> Not a fair question [what messages it has] as it's only a minority history – money started it and [the family] trusted it off. Not an example of England's history as a whole.
>
> (CH312, male, over 60, water-well drilling)

Get the impression that the servants were kept down and apart from the gentry; a very cold place – not the temperature but emotionally.

> (CH209, male, over 60, engineer)

Old England was tough for the working class but very grand for the wealthy.

> (CH341, female, 13-year-old accompanied by parent, a financial advisor)

Speaks huge volumes about wealth and power and control. Especially control of the landscape, class is the natural order of the world so therefore if you control landscape you are in control of everything.

> (CH251, male, 40–59, artist)

Not only were people critically reading the landscape and other symbolic messages of the country house, they were also critically aware that they were expected to be an audience to a particular set of messages and meanings. This is illustrated by one respondent who dismissed the house, he was visiting as 'another National Trust production – I prefer the National Coal Mining Museum and hands on museums' (CH187, male, 40–59, salesman). Others commented on the sterility and sanitization of the houses, as CH310 noted: 'It's important to be able to experience places like this and have connections with the past – hope to put [things] in a sense of history. I love kitchens and prefer the servants – all you see is the opulence, which is so sterile' (female, 40–59, print maker).

The small handful of people who did have direct links to the country house were not actively critical of the country house, but often appeared quite disengaged from the wider ambiance or sense of place of the house and appeared quite focused on reminiscing about family history or personal memories. As one of these people remarked: 'The kitchen is most interesting. My mother and grandmother were in service in grand houses – because of this link it is [the house] no longer history but personal' (CH390, male, over 60, postman). The houses' wider historical and, by inference, national meanings were not relevant for this person, who identified heritage as: 'What makes us who we are' and that it is 'very important to know where you have come from – that's what heritage is about, roots, what came before equals who you are' (CH390). While another noted that they 'liked visiting places like this as my ancestors were in service . . . family steeped in service – mother, grandmother, great grandmother, males as chauffer and game keepers in London area and royal establishments' (CH270, male, over 60, stores manager, Ministry of Defence). While another stated that 'my grandmother was in service, she was a cook', they expressed disappointment that 'this place does not open up its servants' quarters', while noting that they felt 'overwhelmed at the work servants had to do' (CH195, female, secretary).

Although none of these people were expressing an active sense of dissonance, what is interesting is that they were using their visits in quite personal ways to re-engage with family, rather than national or class history, and that this handful of people bring yet another layer of meaning to the country house visit.

Although a dissonant reaction to the county house was not frequently expressed in visitor responses, it is important to note that they were there and that tensions were expressed over what the houses meant to people. What is also important here is not just that people were critical, but more importantly that they were critical at the places they were at. The expression of this critique while people were undertaking their visits suggests, more than anything else, that people were not necessarily mindlessly engaging with a sense of place, but were actively negotiating its meaning. While this may have resulted in the majority accepting, at some level, the message and meaning of the country house sense of place, it is important to note that the 21 per cent who wanted more information about the servants were saying that they wanted their sense of place expanded to be more inclusive of a wider sense of class experience (Table 4.10). This does suggest an active engagement with the house, and that some form of negotiation of meaning and message was going on – what of course is discomforting is the apparent degree to which the conservative and elegantly packaged messages of class and nation seem to have been comfortably and banally accepted.

Conclusion

The performance of the country house visit has been identified by Hewison (1987), Wright (1985) and others quite correctly as a dominant form of heritage in the United Kingdom, and is criticized by them for its political conservatism and lack of authenticity – as Mandler (1997) points out, this wide scale visitation of country houses is quite specifically a latter twentieth-century phenomenon. However, for many of the respondents we questioned this performance was seen as 'authentic' as it engendered what for many were real feelings and emotions that helped them make sense of, legitimize and feel comfortable about their social experiences and sense of community. The heritage performance was thus not authenticated through a notion of time depth or an archaeologist's or a historian's concern for historical 'accuracy', but rather its authenticity was judged on the legitimacy and relevance of the contemporary meaning it had in people's lives. For a significant number of visitors, the country house performance engendered a sense of comfort, belonging and a reaffirming sense of social deference. A 'community' or 'club' of country house visitors was actively created by the public perform-ance of participating in the conservation and preservation of England's heri-tage, and by the shared experiences and memories of visiting country houses. The creation of a community of shared experiences and memories of happy and pleasant visits to comfortable localities made a statement about the wider social identity of each performer. These shared experiences, because they were collective experiences and shared with other performers/audiences of the country house visit, were able to 'diffuse out' into everyday life to help underpin a sense of middle class membership and identity (Abercrombie and Longhurst 1998). Visiting country house sites 'is a middle class thing to do', and that visiting reaffirmed their social and national identities as middle class English subjects.

This survey's results are similar to marketing surveys that reveal that most visitors to such sites fall within the professional or managerial occupation categories. Visitors reported that it made them feel comfortable that they would encounter 'like people' (i.e. culturally and socially identical or very similar to themselves) undertaking similar activities as themselves at these sites. A very strong motif in many responses was the idea of 'comfort' – respondents most frequently reported that these places made them feel comforted, comfortable, safe and secure. It is important to note that these comments did not just refer to a physical sense of security and comfort, the context of responses clearly referred to a social and cultural sense of security. Visiting these places made people feel socially secure, they were affirming their social identity and 'place'. Aligned to this is a strong sense of deference to the aristocracy – often cosily referred to by the majority of respondents as 'the family', as one respondent uncritically remarked, 'it gives us something to tip our hats to', and visiting such houses becomes a process of remembering both one's social and cultural place in the world.

It is also a process in which memories of the visit are themselves created and treasured – visiting was also often seen as something important for children to remember, and the messages and impressions or memories most often taken away tended to centre on the sense of awe and wonder engendered by the properties, which tended to facilitate a disabling sense of humility, deference and propriety. People were learning their place – at one level their place as middle class people was defined through possession of the cultural literacy or capital to read the aesthetic qualities of the house through the performance of visiting and their willingness and ability to part with what were often quite high entrance fees. While, on the other hand, the act of 'visiting' disbarred them from any aspirations to join the ruling class. They could take tea in 'the warm parlour of the past' (Bickford 1985), but that tea was inevitably taken in the stables or ex-servants' domains.

This sense of comfort and identity is linked to conservative and nostalgic messages about the past that often identify the country house as a significant national cultural achievement, and as uncritically representative of English history. As Hall (1996: 118) warns, 'if icons are allowed to float free they will attract like magnets those master narratives that are so deeply embedded in contemporary culture'. This was particularly evident in the frequency with which the houses were positively compared to similar places in Europe and

America – where it was often bizarrely claimed that these countries had no such traditions. These comparisons were used to underwrite a sense of English nationalism and patriotism. A strong sense in many of the nostalgic responses to questions is that of a reactionary acceptance of class difference and the historical, social and political legitimacy and dominance of the aristocracy.

However, there was also a significant undercurrent of dissonance occurring. Across all properties surveyed, this undercurrent was most evident in the frequency with which people actively voiced a strong desire to see more interpretation of estate workers, servants and/or slaves, with the occasional request to learn more information about where, and exactly how, the owners of the houses accumulated their wealth. While very few actually went on to criticize further, a small number of these people actively identified with the country house they visited because members of their family had worked in service. In these instances, the houses become personal sites for reminiscing about family memories. Still other visitors, although a small minority, did actively engage with the house to make or reaffirm critical social commentary on the inequities of British life.

The dissonant undercurrent is important, especially in the context of increasing public debate about the nature of Britain's multicultural past and present, which have been facilitated by the current Labour Government's policies on 'social inclusion'. What I have identified as dissonant views may represent the beginnings of change in the way visitors are viewing and engaging with received messages about nation and class found at and associated with these houses. However, the emotional and cultural power of the dominant country house performance to resist such dissonance needs to be considered. The ability of the country house visit to engender feelings of social comfort and security that underlines the collective identity and experiences of 'like' people is a very powerful phenomena. Here, identity is being forged through not only comforting and pleasant experiences, but specifically through a sense of engagement with 'like people'. The possibility of challenging the historical and social narratives intertwined with these experiences becomes highly problematic in the face of their emotional and cultural power. The possibility of multi-vocality in the interpretation of these houses, with the reminders of the discomforts and inequities of English history that this must bring, is made more difficult given the emotional and cultural capital invested in the dominant country house performance. The cultural work that the country house performance does is, ultimately, to divide and exclude, at the same time as it works to bind (some) together, and to represent the best of the 'nation'. Who is now 'included' in that performance may have broadened considerably over the last 100 or more years; however, the vision of English life that it offers and rehearses is not one that finds synergy or sits comfortably with multiculturalism or critical class consciousness.

Overall at the country house the cultural process and performance that *is* heritage was being used, often with the active consent of the country house audience, to negotiate and embody a sense of historical and social legitimacy for the ruling classes and a sense of what it means to be middle class. While many people took the country house message and rendered it meaningful for their own sense of middle class or personal identity, and while this message may be negotiated and occasionally challenged by some, and while the messages and meanings of the country house *visit* express a range of contemporary meanings, the meanings of the country house itself have not substantially changed since they began to be built over 400 years ago, as Noel Coward so eloquently observed in 1938:

The Stately Homes of England
How beautiful they stand,
To prove the upper classes
Have still the upper hand.

5

FELLAS, FOSSILS AND COUNTRY
The Riversleigh landscape

Master narratives about class and nation underwrote the ways in which the English country houses, discussed in the previous chapter, are used as sites of heritage. As 'heritage', the houses became symbolic focal points in the negotiation and expression of overlapping identities based on both national and class allegiance. While that chapter revealed the ability of the AHD to underpin and validate these narratives, it was also demonstrated that these narratives are neither static or uncontested. This chapter explores these issues further, and examines how the Australian AHD's representation of nationhood and national identity are themselves performed, negotiated and ultimately contested. The chapter argues that the AHD and the forms of national identity it constructs are inevitably multilayered and underpin authorized sub-national identities. However the AHD inevitably sits within a web of competing national and sub-national interests, and in mapping the way various dissonant interests use the AHD to assert their identities and claims to heritage resources, the chapter aims to explore the consequences of this dissonance for understanding the nature of heritage and its use. This chapter reiterates the argument that 'heritage' is a cultural process of meaning making and, in identifying and examining the ways in which different meanings about an item of 'heritage' come into conflict, explores how the power and authority of certain meanings and understandings about the nature of the Australian past are created, reinforced and legitimized – or alternatively marginalized.

The authorized heritage examined in this chapter may not be immediately recognizable as a site of authorized heritage within the terms of the European AHD. 'Riversleigh' is the name given to a landscape, often characterized as a 'natural' landscape, in far northwest Queensland (Figure 5.1). This landscape has been listed as a site of natural heritage on the World Heritage List for its values to scientific research. It is an area containing significant fossiliferous Cainozoic deposits, which have contributed to palaeontological knowledge about the evolution of Australian fauna. The idea that a 'natural' landscape could be identified within the AHD would appear contradictory to the argument developed in Chapter 1. Certainly, the idea of cultural landscapes

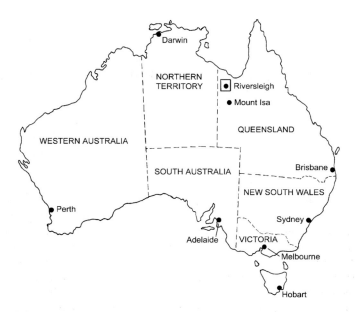

Figure 5.1 Riversleigh World Heritage Area – locality map (A. Marshall).

is one that has only relatively recently been included within the assessment values for the World Heritage List; while the divide between 'nature' and 'culture' within general Western definitions of heritage, although assailed in recent years, remains largely intact (Titchen 1996; Head 2000b; Cleere 2001; Waterton 2005a). However, in Australia, as argued in more detail below, the 'natural' landscape is one of the defining icons of Australian national identity. The idea that such a landscape may be identified as part of the cultural heritage of the nation is not necessarily straightforward or uncontested within the Australian AHD. However, in examining the way the Riversleigh landscape has become part of Australian cultural heritage the mutability of the AHD, and the way its authority is constructed and reconstructed in the face of dissonant and competing heritage discourses, will be illustrated.

Riversleigh World Heritage Site

The Riversleigh World Heritage property is a component of the Australian Fossil Mammal Sites World Heritage Area, listed in 1994 for its outstanding natural heritage values. The Riversleigh Fossil fields, jointly listed with the Naracoorte caves, some 2,000 km away in South Australia, is characterized as containing 'one of the world's richest Oligo-Miocene mammal records' (DEH 2005). The deposits span a period from 25 million years ago through the

Pliocene and into the Pleistocene to possibly about 20,000 years BP (Archer et al. 1989; DEST 1993: 14). Riversleigh is located in far northwest Queensland, approximately 250 km northwest of the city of Mount Isa (Figure 5.1). The World Heritage Area comprises about 10,000 hectares within the watershed of the Gregory River and within the boundaries of Boodjamulla (formally Lawn Hill) National Park. The area is only accessible by four-wheel drive during the dry season (May–October) and is about 4–5 hours drive from Mount Isa.

The fossils occur in discrete locations in limestone deposits and are considered to be remarkably well preserved (Luly and Valentine 1998: 23). The landscape of Riversleigh is characterized by vast limestone plateaus vegetated by sparse Eucalypt woodland and spinifex grasslands (Figure 5.2). The Gregory and O'Shannasy Rivers cut through the region, and the narrow bands of riparian forests that grow along their banks provide an oasis in the otherwise semi-arid Riversleigh landscape (Figure 5.3). In the popular literature about Riversleigh, these rivers are identified as being reminiscent of the rainforest that occurred over the region in the deep past, when many of the animals now fossilized were living (Archer et al. 1996).

The fossils were first reported in 1901, and were initially thought to be post-Tertiary in age (Cameron 1901; DEST 1993: 5). Further exploration of

Figure 5.2 The Riversleigh landscape: basalt plains and limestone mesas vegetated by sparse eucalypt woodland and spinifex grasslands. The rugged, arid nature of this landscape is significant in the iconography of Australian national identity.

164

Figure 5.3 The Gregory River. It forms the southern boundary of the World Heritage Area and provides a cool, calm oasis in an otherwise arid landscape. The bands of lush vegetation on either bank extend for only short distances before giving way to spinifex grasslands.

the fossil deposits then did not occur until the 1960s, when they were assessed as belonging to the Miocene (Luly and Valentine 1998: 23). The palaeontologist Professor Michael Archer, Dean of Science at the University of New South Wales and former director of the Australian Museum, began research at Riversleigh in 1976 when he was at the Queensland Museum, and conducted almost annual field research trips from that period through the 1980s and 1990s, with research continuing there today. Professor Archer's career is intimately linked with Riversleigh, the fossil discoveries essentially making his 'name' both in the professional and public arenas. In most field trips new fossil sites tend to be found by the palaeontologists (DEST 1993: 6; see also Archer et al. 1996). The significance of the fossil fields lays not

165

only in the state of their preservation, but also in the diversity of vertebrate animals occurring in the fossils and in the geological age range that they cover (DEST 1993; Archer et al. 1997; Luly and Valentine 1998). The fossils have been vital in profoundly altering and developing scientific understanding of the origin and diversification of the distinctive Australian mammal fauna (Archer et al. 1989, 1996), and have contributed to debates about current mammal conservation (Australian Museum 2002; FATE 2005). Research has been able to examine how the environment at Riversleigh has changed from a rich rainforest community to semi-arid grasslands, and how this has affected faunal evolution and diversity (Archer et al. 1996, 1997; Creaser 1994). Discoveries at Riversleigh have been extensively reported in the Australian media and the fossils have become a significant attraction to both domestic and international tourists (see below). Although many of the fossils are difficult to identify to the untrained eye, a few of the fossils are conspicuous (Figure 5.4), and one site, 'D Site', has been interpreted for visitors. In Mount Isa, the Riversleigh Fossil Centre provides details about the natural history of the region, including exhibitions of fossils, reconstructions of past landscapes, and details about palaeontological work and research.

The nomination of Riversleigh to the World Heritage List was based on the outstanding scientific values of the deposits, particularly as an 'example of significant ongoing ecological and biological processes' (DEST 1993: 43). Under Article 2 of the World Heritage Convention, 'natural heritage' is defined as:

> Natural features consisting of physical and biological formations or groups of such formations, which are of outstanding universal value from the aesthetic or scientific point of view;
>
> geological and physiographical formations and precisely delineated areas which constitute the habitat of threatened species of animals and plants of outstanding universal value from the point of view of science or conservation; natural sites or precisely delineated natural areas of outstanding universal value from the point of view of science, conservation or natural beauty.
>
> (UNESCO 1972)

Thus, under this listing, Riversleigh is defined as a physical landscape, understood primarily for its palaeontological scientific values. Consequently, any cultural, social, political, or economic values it may have are both circumscribed and relegated to secondary importance. However, no landscape may be entirely understood or defined by its 'natural' values. As Lesley Head argues, the classification of Riversleigh as a scientifically important locality is itself a cultural process that rendered the fossils significant, while

Figure 5.4 An example of one of the more conspicuous fossils at Riversleigh. This is the fossilized leg bone and gizzard stones of a giant flightless bird eroding out of a limestone boulder. Dromornithid fossils are only found in Australia; these birds were not related to the emu, and became extinct about 26,000 years ago (Archer et al. 1996: 80).

classification of this site as 'natural' works to make the 'human labour of science invisible' (2000b: 90). She also goes on to note that the fact of its listing would not have been possible if the idea of 'Riversleigh' had not been constructed within the public imagination (2000b: 90). The discoveries of quite bizarre animals amongst the fossils include marsupial lions, the giant diprotodontoids, carnivorous kangaroos, or the whimsically named 'thingodonta', with its strange horizontally protruding incisors, or the equally mysterious and enigmatic 'weirdodonta', has had a certain appeal to the Australian imagination (Archer et al. 1996).

During the process of listing Riversleigh as a World Heritage Site, and in the ensuing development of its management plan (Manidis Roberts 1998), a number of groups identified themselves as having a stake in how Riversleigh is understood, valued and managed as 'heritage'. The Riversleigh landscape has since become defined by dissonance, and it is the focus of a range of competing values and conceptualizations of what it represents and means, all of which interact in a range of ways with the 'natural' values of the region. Stakeholder groups include palaeontologists, the Waanyi Aboriginal community, tourist operators, local government, mining companies, local pastoralists who have both a cultural and economic interest in the area, and the Queensland Parks and Wildlife Service.

The Australian landscape as authorized cultural heritage

As argued in Chapter 2, landscapes are places of symbolic importance and can also embody a sense of place. Landscapes are defined and shaped by cultural perceptions and practices, and may in turn structure and shape social and cultural experiences (Head 2000b; Tuan 2003). Cultural and social beliefs and values can also become embedded and symbolized by landscape forms (Crang 2001). The temporality of the idea of landscape is also significant, as in the conceptualization of landscape the past becomes linked to the present (Inglis 1977, quoted in Bender 1992: 736; Ingold 1993), and as such landscape offers a vista wherein a range of histories, chronologies, events and meanings may be viewed and displayed. As also argued in Chapter 2, the idea of landscape embodying a sense of place opens up the conceptual field, and allows for a greater range of interconnecting meanings and values to be identified and explored. As a palimpsest, written over both by human physical and cultural interactions, a landscape:

> tells – or rather *is* – a story. It enfolds the lives and times of predecessors who, over generations, have moved around in it and played their part in its formation. To perceive the landscape is therefore to carry out an act of remembrance.
>
> (Ingold 1993: 152)

In a pragmatic sense, no landscape can be described as 'natural'; certainly, the landscape of Australia has been managed and shaped by at least 40,000 years (and possibly 60,000 years) of human habitation (Lourandos 1997). However, as Head (2000b) argues, the processes by which landscapes are conceptualized and understood are entirely cultural and are themselves acts of meaning making. The identification of the natural characteristics of any landscape is of itself a statement of meaning and value. As Lowenthal (2005) notes, 'natural' values are often prized over 'cultural', which in itself is a cultural judgement and expression of cultural value. The 'naturalness' of the

Riversleigh landscape is key to its value as a cultural tool of remembrance. The very reading of the landscape as 'natural' is important to the symbolic values it holds to the sense of Australian identity.

The Riversleigh landscape is often described by both locals and visitors to the region as 'barren', 'rugged' and 'isolated' – an 'untamed wilderness'. These are terms, as Jay Arthur (1999) argues, that are significant in the geographical colonial lexicon of Australia. The barrenness of the Australian 'outback' is symbolic in a range of ways to the conceptual construction of 'Australia'. It defines who Australians are not – as Arthur observes, the 'colonist created this new country haunted by the image of the Default country [England], which was narrow, green hilly and wet – which meant that *Australia* was understood as *vast, brown, flat* and *dry*' (1999: 73, original emphasis). Significantly, the imagery of the rugged 'outback' is also an important agent in one of the defining myths of Australian cultural character and nationhood.

In 1958, Russel Ward's *The Australian Legend* identified one of the enduring myths of Australian national identity – that of the bushman. It is a myth of particular relevance to non-Indigenous white Australians whose ancestors came from Britain and Ireland (Curthoys 1999: 4). However, the Australian bushman legend is one that tends to underpin the Australian irreverence for and distrust of authority, egalitarianism, laconic mateship and a concern for the ordinary Australian 'battler'; it is one that both draws upon and is performed against the brutalities of the Australian 'natural' landscape (Curthoys 1997, 1999). The image of the bushman, and all it symbolizes, began in the 1880s in the pages of the Australian magazine *The Bulletin*, with a conscious attempt to create a distinctive national character (White 1992: 25). There are many ironies tied up in this creation, not least because this was an urban magazine promoting an image based on the idealized characteristics of the itinerant pastoral worker to what was then, and is now, a heavily urbanized nation.[1] The image was created and expressed within the poems and writings of A.B. 'Banjo' Paterson and Henry Lawson, two iconic figures in the history of Australian literature, and in the artwork of the acclaimed Heidelberg School. The landscape of the 'untamed' bush and barren outback are landscapes that white Australians fear and must overcome (Lattas 1992: 52). In the face of the wide open barrenness of the landscape, where the impersonal force of nature is brutally apparent, the insignificance of individuals is laid bare, but from endurance and through mateship and an understanding of egalitarian values fear is overcome, and a sense of place in the world for both individual and the Australian nation is created. As White notes, the image of the Australian landscape is emotionally very powerful, and rests in part on the conceptualization of its uniqueness (1992: 25; see also Meaney 2001: 83). It also rests on its authenticity, which is based on its conceptualization and characterization as untamed wilderness – as a natural landscape. Central also in this myth is the sense that wholeness and well-being will be derived from

169

interaction with this landscape, as the modern 'bushman' Paddy Pallin[2] is quoted as saying: 'cities are very convenient and good culturally, but they sap your spirit. You have to get out and expose yourself to natural hazards if you are going to become truly alive' (quoted in Lattas 1992: 51–2). This sense of the bush making you well and whole is expressive of the sense in which the Australian landscape provides identity and a sense of place, and is encapsulated in the following stanzas of Paterson's famous (in Australia) poem, *Clancy of the Overflow*, published in *The Bulletin* in 1889:

> I had written him a letter which I had, for want of better
>   Knowledge, sent to where I met him down the Lachlan, years ago,
> He was shearing when I knew him, so I sent the letter to him,
>   Just 'on spec', addressed as follows: 'Clancy, of The Overflow'.
>
> And an answer came directed in a writing unexpected,
>   (And I think the same was written in a thumbnail dipped in tar)
> 'Twas his shearing mate who wrote it, and verbatim I will quote it:
>   'Clancy's gone to Queensland droving, and we don't know where
>   he are'.
>
> In my wild erratic fancy visions come to me of Clancy
>   Gone a-droving 'down the Cooper' where the western drovers go;
> As the stock are slowly stringing, Clancy rides behind them singing,
>   For the drover's life has pleasures that the townsfolk never know.
>
> And the bush hath friends to meet him, and their kindly voices greet him
>   In the murmur of the breezes and the river on its bars,
> And he sees the vision splendid of the sunlit plains extended,
>   And at night the wondrous glory of the everlasting stars.
>
> I am sitting in my dingy little office, where a stingy
>   Ray of sunlight struggles feebly down between the houses tall,
> And the foetid air and gritty of the dusty, dirty city
>   Through the open window floating, spreads its foulness over all.

Linked to the bushman mythology is also that of the 'pioneer' myth. Also created in the late nineteenth century, this myth is about the struggles of early European settlers to battle with and subdue the hostile land for farming and civilization (Curthoys 1997, 1999). In this conceptualization, the colonizing activities are not seen as destructive, but rather as completing the incomplete character of the landscape (Arthur 1999). This is linked to the idea of *terra nullius*, the legal British fiction that identified Australia as vacant and unoccupied land at the time of British settlement (Reynolds 1987, 1989). Under the doctrine of *terra nullius*, Aboriginal people were seen to be vague wanderers over the landscape, which they had failed to shape and improve. This initial definition of the Australian landscape has tended to underwrite subsequent understandings of it, particularly the enduring idea of its wilderness and natural qualities. The ability to tame and improve the landscape became part of the justification of European occupation of Aboriginal Australia. In the Australian discourse, the ability to change the land from an indigenous to a colonized use is to improve it (Arthur 1999: 74). The pioneer legend and bushman legend become intertwined through the motif of landscape – the ability to survive in and tame it – and these legends not only have the power to offer a sense of identity, but to justify the very occupation of Australia by non-Aboriginal people. These myths are inherently politically conservative, as they tend to facilitate the obscuring of colonial brutalities, they celebrate individual rather than collective achieve-ment and gloss over class and other forms of social inequality (Hirst 1989). Both images, and the bushman one in particular, are intensely masculine. 'Real' Australians in the bushman legend are men – women are absent in this characterization of 'Australia'. Although women are not absent in the pioneer myths, they are represented here as either a civilizing influence or 'God's police' (Summers 1975; McGrath 1997) or an essentialist natural force, an embodiment of the landscape that must be subdued and put in her place (Schaffer 1988).

In recent times, heated historical and public debate arose in Australia over the validity of what the conservative Australian Liberal Prime Minster John Howard refers to as the 'black armband' view of history, and what Ann Curthoys calls the 'white blindfold' view (1999: 1–2). In the former version of history, the colonial realities of forced land seizure, warfare, child removal and cultural assimilation that attended British occupation of Australia are identified as foundational aspects of Australian history, and white racism is exposed. The other view emphasizes the social, economic, cultural and technological achievements of the settler society. As Curthoys (1999) notes, underlying the uneasiness towards the first view is the sense to which Australians see themselves as victims – struggling against adversity in a hostile land – and it is difficult for those wedded to this image to see them-selves also as oppressors. However, what emerges from this contemporary debate is the problematic place of Aboriginal people in Australian images of landscape and national identity.

There are two central themes, those of naturalization and appropriation, which are important here. The first tends to naturalize the Indigenous popu-lation as part of the Australian landscape – as part of natural Australia that must also be overcome and subsequently assimilated. As Lattas (1992: 53) observes, one of the enduring images of Australia is its portrayal 'as a prim-ordial landscape whose flora, fauna, and Aborigines are the living relics of an ancient evolutionary time'. The time depth of this conceptualization not only helps to naturalize Aboriginal people as part of nature, but also provides a sense of time depth to Australian national identity. Colonized only in 1788, there is an enduring Euroaustralian insecurity about the lack of temporal depth to non-Indigenous culture (Lattas 1992: 56). In locating Aboriginal people as part of the natural landscape, which Australians themselves have a unique affinity and ability to 'tame', a sense of antiquity is added to Australian identity. An example of this was the Jindyworobak movement of the 1930s and 1940s, which was a literary movement that aimed to bolster Australian nationalism, drew on the motifs of the environment and landscape, and stressed the uniqueness of the Australian wildlife. In this movement Aboriginal people, as the 'noble savage', were defined as living in harmony with the landscape and as one with nature – here again located as part of the natural landscape of Australia. The importance of the uniqueness of the marsupial and monotreme fauna of Australia to Australian identity is also displayed in the Australian currency's coins. As banal and quotidian symbols of nationalism, Australian coins are highly illustrative and suggestive. Each coin bears an Australian animal: the koala on the 5 cent, echidna on the 10 cent, platypus on the 20 cent, kangaroos on the dollar coin, and the visual cliché of a bearded male Aboriginal elder is on the two-dollar coin. The naturalization of Aboriginal people and culture not only provides a sense of temporal depth to national identity, it facilitates the appropriation of Aboriginal culture as 'Australian'. The tendency to naturalize Aboriginal people as part of the landscape is also linked back to the fiction of *terra nullius*.

What is now popularly known as the 'Mabo decision' marks a very important moment in Australian and Indigenous politics. In summary, the Mabo decision refers to the High Court's 1992 determination in *Mabo* v. *State of Queensland* that Native Title to land had not necessarily been extinguished by colonization, and that Australian common law could recognize Native Title – that is, Indigenous laws over land (see Bartlett 1993; Butt and Eagleson 1993, for more details). This decision legally overthrew the legal legitimacy of *terra nullius* and the role this concept played in the legitimization of Australian 'settlement'. However, while legally the impact of this decision was significant, it has so far had little flow on effects for the nature of Australian cultural master narratives discussed here. This is in part because the judgement has had no material impact on the majority of Australians. A situation ensured by the enactment, in response to the Mabo decision, of the Commonwealth *Native Title Act 1993*. This Act establishes legal mechanisms to determine Indigenous claims to land, validate various land titles, and to extinguish Native Title over freehold lands – in effect, retrospectively validating non-Indigenous occupancy and land tenure. Although both the Mabo decision and the Native Title Act have had wide legal and political implications, the challenge to *terra nullius* has not seen any major cultural modifications to the underpinning perceptions of the Australian bushman or pioneer legends, which still ultimately treat Aboriginal people as a feature of the Australian landscape. It has, however, perhaps increased the importance of the second theme – that of cultural appropriation.

The appropriation of Aboriginal culture is important for the recreation of non-Indigenous Australians as themselves indigenous. As Arthur (1999) notes, part of the colonist imagining has been the creation of a new world in which the colonist could become indigenous. As part of this, and to cement links to landscape and to reinforce rights of possession, a twentieth-century rendering of the bushman myth has seen the need to 'overcome the haunting emptiness of the landscape' by discovering the 'unique spiritual meanings which Aborigines read into the land' (Lattas 1992: 52). These appropriations are often expressed as correcting or fulfilling Australian spiritual deficiencies, of bringing cultural and spiritual wholeness and well-being (Lattas 1992; Read 2000).

The Riversleigh sense of place

This section traces the various, and often dissonant, ways in which Riversleigh is used as a place. The various values and meanings that are associated with and embedded in this landscape are given value by virtue of their association with the cultural authority of the Riversleigh landscape. A range of groups use the landscape in similar, but at times conflicting, ways to help them make sense of their cultural and social experiences and to embody, and thus legitimize, their sense of place and the identities that they derive from that. All but one of these groups utilize or sit within the authorized heritage discourse of Australia, which recognizes the sense of place afforded to the Australian psyche of a 'natural' landscape. Within the Australian AHD a landscape, although conceived as natural, is clearly understood as significant to national identity – as White notes, reactions to the Australian landscape are often used as a test of patriotism (1992: 25). Each group utilizes the AHD in different ways to construct their own sense of self and identity; however, as is illustrated below, despite their shared association with the AHD, and the values embedded within it, these groups come into conflict. This is because the particular use each group makes of the AHD to take meaning from the landscape often clashes with the aspirations and needs of other groups. One group, the Waanyi, sit outside of the AHD, but the sense of place that they construct as Indigenous people is appropriated and given new meaning within the AHD by other interests or collectives.

The following discussion is based on informal interviews and conversations during 1998, 1999 and 2000 with individuals from Mount Isa local government, tourist organizations and operators, government land managers, pastoralists and with members of the Waanyi community. All interviews used below are unattributed to keep them anonymous.[3] It is also based on observations of palaeontologists with whom I worked on archaeological issues during one research season in 1998. A qualitative survey of 92 visitors to the Riversleigh Fossil Centre and to 'D site' at Riversleigh was also undertaken. The methodology used here was identical to that described in the previous chapter.

Riversleigh as country

The Waanyi are the traditional Aboriginal owners and custodians of the Riversleigh–Boodjamulla area. It is their country. 'Country' is a term Indigenous Australians use to refer to the land associated with their particular community and personal identity. Europeans and other Westerners identify their national identity by asking each other 'what country do you come from?' and then identifying their country of origin when they say 'I come from England', or from France or America or Australia, etc. In this instance, however, country refers to the area or region of Australia from which Aboriginal people draw their identity and a sense of place and community. Aboriginal people also talk about 'caring for country', that is, caring, managing and maintaining the landscape and its resources, and who has responsibility to care for country is carefully defined along clan, kin, age and gender lines (see Birckhead et al. 1992; Rose 1996; Deveraux 1997; Tarran 1997; Head 2000a).

The Waanyi conceive of the Riversleigh fossil fields as part of a landscape defined by personal histories, individual and collective memories, kinship relations and cultural knowledge. The fossil fields were known to the Waanyi prior to palaeontological 'discoveries' and investigations, and are sometimes referred to as the 'bone hills' or the 'skeleton hills', while human burials have also been reported to occur in these areas. Cultural knowledge, often popularly referred to as 'Dreamtime knowledge', is important in defining the meaning of the landscape for Indigenous Australians and the sense of place that it represents. Waanyi cultural knowledge of the region incorporates memories of living fossils, with accounts of giant kangaroos inhabiting a landscape in which palaeontologists have found fossils of giant macropods.

An extensive range of cultural sites and places occur across the region including occupation sites, burials, middens, art sites, stone arrangements, cave deposits and places of sacred significance to Waanyi. Some of these sites have been recorded in close association with the fossils (van der Meer 1997). Although many Indigenous Australians argue that they have always been in Australia, and thus their arrival into the country as a whole and particular regions of it cannot be dated, archaeologists have dated Indigenous occupation of the area to at least 15,000 BP, although they concede an earlier date is highly likely (Hiscock and Hughes 1984; van der Meer 1997). The existence of cultural sites in the landscape is not only evidence of Waanyi occupation and physical interaction with the landscape, but also material evidence of their prior sovereignty as Indigenous peoples of Australia. Waanyi have been very active in negotiating their rights as active agents in the management of both the World Heritage Area and the surrounding Boodjamulla National Park (see Manidis Roberts 1998; Smith et al. 2003a). The ability to control, or at least have a more than tokenistic say, in the management of the Riversleigh landscape is important not only for cultural reasons for Waanyi, it is also a tacit recognition of their rights over land and other resources that will inevitably have economic implications.

There have been calls by some in the Waanyi community for the fossils to be returned to the Riversleigh area once palaeontologists have finished studying them. Needless to say this request is at odds with palaeontological scientific values – as fossils removed from the landscape they are, to many palaeontologists, scientific samples devoid of any other value but their scientific meaning. Their removal from the landscape has transformed them into individual items of data and they have, for the palaeontologists, ceased to be understood as ongoing parts of the landscape. However, for Waanyi the fossils do not necessarily have meaning as individual 'fossils'. Rather they are regarded as part of the landscape, or part of country, and they will remain so regardless of their removal and transformation into individual 'fossils', and as such they should rightfully be returned so that the holistic meaning of landscape and country is retained.

The Waanyi conceptualization of the Riversleigh landscape sits outside of the AHD. It does so in part because the Waanyi cultural understanding of Riversleigh is simply so very different to non-Indigenous understandings, in part because the Waanyi are seen, alongside other Aboriginal Australians, as part of the landscape which must be managed and controlled, and in part because their claims about the meaning of the landscape are viewed as highly political. The cultural politics of identity in which Waanyi engage, sometimes in quite overt ways, are often understood by other stakeholders as irrelevant to the 'natural' and scientific values of the Riversleigh landscape. The natural values, enshrined in the region's World Heritage listing, are viewed as separate from cultural values – these values belong on a different, quite separate, World Heritage List after all. However, as will become clear, all other groups involved with Riversleigh are engaged in identity politics of one sort or another; ironically, however, these are often rendered invisible because they are 'naturalized' within the AHD. They are obscured because they are constructed by the AHD and speak to white Australian mythologies that are so intrinsic to Australian collective identities that they 'just are' and are thus not subject to reflection. Indeed, for some of the stakeholders in the Riversleigh region the Waanyi values and meanings have become themselves mined and appropriated – are in fact part of the resources offered by the Riversleigh landscape that are drawn on in the construction and negotiation of place and the identity politics played by other groups.

Local, non-Indigenous or Euroaustralian residents of the region often refer to the wider gulf area of Queensland in which Riversleigh is located as 'The Gulf Country'. The use of the term country is significant, as this is the 'real' Australian country – the real national character, symbolic of the rugged and dangerous bush that 'made' 'Australia'. Here the rugged and tough landscapes of the gulf region are part of the mythology wherein human, but particularly male, interaction with the hostile landscape created the cultural character and values that represent the Australasian nation. As local residents have observed about the Riversleigh landscape:

> It is a real testing ground, it brings out the real you. You sort out your shit out here.
>
> (Male, local resident)

> You become tough and independent people out here. You develop into strong characters living out here.
>
> (Female, local resident)

> The rugged run, it's a tough place, but rewarding.
>
> (Female, local resident)

> Nothing artificial, you get right down to basics out here.
>
> (Female, local resident)

In discussing the importance of Riversleigh, Aboriginal imagery and discourse was often invoked by locals. In particular, the Riversleigh region was referred to as 'our country':

> I feel a custodianship of that country − I feel that the universe revolves around that area, it is so important to us.
>
> (Female, local resident)

> It is our country, it belongs to us.
>
> (Female, local resident)

This sense of place was important in defining identity not only for individuals but also the region. Again and again locals defined the Riversleigh landscape as their heritage and their country. It not only defined the region by drawing on the region's ability to represent and personify the national character, but the Riversleigh 'country' was itself definitive of local identity, an identity that had taken on world importance through the World Heritage listing of the fossils; as one local expressed it:

> In this area people see Riversleigh as part of our heritage. It is our area but it's something we can share with the world. That we have got maybe a little bit of control over. It's so important, really. Do you recall that *Roots* thing that was on TV a few years back? That Haley's *Roots* thing? And people got so interested in their backgrounds and even a bit of national sort of fervour in places where they go back in a particular area for a long time and being part of a group of people. This Riversleigh area has got a lot of the secrets of the past and we see

the importance of it as being our, maybe our roots, not people from any particular country or anything, but it's in our region. But from there [Riversleigh] there is information for the history of the world and a very important history . . . you get a feeling for the importance of life, some people here then feel an affinity with – uh – their connection to life itself.

(Male, local resident)

This sense of identity linked to ideas of landscape as country elicited very strong emotional responses and experiences, which in turn reinforced the sense of place:

It's quite dramatic, it's very old, makes me feel – it just looks ancient and dramatic and harsh and unforgiving.

(Female, local resident)

If you look at the landscape and you go to Riversleigh and Lawn Hill [Boodjamulla] it's almost a religious experience because you realize that in time you're nothing as this has been here for millions of years and it's going to continue and regenerating . . . it puts in your mind the reality of life and in a million years no one will know you were here, in a thousand years no one will know. So nature's out there, the magnificence and energy of nature, it's experienced . . . you have got the connection with that, with the remains of the animals of that . . . you could almost expect to see the animals still alive – you really could.

(Male, local resident)

In all the observations above about the qualities of the Riversleigh sense of place, the AHD about the heritage and nature of the Australian character is rehearsed, in so far as images of a rugged landscape 'that makes you' are appealed to and invoked, but this is given extra spiritual dimension by appeals to the discourse of country, deep time and spiritual connection with the land – usually a discourse associated with Indigenous Australians. As Lattas (1992) observes, the use of these values and images by white Australians means that the emptiness of the landscape has been made culturally mean-ingful, safe and whole. Here, the colonists, in the form of non-Indigenous Australians, are invoking images of the landscape in which they have also become indigenous. As Arthur (1999) argues, the incorporation of a sense of indigenaity is integral to Euroaustralian imaginings of the Australian land-scape. The consequence of this is that the landscape comes to represent a sense of experience about what it means to be a member of both the Riversleigh–Mout Isa community, and of the Australian nation, that at one hand appropriates the Indigenous sense of place, while naturalizing

Aboriginal experiences as part of a natural landscape. The wider consequences of this are discussed below; however, another element of the sense of place that Riversleigh represents needs to be explored.

Landscape of masculinity

Riversleigh put Australian palaeontology on the world map. The research undertaken at Riversleigh has transformed palaeontological knowledge about the evolution of marsupials in Australia (Archer et al. 1989, 1996; DEST 1993). The previously held view of Australia as an evolutionary backwater of marsupials has been robustly replaced by a view of the continent as 'the world's only isolated natural laboratory for mammal evolution' (DEST 1993: executive summary). The research has revealed a diverse and unique fauna central to a reworking of palaeontological understandings of mammalian evolution. Riversleigh has been constructed as a 'cradle of life' (Creaser 1990), originally a lush, rich and fertile rainforest, which nurtured the evolution of the mammalian taxa, now adapted to Australia's more recent harsh, dry environments (Archer and Hand 1987; Archer et al. 1988, 1989). This argument is embodied by the juxtaposition of the oasis-like Gregory and O'Shannasy Rivers against the arid limestone and basalt plains of Riversleigh (cf. Figures 5.2 and 5.3). However, it is not just scientific knowledge, but the nature of that knowledge that is made material and embodied in the landscape. The hand of science that rocks the 'cradle of life' is personified by the masculinity of the Riversleigh landscape.

The listing of the region on the World Heritage List has placed it among some of the most well-known sites of scientific significance, including the Burgess Shale, Dinosaur Provincial Park, and Messel Pit fossil site. As Kirshenblatt-Gimblett (2004: 57) observes, the listing of places on the World Heritage List places a site or place in a context of other 'outstanding' sites, cementing its universal values in relation to everything else on the list. The listing, undertaken for its scientific natural values, universalizes and legitimizes the palaeontological conceptualizations of the landscape and the values it symbolizes. These values are obvious – for palaeontologists Riversleigh is of immense scientific value. However, it is also significant in a more subtle way, as the Riversleigh fossils have also legitimized the Australian palaeontological disciplinary identity by locating it in a place of world importance. Riversleigh provides not only a sense of place for the universality of scientific values, it provides a sense of place for palaeontologists generally, and more specifically those palaeontologists associated with the region. Palaeontology becomes not just a label for research work that is done, but an identity in which a range of values and meanings are constructed and make sense – all of which tend to be universalized due to the authority vested in science, but which are materially authorized by the listing of Riversleigh as a World Heritage Site.

Scientific sites, discoveries or particular objects or specimens can take on significant prestige within a discipline (Lahn 1996; Smith 1999; Fforde 2002). So much so that they can, and do, become synonymous with the researcher or scientist who discovers them or discovers something important about them. Scientifically important sites, or sites that appeal to popular romantic imagination – sites like Riversleigh – become associated with the careers and both personal and disciplinary identity of individuals. As van deer Meer notes (Smith and van der Meer 2001), Australia in the 1970s was fertile ground for a number of overseas-educated palaeontologists ready to stake a professional claim. Riversleigh has come to be associated with and represent both a successful scientific career, and the reinforcement of the importance and value of palaeontological research in Australia. A large and active vertebrate palaeontology group was established at the University of New South Wales on the basis of the work undertaken at Riversleigh. Numerous PhDs have been written on fossil materials obtained from the region (DEST 1993), and according to van der Meer, a former student at the University, undergraduate students aspire to work there and thus become 'real' palaeontologists (Smith and van der Meer 2001). Many palaeontologists now in post-doctoral positions in Australia or managing other fossils sites throughout the country cut their professional teeth at Riversleigh. Further, van der Meer notes that students also compete with each other for the privilege of undertaking fieldwork and complex political networks have developed over access to the fossils, especially over who gets to work on the fossils regarded as belonging to the 'small furries' versus the more glamorous 'carnivorous nasties'. Indeed, Riversleigh partly defines the Australian palaeontological disciplinary identity. The research practices conducted at Riversleigh have strongly fostered the development of a palaeontological culture at Riversleigh. A study commissioned by the Federal government assessed the impacts of these research practices on Riversleigh's World Heritage status (Luly and Valentine 1998). The continued management of the World Heritage Site for its natural values, specifically its palaeontological values, was recommended by this assessment, which noted that: 'the values for which they are recognised are best conserved by treating them as living research sites, where knowledge can be continuously refined and tested by continued excavation' (Luly and Valentine 1998: 7). This is not to say that continued research at Riversleigh is not important, but rather what has also become regulated and validated by the World Heritage listing, and subsequent management of the region, is not just scientific values, but the disciplinary culture.

The excavation practices employed at Riversleigh can include the use of explosives due to the extreme hardness of the limestone deposits. Of necessity, the excavation practices used at Riversleigh leave behind large craters that are left to dot the fossil fields; however, these craters become material demonstrations of palaeontological presence, control and domination of the landscape. In popular accounts of Riversleigh work, graphic descriptions about the hardness of the limestone are set against the determination and resolve of scientists to penetrate and open the landscape. These images recall wider masculine Australian images about the mastery of the landscape, and are often reproduced in the context of descriptions of how sheer strength is needed to break apart the rock, and of sledgehammers like 'Conan' who help to subdue the landscape, for instance:

> With sweat streaming into my eyes, I belted the boulder yet again with 'Conan' the monster seven-kilo sledge, infamous on Riversleigh expeditions for laying low the macho and muscles of mortals foolish enough to swing this juggernaut more than once. Unfortunately, some of Riversleigh's 20-million-year-old fossil-rich limestones are uncommonly hard and few can be 'opened' with anything less brutal than a sledge.
>
> (Archer 1990: 334)

The macho imagery draws attention to the ruggedness and barrenness of the Riversleigh landscape and the ability of the palaeontologist to tame, subdue, open it and make it fertile and meaningful – it represents the machismo of what it is to 'be' a palaeontologist in Australia. This imagery draws on Australian cultural mythologies of rugged bushmen, individualistic, but bound by mateship. To be a palaeontologist is to be rugged, tough, dedicated and bound to scientific values. This is by no means a new phenomena, feminist philosophers have documented the machismo values and field culture of the physical sciences and noted their utility in the maintenance of disciplinary cultures and values (for example, Harding 1986; Wylie 1992). The same sense of the ability of masculinist values to tame and name the Australian landscape has also been examined in relation to the Australian archaeological disciplinary identity (Clarke 1993; Hope 1993; Moser 1995; Smith 1995). Indeed, the archaeological discipline more widely has been identified as using a popular macho image of itself to help legitimize scientific values within the discipline (Silberman 1995; Zarmati 1995). Indiana Jones, although often reviled by archaeologists (see McBryde 1993), draws on masculine and highly adventurous stereotypes that have a real presence and a long history in the archaeological discipline (Ascher 1960; Zarmati 1995). The association of these types of image with the Riversleigh landscape, and the ability of palaeontologists to stage public performances in the popular media and literature that appeal to these images, enhance both a sense of the adventurousness and masculinity of palaeontology and those associated with the landscape. The image is that you need to be tough to work in the harsh, hot, arid, dangerous and isolated environment of the palaeontologist. The popularity of this image is reflected in the growing number of tourists visiting Mount Isa and Riversleigh to see the fossils. One male tourist operator explained (interviewed 1999) growing tourist interest in the region as a response to the romance and glamour invoked by not only the fossil discoveries, but also by the performances of their discoverers:

> Oh well, I suppose you could say things like the Jurassic Park movies and that where archaeologists and palaeontologists are sort of . . . um . . . you know . . . people think Indiana Jones is a pretty good sort of a fella. On TV the other night they were saying Mike Archer [the senior palaeontologist] was the Indiana Jones of palaeontology. . . . [there is] romance and glamour and all that.

Although a popular image, it is one that gains authority through its very popularity and its appeal to a sense of mystery and romance. Its popularity ensures that disciplinary culture and values exhibited in the field are extended to and accepted within the public domain. Sir David Attenborough encapsulates part of the popularity of this image when he observes:

> Hit a block of rock with a hammer. It splits apart. And there, glinting in the first rays of the sun to shine on it for twenty five million years, protrudes the gem-like tooth of a fossilised creature. You are the first human being ever to see it. Few hearts do not beat faster at that enchanting moment.
>
> (Attenborough 1991, Foreword to Archer et al. 1996: 5)

The privilege of being the first human being to experience these moments is maintained by adherence to a disciplinary culture that becomes synonymous with the place of its doing. The territorial rights to this place are defined by the authority of the meanings that can be invoked about them, which are materially demonstrated in the landscape by the scars left after excavation by sledgehammer and explosives. Other symbolic and material changes to the landscape also help to maintain the palaeontological sense of place. Features in the fossil-bearing landscape have been isolated and named after individual researchers – for instance, there is now Godthelp Hill, Rackham's Roost and Neville's Garden. More imaginative names, such as Camel Sputum, Rat Brain Regurgitation Site and Turtle's in Trouble Site (TITS . . .), also reinforce a sense of place linked explicitly, in these cases, to the experiences and masculinity of the disciplinary culture. The naming rights to fossil sites is awarded to the discoverer of the site, and these names are then published in the scientific literature, and name-plaques are even glued to the limestone in the field. The performance of naming fossil deposits provides a system within which palaeontologists relate to the landscape and to each other. This practice also stakes a claim over the existence of other conceptual systems through which other groups and stakeholders may relate to the landscape.

The palaeontologists also stake a claim over the Riversleigh landscape through their abilities to invoke a sense of mystery that they alone can unlock and reveal. Archer, in particular, has created for himself the role of master storyteller in which science reveals not only the big picture of mammalian evolution in Australia, but also the micro picture of individual fossil 'events'. Archer, in publicly describing and explaining the value and importance of the Riversleigh fossils, is highly skilled in engaging public interest and imagination. For instance, one evocative story, which has been published in a popular nature magazine and is the feature of a large display at the Riversleigh Fossil Centre at Mount Isa, describes the death of a female diprotodontid and the baby she is thought to have carried in her pouch. It is entitled the 'Miocene Madonna and child', and like the 'cradle of life' image, this is a curiously religious reference from a scientist who is often critical about creationism and similar issues (see, for instance, Catalyst 2002, 2005). However, the image does encapsulate a useful sense of pathos and romance. The fossils of both the adult and pouched young were found in deposits that had been a water hole. It is hypothesized that a limestone crust had formed around the edge of the water hole and that the diprotodontid had fallen through this crust in her search for food or water and drowned. Many of the fossilized animals at Riversleigh are thought to have died by walking onto limestone crusts formed around the edge of water courses and then falling through these crusts into the water where they drowned or were killed by crocodiles, their remains then falling to the bottom of the water course to be covered by deposits and fossilized (Archer et al. 1996: 48–9). However, this story of fossilization is poignantly retold using evidence that the mother died with her nose next to her infant:

> A deer-sized diprotodonid . . . cautiously sniffed the air . . . she nibbled the pale tops of several fern fronds before noticing the bright yellow flowers that beckoned from the tangle of root and earth . . . As she stretched her nose towards the bright morsels, she felt a stirring in her pouch. It was her six-month-old pouch-young . . . As she leaned over the water-filled crater towards the orchid, her pouch skin tightened over his warm, milk round body. Suddenly the earth below her forefeet gave way, tipping her headlong into the crater. He heard his mother's sharp cough of alarm. Frightened and confused, he tried to scramble free but her right rear leg had folded up against the pouch entrance. All he could manage to do was force his head out. She dug her short toes into the steep bank trying to halt her descent but the sides of the pit were now a slippery-dip of loose mud. The end came quickly. With one last call of distress, she and her trapped young slid into the cool water below. The last thing she saw was the yellow flame of the treacherous orchid that had lured her to this end. The muscles of her pouch

contracted in a vain effort to seal her infant from death but it was already too late. She forced her nose towards her pouch where she felt the heat of life leaving the face of her young one. There they both stopped, nose to nose, nuzzled together in their last moments, 20 million years ago.

(Archer 1996: 70–1)

The authority of the storyteller is reinforced by the palaeontological identity as masculine master of the rugged outback Australian landscape. This ability helps to cement the public claims of palaeontological 'ownership' of Riversleigh established through the masculine mastery of the landscape. The palaeontologist becomes both guardian and interpreter of the landscape, a role that helps to secure funding for continued research.

The palaeontologists are a highly visible and vocal claimant of the World Heritage Area, and the meanings they construct about the Riversleigh landscape actively contribute to notions of Australian identity. The primordial landscape of Riversleigh, its unique, and often quite bizarre past life forms underline and validate the sense of the uniqueness of the natural landscape that Lattas (1992) identifies as one of the elements central to Australian national identity. Time depth is also given to the national identity, and the identity of the Mount Isa community is seen to move beyond the mining industry for which it had been primarily known prior to the Riversleigh discoveries. Underlying the value and meaning placed on the World Heritage Area lies a palaeontological disciplinary identity which has become both authorized by, and in turn authorizes, the values and discourses of 'Australian heritage'.

The masculinity of the palaeontological image is, of course, one that speaks to both the regional and national sense of identity. Its appeals to masculinity make it nationally palatable in terms of the AHD, and this has had useful consequences for the ability of tourist operators in the region to realize the economic values and benefits of the Riversleigh area. These values are intimately linked to the ability of place to speak to and make sense within the cultural experiences of both locals and visitors to the region from other parts of Australia. How the economic values of heritage are realized is discussed below. However, to understand the wider significance of the masculine image and the masculinity of the experiences engendered by the Riversleigh sense of place, it is important to illustrate local perceptions and values about the masculinity of place – perceptions and values that the palaeontologists both unconsciously draw on and reinforce.

The taming of the Riversleigh landscape by masculine palaeontological types, a taming that leaves behind the visible scars of excavations and other penetrations into the fossil-bearing deposits, calls on the cultural currency of an image very real in a region where a local rural outfitter names itself 'mansworld' (Figure 5.5). One woman in discussing the meaning of the

Figure 5.5 'Mansworld, a Mount Isa rural outfitters selling 'menswear', which includes equipment, clothes, shoes and other necessities of rural travelling, leisure and work life. The landscape of the Mount Isa–Gulf region resonates with the masculinity of the Australian bush hero.

Riversleigh–Gulf area to her and her family explained her sense of place in a manner that both invoked the idea of 'country' and the Australian AHD about the meaning and nature of landscape:

> You feel well when you are there . . . Living in Mount Isa is ok, but you go home [to the Gulf Country] and you get well again. It's particularly strong in the men. Like the men from that country . . . they just exist when they leave there. Alright it's nice to have all the services and things that can be supplied in Mount Isa, but their hearts and their minds are not here [in Mount Isa]. They may be going from day to day whatever, but their hearts and minds are still up in the Gulf.

She then went on to talk about a woman she knew who was 'not from this country', meaning the Riversleigh region, but who had married a man from the region. She reported that her friend told her that her husband:

> 'he just gets so well when he comes back up here'; she didn't understand it, that was just part of him having been a part of that country, it was still in him. To be a Gulf Man is very important to them – the Gulf Men. It's all part of our culture – their culture, because they lived it for so long.

In this discussion, the AHD about the heritage and nature of the Australian character is again rehearsed, but given an extra spiritual dimension by

184

appeals to the discourse of country. The masculinity of the bushman is given temporal depth and spirituality through the discourse of 'country' and the masculine culture is made 'indigenous'.

Landscape as theatre: The Riversleigh performance

The sense of place that is 'Riversleigh' is a cultural experience that speaks to and invokes a range of values and meanings. As one male tourist operator noted: 'Riversleigh is not only the actual fossils – it's the whole environment, the impact of the O'Shannassy and Gregory Rivers . . . the whole combination . . . it's a spectacular place . . . well to me it has an addiction, I just crave to go back there.' Another tourist operator reported that tourists consistently feel amazement and awe at Riversleigh, not just because of the fossils, but also because of the landscape itself. The experience that is Riversleigh is one that is marketable as a tourist resource because of its ability to speak to Australian cultural narratives, rather than any intrinsic value to natural history. It is eminently marketable as a heritage experience because of its ability as a place to perform and experience the meanings of authorized cultural narratives.

The major industry in Mount Isa has been the mining of copper, lead, silver and zinc; however, as the mining industry begins to employ less and less people local government has actively encouraged the development of tourism. The tourist industry has developed around the annual rodeo, tours of the Mount Isa mines and the attraction of watching the evening slag pour. However, the fossil discoveries and the listing of Riversleigh on the World Heritage List is viewed by many in local government and the tourism industry as offering a significant opportunity for tourism development:

> You see the tourist numbers growing up here [in Mount Isa] because the promotion that is done . . . [a number of tourist resources have been built] to encourage tourism to the fossil fields and as a viable industry for the northwest. You know the mining industry is employing less and less people these days due to technological changes in production . . . they are using more robotics, more mechanised processing. The city fathers, so to speak, are wanting to preserve the city and hopefully see it grow, but it is going to have to be without mining, the thing that is going to keep Mount Isa going is tourism.

> (Male tourist operator, 1999)

Both local government officials and several tourist operators stated that 'Riversleigh could become to Mount Isa something like Ayres Rock [Uluru] is to Alice Springs' (see also *North Western Star* (NWS) 1993a, 1994a, 1994b). The local Mount Isa newspaper, *North Western Star*, has been active in promoting Mount Isa, as the 'port for Riversleigh' (NWS 1994b: 1) and has consistently argued that the region must capitalize on the romance and mystique of the fossils (see also NWS 1993b, 1993c, 1994c, 1995, 1996, 1997). One of the issues presented by the fossils, however, is that they are hard to see – conspicuous sites like that Illustrated in Figure 5.4 are rare as most fossils are only visible as small bits of unarticulated bone fragments. As tourist operators note, people need to be guided on fossil tours so that they not only see them, but also do not souvenir them or otherwise damage them or the surrounding landscape. The need to guide visitors to the fossil sites dovetails nicely with the desire for operators and local government to foster and control tourist spending. However, it is not simply the fossils that tourists are interested in seeing. A survey of tourists taken at both the Riversleigh Fossil Centre in Mount Isa and out at the 'D site', the one fossil locality easily accessible to visitors, revealed that many domestic tourists or visitors to the region were undertaking a leisure activity that was also about 'getting in touch', as several respondents noted, with the Australian bush. The majority of domestic visitors were unaware that Riversleigh was a World Heritage Site, and were travelling through the region to experience, at some level, what it was to be 'Australian', while others characterized travelling through the Riversleigh landscape as being about 'seeing real Australia'.

The majority of tourists saw the Riversleigh landscape, its desert plains, mesas and rivers, as epitomizing Australian identity and history and their presence in the landscape was affirmation of their own personal and national identity. The fossils did specifically attract the people surveyed to the region, but for many their presence, even as hard to see tiny bones, was further evidence of the antiquity of the Australian landscape and the uniqueness of the continent's flora and fauna. The fossils were important as focal points, points of connection to an ancient landscape full of bizarre and unique animals, but a landscape that is part of Australian identity and often invoked a sense of national pride in many visitors; as one visitor noted:

> Riversleigh is our Australian history; it shows the world that we are not a young country, that we have history, something to be proud of. You go to places like Egypt, Greece, England and such and they have old histories like the pyramids, Parthenon and Stonehenge and stuff, but what we have is much older, more important. We can show the rest of the world that we are Australian.

In this response, 'natural' and cultural history are conflated. However, this is the point of the performance of being in the Riversleigh landscape. It is about embracing or appropriating the 'natural' as part of the 'cultural' through experiencing the rugged machismo of landscape, the contrasts between the plains and the rivers, and understanding the deep age of the landscape which gives temporal depth to identities drawn from and

186

experienced in the landscape. It is about touching or seeing fossils that represent the uniqueness of the Australian fauna, the carnivalesque nature of some of their names – thingodonta and weirdodonta – that speaks to the larrikin[4] spirit of Australian identity and culture.

While many of the tourists passing through Riversleigh are participating in a performance that allows them to create experiences and memories to remind themselves of what it means to be Australian, others in the Riversleigh landscape undertake similar performances. The annual performance of the palaeontological field season may also be viewed as an event that recreates both a sense of disciplinary identity, but more importantly places the palaeontologists as players in the landscape. The ability to place oneself in the landscape, and to demonstrate control over your place in that landscape, is an important statement of authority. The ability to control the experiences an individual or collective has in the landscape becomes important for claims to identity, but also claims to the resources the landscape represents. Although many of the identities constructed at and by the Riversleigh sense of place and its performance are often framed within the AHD – they nonetheless come into conflict with each other. Consequently, one of the key performances undertaken in and against the backdrop of the Riversleigh landscape are those of dissonance, wherein the authority of certain constructions of identity and experience are negotiated and legitimized, or conversely delegitimized.

Landscape of dissonance

It is important to note that the various ways in which Riversleigh is understood, conceptualized and used as a place are used to underpin the identities of a range of interest groups and collectives, all of whom have a stake in the management of the World Heritage Area. All these groups feel very passionately about Riversleigh, and while many come into conflict with each other, the arena of conflict is entirely mutable, with various groups aligning and realigning. At the heart of the conflict over the meanings and value of Riversleigh is the issue of who should control those meanings – who should have most say in the management of the World Heritage Area. How the landscape is managed, and thus understood, becomes significant not only in legitimizing the sense of place and identity a particular group draws from the landscape, but also more pragmatically in terms of who will most benefit from access to the resources the landscape represents. How the landscape is valued and defined will privilege how it is conceived as a resource, and this in turn will feed back to legitimize – or not – the various cultural and social values linked to sense of place. For palaeontologists the resource the landscape represents centres on the fossils; for local government and tourist operators it is the economic resource the fossils and wider landscape represent as a tourist destination; for Waanyi it is linked to claims to land and sovereignty;

for local pastoralists it is linked to claims to land and livelihood; and for other locals and for tourists and visitors to the region it is about access to a leisure resource which has both recreational and cultural meaning. Each of these groups constructs a sense of place from the landscape that sustains their sense of identity, which in turn legitimizes the understanding of the landscape as a particular resource that can be used in particular ways.

Some members of the Waanyi community view the listing of the Riversleigh World Heritage Area as an appropriation by palaeontologists and land managers of what is part of Waanyi cultural heritage, and have reported that they are concerned that adequate consultations and negotiations about the use of their land and cultural heritage have not been undertaken. They are concerned that palaeontologists and their methods of excavation are not sensitive to the landscape, and that their understanding of the past and the meanings it has are not being adequately considered (see also Smith and van der Meer 2001; Smith et al. 2003a, 2003b). The request, by some members of the Waanyi community, to have fossils returned to Waanyi country after completion of study is borne out of both a conceptualization of the landscape that sees their removal as culturally problematic, but also the importance of symbolic politics of recognition. As Nancy Fraser argues, struggles for recognition of cultural identity and other forms of identity politics can have material consequences in facilitating the redistribution of power and wealth (2000: 2). The return of fossils to the Waanyi community, the ability of the Waanyi to be adequately consulted, and the recognition of their rights to make binding management decisions over the region, are all important elements in their struggle for political and cultural legitimacy in post-colonial Australia. Any return of the fossils to the region under the custodianship of the Waanyi would be a material and symbolically important acknowledgement of Waanyi sovereignty, and the legitimacy of cultural identity claims. This in turn would have flow-on effects in wider regional political arenas and negotiations concerning the allocation of a range of economic and other resources. It is subsequently highly important that Waanyi assert their cultural identity, and have it legitimized through their recognition as an active player in the management and care of the Riversleigh area.

For palaeontologists, however, the idea that fossils should be 'returned' is difficult to conceptualize. For the fossils to be stored or displayed in any keeping place not under direct or indirect control of palaeontologists would be a symbolic act that recognizes the cultural values of the fossils. This would undermine the legitimacy of palaeontological claims to what they understand as a natural phenomenon. Its 'naturalness' is a value that is highly prized and important in underpinning disciplinary identity and the authority of scientific knowledge. However, for Waanyi, the ability to publicly claim custodianship of fossils and then have that claim publicly accepted through a symbolic return of fossil material would be a tacit recognition of the cultural values that a piece of a 'natural landscape' has. This process subsequently becomes symbolically important in challenging the AHDs naturalization of Waanyi, as Aboriginal Australians, in the Australian landscape. This naturalization is important to challenge as it tends to either render Aboriginal people invisible in national narratives of meaning making, or renders their cultural knowledge able to be appropriated by non-Indigenous attempts to make their own sense of identity 'indigenous'. Either way, the consequence of their naturalization is to make Indigenous Australians culturally and politically 'safe', so that their presence in the wider Australian landscape does not trouble the post-colonial national conscience.

Another issue for the palaeontologists is the Waanyi claims that they had knowledge of the fossils prior to the palaeontological arrival in the region. This challenges the palaeontological claims to have 'discovered' the fossils and all the attendant kudos that goes with the ability to claim the identity of 'the discoverer'. It also challenges the claims of palaeontologists to be the master storytellers for the region, and ultimately their sense of 'ownership' of the fossils and the Riversleigh landscape.

The naturalization of identity within landscape, however, is a process that appears to have been actively used by another interest in the Riversleigh region. The name Riversleigh derives from the leasehold pastoral station on which much of the World Heritage Area now stands. In the creation of the World Heritage Area, and in extending Boodjamulla National Park, some pastoral lands were excised. The pastoralists in the area tend to run cattle, and do not own their land or 'stations' freehold, but rather lease them from the state or, more often, manage the leasehold for larger pastoral corporations who 'own' the actual lease. Many local pastoralists viewed the excising of land from Riversleigh station as a symbolic act that rendered illegitimate their cultural or historical connection to the region. The economic implications of loss of land and thus loss of, or curtailing of, livelihoods are of great concern to both local pastoralists and those from adjoining areas. However, their concerns were often forcefully expressed in terms of what this act meant to their sense of place, and the impact that it would have on what they called their 'pastoral culture'. Some of the local pastoralists are descendants of the Europeans that first extended the colonial frontier into the Mount Isa–Riversleigh region in the 1870s (Slack 1998), and the World Heritage Area and Boodjamulla National Park is littered with the material evidence of their history. As one pastoralist noted, 'local people feel a sense of intrusion that the place has been taken away from them by it being turned into World Heritage' (interview 1999). This sense of intrusion in part results from increasing tourist numbers to the region, and some pastoralists complain that their lifestyles have been 'put on show' for the tourists. Tourists are also seen as representing a nuisance factor, especially when they come unprepared for the local, very extreme driving conditions, and have to be towed out of bogs or across fords, or asked to leave lands to which they do not have access, or are seen to strip the region of firewood and leave litter behind. In part, the World Heritage listing has meant the pastoralists and other locals have to share the region on a scale they have not had to do previously and this has had an adverse impact on their sense of privilege and their lifestyles. However, the alienation that was expressed was also about the lack of legitimacy given to their sense of place and associated sense of identity as pastoralists. As another pastoralist noted:

> The landscape is our heritage. It needs to be managed properly. The tourists and tour operators shouldn't go there as they don't look after it.

Underlying this tension with the tourists is competition over resources and fear of loss of control of the landscape as an economic resource. As one pastoralist expressed it, the world heritage listing meant 'locking up the land for another group'. However, assertion of rights to have a stake in the management of the landscape was often expressed in terms of cultural heritage, particularly in terms of the abilities of pastoralists to look after the land because they had a special cultural affinity with it. Repeated again and again in interviews, and in meetings I attended about management issues of the region, pastoralists asserted that as 'people who lived on the land' they had a special connection and understanding of it, and that the land had made them who they were – it was part of their culture and it was their 'country'. At risk of alienation by the World Heritage listing, and the subsequent loss of land and the influx of tourists, was also the legitimacy of the pastoral claims to a special place in the Australian pioneer and bushman legends. In talking to pastoralists about Riversleigh, it became apparent that pastoralists were expressing their cultural affinity with the region in terms of standard Australian bush mythologies, but also remaking and reasserting that mythology in response to the deprivileging of pastoral landscape values when the region became managed for its palaeontological rather than pastoral values. This remaking particularly hinged on allusions to the World Heritage Area as pastoral 'country', and thus the appeals to the indigenaity of pastoral culture gave greater temporal depth to their appeals to the bushman narratives.

In this sense of place, the pastoral way of life – the 'pastoral culture' – becomes part of the landscape and as such an aspect of the landscape which must also be preserved and managed – alongside other indigenous forms of identity. As one pastoralist noted, one of the 'major management issues is managed preservation of the landscape, but also the [pastoral] culture that goes with it'. The pastoral identity becomes synonymous with the landscape, and is legitimized by appeals to wider Australian cultural mythologies, and by its naturalization in the landscape itself. By embedding identity in the landscape it becomes part of the natural values of the region – part of the values to be, hopefully, protected and nurtured. Here, pastoralists are placing themselves in the naturalized position often occupied by Indigenous Australians. The pastoralists in this situation feel themselves to have been disempowered by the management decisions over the World Heritage listing, despite the fact that they are usually an interest that is vested with political legitimacy and power in wider Australian social and political negotiations and debates. Here, the AHD is used to make an appeal to the legitimacy of pastoral identity, aspirations and rights to resources. However, it has not been successful in giving primacy to pastoral values, and thus the AHD has been extended in this case by the appropriation of Indigenous conceptualizations and discourse. This use of a subaltern discourse in conjunction with the AHD is part of shifting perceptions in some sectors of rural Australia of where cultural and political legitimacy, and thus political power, are seen to occur.

During the 1990s, pastoralists across Australia began to perceive a new political legitimacy given to Aboriginal discourses and cultural claims in the wake of the 'Mabo decision' discussed above, but more particularly, in the wake of the 'Wik decision'. In 1996, the High Court in *Wik* v. *State of Queensland* acknowledged that Native Title could exist over pastoral leasehold lands. Although the Wik decision resulted in major amendments during 1998 to the Native Title Act that extensively eroded the power of Indigenous Australians to assert the rights granted by Native Title over these lands – a very strong fear and perception of the power of Aboriginal cultural claims remains in rural Australia. While the Mabo decision was a significant turning point in Aboriginal politics in Australia, the Native Title Act and the amendments that have been made to it by the Conservative Howard Government means that the jury is still out on how much this Act has really legitimated or otherwise privileged Aboriginal discourses and aspirations. Nonetheless, the strong *perception* in Australian pastoral communities is that Aboriginal cultural claims, especially to land, do carry authority, or at least have the potential to do so. The adoption of appeals to 'country' in the AHD of pastoralists and other locals residents in the Mount Isa–Riversleigh region marks the shifting nature of the AHD as it responds to, and becomes part of, wider cultural and political negotiations over resources.

Conclusion

This chapter has illustrated three things. Firstly, it again demonstrates how the AHD works to underpin and validate national narratives. However, different groups can put these narratives, and the AHD within which they are expressed, to use in different ways. This may be an obvious point; however, it illustrates that dissonance does not simply occur in opposition to the AHD, and that dissonance does occur within the discursive field marked out by the AHD. Dissonance, then, must be understood as integral to all expressions of 'heritage', as heritage in expressing identity is inherently an expression of not only who you are but also who others are not, and this will always provoke opposition and, at times, confrontational exchanges between groups even though they may share similar meanings and values created by a shared AHD.

Secondly, the chapter reveals that the AHD is mutable. It illustrates that concepts of heritage may be and are deployed in flexible ways that are designed, however unconsciously, to help legitimize special claims to resources. In short, heritage is part of the political discourses and strategies deployed by different groups and interests to help them legitimize and assert cultural, social and economic aspirations. What it reveals is that claims to heritage are never non-political as they are tied to claims to and expressions of power. This power may rest on a group's or interest's ability – or inability – to appeal to or claim a special place in authorized cultural narratives. The ability to demonstrate the legitimacy of a group's identity and experiences within the context of an authorized narrative will often carry substantial gravitas and cultural capital. However, cultural and political negotiations of this sort always result in changes to the sources of power that interests and groups call upon, and this in turn will see shifts and changes in the AHD. The AHD is, in effect, part of the resources of power that groups can and do call upon in political, cultural and social negotiations over, in this case access to land, but ultimately a range of material resources.

The third point to emphasize is that this chapter also illustrates the consequences for subaltern groups of the existence of the AHD and of their placement outside of it. The AHD as a source of political power has the ability to facilitate the marginalization of groups who cannot make successful appeals to or control the expression of master cultural or social narratives. Heritage items, whether they are landscapes, fossils or other items or places, become important objects in the symbolism of identity politics. The ability to challenge marginalization and assert the legitimacy of both identity and associated material aspirations will in part rest on the ability of a group to assert the legitimacy of the value and meaning of their heritage. This can be very problematic for those groups whose understanding of what actually constitutes heritage, let alone what that heritage may mean, is very different to the AHD. The next section of this book explores this last point, and examines how heritage is both used to contest received ideas of national narratives (Chapters 6 and 8) and how different conceptualizations of what constitutes 'heritage' (Chapters 7 and 8) are used to contest and subvert the power of the AHD.

Part III

RESPONSES TO AUTHORIZED HERITAGE

6

LABOUR HERITAGE
Performing and remembering

Within the heritage industry critique, heritage and tradition emerged as commodities that could be packaged and sold to largely uncritical mass audiences (Strangleman 1999: 741). While the elite house museum was criticized in this literature, it was also concerned with concurrent radical changes occurring in curatorial attitudes within museums, and the burgeoning numbers of museums themselves. During the 1960s and 1970s, the idea of 'museums' changed radically, and the 'new museology' challenged the traditional ideas of curatorial expertise and objectivity, and occasioned the usual intellectual angst and insecurities these challenges inevitably give rise to. The museum industry expanded, the range of different types of museums grew, and the numbers of museums overall (in particular ecomuseums) and heritage centres catering to specific regions or historical or cultural themes and/or periods dramatically increased. The ways in which exhibitions were presented and interpreted also changed radically in this period. Technological innovations facilitated the new desire for more interactive audience participation, which was being fostered by changing curatorial agendas, and a wider range of interpretive strategies were introduced (Knell 2003). These included the use of costumed interpreters and demonstrators, actors and other dramatists, whilst community outreach and other innovative community education policies developed and expanded. Although many of these changes were, and continue to be, viewed positively within sectors of the museum literature, the advent of the new museology, together with the rapid expansion of museum types, and thus audience numbers, drew sustained criticism – if not a backlash. This critique viewed such developments as 'inauthentic', catering to a synthetic and sanitized view of the past designed simply to generate tourist revenue through, at best 'infotainment', and, at worst, 'Disneyfication'. While this may not have been a new issue in museums, it was a critique that came to be specifically directed at attempts to incorporate diversity of viewpoints and other innovations into museum practice.

As with the country house literature, there is not a long tradition of asking what visitors 'do' at museums in terms of identity and other cultural work.

Merriman's extensive survey of museum users in the late 1980s identified the middle class profile of traditional museum visitors, and shows that what he identifies as 'lower status' individuals were far more interested in local or family histories – the sort of social history favoured at ecomuseums and social history museums (1991). While a substantive tourism literature exists that analyses visitors to non-traditional museum types, including social history museums, it tends to focus on visitor motivation, often only in terms of marketing issues, and little qualitative work has been done in this area (see, for instance, Prentice 1996, 1998, 2001; Kawashima 1999; McIntosh and Prentice 1999; Light 2000). What this literature does reveal, however, along with the work of Longhurst et al. (2004) and Bagnall (2003) and others discussed in Chapter 2, is that visitors are often much more 'mindful' and critical than much of the museum literature and the heritage industry critique usually allows. A range of authors have identified the need for deeper analyses of museum visitors to identify not only motivations, but the cultural and social work and meaning that such visits have for them (see, for instance, Prentice 1996, 1998, 2005; Cameron and Gatewood 2000; Macdonald and Shaw 2004; Newman and McLean 2004; Newman 2005a).

This chapter analyses the results of an in-depth qualitative questionnaire survey of 273 visitors to three industrial era social history museums during the summer and autumn of 2004. The museums at which surveys were undertaken were the National Coal Mining Museum in Wakefield (NCMM), West Yorkshire, the Tolpuddle Martyrs Museum in Dorset, and the colliery village exhibit within the North of England Open Air Museum, Beamish, Co. Durham. The questionnaire used was identical to that used in the country house survey reported in Chapter 4 – although minor terminological changes were made where necessary, the substantive content of the two questionnaires was the same. These museums, and the colliery exhibit at Beamish, deal directly or indirectly with working class social history, and it is interesting to note that Beamish in particular came under specific criticism within the heritage industry critique for offering a sanitized and inauthentic view of the past. The growth in labour history museums has also been described as a 'sop' to deindustrialization, in that the advent of these museums is seen as a process designed to sooth social distress at the loss of industry, and to offer minimal employment for local community members as a form of economic 'compensation'. Both the NCMM and Beamish offer employment to locals as interpreters/demonstrators, with both the NCMM and Beamish employing ex-coal miners to take visitors on a guided underground tour of an ex-coal mine. However, what the survey reveals is that the criticism that museums like these offer sanitized titillation or are sops to deindustrialization cannot be sustained. Rather, visitors critically and actively utilize these places as cultural and social tools in remembering and memory making that underwrite a self-conscious sense of class and regional identity.

Museums and heritage

To understand the critical tensions over the existence and nature of social history museums it is useful to briefly review the history of museums generally. The development of museums from 'the cabinets of the world' and 'cabinets of curiosity' has a long history (Hopper-Greenhill 1991; Pearce 1992); however, it was not until the nineteenth century that museums as public, rather than private, institutions were founded. The development of the public museum is attributable, as Walsh (1992) observes, to a number of interrelated factors. In particular, the modernist idea of progress and scientific rationality are identified as integral to the ideological context of their development (Walsh 1992: 22). As Hollinshead notes (1997: 174), the traditional assumption about museums is that they present the 'truth'. For Walsh, museums emerged as sites within which Enlightenment ideas of rationality, progress and linear time found expression and form, the industrial revolution and urbanization both reinforced by and reinforcing modernity, while museums became locales in which these changes could be explained and made emotionally stable and understandable. Also integral to the development of museums was a liberal sense of pastoral care that the emergent historical disciplines and Victorian society as a whole identified as important in fostering national pride and social order. Bennett (1995) emphasizes this role for museums, and the degree to which they participated in the governance and regulation of the social order, personal conduct, moral improvement and national identity in a period of increasing urbanization and social change (see also Hall 1999: 4). Walsh, however, notes that while museums did and still do play such regulatory roles, they also continue to fulfil a more emancipatory role through the insights and opportunities they can offer for visitors to contextualize their own experiences historically and culturally, and to engage with and understand the experiences and views of others (1992: 38). Thus, he views museums as important elements in the maintenances of a sense of place and identity.

Nationalism is of particular importance to the sense of identity traditionally invoked by museums. Museums in the nineteenth century also developed in the context of tensions over nation-state formation, and became inextricably bound with the expression of national identity – as 'national museums' formed to help define and express what it meant to be a citizen of a particular nation (Pearce 1992; Bennett 1995; Macdonald 2003). As Hodgkin and Radstone (2003b: 12–13) state, 'memorials and museums represent public statements about what the past has been, and how the present should acknowledge it; who should be remembered, who should be forgotten; which acts or events are foundational, which marginal'. However, museums also have a role in defining 'who' should do the remembering and forgetting. Surveys of museums, and heritage site use in a number of countries, have tended to reinforce the dominant idea that the traditional museum audience draws from the well-educated middle classes (Merriman 1991; Falk and Dierking 1992; Kawashima 1999; Malcolm-Davies 2004). In terms of the arguments developed by Wertsch (2002) and outlined in Chapter 2, museums and galleries may be historically understood as cultural tools of the comfortably educated to help them remember and define their sense of social and geographic place. As Macdonald (2003: 3–5) observes, museum visiting is a performance that helps to identify and enculturate the performer. The artefacts on display give material form to the past and anchor authorized and official collective memory (Davison 2005: 186).

Bourdieu's idea of 'cultural capital' has been a dominant framework for understanding visitor motivation in the critical museums literature. The ability to 'read' the cultural messages, and thus both acquire and exhibit cultural capital is crucial in demonstrating cultural middle and upper middle class identity (see, for instance, Merriman 1989, 1991; Pearce 1992; Walsh 1992; Mason 2004). However, some in the heritage museums litera-ture have identified the idea of cultural capital as too narrowly defined, and suggest that it may prevent understanding the degree to which museums may facilitate or play a role in the expression of non-authorized identities (Longhurst et al. 2004: 121; Pendlebury et al. 2004). Newman (2005b), for instance, argues that a range of other types of 'capital' are acquired and expressed at museums that may not solely be about the expression of class identity. The point to note here, however, is that critical analyses of museum audiences, and what it is people actually do in terms of cultural and social work at museums, is not well developed or extensive. The traditional view of museum visitors is one that owes its legacy to the nineteenth-century incep-tion of public museums, and the 'duty of care' ethos that became embedded within museology at this time, which emphasizes the educational role that museums are assumed to play. One of the dominant views about museums is that they are, by their nature, educational, and that as such the average visitor is a passive receptor of the message or lesson the museum is offering (Malcom-Davies 2004). The assumption of the passivity of museum visitors is being challenged in the museums literature, but the dominance of this perception has tended to retard critical examination of how and why visitors participate and inter-relate with exhibitions and the museum experience overall (Mason 2005).

The advent of the 'new museology', as marked by Vergo's (1989) edited collection of the same name, has been facilitated by and grown out of changes in traditional museum practices and agendas and by developments in new social history agendas (Handler and Gable 1997). Certainly, greater audience awareness and reflexivity has been facilitated by what Ross (2004: 84) notes as the attempted move by curators to adopt, in Bauman's (1987) meanings of the terms, a more interpretive rather than legislative role in their work. However, this development has not been entirely organic, as interviews with museum professionals undertaken by Ross reveal that the wider political and economic shifts that have thrust museums into the marketplace have been the principal element in facilitating these changes (2004: 100). As noted earlier there has, since the 1970s, been a major expansion in museum numbers, with the growth of ecomuseums or open air museums concerned with holistic representations of regional history and culture, social history museums, folk museums, heritage centres and so forth that have challenged traditional ideas of state-sanctioned and national museums. With this expansion has come a greater range of interpretive techniques and methods, in particular the use of costumed interpreters and demonstrators. Many, both within and outside of the museum profession, saw the increase in heritage tourism during the 1970s, and the increasing diversity of museums and interpretive methods that arose in part as a response to this, as a negative issue, expressed in their fear that museums were becoming simply vehicles of entertainment and spectacle. However, the developments in museums can also be viewed in the context of wider social and global processes. Certainly, increasing concern with the local is a well-understood response to globalization (Escobar 2001), while the development of social history museums must be seen as inter-related with the development of social and public history programmes and concerns (Handler and Gable 1997; Davis 1999; Crang 2001; Macdonald 1997). As Poria et al. (2001, 2003) also note, many people participating in heritage tourism are not simply indulging in entertainment, but are visiting heritage sites and museums because they perceive the sites visited as part of their heritage. Consequently, the visit must be understood to be more meaningful than simple recreational entertainment.

As demonstrated in relation to country houses in Chapter 4, social and cultural identity work does occur even though the ostensible or only conscious reason for the visit was recreational. Nonetheless, the changes that accompanied the 'new museology' challenged the traditional authority and expertise of museum curators and the disciplines, such as history, anthropology and archaeology, whose knowledge both guides and is given material form and authority within traditional museum displays. This challenge, and the insecurities it creates, has tended to sustain certain tensions over the use, in particular, of costumed interpreters and the nature of labour/social history museums. The use of costumed interpreters, the instigation of rides at the Jorvik centre at York, and other interpretive and technical changes were considered by some as devaluing the educational role of museums by inserting elements of entertainment (Schadla-Hall 1984; Hewison 1987). Although the use of entertaining and emotionally engaging interpretive methodologies does not necessarily reduce the educative role of museums, and in many ways can actively enhance it (Uzzell and Ballintine 1998; Hjemdahl 2002; Malcolm-Davies 2004), these developments may be viewed as broadening the types of 'cultural capital' visitors were required to draw upon. The advent of social history museums broadened the museum-going audience, and again drew on and addressed a different range of experiences than those of traditional museum goers.

The North of England Open Air Museum, Beamish, opened its first displays in 1971, and was one of the early pioneers in the use of costumed interpretation in Britain. This museum, located in Northumbria, identifies its mission as providing social and industrial history of direct relevance and resonance to the local North-East region of England. As with other open air museums of its type, it consists of a collection of in situ and reassembled buildings, including Pockerley Manor house, railway/waggonway, home farm, town, railway station, and a colliery village reconstructed around an extant drift mine. The site covers over 300 acres, and each element or display is separated by green fields and connected by tramlines or period buses. Each display is designed to represent an aspect of North-East social history at a particular time, and is not meant to be read as a complete representation of North-Eastern history and heritage. Most of the exhibits are set within the year 1913, when the North-East Region of England was at its industrial and economic height, although the manor house and railway/waggonway depict the period between 1815 and 1825 (Cruddas et al. 2004). The colliery village exhibit, at which the questionnaire was administered and directed, includes the drift mine, pithead and winding gear (unrelated to the drift mine), row of miners' houses and outbuildings, Methodist chapel and school.

The museum, often characterized negatively as a 'theme park' in the critical literature, has minimal interpretive panels, and uses costumed demonstrators to engage with and discuss elements of the exhibits with visitors. The policy at Beamish is to employ local people as social history demonstrators, who, unlike at sites such as Colonial Williamsburg, are actively discouraged from playacting or pretending to be people from the periods represented. The demonstrators are provided with historical information supplied by the museum, and are also encouraged to undertake their own research into the exhibitions with which they work. Rhiannon Hiles, Assistant Keeper of Interpretations (interviewed October 3 2004), noted that many demonstrators bring their own interests and insights on local history to their work. They are discouraged from inserting their own personal experiences or political opinions of either the past or the present into their interpretations, and are required to talk in the third and not the first person. While the inclusion of personal opinion and judgements can never really be excised from interpretations, Hiles does note that Beamish staff are 'well aware that we are presenting *a view*' of the past. She stated that demonstrators are encouraged to make visitors aware that interpretations are presented 'in terms of this is our view [and] to the best of our knowledge how it *may* have looked and been' (interview 2004). In the 1980s and 1990s, Beamish had been heavily criticized for sanitizing the past, belittled as a form of entertainment, for privileging 'things' for their own sake and depoliticizing history. Hewison (1987: 95), for instance, notes that 'there is no need for personal nostalgia' at

Beamish as 'the displays do it for you'. Walsh notes that the absence of interpretive signage means that visitors are left to simply admire the object for itself (1992: 98). While the cult of object is not a new phenomenon in museums, the demonstrators do offer information about objects on display, and during the survey undertaken for this chapter were noted on a number of occasions engaging in detailed and quite complex two-way discussions with visitors. In these discussions not only were debates about the meaning of artefacts had, but also the processes of interpretation itself were often discussed and explored – a process dialogically more open than traditional museum displays.

Bennett (1988: 73–4) is concerned that popular memory is restyled and rewritten at Beamish to create a sentimentalized past where class, organized labour and gender issues are depoliticized or obscured. Indeed, he argues that the lack of conflict depicted between exhibits such as the colliery village and the manor house exhibit must result in a message that sees the industrial development of the North-East as 'a process that is essentially continuous with the deeper and longer history of a countryside in which the power of the bourgeoisie has become naturalized' (1988: 69). Walsh, too, is concerned that the museum relies heavily on the 'promotion of selective memory or nostalgia' (1992: 98). While he notes that this is not necessarily problematic if those doing the remembering have first-hand memories of the period, and thus the ability to critically contextualize what they are seeing, he is concerned about the 'second-hand' nostalgia of the children and grandchildren whose memories of this period have been simply passed on, and thus may become de-contextualized and depoliticized nostalgia. In some ways, this concern invokes the anxieties around Nora's argument that modern memory is all archival (1989: 13), and modernity's concern is with 'eyewitness' accounts to document and legitimize the authenticity of memory and meaning.

This concern over the eyewitness may not adequately understand the way collective memory actually works and is transmitted; for example, as Ashton (2005) observed, many in Australia thought that the national memorial celebrations that occurred as ANZAC Day would lose meaning with the death in 2002 of the last Australian ANZAC soldier to fight at Gallipoli. Instead, these meanings have multiplied, for some they remain unchanged and for others new meanings have developed, reinforcing Mason's (2005) observations, that participants in performances of memorializing and commemorating will draw on their own experiences to interpret the values and meanings of collective memory and remembering. However, the idea that museums of this type generate uncritical nostalgia of the 'it was better back then' kind is a dominant critique, and makes a range of assumptions about what it is audiences 'do' or do not 'do' at these sites. Certainly, the idea that Beamish and similar open air museums are artificial places or 'constructed time capsules' that 'represent a form of historical bricolage, a melting pot for historical memories' (Walsh 1992: 103) are criticisms that may be levelled at any museum. Beamish offers – as does any museum – a particular view of the past. Artefacts and whole buildings are presented as pristinely nestled within the rural idyll of green fields – recapturing both a sense that England's heritage must be signified by rolling green acres, as typified by the country house and English Heritage maintained ruins (see Chapter 4) – but also a traditional museum 'glass case' view of artefact display. In summary, Beamish represents a particular genre of museums, much like national museums or country houses represent their own particular genre. The incomplete story that Beamish offers may, as both Bennett (1988) and Walsh (1992) warn, lead to uncritical second-hand nostalgia, or alternatively its incompleteness may, as Brower (1999: 94) suggests in the context of another, similar museum, present the opportunity for critical memory work. What memory work visitors actually do at Beamish can only, however, really be explored through asking visitors themselves about the meaning and value of their visit – see discussion below.

The depiction of social history, and in particular industrial issues, has its own particular tensions within the heritage and museums literature. Early attempts at preserving and interpreting industrial sites have been criticized for the tendency to present these sites and their histories for either their technological and economic achievements, or as monuments to the barons of industry that owned them (see, for instance, Spearritt 1991; Johnston 1993; Stratton and Trinder 2000; Oliver and Reeves 2003; Debary 2004). Although there is a longer tradition of concern with displaying social history, and in particular working class history in the United States, in Britain there has been less institutional attention paid to the artefacts from working class movements (Mansfield 2004; Pickering 2004: 103; similar criticisms have also been made in the Australian context – see Oliver and Reeves 2003). Barthel (1996: 125) argues that this tendency is due to the historical influence of British elites in the heritage management processes, and that organizations such as English Heritage and the National Trust serve largely national interests. Moreover, any critical interpretations of industrial history that include a consideration of its social costs 'run counter to the ideology of many political and economic interests involved in preservation' and conservation (Barthel 1996: 69). Although elites have also dominated preservation history in the United States there is, she suggests, more awareness of cultural pluralism in a country where there is stronger grassroots participation in heritage issues than in the UK. This participation, she argues, ensures that a greater diversity of heritage and history is identified and interpreted (1996: 6f., 125). Certainly, there is far more consideration of cultural pluralism and ethnic diversity in the post-colonial nations of North America and Australasia, while Britain has been identified as still struggling with issues of multiculturalism (Hall 1999; Ling Wong 1999, 2000; Deckha 2004: 419; Littler and Naidoo 2004).

Whatever the case, there are significant tensions within the heritage literature framed by the AHD, as well as in the heritage industry critique, about the depiction of non-authorized history and heritage that explores the diversity of experiences based on gender, ethnicity, class, disability and sexuality. Tensions over the depiction of working class life and labour movements are relevant to this chapter. A characteristic assumption of many heritage professionals is that the traumatic, the socially uncomfortable or the otherwise problematic does not make popular heritage or grist for the museum mill. Barthel (1996: 68–9) herself makes this assumption when she observes that industrial sites are too confronting to interpret as 'layers of dirt and grime violate tourist expectations'. This assumption, although not adequately tested in the heritage and museums literature, is one that tends to dominate. Brower (1999), citing Santner, argues that many societies are unable to deal with historical trauma or painful pasts as heritage because it is simply too problematic, especially for expressions of national identity that so often underwrite authorized versions of heritage and history. Indeed, Debary (2004) argues that museums are fundamentally more about memorializing the past so that it may be forgotten than actually remembering the past – particularly complex pasts of class inequality.

This assumption also underwrites the argument that social history museums, particularly those dealing with industrial issues, if not created to do so, have certainly become panaceas to ease the emotional and economic losses associated with 'the end of work' and deindustrialization: 'As industries die, the heritage solution is increasingly applied' (Hewison 1987: 95). The linking or inclusion of these museums within economic regeneration projects is viewed as an attempt to provide local forms of patriotism, while making previously highly industrial local areas more attractive, through tourism revenue, to both investors and new 'white collar' home buyers (Davis 1999: 39; Lumley 2005: 20; Whitehead 2005). As Crang notes, when, in the context of deindustrialization and the return of 'professionals' to cities, landscapes of labour become commodifed as landscapes of leisure, conflicts over historical and contemporary meaning will occur (2001: 128). This will especially be the case when redevelopment processes involve the erasure of past associations of landscape in order that they can be more comfortably marketed for leisure and tourism (Crang 2001: 130). Further, this can be particularly problematic in landscapes dominated by industries, such as coal mining, where the job implies a whole way of life around which communities are formed and maintained (Crang 2001: 143; see also Nadel-Klein 2003: Chapter 7). Subsequently, social history museums are often identified as either sanitizing a half-forgotten past, or as being memorials containing collections disassociated from continuing traditions and contemporary cultural meanings.

The National Coal Mining Museum for England (NCMM) is situated on the western edge of the Yorkshire coalfields, and is built around and incorporates the Caphouse Colliery. The Yorkshire industrial landscape has changed dramatically since the 1970s as mines began to close, a process accelerated in the aftermath of the 1984–5 Miners' Strike and the then Conservative British Government's attempts under the leadership of Margaret Thatcher to break the British union movement through its attacks on the National Union of Mineworkers (for fuller discussion of this history see, for instance, Richards 1997; Milne 2004; Hutton 2005). The impact of the strike on coal-mining communities and the Thatcher Government's response to it cannot be underemphasized. Communities were fragmented, not only through the economic effects engendered by pit closures, but also through active government attempts to challenge and undermine community identity, cohesion and pride. As one community historian observes about her own experiences living in a mining community:

> Miners, miners' sons and daughters . . . created and sustained a local economy that was buoyant, thriving and self-sufficient. When they were all flung out of work our bustling town centre became little more than a collection of charity shops and building society branches. It remains so to this day. Quite apart from the crass cruelty of deliberately plotting to throw thousands out of work, to decimate close family communities and send self-esteem crashing through the floor, the economic vandalism contained in a policy of shutting down pits and buying coal from abroad is wholly unforgivable. A strategy to rub out what worked well and replace it with nothing at all is criminally insane.
>
> (Pickles 2003: 9)

Pit closures are still a feature in Northern England, with mines in the Selby coalfields, North Yorkshire, closing in 2002 with the loss of 5,000 jobs (Macalister 2002). It is in the context of both economic and cultural loss that both Beamish, and in particular the NCMM, resides. The Caphouse Colliery was closed in 1985 after its coal deposits were exhausted, was reopened as a museum in 1988, and later gained national museum status in 1995. The museum contains collections associated with mining technology and the day-to-day lives of miners and their families within both the workplace and community. Exhibitions include information about the history of mining, leisure activities including sport, music and visual arts, the daily life of men, women and children, pit disasters, safety issues, technological and scientific developments, gala days, the 1984–5 and other strikes and so forth. A significant feature of the museum is the underground guided tour of the mine. These tours, which take just over an hour, are lead by ex-miners, some of whom worked at Caphouse itself. The museum also employs first-person live interpreters who engage visitors and school groups in role-playing, and then critical and informed discussions about community life and experiences (personal observation). The following observations of a miner identify both the cultural and social context within which the museum resides, and the inherent limitations of any museum exhibition:

> What have we got as an alternative to those family days? Well there's the national Museum of Mining at Caphouse. I am all in favour but you have to remember that it is intended to give an impression of the history, not modern conditions. It cannot show what it is like working down a producing pit. It cannot give an impression of the noise, the rushing air or how dirty it all is, or of the great distances travelled either on conveyors, man-riders or by walking. Nor can it show the humanity of such places.
>
> (Anon, quoted in Lewis 2003: 21)

The Tolpuddle Martyrs Museum in the village of Tolpuddle, Dorset, tells the story of the arrest in 1834, and subsequent trail and transportation to Australia, of six farm labourers who were accused of taking an illegal oath. The Tolpuddle Martyrs had taken an oath as part of their attempt to form a union, but were arrested on information obtained by the local squire and charged under a 1799 act 'for the more Effectual Suppression of Societies Established for Seditious and Treasonable Purposes' and the 1797 Mutiny Act, which made it illegal to administer an oath preventing another to reveal a confederacy (John Carr and Associates 2000: 16). Following a rigged trial, all six were deported to the Australian penal colonies for seven years; however, after widespread protests they were given conditional pardons and returned to England after three years' absence. The martyrs are iconic figures in the history of organized labour and the union movement in not only Britain, but also Australia and Canada, where five of the six eventually settled. The museum is contained within one small room, the former library, of the Tolpuddle Martyrs Memorial Cottages, which were built in 1934 to mark the centenary of the arrest and conviction of the martyrs. The museum contains very few artefacts and consists almost entirely of printed interpretive panels and interactive computer terminals telling the martyrs' story. The museum, as it currently exists, opened in 2000, though prior to that date an ad hoc display of memorabilia existed in the library rooms of the Memorial Cottages (Tolpuddle Martyrs Museum Trust 2001). The Memorial Cottages, which house retired agricultural workers, are built at one end of the village of Tolpuddle, and the museum may be visited along with other landmarks in the martyrs' history. These include the cottage where the oath took place, the sycamore tree under which meetings are thought to have been held, the Methodist chapel, and the cemetery where one of the six is buried. The village of Tolpuddle is a highly picturesque village, and although the museum attracts a high number of visitors into the village, some of the surrounding residents are uncomfortable about the museum's presence. One local farmer that I spoke to expressed discomfort about the content of the museum, noting that 'things' (relations between landowners and agricultural workers) had changed for the better now so he did not see the point of the museum. One worker at the museum observed that the end of the village where the museum occurred was often derogatorily referred to as the 'red end'.

All three museums surveyed for this chapter, Beamish, NCMM and Tolpuddle, attract visitors from a wide range of social backgrounds; however, those from which figures are known tend to attract a significantly higher proportion of people from working class backgrounds than do more traditional or national museums (Selwood, NCMM personal communication; Anon 2004). Since the introduction of social inclusion policies with the election of the 'New' Labour Government in 1997, museums, and the heritage sector generally, have been under pressure to implement policies and strategies to broaden the visitor base to include non-traditional visitors – that is, people from working class backgrounds and ethnic minorities (Belfiore 2002; Merriman 2004, Newman 2005a). The issue of widening participation in museums is not confined to Britain, it is a subject of debate across the world, taking on particular urgency in post-colonial countries following sustained criticism by Indigenous peoples and ethnic groups about museum elitism (Fforde et al. 2002; Fforde 2004; Mason 2004; Harrison 2005). A response to these pressures has been an increase in the emphasis museums place on their perceived educational function (Harrison 2005). This response derives ultimately from the assimilationist assumptions underlying many social inclusion and outreach policies.

These policies, particularly in Britain, and many of the practices enacted to implement them, are based on the assumption that non-traditional museum and heritage visitors must simply be encouraged to understand the values of museum visiting. While a key element in the implementation of these policies is to make museums less likely to inhibit non-traditional users there is, nonetheless, the assumption that these visitors need to be simply led into the museum and heritage fold, so that they can be educated and informed about the cultural delights from which they have been traditionally excluded. This is assimilationist because it is assumed non-traditional users need simply to be encouraged to go and visit – rather than reconsidering the nature of museums and heritage attractions themselves. This reconsideration is rarely undertaken because one of the dominant assumptions made, both in the critical literature and in the application of social policies on inclusion, is the idea that museums are about aesthetics. This is in large part because, as Kawashima (1999: 33) notes, the historical assumptions that the values of artefacts are inherent are still very active within the museums literature and practices. It is no accident that social inclusion policies in Britain, at least, are specifically aimed at museums and heritage sites that have a high proportion of middle class and upper middle class visitors – they are encouraged to increase their visitor base, as indeed they should. However, there is often little or no corresponding expectation that museums and heritage sites that attract high numbers of visitors from non-traditional social and cultural backgrounds need engage in social inclusion policies – that is, encourage traditional middle class museum goers to consider a different type of museum experience. This may sound like a petty point, but it reveals the degree to which it is assumed that social inclusion can be achieved through the assimilation of a wider audience base into the dominant heritage discourse and a consensus view of history and heritage. It also perhaps indicates the degree to which social history and ecomuseums remain outside of the dominant assumptions and discourses about the nature and meaning of museums.

If social inclusion is, however, to refer to more than equitable physical access or audience development then there needs to be, as Sandell (2003) argues, a paradigmatic shift in the way museums regard their role in and relationship to society. One of the impediments to this shift, however, is the lack of information and clarity about the way heritage acts upon individuals (Newman and McLean 2004: 169). Social inclusion that does not reduce itself to cultural assimilation, but that can recognize and accept the legitimacy of different cultural and social experiences, can only be developed once a more nuanced understanding exists than it currently does about what people do at and with museums and other sites of heritage.

Methodological note

To explore what people do at industrial era social history museums, and the sorts of identity and memory work undertaken, an identical questionnaire to that used at the country houses, and described and discussed in Chapter 4, was implemented at the three museum sites discussed above.[1] A total of 273 surveys were undertaken, with 128 collected at Beamish, 85 from the NCMM and 60 from Tolpuddle. All surveys, as at the country houses, were undertaken one-to-one, with the interviewer taking verbatim notes. To derive descriptive statistics from the open-ended questions, each question was read through and themes identified. All questions were re-read and coded according to these themes. These codes were then entered into the Statistical Package for the Social Sciences 11 (SPSS) to derive descriptive statistics. In the discussion below, extracts from interviews are referenced with an interview code (place of interview and number interviewed) alongside the gender, age and self-identified occupation of the respondent being quoted.

'Better rememberings from here': Remembering and the negotiation of social meaning and identity

The survey results obtained at the three museums are discussed collectively below. Although very similar memory work was undertaken at Beamish and the NCMM – often around mining work and community life – a slightly different type of memory work was undertaken at Tolpuddle. At this museum, memory and identity work centred on issues of organized labour, and a wider range of memories about work and community experiences than at the other two museums. However, the analyses are combined because how this work was used, and the social and cultural meanings it had for respondents, do not necessarily cross reference to the particular site or museum at which the survey was undertaken.

A comparison of Table 6.1 and Table 4.1 illustrates that at these museums visitors were three times more likely to come from occupations traditionally associated with the working class than at the country house sites discussed in Chapter 4. The dominance of these occupations was especially notable at Beamish and the NCMM, while the Tolpuddle museum tended to attract many teachers, as the National Union of Teachers advertises the museum to its members, and a number of teachers interviewed were also visiting to assess the site for school excursions. A third of respondents were educated to university level, but respondents at the Tolpuddle museum were more frequently educated to this level than at the other two museums. The majority of people surveyed self-identified as English or British, with only a very small handful of overseas visitors included in the survey (5 per cent), and only three

Table 6.1 Industrial museums: Profile of survey population

	Frequency	%
Occupation		
1.1 Senior managerial	14	5.1
1.2 Higher professional	33	12.1
2 Lower managerial/professional	77	28.2
3 Intermediate occupations	53	19.4
4 Small employers/own account	19	7.0
5 Lower supervisory/technical	13	4.8
6 Semi-routine	23	8.4
7 Routine	32	11.7
8 Unemployed/students	9	3.3
Total	273	100
Education		
No response	0	0
'O' levels/GCSE	38	13.9
'A' levels (Matriculation)	22	8.1
Undergraduate degree	59	21.6
Postgraduate degree	32	11.7
Technical qualifications	47	11.2
HND/HNC	20	7.3
No formal qualifications	55	20.1
Total	273	100

Note For description of occupation categories, see Office of National Statistics (2004).

British visitors identifying as coming from ethnic backgrounds other than 'White-British'. Of those people surveyed, 51 per cent were men, 43 per cent were repeat visitors (a similar percentage to country house visitors), 32 per cent were members of amenity societies (a smaller proportion than for country house visitors) and 60 per cent had travelled from a home address – 33 per cent identified themselves as 'locals' to the museum in question. These latter two statistics are slightly lower in proportion to the country house sites, in large part because Beamish attracted a regional (rather than 'local') audience, and as Tolpuddle attracted almost entirely people who were travelling – as the museum itself notes, most visitors to Tolpuddle are often on a pilgrimage to the site to commemorate the martyrs. As respondents to the survey observed, the visit is indeed 'a type of pilgrimage' (TP53, male, 40–59, local government) undertaken to foster 'kinship and comradeship with the past' (TP34, male, 40–59, train driver).

What is heritage? The AHD and its tensions

Visitors to these museums were less likely to reproduce the AHD when attempting to define what heritage meant to them than visitors to the country house sites. The AHD was still present, but its boundaries were pushed by the inclusion of notions of intangible heritage, and also because people tended to have conscious tensions with it. Table 6.2 summarizes the range of definitions and the frequency with which they were expressed by respondents. As with country house visitors, a significant percentage of respondents identified heritage as the process or act of conservation and preservation, so that heritage was understood as 'looking after what we have for generations to come. Saving knowledge and the countryside so it does not get lost' (NCMM1, male, over 60, miner). Or, more simply, 'preserving things from the past' (OAM71, male, 40–59, joiner) and 'Preserving and learning from the

Table 6.2 Industrial museums: What does the word heritage mean to you?

Response	Frequency	%
No response	4	1.5
Educational aspects	6	2.2
History in general	42	15.4
Identity – personal link	27	9.9
Material things from the past	29	10.6
Non-material past	82	30.0
Negative word/connotations	0	0
Patrimony/preservation	60	22.0
Royalty/aristocracy	0	0
'The past'	21	7.7
Total	273	100

past' (OAM102, male, over 60, retired fire-fighter). However, the most frequent definition of heritage, reported by one-third of respondents, identified heritage as either non-material or a mixture of material and non-material. While definitions incorporating notions of intangible heritage were also offered at country houses, people at the museums were much more likely to consider intangible or non-material definitions. The intangible heritage that people identified included things like memory, skills, workplace experiences, traditions, ways of life, family history, local and national culture and so forth; although in identifying these elements they were often also identified alongside material elements as well:

> Things we have that we want to keep going – like mining.
> (NCMM6, male, over 60, decorator)

> Me and mine and how the family used to live. Appreciate what you have now.
> (OAM9, female, 40–59, nurse)

> Family history and where we are from.
> (OAM126, female, over 60, deputy head teacher)

> Family background.
> (TP36, male, 40–59, teacher)

> A living history of how we got here socially. Growth and change.
> (OAM116, male, 30–39, scientist)

> What has gone on in the past . . . architecture, industry and socio-economic change.
> (OAM26, male, 40–59, electrical engineer)

> Traditions from the past.
> (TP4, female, 71, retired social worker)

> Traditions that have been handed down.
> (TP8, female, over 60, teacher)

Far more tension was expressed over the actual definition of 'heritage' in this survey than in the country house survey. At country houses tensions generally occurred in terms of the difficulty some respondents had in putting the feelings and the emotions that heritage engendered into words. The tensions at the museums were far more explicit or pragmatic, and tended to centre on the discomfort respondents had with traditional views of heritage. Some respondents actively identified what they saw as a dominant view of heritage – a view which was almost inevitably signified by the country house or stately home – and which they quite explicitly saw as oppositional to their own sense of what heritage was or should be. In short, many respondents identified dominant or authorized definitions of heritage that they considered as irrelevant to their own sense of the past or cultural and social experiences:

> When you hear a lot about heritage it's not usually the heritage of the whole country, it's exclusive, it excludes people. Such as stately homes, they represent the upper echelons of society and not the majority; here [Tolpuddle] it is more inclusive of people's heritage.
>
> (TP35, female, 40–59, teaching assistant)

> Stately homes is a dominant idea [of heritage], but for me it is the whole history – more than just kings and queens and politicians. The traditional view of heritage represents only the top level of society. . . . this is the other side of history than was taught at schools or traditionally seen as heritage. The nineteenth century as taught in schools in my day was about Empire and how great Great Britain was – this is the other side of that history.
>
> (TP39, male, 40–59, accountant)

> This [colliery village, Beamish] is not like a stately home, it has more relevance to more people – this is the background to most people and they mean more to people than stately homes.
>
> (OAM126, female, over 60, deputy head teacher)

> [The Tolpuddle Martyrs Museum] focuses on what people had to give up to achieve for today. It's very important that these places are kept, even more so than for stately homes. I love stately homes, but it is only a building and a way of life for a few, here it really gets down to our roots.
>
> (TP8, female, over 60, teacher)

> You go to a place like Longleat and you come here and it is just miles apart.
>
> (TP41, female, over 60, teacher)

Both the emphasis on intangible heritage and the rejection of authorized accounts of heritage are a significant feature of the responses from the museum visitors. These issues are likely to be interconnected as notions of intangible heritage are, as discussed in Chapter 1, external to Western authorized accounts of heritage. The interconnections of both these views are clearly encapsulated in this response, where working class history is understood to include a range of experiences and not simply material culture:

[heritage is] working class history as opposed to seeing a stately home where the landed gentry live [said sneeringly], country houses are interesting in themselves but there is only so much you can learn from them, and why would I pay someone to look around their house – they can pay me 10 quid to look around mine.

(NCMM5 male, 40–59, miner)

As will be elaborated on below, the significant themes that emerge in the responses to the questionnaire at the industrial era museums are those centred on memory and commemoration. It is important to mention this here, however, as the emphasis on intangible heritage, especially memory and experience as heritage, suggests a very different sense of patrimony and preservation than that expressed by respondents at country houses. In both surveys, the act of preservation was frequently defined as 'heritage'; at country houses, this sense of heritage was intertwined with the act of visiting the house and traditional concepts of physical conservation. At the industrial museums, the act of preservation was not so much the visit to the place, but rather the act of passing on memories, family histories and work experiences. The museums became sites of heritage, places that facilitated remembering, commemorating and passing on – all of which may be viewed as an act of heritage – this sense of heritage is illustrated here:

You have to know about the past to see how we got here. It is important for children to see this, but children don't have a real concept of time, they think only very old is history, but this is history too, and it can teach them things about their values, their ancestors – but it will fade out, telling the grandchildren about my grandparents working down the pit means little, but the place makes it a bit more real. It is hands on.

(OAM64, female, 40–59, teacher, from mining family)

Better rememberings from here than anywhere else in the country. I can see me mam making rugs – clipping mats and rag rugs.

(OAM69, male, over 60, mining engineer)

Being here brings memories back and it's nice to share them with the family.

(NCMM14, male, over 60, factory worker, ex-miner)

Being here means knowing one's past, otherwise you have no memory, memory is important, it's in the landscape and buildings.

(TP30, male, over 60, teacher)

Sentimental – it reminds me of things I have forgotten. Things have drifted away and you don't notice they have gone until you see them here.

(OAM89, male, 40–59, lab technician)

For a short time feeling part of history, even recent history . . . It just brings things home – it reinforces how you feel about the past.

(OAM85, male, over 60, accountant)

Thus the focus is moved to remembering and commemorating – a process that may be triggered by landscapes, artefacts or buildings – but which is fundamental to many people's sense of 'heritage'. For many respondents this aspect of heritage underwrote their own personal or family identity, and visiting these museums was simply about reminiscing. As one respondent noted, 'It's important for me to see this place, my father and five brothers were miners. In them days if your father was a miner you were too. I have been here two hours and I have just walked around reminiscing' (NCMM74, male, over 60, retired miner). Many talked about this process in terms of 'nostalgia', which was shorthand for 'I am remembering my own or my family history and passing this on to my children or grandchildren' or 'I am remembering stories my parent or grandparent told me'. This idea of nostalgia was not necessarily, although in a few cases it was, tied to a 'it was better back then ethos', as in many cases it was linked to the recollection and commemoration of memories that were not all good or positive, or to memories that were used to frame critical commentaries on both the past and present (see below).

While the sense of heritage that emerges from this survey tends to emphasize personal and family identity and memory work, it is important to note that this was also often tied into wider narratives about workers' achievements and class experiences. While people noted they were remembering their own experiences, or the stories told to them by their parents, these would also be framed or understood in terms of narratives about workers' achievements and how these in turn underpinned national identity and economic growth and development. For some, being at the museum and remembering and commemorating was also 'to be part of something' (NCMM13, male, 30–39, paint sprayer). It placed the personal into contexts where work mattered and underpinned technological, social and economic growth: 'a lot [of the museum] is very personal, as it is based on the lives of actual people' (NCMM36, male, 18–29, student). The heritage work undertaken at the industrial museums demonstrated that the personal mattered, through illustrating:

That our ancestors worked damned hard – the life we have now is due to the hard manual labour that they did. The technology has moved on because of their labour.

(NCMM84, female, 30–39, bank clerk)

It underpins a lot of being British and seeing where we came from technologically and culturally.

> (NCMM61, male, 30–39, solicitor)

The realization that the people who lived this hard life made all the changes and made it different for us now.

> (OAM13, female, 40–59, unemployed)

Being part of a long tradition is good and that the struggle for unions is an ongoing thing.

> (TP55, female, 40–59, clerical officer)

There was also a significant element of validation in this process of remembering and commemorating, validation at least in terms of understanding that personal experience had wider social consequences and resonance in working class experiences overall. As one respondent at Tolpuddle observed, 'Visiting a place where history was made or at least linked' is important as 'visiting supports and commemorates their [martyrs'] memory and what unions stood for' (TP56, male, 40–59, trade union official). For him, the visit commemorated the personal and reminded him about wider social and industrial issues that impact upon his life. As he went on to note, his visit was about 'revisiting and revising and reinforcing my knowledge' (TP56) and knowing that this knowledge, and the values underpinning it, were important and historically significant. He went on to observe that, 'Marx came to study the English working class, those associations are important' (TP56). While another respondent observed 'that it was the working class who had the more interesting history and probably did more to help us have the society we have today' (TP57, female, 40–59, teacher). Here, knowledge and values were consciously considered, reaffirmed and validated by the commemoration of the memory of the Tolpuddle Martyrs. This type of work was also undertaken at both Beamish and the NCMM, although in this case it was often in terms of how people's working lives in the past had been vital in creating the living standards that people enjoyed today.

That this sort of work was consciously critical is significant, and influences the sense of place, discussed below, that was constructed at the museums. However, this idea of heritage had generational boundaries. For many in the older age groups, the NCMM and Beamish were identified as 'memory joggers' for themselves, but specifically places of education for younger people because younger people had no first-hand knowledge of what the exhibitions at these museums illustrated. As one woman observed about Beamish: 'Memories – this place reminds me of my childhood. Nostalgic, as it is not old enough to be historic. My thirteen-year-old daughter thinks it is educational, as it is for her, but not for me. Rather, it is nostalgic because of memories' (OAM63, 40–59, factory worker). This woman was not alone in identifying Beamish and the NCMM as depicting periods that were not 'historic', but rather 'nostalgic', because the periods were not deep in the past, and thus for the visitor more personal and personally relevant than authorized history tends to be. The periods and events displayed at both museums exist outside of official and authorized accounts of Britain's history and heritage, and heritage is here defined by personal memory, and it becomes educational when that memory is no longer first-hand: 'The more places around like this the better, particularly for children. I can remember things like this, but the children can't' (OAM62, male, 40–59, technical inspector). While the heritage industry critique is concerned that once first-hand memories are gone, places like Beamish and the NCMM will become places of second-hand reactionary nostalgia, older visitors to the museums were more hopeful about the critical nature of the education children and younger people will gain:

> Educational for children as they don't know how easy they got it and they can see how hard their ancestors worked.
>
> (OAM67, female, 18–29, social worker)

> Good for children to see what life was like and to value what things they have gained. People are too cosy about the past.
>
> (OAM72, male, 40–59, nurse)

> [This place is] very important for people like my daughter, as she never visited her grandparents when they lived in places like this. It teaches them more about the past than my generation.
>
> (OAM74, female, 40–59, housewife)

> It's important that young children see what life used to be like – even in the 1920s and 1930s and see how it was.
>
> (NCMM72, male, 40–59, vehicle inspector)

> Well . . . it's important for youngsters to learn what life was like for the grandparents as kids today have little idea of what life was like.
>
> (NCMM73, male, over 60, fitter and turner, Australian)

> A lot of importance because people growing up today don't understand mining as most of the mines have gone, the only way to know about it is to come and see it.
>
> (NCMM74, male, over 60, retired miner)

> I hope the children learn how hard it was for children their age. They [the children the respondent was with] were shocked that children their age worked in mines.
>
> (NCM85, female, 30–39, teacher)

One respondent worried that once first-hand memories were gone, Beamish would simply become a 'museum', for which read dusty and without meaning, when she notes: '[Beamish] reminds you of your roots, where we have come from and how things developed. Worried that kids will say "so what" as they won't remember any of this, they won't relate to it. For the next generation it will be a museum, but for us it's an experience' (OAM75, male, over 60, church worker). However, as Tolpuddle demonstrates, first-hand memory is not necessary for the process of critical collective remembering and commemoration to continue.

A sense of place

All museums attempt to construct an experience, or sense of place, for their visitors. What emerges from the surveys is that many visitors were critically aware of this, and quite consciously engaged with or constructed and negotiated their own sense of place during their visits. Although Table 6.3 illustrates that one of the most frequent reasons for visiting, chosen from a range of options offered by the questionnaire, was recreation, as at the country house sites deeper interrogation through the open-ended questions revealed more nuanced and complex processes going on during the visit. However, an equal proportion of visitors chose the primary reason, 'for the experience of seeing how working people lived in the past' (offered at NCMM/Beamish) or 'to celebrate the history of the Trade Union Movement' (offered at Tolpuddle), which suggests a conscious desire to actively and self-reflexively engage with identity production and sense of place. This critical work becomes more evident in the open-ended responses, but may also be reflected in the degree to which education is also nominated as a reason for visiting. 'Education' was not, as may have been expected within the frameworks of the AHD, a discourse that was conspicuous in the context of the country house survey; however, here 15 per cent of people chose education of themselves as the

Table 6.3 Industrial museums: Reasons for visiting (chosen from a list supplied)

Response	Frequency	%
Recreation	72	26.4
Education	41	15.0
Aesthetic interest	8	2.9
Technical/architectural merits/interest	0	0
To see the collection in the museum	21	7.7
Experience of seeing how working people lived	75	27.5
Taking the children	39	14.3
To see a specific exhibition	3	1.1
Other	14	5.1
Total	273	100

primary reason for visiting. A further 14 per cent were visiting 'to take the children', a figure which was made up of 12 per cent who further nominated that this was because they hoped to educate their child/children, while 2 per cent were keeping the child/children occupied. Note that no one chose 'technical interests or merits', which given the nature of the mining exhibits could have been expected, and only 3 per cent nominated 'aesthetic appeal' as a reason. That people considered they were engaging with a sense of place that mattered to them is evident in the response to the question, 'Whose history are you visiting here?' (Table 6.4), when 45 per cent identified they were visiting either their own/family's history or that of working people. When asked if they felt they were part of the history represented at the museums they were visiting, 55 per cent of respondents also answered 'yes', that they were.

Respondents were critically aware that they were in a museum where the artefacts and other displays they were engaging with had been removed from their contexts. Respondents at Beamish frequently noted that the buildings they were wandering through were not in situ and that it was much dirtier and grimier in the past than the displays at Beamish suggest. For instance, the following observations were made by people who were actively engaged with reminiscing, commemorating or passing on stories to their children:

> [We are] rekindling memories — we have young grandchildren and will bring them here when old enough to show them. . . . Reminding us how things were, it's something we should not forget. . . . It's too clean — no coal dust — houses were always dirty in our community.
>
> (OAM 79, female, 40–59, civil servant)

> It's my past. My father was a miner and I am a Methodist preacher.

Table 6.4 Industrial museums: Whose history are you visiting here?

Response	Frequency	%
No response	10	3.7
Architectural history	1	0.4
Industrial	29	10.6
Local/regional	31	11.4
My own – family's/working people	125	45.7
National	22	8.1
No one's	5	1.8
Period specific	12	4.4
Trade Unions/Unionism	18	6.6
Working class	20	7.3
Total	273	100

Really, in some respect it [Beamish] is awesome. The houses are a bit too clean – but we are dealing with a museum, but they should be more untidy and dusty. I like the outhouses, they look lived in and used. [The message I take away is about] industrialization and the use of coal – Mrs Thatcher should be ashamed for destroying that community. . . . [The impressions I have are] what the lives of the miners were like, and a sense of the difficulties . . . I like the out-buildings they have added, it is not just twee interiors. Pity they don't have a pub here, they have the chapel.

(OAM 4, male, 40–59, surveyor)

[Beamish is important to] children so that they can understand their way of life. [My dominant impression is] how clean it all is, coz it wasn't, the buildings are all clear and not sooty.

(OAM 17, female, 30–39, academic)

I'm reliving what people went through – it was just a job, but it makes you realize how bad a job it was. This place brings that home. I'm trying to see what it was like for the men in my family for the sake of a wage. [The message I take away is] just how lucky we are these days. However bad we think it is today it's not as bad as it was. It [the NCMM] reinforces how dangerous and grim it must have been. No matter how much people tell you how bad it was you don't ever really get a good sense of that. [The museum is] never going to be a true representation as it is only going to give snatches, and while it is clean and bright it will never give a true impression. [This place] makes me feel humble.

(NCMM20, female, 40–59, shop assistant, husband and brothers were miners)

While many people made observations about inauthentic cleanliness and the staged nature of museums, these were often simply remarked on in passing and were not seen as very significant. Instead, what was significant for many was the emotional authenticity their visit engendered – how well the place triggered either memories or stories to pass on, or invoked stories that had been told to them. People appear to be quite mindfully using the museums as what Wertsch (2002) calls a cultural tool for remembering.

There were two significant emotions engendered by visitors to the museums. If 'comfortable' and 'safety' were the defining discourse at the country houses – 'humble' and 'nostalgic' were keywords at the museums: 36 per cent expressed some form of empathy with people in the past through an expression of how *humbled* they felt for what people had done, achieved or endured in the past so that things could be better now, and 20 per cent of people talked about feeling nostalgic (Table 6.5 and cf. Table 4.6). It is

Table 6.5 Industrial museums: How does it make you feel to visit this place?

Response	Frequency	%
No response	13	4.8
Aesthetically engaged	0	0
Comfortable/comforted	8	2.9
Creating/maintaining links	10	3.7
Cultural capital	0	0
Dissonance	21	7.7
Humbled – deferential sense	0	0
Humbled – positive sense, expressing empathy	99	36.3
Interested/education	35	12.8
Nationalistic	1	0.4
Nice day out	5	1.8
Nostalgic – reactionary	5	1.8
Nostalgic – social memory	56	20.5
Numinous	1	0.4
Privileged to be allowed to visit	6	2.2
Proud of workers' achievement	13	4.8
Total	273	100

important to note that 'humble' and 'nostalgic' were common terms also used at the country houses, but that these terms were used very differently in each context. At country houses, these feelings were often expressly linked with reactionary social messages and meanings tied to aristocratic deference and the idea that things were 'better back then' (see Chapter 4). The sense of humility and nostalgia expressed at the industrial museums was, unlike at the country houses, not at all disabling, but rather centred on an active process of remembering. The word nostalgia, as noted above, was used by many respondents interchangeably with, or as shorthand for, a sense of reminiscing or remembering:

> Very nostalgic ... memories ... Pegging rugs and fireside oven reminds me of my grandmother. I was brought up in a colliery area – grandparents – brings a lot of that back.
>> (OAM28, male, over 60, pilot, great uncle a miner)

> Nostalgic, never get tired of remembering our childhood and how we used to live. . . . [This place is] nostalgic to me, to my grandchildren, [it's] important.
>> (OAM69, male, over 60, mining engineer)

> Nostalgic, makes you grateful for the life you have now.
>> (OAM74, female, 40–59, housewife)

Nostalgic, it reminds me of going to visit grandparents when I was a child. . . . I appreciate how hard life was . . . when I was in the house [one of the colliery village houses] I was taken back in time, as the cooker they had was one we had and I stood there remembering for a long time.

(OAM125, female, 30–39, police officer)

Brings back a lot of memories – nostalgic. When places like this [Caphouse Colliery] were on the go I was a child and it brings back memories of the sound of the clogs as the miners went to work.

(NCMM7, male, over 60, nurse)

The importance of memory is also illustrated in the response to the question, 'What does being here mean to you' (Table 6.6). While many respondents in the country house survey found it difficult to answer this question, and no clear themes emerge in response to it, respondents at the industrial museums were much more decided in their answers to this question. For a third of respondents, being at the museum was about memory work – remembering and commemorating individual and collective memories, while others were commemorating by expressing empathy or kinship with people in the past (14 per cent), and an equal proportion were also being educated (14 per cent). The emphasis on memory is perhaps not surprising as these museums obviously have a close and personal link with their visitors – many of whom were miners or came from coal-mining families or communities, or in the case of Tolpuddle, had close personal or family associations with organized labour. However, understanding what was being done with these memories is important. Most memories were highly charged emotionally, and many were using both the memories and emotions to engage in critical reflection. At Beamish and the NCMM it was often personal or family memories that were the focus of their emotional response to place. When people had no personal memories to draw on, the dominant emotions, as they were at

Table 6.6 Industrial museums: What does being here mean to you?

Response	Frequency	%
No response	60	22.0
Educated/interested	38	14.0
Empathy with people in the past	37	13.6
Memory	94	34.4
Nationalistic feeling	3	1.1
Numinous	6	2.2
Reactionary nostalgia	5	1.8
Touristic meanings	30	11.0
Total	273	100

Tolpuddle, were the feelings of humility, empathy and/or a sense of gratitude to the past. In reporting feelings of being humbled people were noting a sense of kinship, affinity and gratitude; these feelings, as with those of nostalgia, were also used to frame reflections on past and present:

> Quite humble – would I have had the guts to do what they did?
>
> (TP3, male, over 60, truck driver)

> Difficult to define – a bit in awe of what they did and how they were treated. . . . I think people need to know about the martyrs, as people are so bullied they don't learn about the background of trade unions.
>
> (TP4, female, 71, retired social worker)

> Humbling. I'm trying to restore faith in trade unionism [by being here].
>
> (TP21, male, 40–59, civil servant)

> Extremely sad and humbled. [Being here means a] realization of what people suffered. I suppose I was never in agreement with trade unions, but after being here and seeing what they are about I agree with them now.
>
> (TP24, female, over 60, receptionist)

> Humble. I think there was injustice between the classes and this was the start of the correction of that injustice and lessening of the divide between the classes. . . . My father was a farmer and he employed people; hopefully we treated them in a reasonable way.
>
> (TP49, female, 70, doctor's wife)

> Lucky and humble . . . I've been reflecting on what it was like, it brings on lots of emotions; I have been thinking about my son and what life would have been like for him if he had been born then.
>
> (NCMM28, female, 30–39, nurse)

> Humble, they worked hard and it opens your eyes.
>
> (NCMM73, male, over 60, fitter and turner, Australian)

> Humble. The technological changes and the hazardous life of the miners.
>
> (NCMM77, female, 70s, teacher)

> Humble, and that I have it lucky now – I feel more enlightened.
>
> (OAM13, female, 40–59, unemployed)

221

Humble to what they had to do and live and how we now live.
(OAM77, male, 40–59, RAF officer)

Humble. Making me realize how fortunate we are.
(OAM78 female, over 60, administrator)

At the country house sites the master narratives of national and class legitimacy appear, in large, to have been uncritically embraced. However, at the industrial museums there appears to have been a far more critical sense of engagement, in which individual and collective narratives and meanings were under negotiation. These were used either as critical commentary on the present, or as acts of commemoration in which people expressed thanks that things were better now. The way this emotional response framed critical reflection is well summed up by a respondent at the NCMM, who stated that visiting made her feel:

Humble. It gets to you there [punches chest] as well as up there [points to head]. Going down pit is a shock to the system. I went down a pit 40 years ago and I still remember it.
(NCMM77, female, 70s, teacher, husband a miner)

The experiences people sought in terms of the sense of place offered by the museum are interwoven with the emotions engendered by the visit and the narratives people were constructing about the past. Table 6.7 summarizes the responses to the question about the experiences people valued on their visit. Expressing empathy or actively creating empathic connections or links with people in the past was the most frequent response (28.6 per cent). These links were created through 'connecting with how people used to live. Seeing how people got on with their lives and made the best of it' (NCMM41, female, 40–59, librarian) or 'seeing how things have changed today for the working class' (NCMM55, female, 40–59, clerk). For many at Beamish and

Table 6.7 Industrial museums: What experiences do you value on visiting this place?

Response	Frequency	%
No response	41	15.0
Active identity – memory work	48	17.6
Educational/informational	41	15.0
Empathy with people in the past – active	78	28.6
Gaining cultural capital	5	1.9
Passive connection with the past	25	9.2
Physical sense of being at, or visiting, museum	29	10.6
Touristic/recreational	6	2.2
Total	273	100

the NCMM, visiting was seen as a 'graphic history lesson' (NCMM78, female, 70s, teacher) where learning about and creating links with the past was 'hands-on' or 'a tactile experience, touchy feely' (NCMM57, male, 40–59, quality engineer):

> It's a way of bring history to life, it's a way of touching it rather than reading about it – it's living history. We had been to Beamish and thought we could come here [NCMM] after going through the drift mine.
>
> (NCMM84, female, 30–39, bank clerk)

The experience of the underground tour at the NCMM or going through the drift mine at Beamish and walking through the associated miners' houses was an experience many people used to get a 'better understanding of how things developed and the way people lived' (NCMM77, female, 70s, teacher) or 'to see how well off we are now compared to then' (NCMM25, female, over 60). At Tolpuddle, this connection was forged through 'putting yourself back into the era represented' (TP7, female, 40–59, probation service) and asking 'What would I have done, if I had been strong like the martyrs? If I was wealthy would I have done what the landowners did?' (TP5, male, 30–39, unemployed) or by 'trying to relate it [what was seen and read] to experiences you have in your life' (TP13, male, 30–39, engineer).

For a further 17 per cent of respondents, active identity and memory work was identified as a valued experience. For some, this was remembering 'past experiences – remembering when I was a miner 30 years ago. I miss the community spirit, it's not like that in the factory I work in now' (NCMM14, male, over 60, factory worker). For another, it was remembering 'a lot of friendship, another world, when we were down the pits we were very close and watched each other's backs . . . it reminds me of what I worked on, what I did' (NCMM8, male, over 60, retired miner). For others, it was passing on these memories to children or other family members: 'I brought the grandkids, as I like them to see how things was in the past' (NCMM72, male, 40–59, vehicle inspector) or, as one man observed, 'educating the daughter' about family history:

> This place has great importance because mining has been the back-bone and structure of society and now it's all gone and it's important for my daughter to come and see.
>
> (NCMM62, male, 40–59, retired miner)

> It was our lifestyle and we like to pass it on to our grandchildren so that they will know what it was like.
>
> (NCMM9, female, over 60, from a mining family)

This process of passing on and affirming family memories was also demonstrated by one interaction with a family group at Beamish. A woman in her sixties (OAM128) was discussing some of the memories invoked while walking around the colliery exhibit. Although not from a mining family, she identified the exhibit as part of her heritage and observed she had been 'thinking about my mum working in the mills in Manchester', at which point her young grandson interjected and recounted the family story of his great-grandmother losing a finger in the mills.

The experiences people valued at the museums are firmly linked to the messages that people took away from the three museums. As Table 6.8 illustrates, the most frequent (39 per cent) message taken away was about how hard it was in the past for people and how much better it is today – often expressed as a sense of gratitude or historical debt. Although these messages are relatively simple observations about social and historical change they were, however, graphically underscored by both the memory work people were doing at these places and/or the experiences and feelings of empathy, humility and gratitude that many expressed:

> Conditions are better now – appreciate social wages.
> (NCMM49, male, 40–59, local government)

> How dedicated people were in doing this job [mining] so other people could live in comfort.
> (NCMM12, female, 40–59, unemployed)

> To be grateful and thankful for all the work they have done. How hard it was and that it is a shame they are shutting down the pits.
> (NCMM30, female, 18–29, student)

Table 6.8 Industrial museums: What messages do you take away from this place?

Response	Frequency	%
No response	19	7.0
Confirms aspects of personal identity	29	10.6
Conservative social message	6	2.2
Critical engagement	32	11.7
Gratitude/historical debt	107	39.2
How society has changed	17	6.2
Nationalistic	1	0.4
No message	3	1.1
Preservation message	12	4.4
Sense of loss	10	3.7
Vague or specific historical information	37	13.6
Total	273	100

That people worked very hard and in poor conditions.

> (NCMM32, female, 30–39, bank clerk)

How lucky we are these days – things have moved on. I have a cushy job in comparison.

> (NCMM34, male, 30–39, business analyst)

That miners had a hard life, and deserved every penny that they got.

> (NCMM35, male, 40–59, local government)

Makes you think how difficult it was in the past to work.

> (OAM1, female, 40–59, receptionist)

People had a very hard life, especially in them days. Britain may have lead the world – but at a price.

> (OAM28, male, over 60, pilot)

How we came on since then – we have progressed and are lucky.

> (OAM3, female, 40–59, cook)

It just makes you understand how people had to live there – makes you appreciate what you have today.

> (OAM5, female, over 60, cook)

That cultures change over such a short time. This era only belongs to our parents' generation, and we have moved forward in such a short time.

> (OAM6, male, 40–59, engineer)

A small percentage (2.2 per cent), and all of these were recorded at Beamish, took away the opposite message that things were better in the past than the present, and that they desired a return to past values. These messages are those predicted by the heritage industry critique, which Beamish in particular has been identified as purveying. However, the low frequency with which they were expressed or taken on board by respondents reduces their impact:

Seeing how things have changed. It was better then, we should go back to the values back then.

> (OAM71, male, 40–59, joiner)

Times were not easy but in some ways it was nicer than it is now, less hectic then and they had better values.

> (OAM73, female, 30–39, teacher)

Uniform cities a shame, losing national character, far too cosmopolitan.

> (OAM95, male, 40–59, company director)

A lot more attention to detail back then – thoroughness. Education was far superior back then.

> (OAM31, female, 18–29, office administrator)

See how history has been rewritten – there's material in [the] school about the Boer War and now we have rewritten history, we don't teach that now, kids today don't know about the Boer War – we have rewritten the history, we have no heroes now.

> (OAM93, male, 40–59, company director)

Although many took away specific or quite vague historical information from these sites (14 per cent), two other themes are worthy of note. Some used the sense of place engendered by their visit to make or engage with critical social messages, while others used the sense of place to confirm aspects of their personal identity. The critical messages that many constructed and took away were about issues of class inequity that tended to be underlined with a sense of class solidarity:

> It's about class struggle and how much people had to fight to get better conditions. Also the school [in the Colliery village] shows all the empire stuff and how children had propaganda put on them.
>
> > (OAM72, male, 40–59, nurse)

> Huge differences between the middle and lower classes.
>
> > (OAM114, male, over 60, managing director)

> That we are still faced with a bunch of politicians who are scallywags and that we still live in a society of have and have nots.
>
> > (TP10, male, 40–59, teacher)

> Understanding that it wasn't all a green and pleasant land for all people, it was hard work but they had the guts to stand up. Politics affects everybody, it's not just Parliament.
>
> > (TP19, female, 30–39, teacher)

> That we must not forget – not to trust the elites, never trust the elites!
>
> > (TP31, male, over 60, diplomat, self-identified as coming from a working class background)

> It just reminds me not to forget what happened and to keep on my

guard . . . That the ruling classes didn't give a damn about anybody except themselves . . . Yes, I'm in a trade union and I know that in a smaller way these things are still going on and that we are still fighting to stop management taking advantage of their workers.

(TP34, male, 40–59, train driver)

The extent and injustice of the class divide dominated most messages; however, the one respondent who considered that 'the class division has broken down now' expressed curiosity, but emotional detachment at visiting Beamish. Interestingly, he noted that his 'wife is from county Durham and [has] antecedents in the coal industry. She was a [family name] which was a great name around here' (OAM93, male, 40–59, company director). His wife noted, 'my ancestors owned mines, we made our money mining. I have gained a slight feeling of [long pause] what they [miners] went through [very hesitant here, long pause], but that's changed now [said forcefully] (OAM93, interjection by wife).

In constructing a sense of personal and family identity, the messages that many respondents constructed here were once again focusing on remembering and passing on memories to other members of their families. However, for others the message of the sense of place they found or constructed at the museums was about affirming the legitimacy of their own identity. This affirmation was expressed in two ways. Firstly, in terms of asserting the wider social relevance and legitimacy of working people's lives and experiences; as one respondent observed, 'museums like this they never did this before, but now they look at how people live, now we can learn about our history' (NCMM16, female, over 60, retail, from a mining family). Others questioned the universal relevance of standard definitions of history and heritage:

I feel that they really haven't done enough in this area and have only dealt with it because they have had to – you know they have all their castles and stuff. Dealing with it now as people are getting more interested and it is part of their history.

(NCMM70, female, 40–59, homeduties, husband was a miner)

Our past is nothing to be ashamed of, we should remember it.

(OAM21, female, 40–59)

Pleased that trade unionism and the sacrifice of those men is given credence.

(TP55, female, 40–59, teacher)

The social influences that the history of this country had . . . are important.

(TP56, male, 40–59, trade union official)

227

Secondly, affirmation was expressed through the validation of memories that had been passed on: 'It brings it home about what my dad went though' (NCMM22, female, 40–59, nurse, daughter of a miner) or 'It fetches it home as I have had family that worked in the mines, and I appreciate what they have done' (NCMM22). While another observed: 'I can relate it talking to me grandmother and link it to the stories she told me' (OAM70). And from a less personal perspective:

> I'm here to get background on legal issues and get a feeling for what these guys went through, and get a feeling of the industry and working life. I am a lawyer and represent ex-miners and I am here with three colleagues who represent ex-miners and we came to find out more about their working lives.
>
> (NCMM81, male, 30–39, lawyer)

The expression of identity that emerges from the sense of place experienced and constructed by respondents at the industrial museums tends to centre on personal and collective family memories. However, these are inevitably contextualized through narratives about the nature of working class experiences, and through an understanding of how and why living and work conditions have changed. This change, viewed most often as being for the better, was identified as being brought about by the hard work of working people in the past. Links of 'Kinship and comradeship with the past' (TP34) are forged through the emotions engendered both by the sense of place and the memories it provokes and affirms. For 43 per cent of respondents, the meaning these museums had in modern England (Table 6.9) centred on their role as aids to memory that affirmed and maintained personal and family identity. However, for a third of respondents, the sites were primarily seen as educational and historic resources, often in terms of the education of younger members of their own family or children generally. This point was reinforced when

Table 6.9 Industrial museums: What meaning does a place like this have in modern England?

Response	Frequency	%
No response	5	1.8
Aid to memory – personal identity	116	42.5
Circular heritage statements	8	2.9
Critical identity work	12	4.4
Educational resource	94	34.7
Nationalism/reactionary nostalgia	9	3.3
Should conserve – vague statements	6	2.2
Shouldn't forget – vague statements	23	8.4
Total	273	100

respondents were asked about their impressions of the museum, with 36 per cent of respondents noting that their main impression was they were more informed by their visit to the museum; although 63 per cent noted that their views of the past had not changed but had simply been reinforced. However, a greater frequency of people at the industrial museums than at the country houses considered their views had been changed (at country houses the 'no' response was 85 per cent). A total of 23 per cent had had views changed or felt they had learnt something new, and this percentage includes 11 per cent who noted that they had had what equated to a cultural epiphany. While many people's views of the past, or more precisely their memories and the meanings those memories had, were reinforced, it is important to note that the museums were also seen as educational tools for those without first-hand memories and that for some, at least, the museums were successful in providing experiences that changed people's views of the past.

Remembering and performativity at industrial social history museums

The performativity of going to and being at the museum – doing the museum visit – is focused on acts of remembering and commemoration. When asked what aspects of the site 'spoke to' people, 23 per cent identified that these were places that were helping them to remember and/or commemorate (see Table 6.10). Although 25 per cent said the sites did not speak to them, 14 per cent identified the sites as part of their own history and/or heritage, while 10 per cent once again identified feelings or sentiments expressive of empathy, and a further 10 per cent were participating in critical reflections about the past or the present. However, these critical and

Table 6.10 Industrial museums: Does this place speak to any aspect of your personal identity?

Response	Frequency	%
No response	17	6.2
Does *not* speak to them	69	25.3
This *is* my heritage	39	14.3
Aspiration/cultural capital	4	1.5
Critical reflection on past for commentary on the present	26	9.5
Elicited tourist response	1	0.4
Empathy with people in the past	26	9.5
Find it educational	8	2.9
Part of my English/British identity	4	1.5
Personal reminiscing/affirming nostalgia	15	5.5
Social memory – commemoration/remembrance	63	23.1
Trivial observation	1	0.4
Total	273	100

empathic statements emerge not only in response to this question, but are a significant and recurring feature of the survey results in general. What the performance of the museum visit overall does is to trigger, validate and affirm individual and collective family memories, and to contextualize these in wider narratives about working class experience. While the affect of this is to define and maintain personal and family identity, it also does more – it provides a framework or baseline upon which to critically reflect upon present-day social and work experiences:

> I'm from a mining village and [I am thinking about] the major ramifications culturally and socially that the closing of the industry has had.
>
> (NCMM83, male, 30–39, sales assistant)

> It were a great community. We also feel hatred to Mrs Thatcher when we come here – well . . . felt that before we came here too! [This place speaks to me about the] traumatic effects of the miners' strike – it affected me and everybody in the North and people in the South were totally unaware of it – and I am originally a southerner!
>
> (NCMM82, female, over 60, social services)

> Communities were destroyed [during the 1984–5 strike] and animosities are still present from the strike. I went to work then, and people I went to school with won't speak to me 20 years after the strike.
>
> (NCMM38, male, over 60, miner)

> Commemorates how they supported one another and their families – we have lost that sense of community, no job has that sense of community now.
>
> (NCMM84, female, 30–39, bank clerk)

> Even though this is a different era – what these people went through still has an impact on your life, you got to remember that.
>
> (NCMM55, female, 40–59, clerical officer)

> [This place is] important otherwise other generations who did not know what coal was about wouldn't appreciate the workers, so it will give them an idea. Also make the industry think again about how they employed people and killed them.
>
> (NCMM81, male, 30–39, lawyer)

> I come from a mining community. My dad was a miner, I was raised to work as a miner, basically we were fodder for the factories and

mines. This place brings back memories of my family, it's nostalgia, and I was showing my wife around and telling her about my grandfather, the wood smoke and the backyards of the cottages, took me right back to thinking about him.

(OAM89, male, 40–59, lab technician)

Been lucky to have come from a mining background and have had the opportunities I've had, I wasn't sent down the mine at 12/13.

(OAM109, female, 40–59, nurse)

I think about my own kids and then the kids in the past.

(NCMM32, female, 30–39, bank clerk)

That people worked so damned hard and we are so lucky now. Women stayed in the house then – the role of women has changed so much. We are so lucky now as women.

(OAM81, female, 40–59, antique dealer)

Yes – practically everything has changed my view on how hard life was back then. It's hard to imagine how women actually provided for their families.

(NCMM73, male, over 60, fitter and turner, Australian)

Yes – nostalgic side takes you back, makes you think and brings you back to reality.

(OAM111, male, 40–59, police officer)

It's important that people defend their rights and sometimes you pay a high price for that.

(TP10, male, 40–59, head teacher)

I have sympathy for the martyrs. We needed these people at that time, and even now we need them, we need more rights as working people. It went too far in the 1970s, we still need more rights.

(TP13, male, 30–39, engineer)

It speaks to me about my role in bringing back my traditions and spirituality to my people on the East Coast of Canada, and it gives me more courage to continue speaking out about inhumane people and not to be afraid to take a stand.

(TP16, male, over 60, counsellor, Native American)

Yes, I came from a working class background, I was the first in both families to get a higher education – it reminds me how lucky I was to live well in times after the Tolpuddle Martyrs.

(TP31, male, over 60, diplomat)

I have always been a union member so would like to believe that what they did and achieved could have meaning today, but unfortunately for many I don't think it does.

(TP32, male, 40–59, civil servant)

It's easy for young people to not understand the importance of unions, but if you can see yourself as part of a historical movement then you can understand how you fit into ongoing struggles.

(TP56, male, 40–59, trade union official)

Between my first visit [to Tolpuddle] and this I have done more things within my union and understand more about trade unionism, so it spoke to me and inspired me, especially my first visit.

(TP55, female, 40–59, teacher)

I work as a magistrate, and this place shows how powerful we – that is magistrates – were and how that has changed. We administer the law, and don't make them up! I work with unions as a magistrate, and it is interesting for me to see this history of trade unions and it stirs me, these brave people, and that unions still stand up for people's rights.

(TP38, female, over 60, magistrate)

Sad that the aristocracy are still doing what they do. In terms of the law things have changed, but the attitudes of landed people not at all. . . . Yes, both myself and my wife are very conscious of unionism and strong believers in equality and unionism. At the moment the debate on hunting – this is the same issue really, as we suspect that a lot of rural people say they support hunting as they live in tithed cottages and feel that they have to support it. These relations [between agricultural workers and landed classes] shown here still happen in rural England. We live in a rural area and are told we don't belong because we don't hunt and don't go to church.

(TP39, male, 40–59, accountant)

Very important that people are aware of why they have the rights they have today. This [Tolpuddle] has resonance with Thatcher and the miners.

(TP50, female, 30–39, teacher)

232

The performativity of the museum visit is linked, as it was at the country houses, back to the definitions of heritage that many people appeared to be utilizing either consciously or unconsciously. The important point here is that heritage, as inclusive of intangible heritage, was about memory and the act or performance of remembering, commemorating and passing on memories to family members. These performances and the meanings they engendered were made meaningful and significant by the place of their doing – surrounded by hands on exhibits that embodied the memories of parents, grandparents, and working people more generally. While active claims to class identity were less conspicuous in the industrial museums than at country houses – people did not claim, as they did at the country houses, that what they were doing was specific to their social class – nonetheless, a strong sense of class identity emerges. This is evident in the sense of solidarity, often expressed as empathy, humility and gratitude, that was being used to bind or link people in the present with people in the past. The links thus forged were about proclaiming a class identity that was made meaningful and relevant to the present through the critical work of social commentary that many respondents undertook – in short, reacting emotionally, but using that to think and reflect. Although many took away knowledge and messages that things were better now than in the past, a sub-text emerges that these gains must be maintained through ensuring that 'we don't forget' or, as one respondent put it, 'It's important not to forget so it doesn't happen again' (TP3, male, over 60, truck driver). Subsequently, the educative value of the museums and the memories they recall were also stressed, so that children and younger people will, to paraphrase respondent TP34 (quoted above), not forget what happened and to keep on their guard.

The messages and meanings many took away from the museums were as much a result of the active engagement or performativity of the visit as they were of the sense of place constructed by the museum. Senior interpretive staff at both Beamish and the NCMM noted that the inclusion of overt political or social messages in museums was not something that was done, for a range of reasons, at either museum. Yet, at times, quite overt and politicized meanings and messages were constructed or expressed at the sites by respondents. The point here is that many respondents actively negotiated both the sense of place and the performativity and subsequent meanings of the visit. As museum audiences, the majority of respondents to this survey were active and self-conscious in their engagement, an observation that has important implications for the sense of class identity that the industrial museum performance creates and maintains.

Dissonance

The oppositional dissonance found at the country house was not recorded in this survey. Although a few visitors expressed quite reactionary, nostalgic memories of the 'it was better back then' type, these were not oppositional and were simply another view to the more frequent memories and feelings of humility, solidarity and gratitude. Respondents expressing reactionary nostalgic views constructed their sense of place, and the performativity of their visit, to reflect and engage with these values and did not perceive their views as being dissonant. Rather, what is dissonant is the way heritage was used at the museums, as this use exists outsides of the confines of the AHD – a point not lost on some surveyed, who pointed out that the dominant views of heritage in England were exclusionary of their own sense of heritage. Remembering and commemorating are revealed as moments of heritage in a way that makes mockery of the fetish of material authenticity and the critique of the heritage industry. At the museums aspects of working class, and sometimes radical or critical working class identity, are played out in a way that allows self-conscious and sometimes critical engagement with a range of social and political issues – a process that is of itself dissonant both in nature and intent. Here, again, the dissonant nature of heritage is revealed, but in this case as a way of viewing the world and giving work and life experiences meaning.

The dissonant nature of heritage, particularly the heritage revealed here, has significant implications for social inclusion policies and aspirations. Its dissonant nature, itself, makes it difficult as it invokes a sense of social identity that is at odds with authorized social values and meanings. Not only does a sense of heritage that embraces both the intangibility of memory, linked with the activity of remembering and commemorating, sit outside the frameworks of the AHD, it also actively challenges them. The assimilationist nature of current social inclusion policies is based on the universality of the AHD, and the discursive space to accept the legitimacy of different social and cultural experience does not yet fully exist in Britain. Nor can the sense of class identity, values, experience and collective memory that emerges from the survey make any claims to its own universality. It needs to be pointed out that this is a particularly 'white' version of historical and class experience, and only a small handful of respondents came from ethnic backgrounds other than those traditionally defined as 'white British' in the British classifications of ethnicity.[2] At least at Beamish and the NCMM it is also a particularly Northern English experience of work and class. The simple point here is that there are many versions of what heritage 'is' and 'does' and the social meanings and experiences it represents. Without acknowledging and accepting the diversity of social and cultural experiences, heritage policies and practices will simply continue to recreate and maintain a consensus and exclusionary vision of heritage, history and the present.

Conclusion

One of the key observations that emerges from this survey is that many visitors to these industrial museums engaged actively and critically with the performativity of their visit and the sense of place they both found and constructed at the museums. Even for those whose primary reason for visiting was recreational, a strong sense emerges that, overall, they too were aware of and engaged with a process of identity and meaning making. The identities created were based on an act of remembering that was inextricably linked to acts and feelings of commemoration. The feelings engendered by the commemorative nature of the remembering were part of the process of forming ties and links to people in the past – either specific family members or working people collectively, or in some cases the working class specifically. While, for many, family was the focus of their remembering and the links being forged or maintained, these links were contextualized within a critically conscious awareness of class identity and collective experiences. Although at Beamish and the NCMM family memories were often the focus of individual remembering, these memories were narrated and underscored by collective class memories, and remembering of what it meant and currently means to be English working class. At Tolpuddle, and those at the NCMM or Beamish without first-hand or family memories relevant to the sense of place offered by the museum, a process of remembering and commemorating what it meant and means to be working class still occurred – with many drawing on their own or family experience to underscore and validate collective remembering. Put simply, people were not mindlessly engaging with the messages offered at the museums and undertaking uncritical collective remembering, but rather they made sense of and were validating collective memories by drawing on their own experiences. What is also significant is that this remembering, and the meanings and values it engaged with, negotiated and rehearsed, was itself then actively deployed and used by many respondents to critically evaluate and reflect on both past and present social and economic inequities and experiences. The identities constructed and maintained by the performativity of the visit were actively used and interlinked with attempts to make sense of and contextualize contemporary life and work.

The doing of the visit and the being at the sites, even at places like Beamish where material had been moved to its location rather than being in situ, were important in providing a 'theatre of memory' where remembering and commemoration could not only be done, but also be *marked* as legitimate and of significance and validity. The place of its doing grants a legitimacy to both the ritual of the performance itself and the memories which were the subject of that performance – that legitimacy is not necessarily gained through the in situ authenticity of the material culture, or the authenticity of its dirtiness, but in its ability to invoke and signify and connect with people's wider social experiences and knowledge. What was important here was that these places opened up the discursive spaces of what heritage is and does and provided arenas in which non-authorized forms of history and heritage could be explored and experienced. Although many respondents were aware of the 'staged' nature of the locale for their performance of remembering and commemoration, what was more important than its in situ authenticity was the process of heritage making and the feelings and memories it engendered. Authenticity, as others have noted, was entirely negotiated (Bathel-Bouchier 2001; Halewood and Hannam 2001; Apostolakis 2003). The things, artefacts, buildings and landscapes that visitors encountered were an important aspect of heritage – but only an aspect, a backdrop to the central moments of heritage: the memories and feelings of kinship and comradeship reinforced, forged and remade by the performance of remembrance and commemoration.

The active nature of heritage and the understanding that 'heritage' is an act of doing and being, albeit a doing and being connected to place, but nonetheless an act of connection and connecting, challenges the assumptions underling both the AHD and the heritage industry critique. This activity does not necessarily produce reactionary nostalgia – it can, as was illustrated in Chapter 4 – but does not of necessity mean that it will. How heritage is used may thus have more to say about wider issues, such as the politics of class, than it has about the nature of heritage or the so-called industry of heritage itself. Industrial social history museums and/or the acknowledgement of labour or industrial heritage cannot be characterized as a sop for deindustrialization or the 'end of work'. Those surveyed were actively using these places as cultural tools in a process that, while recognizing the past nature of aspects of working and social lives, was nonetheless about the negotiation and renegotiation of the meaning of work, community and family life in contemporary society.

7

THE SLATE WIPED CLEAN?

Heritage, memory and landscape in Castleford, West Yorkshire, England

This chapter examines how a community in Northern England is consciously using cultural heritage to engender a sense of place. Castleford, West Yorkshire (Figure 7.1), is a small town in the throws of deindustrialization. Although known primarily as a coal-mining town, Castleford was also home to a range of other industries, most of which have now closed. The loss of these industries, together with the aftermath of the 1984–5 miners' strike, has shaken community cohesion and pride. The strong social ties that tightly bind communities centred on specific industries, and in particular coal mining, are well documented (see Richards 1997; Crang 2001; Hutton 2005 for coal; and also Bruno 1999; Nadel-Klein 2003; Stenning 2005 for other industries). However, mass job losses and unemployment have threatened the stability of these ties. During the miners' strike[1] the Thatcher Conservative Government targeted and attacked the social and cultural bedrock that underpinned the identity of mining communities. With the closure of industries, many of the industrial buildings, pits, machinery, high-density terraced housing and the 'back-to-backs'[2] that were supplied to mine and other workers were torn down and redeveloped – the slate, so to speak, was wiped clean. The authorized heritage discourse cannot readily recognize that Castleford has any 'heritage' left, as memory alone is untrustworthy without the material evidence. However, many residents of Castleford who, in a range of ways, are self-consciously creating a new heritage and range of memories linked to existing memory and experience, do not accept this. This chapter examines the ways in which heritage is understood and actively used in Castleford to redefine community identity and cohesion.

What is revealed in this chapter is the way the AHD can and does exclude notions of heritage based on working class experiences and values. More importantly, however, the chapter demonstrates that this exclusion is contested and subverted at community levels. Dominant ideas about the heritage values of 'authentic material culture' and the 'built environment' are

Figure 7.1 Castleford, West Yorkshire, England – locality map (A. Marshall).

being rewritten and redefined within a cultural process that privileges the performativity of 'doing' and 'being', rather than the possession of, or association with, material objects. This is not to say that the physicality of place and object are abandoned as important elements in the heritage process, but rather they are de-privileged, and reassigned supporting roles in a process that is fundamentally about providing and creating opportunities for acts of remembering and commemoration, and above all social networking. This process is not based on backward-looking reactionary nostalgia or a unified or consensual view of the past, it is rather about utilizing collective remembering to foster community cultural and economic growth and to recognize and celebrate diversity and change. This is particularly important in Castleford as the community is making an active attempt to overcome the social and economic trauma of the miners' strike and its aftermath.

Castleford is a community whose economic and cultural contribution to the nation has been marginalized or obscured, both through the way history is defined and authorized in England, but also actively so by Conservative government policies and practices during the 1980s and 1990s.

These practices sought firstly to demoralize mining communities during the miners' strike and, secondly, to justify the consequences of their industrial policies during the following decade. Subsequently, any assertion of a sense of heritage in Castleford must be understood as dissonant in two ways. Firstly, it is dissonant because it sits outside of the AHD, while also asserting a sense of community identity and cohesion that is challenging the community's isolation and marginalization in the wider historical and cultural narratives of England. Secondly, it is also a heritage associated with trauma and community distress. Chapter 6 revealed the importance of remembering and commemoration as fundamental to the cultural process of heritage, and this chapter reinforces those observations, but goes on to demonstrate the social and cultural work that this process does at community level. The argument pursued in this chapter is that heritage is something that is actively made in the present in response to cultural, social and economic needs and aspirations. It is a process of doing in which heritage is made and remade through the creation of memories and experiences, and thus heritage in Castleford is ultimately about maintaining and re/creating interpersonal relations that are knitted together to foster community identity.

This chapter is based on interviews[3] with 39 Castleford residents, 17 of whom are members of the Castleford Heritage Trust (discussed below). Ethnographic work with the Castleford Heritage Trust (CHT) was also undertaken during 2003–5, when the author attended meetings and other public events organized by the Trust. Since 2001, the CHT has organized and run the week-long Castleford Festival (discussed below), and in 2004 and 2005 a questionnaire survey of 107 people in the town centre was undertaken during the parade and street performances that mark the end of the festival. The questionnaire asks a sequence of open-ended questions about respondents' thoughts on 'heritage' generally, Castleford's heritage, and their opinion and assessment of the festival and the work of the CHT more generally. In the discussion below, extracts from interviews and the questionnaire survey are given anonymously. The questionnaire was administered one-to-one, with the interviewer recording the answers of the respondents. All but four of the formal interviews were taped and most interviews were conducted one to one; though five of the interviews were either with couples or with small groups of three to five people.

For the most part, the members of the CHT and residents of Castleford interviewed for this work tended to be in the over-40 age group, a group Charlesworth (2000: 2) identifies as having a far more 'coherent way of describing their lives and a sense of what has happened to the working class' than younger people tend to have. Certainly, this chapter makes no claim about the representativeness of those interviewed. Rather, it aims to examine how some people are going through a complex process of drawing on ideas about heritage to frame and understand their own life experiences, while actively attempting to create a sense of heritage to foster community goals, and to instil a sense of shared culture and experience for younger residents of Castleford.

History and place

In the growing field of working class studies, researchers have increasingly argued that class matters in terms of the construction and expression of a range of sub-national collective identities (Bruno 1999; Charlesworth 2000; hooks 2000; Linkon and Russo 2002; Strangleman 2005). Although it is impossible to assert the existence of a single 'working class identity' as matters of race, ethnicity, gender and other issues will cross cut the expression and construction of identity (Gilroy 1987; hooks 2000), class consciousness and class-based community identity are often integrally linked with sense of place (Russo and Linkon 2005: 8).

Castleford, which sits on the confluence of the Calder and Aire rivers, was originally a Roman settlement established soon after AD 71, and a strategically important Roman fort was built there in the third – fourth centuries. The Roman name for Castleford was either Legeolium or Lagentium (Wilders 1995: 15) and a range of remains, including the fort and a bathhouse, has been found in and around Castleford. Archaeologists have excavated a number of sites, and the artefacts found both during these excavations and those found through inadvertent discoveries, including a Roman milestone, have been removed from Castleford and sent to museums in the nearby cities of Wakefield and Leeds. The discovery of the remains of the bathhouse in 1978, and its excavation in the early 1980s, is a significant memory for many residents of Castleford (see below). Although the bathhouse has been covered back over, the desire to uncover it once again, and permanently put it on public display, is an important issue for many Castleford residents. The Roman remains have also attracted the attention of the archaeological television programme *Time Team*, a very popular weekly programme shown on Channel 4 television in Britain. Each episode documents the excavations of selected sites undertaken, usually over a three-day period, by the programme's team of archaeologists. *Time Team* excavated part of the Roman fort in 2002 and supported on air the desire expressed by many residents for the development of a town museum and the return of artefacts held in nearby Wakefield and Leeds (Channel 4 2002). The repatriation of Roman material back to Castleford is a significant issue to many residents and is discussed below.

After the Romans left some form of settlement seems to have continued at Castleford, but very little is known or documented about the town's history until the eighteenth century (Wilders 1995: 17). In the eighteenth and nineteenth centuries, Castleford's population increased steadily as a range of industries developed within the town – attracted to the region by its diverse and extensive natural resources of coal, clay and sand. The rapid growth of the town at this time was also facilitated by the ability to transport both resources and goods along the Aire and Calder rivers (Taylor 2003). Local historian David Wilders (1995, 2003) has documented the growth of Castleford's industries. As he shows, one of the first of these to develop was the pottery works, with the first pottery opening in 1724. Bricks and coarse and fineware pottery were made by a number of potteries, although only Clokies and Hartleys survived into the twentieth century. Glass manufacturing was also an important Castleford industry that developed in the Glasshoughton region of Castleford sometime in the 1700s. In 1915, Hickson and Partners (later Hickson and Welch) built a chemical works that became one of the largest employers in the town (Wilders 1995: 72). Other significant industries included tailoring, flour milling at the Allinson Mill, and confectionary manufacture at Bellamy's (later Macintosh and then Nestlé). Prominent among these industries was coal mining. Although surface mining occurred from the 1500s onwards, the industry took off in the nineteenth century with the opening of Whitwood, Wheldale, Glasshoughton and Fryston collieries.

Although Castleford is best known as a 'mining town' its other industries have also been highly significant to its population. The prominence of mining presents an essentially masculine image of Castleford, however the potteries largely employed women, and ex-pottery workers talk proudly of the artistic skills the workforce possessed in, amongst other things, decorating and glazing pottery (Cas06 2004;[3] Cas10 2004; see also Wilders 2003). Women were also the main labour force at the confectionary factories and in the tailoring industry.

Post-war industrial change, deindustrialization and the 'end of work', however, had a significant impact on Castleford. By 1961, the last of the potteries had closed; followed by the demolition of most of the buildings associated with this industry. In 1983, the last glassworks closed with the loss of 600 jobs. The 1984–5 miners' strike saw 3,000 jobs lost in Castleford, with most mines closing shortly after the strike, others in the mid-1990s and the last (Prince of Wales Colliery) closing in the Castleford-Wakefield region in 2002. The impact of this strike and governmental responses to it were keenly felt in Castleford, with some in the CHT noting that their efforts with heritage matters are an attempt to resurrect community pride which took a severe bashing at this time (Cas18 2004; Cas19 2004). Not only did the pit closures have a major economic impact, they also had an immeasurable consequence for community pride and security. For instance, the police, who were used by the Thatcher Government to break up picket lines to allow strikebreakers into the mines, are to this day not trusted in many mining communities, Castleford included (Cas14 2004). One CHT member noted that it had taken 20 years for Castleford to get over the shock of that period and to remember that Castleford, as a community, mattered (Cas19 2004). In 2005, the Hickson and Welch chemical works, then known as 'C6', closed, with the loss of at least 300 jobs.

The landscape of Castleford has undergone major changes – as each industry has closed most of the industrial buildings have been demolished and
the sites redeveloped. New housing estates have overlain the high-density
terraced and back-to-back housing, changing not only the streetscapes
but also the focus and nature of interactions with neighbours. Interviews
reveal that the focus of community interaction in the terraced housing
and back-to-backs was inevitably the street frontages (this form of housing
either having small backyards or lacking them altogether, and in some
areas requiring communal ablution blocks), and the sense of privacy in this
form of housing was entirely different to that offered by the new estates
characterized by semi-detached housing, many with front and rear gardens
or yards:

> When you was in the back-to-back house, so you didn't have a back
> door, you had a front door. Everything went on in the street and that
> were the entertainment, doing something in the street.
>
> (Cas05 2004: 19)

> [You] used to know everyone in your street, but not now. People get
> in their car and go to work and come home in their car so don't get to
> meet people in their street.
>
> (Cas01 2004: 4)

> There were a lot of neighbourly [feeling], and there was a lot of back-
> to-back houses and street houses and, I mean, people never used to
> lock their doors and they used to keep an eye on them and look after
> kids. You know, take a pride in doing the steps and that, that type of
> thing. So they were very community spirited.
>
> (Cas10 2004: 13)

This is not to say that the removal of the back-to-back and other areas of
high-density housing are lamented, as they were associated with overcrowding
and poverty:

> Although mining's been a well-paid job over the last couple of dec-
> ades, when I was a child it was a poorly paid job . . . most people
> were relatively poor, or very poor in fact, never mind relatively. I
> came from a large family . . . And we lived in a two-up and two-
> down, as many others did. No hot water, no bathrooms of course,
> they used what everybody knows about nowadays, the old tin bath
> hung on the nail in the yard, the back yard, the toilet at the bottom
> of the back yard, which froze in the winter, and well, services were
> pretty bad, and we were pretty poor.
>
> (Cas09 2004: 1–2)

Further, the new estates are often seen as a positive development: 'I couldn't have envisaged this estate when I were in my twenties or whatever . . . So we have really moved on' (Cas15 2004: 6–7). However, the changing landscape has reflected changing work patterns and domestic lives, and has both mirrored and affected the interaction of neighbours, and subsequently individual perceptions of changes to community spirit and belonging.

The removal of industries has also had a significant impact on the town, as not only have the landscape and skylines altered, but declines in noise levels, air quality and the day-to-day presence of pollutants in the form of soot, smog and foam deposits churned up in the river have altered Castleford's ambiance. These changes are not seen as negative by the Castleford community, but it is important to note the degree to which the built environment and landscape of Castleford has changed. The commercial centre of Castleford has also changed, and this change is less well received by many residents. The old market hall, which features prominently in many people's recollections of the town, although still extant, is no longer used as a market and has been replaced by new forms of shopping centres and market facilities. As one member of the CHT noted, the economic and social despondency of Castleford is reflected in the number of charity, cut-price and pound shops that now dot the main shopping streets (Cas19 2004). As documented in the ex-steel milling town of Youngstown, USA, changes in industrial landscapes have a significant and often complex inter-relation with individual and collective memories (Linkon and Russo 2002; see also Mellor and Stephenson 2005). Nor are the memories of workers and their families necessarily ones that everyone wants to commemorate. The desire to forget the brutalities of poor pay and working conditions in dangerous industries has seen some de-industrialized towns or regions actively reject the idea of preserving the industrial landscape (Barthel 1996: 58–9; Donald Insall Associates 2000: 6).

With many of the industrial buildings of Castleford removed, a common observation is that the 'heritage of Castleford is dead'. This remark, recorded in a conversation with five Castleford women not involved with the CHT (9 March 2004), relates to the observations they made that 'Castleford doesn't have a lot of landmarks'. They went on to note that 'Castleford hasn't got any nice buildings – [they are all] pulled down', although on reflection, they concluded that Castleford never had any nice buildings anyway, not even those that had been pulled down. The theme of lost heritage, or the idea that Castleford never had any nice buildings (and thus heritage), was reflected in some of the street surveys. In a response to a request for people to identify the places, buildings or sites important to Castleford, 20 per cent of respondents lamented the loss of the town's built heritage, and thus concluded that Castleford had no heritage, or noted that Castleford simply had no heritage to begin with:

[Castleford's heritage is] Roman, industrial heritage – but all gone now.

(CF5 2004, male, over 60, joiner)

[Castleford's heritage is] Roman and mining, amongst other things we have lost.

(CF80 2005, male, 40–60, civil servant)

Didn't know Castleford had one [a heritage].

(CF106 2005, male, 40–60, ambulance driver)

We've lost most of it, haven't we? There were mining, there were potteries, there were sewing industries. The hospital, we lost that. What else have we lost? Before there was a shopping centre but there's nothing. We'd the best markets in Yorkshire.

(Cas12 2004: 1)

Certainly, the privileging of the grand, aesthetically pleasing and monu-mental in the AHD underlines and frames observations that 'Castleford has no heritage'. This echoes an observation by Denis Byrne (2001: 7, 2003) that a dominant assumption in the heritage sector is that buildings are self-classifying, and that their fabric will simply proclaim identity and signifi-cance. The architectural historian Sir Nikolaus Pevsner observed in his definitive architectural survey of England: 'What can the architectural recorder say about Castleford? There does not seem to be a single building in the centre of the town, which would justify mention' (Pevsner [1959] 1986: 158), and thus he dismisses the town as having no historical and cultural significance.

Today the population of Castleford is approximately 40,000, with a pre-dominantly Anglo population, with less than 1 per cent of residents identify-ing in the 1991 census as being from an ethnic background other than 'White-British'. Twenty per cent of the population of the town occupy the two lowest categories of attainment in health provision, education and unemployment in an analysis of the indices of deprivation for the region (Wakefield District Multi Agency Information Group 2002). Castleford has been the subject of a range of regeneration initiatives to bring employ-ment into the town. The building of the Freeport Outlet Village and the XSCAPE leisure complex has featured in this process. Castleford is also the subject of a new initiative in regeneration strategies and 'The Castleford Project' is one such government-funded initiative. This project involves the collaborative work of Wakefield Metropolitan District Council, within whose boundaries Castleford now lies, the Commission for Architecture and the Built Environment, English Partnerships, Yorkshire Forward, Ground-work UK and the Coalfields Regeneration Trust. The development, progress and impact of this project is currently being filmed for Channel 4 by the production company Talkback UK and will be screened as a documentary series. An analysis by the Office of the Deputy Prime Minister (ODPM) of the regeneration of former coalfield areas concluded that:

> The Castleford case-study area had shown a fragile recovery from the pit closures that extended over a long period of time from the early 1980s to the mid 1990s. Whilst total employment growth resumed in the mid 1990s and unemployment rates approached regional and national averages, there was evidence of disguised unemployment (in the form of long-term sickness) and out-migration and commuting and a decline in GDP and earnings per head for those employed in the area and Wakefield more generally. The area had to contend with a mature economic structure in which high technology/knowledge-based activity was relatively limited, there was a low educational attainment base, the lack of a strong entrepreneurial culture, and an adverse image — as much to do with its industrial roots than with the physical aftermath of the decline of coal.
>
> (ODPM n.d.)

Pendlebury et al. (2004) documented the connection, established in England during the 1980s and 1990s, of the heritage sector to urban regeneration efforts, wherein cultural re-branding exercises became integral to regeneration agendas. Local residents in Castleford are well aware of the negative image of their town and see this as an impediment to economic investment. Those interviewed not only regarded the physical regeneration of the town as vital, but also clearly identified this as interlinked with redefining the town's cultural image. An argument put forward by residents is that attention to both environmental and cultural issues in regeneration policies and activities will mean that fewer younger people will want to leave Castleford, and that it will become a place attractive to outside employers and workers, in particular promoting white collar work opportunities. This is not gentrification, or an aesthetic remake of the town, but a cultural and social process to do with memory in the present and the creation (but not simply re-creation) of identity. In identifying the significance of cultural issues in the regeneration process, those interviewed were not concerned about creating so much a *new* image of Castleford, but rather both bolstering and asserting the extant social and cultural vitality and legitimacy of the sense of community that both in the past and present defined 'Castleford' to its residents. It is useful to note here that there is a startling lack of reactionary nostalgia or sentimentality in this cultural process. The 'better back then ethos' is almost entirely missing, and there is no attempt to romanticize the brutalities of the mining and other industrial pasts. There is, however, a real sense of a lament for community camaraderie associated with mining communities, and it is this sense of community that residents, and the CHT in particular, hope to save and reinvigorate. The brutalities of high-density housing and industrial Castleford are remembered entirely to underline the achievements of the present, and to anchor future negotiations about Castleford community identity to critical class-consciousness. As Alison Drake, Chair of the CHT, notes:

> During the last two decades at the end of the 20th century in Castleford I witnessed the deliberate destruction of the coal industry and the total disregard for the suffering of the mining community by the Thatcher Government. The costs to individuals and the community that I saw caused me to be increasingly driven to strive for improvements in our town environment, social conditions, and local services and community life. This desire grew from experiences as a member of the community, from being part of a large mining family and also as a primary school teacher in some of the most deprived areas. I found that when I voiced my concerns about the state of our local environment, the neglect and decline of what had been a thriving, working, supportive community there were others in the town who also wanted to try to bring about improvements.
>
> (Drake 2004: 1)

However, as Pendlebury et al. (2004) argue, the social values that underlie the processes of heritage management and conservation that have become enmeshed with urban regeneration polices and practices are not necessarily socially inclusive or progressive. As they note, 'partnership building' has been a significant policy feature of urban regeneration, whereby multi-stakeholder involvement in regeneration schemes, as at Castleford, is seen as desirable. However, they argue that negotiations and consultations between stakeholder groups are often too short lived to transform power relations (2004: 26), and thus certain values and aspirations can become naturalized while others are marginalized. Within the regeneration process traditional values about the nature, meaning and value of heritage as defined by the AHD are not only unproblematically assumed, but are actively reinforced. This occurs through the ability of aesthetically pleasing tangible heritage resources to facilitate the regeneration process by improving the aesthetic ambiance of communities, thus aiding re-branding. The examples of urban regeneration based on partnerships given by Pendlebury et al. in Redruth, Cornwall, and Cresswell in the Nottinghamshire coalfield, demonstrate that the conservation of the historic environment played central roles in the regeneration processes of both community and property. However, as they go on to observe, this contribution was coincidental, as these deprived communities happened to have building stock that could be 'considered historic in conventional terms' (2004: 26). So what happens when the slate of the built environment is not only wiped clean, but also when stock that may be valued in conventional terms does not exist? What does *not* happen is a process of substitution; Castleford residents are not attempting to develop a sense of community heritage to compensate for the lack of conventional heritage items. Rather, Castleford offers the opportunity to reveal the existence of other forms and meanings of heritage that exist within Western societies, but do so outside of the boundaries of the AHD. An increase in the expression of sub-national identities is predicted in the literature on globalization and on post-industrial change in the West (Inglehard and Baker 2000: 21). While Castleford is responding to a need to define and redefine itself in these contexts, the expression of identity that residents are attempting to assert is organically linked to community and class experience that does not, and perhaps never did, take its cue from national consensual narratives. Contra to the detraditionalization literature discussed in Chapter 2, tradition here is not abandoned, although it is being used in a very modern sense. Links to the past that draw on past experiences and community traditions are not abandoned, but are used to anchor and underline new forms of community expression.

'But Miss, what's the black lump?' Memory and heritage in Castleford

In this section I want to not only examine how heritage is defined and understood in Castleford, but also to examine the work that this sense of heritage does and how tensions between this and the AHD are worked out, resisted and at times incorporated within community definitions and uses of heritage. Heritage became a public community issue in Castleford in 1999–2000, when a small group of residents campaigned to have the clock put back on the old market hall in time for the millennium. The clock was once an important meeting place and older residents used to organize to meet friends 'under the market clock'. The market hall itself, together with the town library beside it, were important places not only in terms of their primary functions as market and library, but also as meeting places and places of social networking and interaction. The library, one of the most heavily used local libraries in the country, along with the market hall, are often described by residents as central to community identity. Although not architecturally noteworthy in conventional terms, it is the sense of place that they provide that is identified as valuable to residents. When residents were quizzed on which sites, buildings or places in Castleford were most important to them, the market hall and library complex were inevitably top on people's lists. In the street survey, 51 per cent mentioned them individually or collectively as significant sites. When quizzed further, the sense of place represented by these buildings centred both on the roles they played as a resource and as focal points in community interactions and networking.

247

When asked about important or vivid memories of Castleford, 15 per cent of people in the street survey also nominated shopping at the old market hall as an important memory (see Table 7.2, discussed below). As one resident noted, the activity of 'shopping' is central to community interaction and identity:

> Well, I think one of the central things [that is significant] is the town centre and the market because that attracts a lot of people. You can go into Castleford town centre any time, any day, particularly if it's nice, and you'll see lots of people. Now at one time, years and years ago, the market was in a different place, open air market. There's still an open air market today but it's in a different place and it's not the same as what it used to be. And there were hundreds of people always knocking about shopping, particularly on a Saturday. And even today there's people come from as far away as York and miles and miles around. They come to Castleford to do their shopping because they like coming here because the people are so friendly I think, and understanding and helpful, and I've spoke to quite a few people, along with the heritage people [CHT], and I've asked them that question, so they like to come here because they're so friendly and helpful and understanding.
>
> (Cas15 2004: 3)

The importance of the friendly character of the community is a point of pride in Castleford, and many people interviewed on the street noted that the defining feature of the Castleford community was its friendliness. As one resident and ex-miner observed: '[The] community's about neighbours and the street, and everybody being linked in together and looking after each other. Watching out for each other' (Cas14 2004: 3). This friendliness is often sourced to the dominance of the mining industry in the town and the culture of the work in which people watched one another's backs. When people in the street survey were asked about what memories of Castleford were most vivid to them, one of the recurring memories (8 per cent – see Table 7.2, discussed below) was the friendliness of the community:

> People friendly, helpful, understanding, pride in place.
> (CF1 2004, male, 65, bus driver)

> People – good, honest, friendly.
> (CF18 2004, male, 30–40, car painter)

> People. Friendliness of the people.
> (CF53 2004, female, 40–60, laundry assistant)

> I came to Castleford from a village (lived here 40 years), but couldn't
> meet more friendly people – people make the place.
>
> (CF54 2004, female 40–60, funeral director)

The maintenance of the friendly character of the community occurs
through social interaction, networking and communication. In defining the
places most important in Castleford, one woman (Cas10 2004: 12–13) nominated the modern Carlton Lanes shopping arcade because 'It's somewhere
you can go and sit, and it's – that's what I like. Where people sit, because
Castleford people like to sit and talk, you know. I've noticed that, the seats
get full.' Another resident, an ex-miner, also remarked of the same arcade
that it's 'a nice meeting place, is that. That's what we need more of. A town
– I mean that's what it's lacking in some respects is a good town square
where you can meet' (Cas05 2004: 19). While many people identified that
they 'owe[ed] a lot to the library at Castleford' (Cas09 2004: 10) because of
its role in supporting educational aspirations, the library and market complex also represented a point where community networking, entertainment
and sense of identity came together:

> Before there was a shopping centre but there's nothing. We'd the
> best markets in Yorkshire. Not now. There's nothing. It used to be
> the highlight of my day when I were little, about 13, I lived in
> Airedale then. And it were my treat to come down to town on my
> own on a Saturday and I used to stand – I don't know if they're still
> there but there were some steps going down onto where the old
> market used to be – and there was two stalls. One had pots and pans
> and one had bedding, and they used to be shouting one to the other,
> real market – I'd stand there all morning. Nothing, there's no – I
> don't know, they're characters, aren't they? [Name of stall owner]
> she used to get onto her husband all the time and they did rapping
> back at him and he'd be throwing his cups and we'd be stood there
> waiting for them to drop. They were markets.
>
> (Cas12 2003: 1–2)

> All the different industries around Castleford, mainly the men
> particularly congregated because of what they did. I mean the old
> Castleford market where the, around the side of where the library is
> now, where the shops are, they were all open stores, and you can, I
> can guarantee every evening if you walked down you would find
> the men all sat on the stalls smoking and talking. So it was a
> get-together point, as was the old lamp on Bridge Street.
>
> (Cas06 2004: 16)

Residents young and old in both interviews and street surveys frequently identified another 'site' of importance. Known as the Castleford forum, a lamppost used to sit on a plinth in the centre of the intersection of Aire Street and Bridge Road (Figure 7.2). Although it has long since been removed – a traffic roundabout now covers the position of the lamppost – the site remains firmly fixed in Castleford's collective memory. The men of Castleford used to sit around this post, also identified as the 'old men's parliament' (Cas21 2004), discuss work and social issues and resolve conflicts and generally socialize. Oliver and Reeves (2003) similarly report that workers at the Midland Railway Workshops in Western Australia identified as significant to them the flagpole around which workers gathered for stop work meetings and to hear political and industrial speeches. The flagpole had

Figure 7.2 The Castleford Forum or 'old man's parliament'. Once located on the intersection of Aire Street and Bridge Road, but now removed. Photo by Jack Hulme, reproduced here with permission from Wakefield Metropolitan District Council Museum and Arts.

become central to issues of industrial management, and conciliation and arbitration, and thus symbolic of the workers' identity as an industrially active collective. Only the oldest person I interviewed (aged 90) had first-hand memories of the forum, and even though it does not physically exist, it remains significant as a heritage site. Like the market hall complex, the forum also represented and symbolized the stuff of community cohesion – communication and networking, albeit on this occasion a gender-specific section of the community. The significance of the intangible social elements and values that the forum represents have not been diminished by the absence of the lamppost's physical presence and it remains symbolic in the collective memory of Castleford as representative of what heritage is and does.

In 2000, following the success of restoring and reinstalling the clock on the market hall, several community groups came together to form the Castleford Heritage Group (now the Castleford Heritage Trust). Over 400 people attended the first meeting (Drake 2004: 3). The significance of this was underlined by one of the CHT committee members (an ex-Trades Union Congress secretary, active in economic regeneration efforts) who noted that, in the whole five towns Wakefield area important public meetings about economic renewal are often lucky to get 30 people attending, but CHT meetings can regularly attract over 300 people (Cas19 2004). The Castleford Forum Project developed out of the initial meeting in 2000, and the project aims to agitate for the development of a new or expanded library, restoration of the market hall for gallery or other community meeting space, and the development of a community museum. The CHT and the Forum project are also concerned with lobbying local government and other agencies about the significance of Castleford's heritage, and helped persuade Channel 4 to choose Castleford for its series on regeneration. The CHT has also successfully sought money from the Heritage Lottery Fund[4] to finance the initial stages of the Forum Project and the Castleford Festival (discussed below). The vision of both the Forum Project and the CHT is summarized by the CHT Chair:

> We have a rich and varied heritage that we want to pass on to our children and future generations. We want local people to be proud of their roots and enjoy learning about life in our town over previous generations and civilisations. We want community esteem so that local children can grow in self-esteem and value their town and community and in their turn grow up to take responsibility. We want them to learn from the past to value education and the acquisition of skills and knowledge. We see these issues as important considerations in the vision for 'The Castleford Forum'.
>
> (Drake 2004: 5–6)

The point made here about the acquisition of skills and knowledge is an important one, as it emphasizes that integral to the ethos of heritage being developed in Castleford is not only the concept, but also the desirability, of change. 'Conserve as found', even in terms of social and cultural practices and experiences, is not constitutive or applicable to a sense of Castleford heritage. As one community member, not involved with the CHT, observed about the character of the Castleford community:

> Tough and gritty. Adaptable. Look forward to change. I don't think – miners have been described as a bit stuck in the past, that they're wanting the pits back, you know, the industry. But I don't think that's true. I think that these areas – miners have always moved about, they've moved from pit to pit, from coalfield to coalfield. There's communities in Castleford that are originally from Scotland, Wales, north-east, but there's also communities here that come from Ireland. And they've all come and moved all over Britain, sort of thing. And they follow change, it's excited them. So I don't think Castleford's looking towards the past, I think it's looking for something exciting, it's looking for a change, so I disagree with the sort of people who tend to think that we're like moribund, we're passed our sell-by date, and I don't think they're right.
>
> (Cas14 2004: 3)

This sentiment was also echoed by a respondent in the street survey:

> Castleford was a growth town over 100 years ago. Still has that spirit of growth. By growth I mean cultural – not size. Lots of people have come to Castleford in the last 100 years – pioneering spirit and cultural spirit, social spirit. Social spirit is important in terms of people wanting to belong to a community rather than sit in their houses as individuals. There is a definite desire for people to be part of a community.
>
> (CF7 2004, male, 40–60, lab technician)

The sense of 'heritage' that emerges here is one that incorporates both the tangible and intangible heritage, but the emphasis is placed on what heritage does. In the street surveys, when respondents were asked to define their idea of 'heritage', 11 per cent provided answers within the expected confines of the AHD, for instance it was 'grand buildings', something 'belonging to the nation' and so forth ('things from the past' and 'national identity' in Table 7.1). However, 22 per cent identified their understanding of heritage as entirely intangible, nominating such things as 'my family', the community, 'people' or 'a sense of place' (Table 7.1). For instance, heritage means 'family, friends, it just means everyone looking after everyone' (CF71 2004, female, 40–60, housewife, husband an engineer).

Table 7.1 Castleford: What does the word heritage mean to you?

Response	Frequency	%
No response	21	19.6
History in general	19	17.8
It's all gone	1	0.9
Local history	21	19.6
Material things from the past	9	8.4
Intangible (traditions, family history, memories, music, etc.)	23	21.5
National identity	3	2.8
Nothing	6	5.6
Patrimony/preservation	4	3.7
Total	107	100

A strong emphasis on community also emerged from many of the interviews as defining not only heritage in general, but Castleford's heritage in particular. This was often tied to and defined against a background of civic pride in two aspects of the town's history — its Roman period and its industrial history, for instance:

> I actually think the heritage is the people that actually reside in this place at this time, as well as what's gone before, but with the heritage of what's gone before.
>
> (Cas14 2004: 2)

> I think Castleford's heritage is the river, the industry, the Romans, Henry Moore [artist, born and raised in Castleford] and being a nice community. I think Castleford's a very friendly community.
>
> (Cas10 2004: 9)

> Hmmm, on a personal note it's — I look at the individual side of it. To some extent the working class of this area, I suppose, not just Castleford but Wakefield and West Riding I suppose. But Castleford because of the . . . um, I suppose circumstance that were laid down what is it, 60 [or] 300 whichever million years ago, we got loads of bloody coal underneath us that helped and developed the industrial revolution that we did.
>
> (Cas05 2004: 5)

> Well, heritage I think, to me, it means — what the area you live in. What it's been in the past. What's gone on in the past such as the coal mining, glass bottle making, and different industries like that. Potteries. There were two or three pottery works. Chemical works,

but one of the most important heritage things, I think, is the Roman scenario and in fact we've got – someone found a Roman milestone years and years and years ago, and that's been taken there – it's made its way to Leeds somehow, but we've asked for it back. It's a vast object and it's very important.

(Cas15 2004: 1)

The Roman and industrial history of the town are collectively regarded as highly important in defining Castleford's heritage. In the street survey, 29 per cent of people defined Castleford's heritage as both Roman and industrial (a further 19 per cent defined it as only 'Roman' and 17 per cent as 'industrial'). The stress on both Roman and industrial heritage is a point of view universally supported by those interviewed. Indeed, one of the major concerns of many residents is the conservation and interpretation of the Roman bathhouse, and the Roman period is often used to give a certain historical patina to the industrial history and heritage of Castleford and the community itself:

[Heritage is . . .] our physical environment, how it's changed over the centuries. The artefacts which have been produced in this area and the factories, which you can no longer see, which my father worked at [name] manufacturers for 29 years – you can't see that any more, but I remember being taken round that factory as a little girl. The importance of our very ancient artefacts, the Roman artefacts and so on. We should be able to show this to the rest of the community and so increase their awareness and their confidence in our heritage, because we may have been poor people, but we were hard working.

(Cas17 2003: 1–2)

The concern for the bathhouse and the significance of the Roman period generally to the residents of Castleford may seem to contradict the emphasis placed on intangible notions of identity based around a sense of 'community', class and family. However, as the above extract reveals, the Romans provide a sense of pride in demonstrating not only the long history of the Castleford community, but that the community and its achievements are anchored or linked to wider narratives of national history. It also needs to be noted that there is an absence of material culture dating from post-Roman and medieval periods in the town, with almost all building stock dating to the nineteenth and twentieth centuries. As one person noted in a meeting of the CHT, there is literally only Roman and industrial material remains in the town. However, nationally the Romans are regarded as historically significant in British national identity and authorized accounts of British and, in particular, English history. As Hingley (2000) has argued, Imperial Rome has been used as an analogy for Britain's own imperial past, and although the image and idea of Rome as the ancestor of Western 'civilization' is shared by many European countries, it nonetheless continues to inform a sense of 'English-ness'. In the extract above, the juxtaposition of the heritage values of the industrial artefacts with those of the Romans is unconsciously used to both legitimize the heritage values of industrial Castleford and contemporary community pride. The juxtaposition of Roman and industrial heritage was one that occurred again and again in both interviews and street surveys. Here, a member of the CHT talks about her memories of the archaeological excavations in Castleford:

> Well I am impressed by the Roman things, and I, I think when you've had a stud put on your hand and they say, 'what do you think that is', 'well it's a stud', 'well, here's the sandal it came out of', they put a sandal on your hand that was Roman, and that feeling is . . . I think it's that sort of thing . . . to remember . . . and when we had children who didn't know what a piece of coal was . . . that nearly floored me I thought, and it's so close . . . it's only '86 when we had four pits in the borough boundary, and we have children today who've never seen coal. Remembrance of that's our heritage to me.
>
> (Cas08 2003: 3)

The discussion of the emotional response the Roman material elicits, and the immediate jump to a discussion of memory and industrial experience as heritage is a rhetorical motif in which the AHD is again used to legitimize non-authorized aspects of heritage. Informed by archaeological knowledge and value, the AHD identifies Romans as authorized and validated heritage, while it excludes the memories that this member of the CHT identifies as equally important. The continual motif of juxtaposing Roman and industrial heritage is a discursive devise that unconsciously validates a community sense of heritage. This is not to say that Roman heritage is not important to Castleford for its own values. However, it also plays an important role in validating the sense of 'other' heritage that Castleford is attempting to assert.

The discourse of heritage that stresses family and community is one that sits in opposition to the AHD. The tension between the discourse of heritage used in Castleford and the AHD plays itself out in two ways, both overtly and covertly. Overtly, there is a very real sense that the Castleford community must demonstrate that it has a heritage and that its heritage is of value. For instance, a member of the CHT, in talking about the importance of the work the Trust is doing in Castleford, states:

> Well first of all I think it makes people realize that their back-grounds are important. They may be from poor mining villages and

mining families, but our heritage is just as important as a wealthy aristocrat's.

The results of the street survey show that one of the messages that respondents hoped the Festival, Forum Project and other CHT activities achieved was to send strong and positive messages both to other residents and to outsiders that Castleford had a heritage of worth. For instance:

Anything that brings Castleford into the public eye is important. There was a lot of despondency in Castleford after the mines closed and it's important that people understand Castleford is as important as it always was.
(CF2 2004, female, over 60, pharmacy technician)

Makes everyone know what's happening in Castleford. It puts Castleford on the map. Remember the pits!
(CF50 2004, female, 30–40, supervisor chocolate factory)

It's important to Castleford's prestige, to give it a sense of esteem. That Castleford is just as important as a community like Pontefract with its castle. [Neighbouring town with a visually prominent castle dated to the eleventh century.] Castleford suffered in the past with its polluting industry – foam off the river – so it's important to let people know that there are things to be proud of in this community. It helps give people self-esteem.
(CF51 2004, female, over 60, primary head teacher)

That we are very proud people in Castleford and that we are proud of what we have and what we have done.
(CF52 2004, female, 30–40, manager)

That we are proud of our heritage and that we are not quiet about it!
(CF59 2004, female, 40–60, funeral director)

That community does matter. Community spirit does matter. That change can be happy as well as hard.
(CF65 2004, male, 30–40, unemployed)

It's very easy for society to concentrate on the negatives and this [the Festival] shows that there are a lot of positive things in Castleford to celebrate.
(CF74 2005, female, 40–60, teacher)

The sense here is that what is valued in Castleford matters to residents very much; however, there is also a strong awareness that what is constituted as heritage in Castleford is either not 'real' or of little value to outsiders. This tension also plays itself out in a covert way as well. Although there is a strong tendency to juxtapose Roman and industrial heritage, and thus use the AHD about Roman history to legitimize other forms of Castleford's heritage, the use of the AHD is not entirely passive. There are very real attempts to subvert, control and assimilate this discourse into a sense of heritage that speaks to and makes sense within the context of the Castleford community. This is evident in the calls for repatriation of Roman artefacts to the town, as it is important for Castleford to control these artefacts and the meanings given to them, as much as it is for any community involved in the repatriation of cultural property. Symbolic control of certain prestigious items is a politically powerful statement of control over the meanings given to the past, and thus the present, which is an issue discussed in more detail in Chapter 8.

This attempt at subversion of the AHD is also graphically illustrated in the use of trades union banners during festivals and parades. Banners are an iconic symbol of labour and working class history and are often highly prized by social history museums (Mansfield 2004). The iconography used on the banners are also themselves symbolic of the values of organized labour and represent a visual discourse that speaks, amongst other things, about the values of unity, solidarity and resistance. In the Castleford Festival the old pit banners take pride of place in the street parade and other Festival activities, and are a significant material aid to memory and commemoration (Figure 7.3). Amongst these banners are also new banners, designed and made by the CHT, depicting Roman and other historically authorized periods of the town's history. Figure 7.4 compares and contrasts one of the pit banners telling the story of the miners' strike with that of Roman Castleford – the iconography is telling, in that the authorized Roman heritage has been translated into a community discourse. In this banner Roman history is retold and reworked in a form that speaks to and is interlinked with more recent community history and experience.

Other important aspects of Castleford's heritage identified by people both in interviews and in the street survey were the actual character of the Castleford community, its friendliness and its people:

> Mining town, bloody friendly place, tremendous community spirit.
> (CF93 2005, male, over 60, factory worker)

> Still a strong community feeling in Castleford.
> (CF18 2004, male, 30–40, car painter)

In addition, a range of forms of cultural life, such as family history, Castleford's rugby league club and musical traditions were also nominated. Two of the younger respondents nominated the XSCAPE leisure complex as

Figure 7.3 Inside the old market hall, Castleford, 2003. Festival exhibition of artwork and pit banners.

their most treasured aspect of Castleford's heritage, and also identified its construction as their most important memory of life in Castleford. The importance of community was also a memory that respondents in the survey nominated (8 per cent) when asked to identify their most vivid or important memory of Castleford (Table 7.2). A notable memory, often mentioned in interviews, and reported by 5 per cent of those surveyed, is of the pollution in Castleford, particularly the chemical foam churned up in the river at the weir below the flourmill, which used to regularly cover Castleford. This foam would blow across the town in massive quantities, reducing visibility and staining clothes. Curiously, this memory is never accompanied by criticism or concerns of the health risk it must have posed – but simply discussed as one of the notable aspects of past life in Castleford.

Memory and commemoration are integral aspects of Castleford's heritage: 'and we have children today who had never seen coal. Remembrance of that is our heritage to me' (Cas08 2003: 3). One of the significant events that galvanized many members of the CHT was the report that during an excursion by children from Glasshoughton's infants school to an exhibition on coal mining that was part of the first Castleford Festival in 2001, a child had asked: 'But Miss, what's the black lump?' (Drake personal communication).

Figure 7.4 Inside the old market hall, Castleford Festival, 2003. The National Union of Mineworkers (NUM) banner in the foreground depicts events in the 1984–5 miners' strike. The banner in the background depicts Castleford's Roman history and echoes the form and style of the pit banners. Its display alongside the pit banners is expressive of the inclusion and reworking of authorized Roman history and heritage into a community context and discourse.

This widely reported incident, in which a child had failed to recognize a piece of coal – something so intimately familiar to adult residents – has entered Castleford's collective memory as a point both of concern and as a rallying cry for community action. In addition to the Forum Project, the CHT has also commenced a programme of recording the reminiscences of residents about life in Castleford, and has published a book in which resident's reminiscences lead readers on four heritage trails across Castleford (Clayton 2005). 'Memory' is a significant motif in Castleford, and is often

Table 7.2 Vivid or important memories of Castleford

Response	*Frequency*	*%*
No response	31	29.0
Disasters (Second World War, explosion at chemical works, etc.)	6	5.6
Festival (2001–2004)	1	0.9
Foam blown up from the weir	5	4.7
Friendliness – sense of community	8	7.5
Industry	7	6.6
Lament about changes to urban landscape	4	3.7
Other	5	4.7
Parades/pageants/gala	3	2.8
Personal memories from childhood	6	5.6
Roman excavation	3	2.8
Rugby achievements	7	6.5
Shopping at the old market	16	14.9
Shopping at the new centre	3	2.8
XSCAPE – its opening	2	1.9
Total	107	100

used interchangeably with heritage and history in the discussion of Castleford's past. As Misztal (2004: 68) observes, the decline in national and religious memories has opened the conceptual space for sub-national memory to become 'one of the main discourses that is used strategically not merely to explain the group past but also to transform it into a reliable identity source for the group present'.

Crouch and Parker (2003: 396) note that *in doing* memories are recalled, and this sense of remembering underlies much of what is done with and understood about the nature of heritage in Castleford. Heritage in Castleford is very much about *doing* and not necessarily only or primarily *having*, the material elements that give the heritage discourse authority and 'reality'. Although exhibitions of mining and other industrial artefacts and photographs are important, one member of the CHT pointed out that 'what is a heritage artefact or place if it is not being used: it is nothing and valueless' (Cas18 2004). A significant part of the doing is the Castleford Festival itself. This festival intentionally invokes the memories of the mining gala days and pageants, often held during 'wakes week' when the pits were closed. Wakes week and other festivals and pageants often feature in residents' memories about Castleford:

> As kids we had wakes week when the mines closed and had a miners' gala, sports and brass bands. I used to look forward to this.
> (CF2 2004, female, over 60, pharmacy technician)

When I first came I liked Castleford – it was a very friendly town and apart from the dirt and the [pollution] it was a good bustling little place. We used to have carnivals, they were nice and involved all the associations in Castleford.

(CF3 2004, female, over 60, pharmacist)

Carnivals. They ran from Airedale to Queen's Park and there were pageants with different lorries from the firms. Wakes week.

(CF7 2004, male, 40–60, laboratory technician)

The festival commenced in 2001; it is a week-long community festival whose primary target audience is the community itself. It typically involves pageantry, a parade (Figure 7.5) and maypole, pottery painting demonstrations led by women who used to work in the potteries, and rag-rug making (Figure 7.6). Exhibitions of children's artwork and the work of current artists from Castleford also feature as part of festival events. The legacy of Henry Moore, a native of Castleford who is celebrated in the Castleford community but whose childhood house has been destroyed, is also seen as being significant. Although there is little tangible material in Castleford to remind residents of Moore's presence in the town (only one piece of his artwork is permanently on display in Castleford), he is actively remembered through the process of giving support to local contemporary artists and their work. Much of the artwork also reflects miners' lives, the strike and the consequences of deindustrialization. The festival is a period when both local past *and* contemporary artists and artwork are commemorated and remembered. Importantly, the festival also includes music, the male voice choirs and brass bands of the mining community are also prominent; while exhibitions of flower arrangements, needlework, poetry, natural history, environ-

Figure 7.5 The head of the closing parade of the 2004 Castleford Festival.

Figure 7.6 A member of the Castleford Heritage Trust shows a group of children how to make rag rugs at the 2004 Castleford Festival. Strips of cloth, cut from old clothes and other items, are pushed through a strip of hessian to create the pile of the rug. The underside of the rug is visible here. Rag-rug making featured in many residents' reminiscences of life in Castleford terraced housing or in the back-to-backs. These rugs, made by women and children, were often used to carpet the floors of these houses.

mental regeneration and archaeology have also occurred. The old market hall is often a central focus of festival activities and the site for exhibitions, music performances, maypole dancing and other activities. The pit banners often are an important feature, and have either decorated the market hall (Figure 7.3) or been carried in the parades (Figure 7.5). The banners are often a point of tension, as many of them are now stored and curated in museums outside of Castleford, and requests to use the banners have often been met with the comments that these items are too valuable to be used. For residents, however, these banners only have meaning if they are being used rather than being stored in museum vaults or displayed in exhibitions outside of Castleford. Their value lies in the memories they invoke about the industrial past, and about community identity, and this is best remembered through using the banners rather than simply viewing them in museum exhibits or through knowing they are kept safe in museum storerooms. As one observer of the 2004 festival parade stated:

[The festival is about] bringing together of young and old and remembering past traditions. The old banners remind us of the camaraderie of people who worked here. It's keeping history alive. I am remembering doing the maypole dances when I was young. It's keeping traditions alive like the maypole.

(CF54, 2004, female, 40–60, funeral director)

Kirshenblatt-Gimblett (1998) considered the paradox that often underpins museum displays – the practice of displaying objects that were never meant to be displayed, or at least not displayed as static objects in a museum glass case. The removal from community contexts and the display of items in museums and other historical or ethnographic exhibits renders, Kirshenblatt-Gimblett argues, the ethnographic object as objects of ethnography. These objects become artefacts of their collection and curation, and their associated meanings and values are transformed and altered. While this process is not necessarily a negative thing, it can, and clearly does in many instances (see also Chapter 8), affect the autonomy and authority of source communities to have the values and meanings they associate with objects validated and acknowledged. When items are particularly iconic, or considered to have symbolic authority, the ability to control or influence how those objects are understood is important in the politics of community and group representation.

Repatriation – the return of artefacts to source community control – becomes a csentral issue in the politics of representation. Kirshenblatt-Gimblett distinguishes between 'museums as a form of internment – a tomb with a view' and live displays (1998: 57). Festivals, she notes, are one such live display, and while museums and festivals are both performances of exhibition and display they represent different genres of display. In traditional museums, the visual sense tends only to be engaged and a sense of reverence and sober behaviour is expected of museum audiences. Festivals, as Kirshenblatt-Gimblett argues, are multisensory and multifocus events. The Castleford Festival is a display, a performance of heritage, that reworks, asserts and creates memories about Castleford and, like the Roman banner shown in Figure 7.4, offers its own discursive reading of history, heritage and memory in Castleford. Its existence as performance, the intangibility of the event – its very transience – is integral to the messages the community both constructs and 'tells' back to itself. These messages are not static – under glass and 'preserved' – but are continually negotiated and remade with each festival and heritage performance.

As with the Roman artefacts, there is also a desire to reclaim these banners and have them repatriated to the Castleford community. Castleford also has only one example of Henry Moore's artwork, and many residents express wistful longing to have more of his work exhibited within the town and the return of art material that once used to hang in public buildings, schools in particular, that were removed because of their value. The desire, too, to uncover the Roman bathhouse, despite the fears that most archaeologists would have about the conservation problems this would pose,[5] is also about the need to use the site and thus give it contemporary meaning, rather than to have it hidden away valued for the sake of 'future generations'. Any 'value' placed in the meaning that this site, or the banners or other objects, may have for future generations is both irrelevant and too distant in time for a community concerned with reinvigorating community cohesion and pride in the present. As noted above, the desire to have material repatriated to the community, so that the community may use it, and by using it assert contemporary community value and meaning, is a material statement about community pride:

> Most of the historical remains, for some reason were taken away by Leeds or Wakefield, and are stored there. In fact most of them are not even open to viewing, so what we do need in Castleford is a large centre where all these things can be brought together to show Castleford's heritage and history so that the children of Castleford have something to be really proud of instead of looking upon Castleford, as some people do, as an old mining town.
>
> (Cas09 2004: 11)

In summary, heritage in Castleford is an active process of doing and remembering. Artefacts, such as the banners, buildings like the market hall, and sites like the currently buried Roman bathhouse, are important, but in terms of how they provide opportunities for experiences and social activities. Their value lies in the uses they have and not because they simply 'are'. These artefacts, sites and buildings also have symbolic value and power in the community, as witnessed by the desire of the community to control that symbolism and meaning through the repatriation of Roman remains, banners and other materials back to community care. However, the symbolic value of tangible heritage is itself quite complex – as this symbolism and what a heritage site may mean to the community do not always need to reside in a tangible object. The meaning for instance of the original Forum, or 'old man's parliament', has not vanished or diminished by that site's destruction. The continuing importance of the forum's symbolism bears witness to the observation that the cultural practices of heritage are not only central to an understanding of what heritage is, but these practices can and do survive, if their meanings are powerful enough, without the object that may give that process an anchor in the physical world. This is not to proclaim that physical heritage is redundant, but simply that the values and meaning of heritage do not always need to be associated with, reside in or otherwise be linked to the physical and, more importantly, that the physical object or place is entirely meaningless without the cultural processes that occur at them. Memories, as Byrne reminds us, need leave no physical traces, and the privileging of fabric will often marginalize the social history and memories associated with place (2001, 2003). The next section examines these processes in more detail. Remembering and commemoration of the past have already been identified as aspects of Castleford's heritage, but what I now turn to is an examination of the cultural work this performance of remembering and commemoration does in Castleford.

Performance, remembering and commemoration: Heritage as community networking

The Castleford Festival is a colourful and lively performance – a week-long community event in which things are done and children learn, amongst other things, to make rag rugs and what those rugs represented, how skilful the women who worked in the potteries were and that their craft required well-developed artistic skills and judgements, what coal is and the meanings that coal has had and continues to have for different generations in Castleford. They touch and play with mining equipment and archaeological artefacts, and see the pit banners given pride of place in the closing parade, and thus remember community pride in their industrial history. Local artwork, including that of school children, is exhibited and brass bands and local choirs give performances. There are a number of interlinked consequences that this sense of heritage and its performance has for the community. The primary consequence is that it generates community identity – however, this is not a simple or straightforward equation wherein heritage creates or becomes symbolic of identity, but rather an acknowledgment that heritage *is* community identity and that identity is made through community experiences. Remembering and commemoration are performances in which the cultural processes of heritage are marked out and identified. This is not simply a process of identification, but a constitutive process in which heritage is made and remade.

In the street survey, the festival parade audience and passers-by were asked about if, and then how, both the activities of the CHT generally, and the festival in particular, were important to Castleford, and what messages they saw the festival events and performances sending out to people. Of the 107 people surveyed, 46 per cent considered that activities of the CHT and the Forum Project (note that this was distinguished from the Castleford Project being filmed by Channel 4) were important for Castleford, and 74 per cent considered the festival important. In discussing the general activities of the CHT, 23 per cent of respondents considered that the CHT provides a positive sense of community identity (Table 7.3). This was achieved through fostering cohesion by bringing the community together (10 per cent), promoting positive statements or messages (7.5 per cent), for both the

Table 7.3 Do you think the Castleford Heritage Trust and the Forum Project important?

Response	Frequency	%
Had not heard of CHT	57	53.3
Brings community together	11	10.3
Engenders community pride/self-esteem	5	4.7
Making a positive statement about Castleford	8	7.5
Educating children about Castleford	7	6.5
Economic benefits	11	10.3
Remembering and commemorating	4	3.7
Generally important	3	2.8
Not important	1	0.9
Total	107	100

consumption of the community and wider audiences, that Castleford's heritage is significant, or raising and promoting community self-esteem and pride (4.7 per cent). For instance, the CHT and Forum Project were:

> Important as it is showing everyone what it means to belong to a community – what's past and what's present.
>> (CF49 2004, female, 40–60, storeperson)

> Yes it's important, it keeps the spirit alive and lets younger generations know.
>> (CF76 2005, male, 18–29, site manager)

> To bring the community together and to ensure the community doesn't lose its background and its individualism.
>> (CF77 2005, female, 30–40, youth worker)

A further 10 per cent considered that the activities of the CHT would bring material gain to the community that would, at some point, translate itself into economic growth and jobs. The activities of the CHT would lead, it was hoped, to material benefits for Castleford either in terms of bringing more people into the town centre to shop or visit, or the development of museums, exhibition spaces and other material benefits. For instance:

> After the economic decline there is a need for regeneration which is slowly happening. Vast change from the 1970s – desolation – and this is why there is so much enthusiasm for the project.
>> (CF1 2004, male, 65, bus driver)

> Without this group nothing would have been done to improve the

heritage of Castleford. I hope they will be able to bring all the artefacts back to Castleford. It's a wonderful group bringing Castleford alive – after the coal strike heads went down and this group has livened the place up.

(CF54 2004, female, 40–60, funeral director)

Make Castleford more important, bring business in.

(CF93 2005, male, over 60, factory worker)

That people come to Castleford and invest their money in it. I don't know what heritage is but that is what it does.

(CF86 2005, male, 18–29, furniture fitter)

Although there is a sense of the 'cargo-cult' of heritage in the last response – identifying important heritage will somehow bring forth riches – other respondents talked more specifically about how identifying heritage would enliven the place, and that this would bring more people into the town to shop. As noted above, 'shopping' is not only an activity that brings economic gain to the community, but is itself important to a sense of community networking, interaction and pride. Subsequently, ideas of material benefit were inevitably linked or intertwined with comments about community identity and cohesion.

Table 7.4 details why people thought the festival was important. The majority of respondents – 53 per cent – thought that the celebration helped to build community identity. For instance, the festival itself was viewed as:

Opportunity for different groups in Castleford to get involved in one annual project. Gives children something to remember when they get older. Memory jogger for older people. . . . Because it gives them a sense of community. Without a sense of community you get antisocial behaviour and crime. It creates and jogs memory. It's

Table 7.4 Importance of the Castleford Festival

Response	Frequency	%
No response	13	12.1
Educational	7	6.5
General sense of importance	7	6.5
Keeping family history alive	2	1.9
Not important	1	0.9
Re/creating community identity	57	53.3
Remembering and celebrating – keeping memories alive	20	18.7
Total	107	100

something to look forward to as an annual event. Best thing about it is that it is communing from the community and not forced on them – it gives them a sense of pride.

(CF7 2004, male, 40–60, laboratory technician)

Everyone keeps to themselves on the new estates, but a thing like this gets people together.

(CF32 2004, female, 30–40, unemployed)

To keep up the community spirit. It was divided during the miners' strike – some families still don't speak. But a thing like this brings people together and gets young people involved in the community and they get to learn about their traditions.

(CF54 2004, female, 40–60, funeral director)

To get people meeting everyone. It's an opportunity for everyone to meet everyone else.

(CF58 2004, female, 40–60, plant manager)

There was such a community feeling in the past. With mining closed there is not such a community feeling now. It's good to see the stalls in the street.

(CF63 2004, female, over 60, secretary)

Because it builds a sense of community and goodwill between people.

(CF65 2004, male, 30–40, unemployed)

So Castleford can maintain its identity. Castleford has a lot going for it and it's important to get that message out there.

(CF67 2004, male, 40–60, bank auditor)

Because we come together as a group and notice each other rather than sitting indoors watching TV. It's the community doing things for the community – but it won't be on TV.

(CF79 2005, female, 40–60, practice manager)

It keeps an interest going – it generates history.

(CF80 2005, male, 40–60, civil servant)

Events like this cut down on crime, reduce feelings of being an outsider. History should not be bulldozed away.

(CF93 2005, male, over 60, factory worker)

See people you haven't seen for ages, wouldn't see each other otherwise. Market days are important for meeting people.

(CF97 2005, male, over 60, machine operator, motorways)

In these responses the festival is seen as important as it provides an opportunity for the community to get together; it is an opportunity to meet and interact with people in the context of a joyous celebration of community spirit and thus bolster community identity. What is important to note, however, is that this celebration is not just of the past, but that the present is celebrated as well – memories are not simply being remembered here (although that was important for 19 per cent of those surveyed, see below), new memories are also being created about community cohesion, friendliness and cooperation. Memorable new experiences are also being produced about what it means to be a community, and once again these experiences centre on socializing and networking. As CF7 above notes, the festival both 'creates and jogs memories'; collective memories are not only being remembered but are also created in the context of an event that marks the importance and meaning of both new and old memories. CF80 notes that the festival generates history, while CF17 also observed of the festival, 'it may be a case of *producing* heritage and creating something now' (2004, emphasis added).

A further 19 per cent thought that the festival events were more about remembering and commemorating past events 'because if it's not celebrated together it will be forgotten' (CF52 2004, female 30–40, manager), or because it 'gives memories a jog, keeps memories alive' (CF92 2005, female, 18–29, unemployed). Some of the past events and things remembered and commemorated included:

Celebrates your grandparents.

(CF27 2004, male, 18, bus fitter)

Lots of people worked down the mine and it's important to remember that.

(CF28 2004, male, 18, nurse)

It's important because you want to know where your roots are.

(CF35 2004, female, over 60, retired)

Because there has been a lot of skills in the past, employment is changing and it's important to remember those skills and old employments.

(CF55 2004, female, 30–40, occupational therapist)

It's important to walk with the banners – so not forgetting the miners. A lot of Castleford's heritage is about miners' lives. It's really for them, to never forget them. My family worked in the pits – it's important to remember them. My mother was the first dancer to open the palladium in 1918 – then she married a miner.

(CF70 2004, female, over 60, husband a miner, three grandchildren in the maypole)

The performance of remembering, however, cannot be divorced from the sense of community cohesion and identity identified by the majority of respondents. Amongst the performance of the festival, many of these memories are discussed and communicated with the audience and performers in the festival events, and become collective memories – their importance marked and reinforced by their creation and rehearsal as collective memories in the context of a public spectacle of celebration. The Castleford Festival is an experience that creates new memories that can be linked to Castleford's past. This process, some saw, as heritage – heritage *was* experience, specifically the experience of being part of a community, of creating and retaining memories about people, their industrial and other work experiences and skills, and of experiencing pride in both the past and present of the community. This sense of experience is continually recreated through the festival and the participation of individuals in the parade as both audience and performer. The line here between 'audience' and 'performer' is blurred; as a community event the audience are very much part of the performance and the performers are also their own audience. The festival creates and recreates meaning and understandings that, in Abercrombie and Longhurst's (1998) terms leak out into the day-to-day lives of Castleford's residents. Memories are created and negotiated as residents engage in rug making, or in getting their children to dress in mining gear, or in the opportunities presented to talk to ex-miners or pottery workers about their work experiences and so forth. Education, especially for children, was also an important issue to some of those surveyed, and again the messages and meanings that many hoped that children and new community members gained is part of the process of remembering past collective memories and making new memories and meanings:

Because with the loss of mines and so on there has been a loss of pride in the area. So it's important for the younger generation to know history. It's also important to get immigrants knowing the history of the region. I'm surprised that many people don't know their own regional history – people should know more.

(CF6 2004, female, 30–40, medical technician)

Education, community responsibility, getting people to rate the surroundings they live in, and so rate the present.

(CF17 2004, male, 30–40, council officer)

270

Brings community together and learning things you never knew about your own community.

(CF49 2004, female, 40–60, storeperson)

For younger ones they get to know what it was like in Castleford in previous years. My daughter is 10 and she hasn't seen the pit.

(CF50 2004, female, 30–40, supervisor chocolate factory)

Need to know what happened in the past to move forward.

(CF100 2005, female, 18, student)

This last comment is particularly telling as it sums up a significant aspect of both what Castleford heritage is and what it does. One of the things it does is centred on creating community cohesion and links to an understanding of the past and present that will foster social, environmental and economic change and growth. What emerges from both the street survey and from the interviews undertaken in Castleford, is that what Castleford heritage 'is' is intimately tied up with what it 'does', and that the two are not mutually exclusive concepts, but rather feed back upon one another. One of the things heritage does is to sustain community identity, but that identity is also the community's heritage – its friendliness, camaraderie and industrial history *is* Castleford's heritage; this is maintained through everyday opportunities and events like shopping or stopping to talk with people in Carlton Lanes or other precincts, or in special events like the festival. The day-to-day events of communication and networking maintain, and are, what makes Castleford recognizable as Castleford to many people. The yearly special events, such as the festival, both symbolically identify the everyday experiences as important, and remind people what heritage is – and thus what it does – in Castleford. This is not a static process but one in which change is inbuilt, in which the past is 'known' and remembered, and where the meaning of the strike and deindustrialization is re-worked to underline not only the achievements of the present, but also to acknowledge and thus embrace community development and growth. The sense of heritage practised in Castleford is expressly linked to community regeneration – not just to the government-led regeneration project, but also to a community-led sense of regeneration and growth. Although there is an element of the 'cargo-cult' phenomena in some people's responses to the importance of the CHT activities and the festival itself – that heritage will bring economic riches to Castleford – this appears to be a minority opinion. There is a much stronger pragmatic understanding that to know and understand the past in Castleford is to know and understand the importance of opportunities to develop and grow, and that the realities of past industrial and everyday life in Castleford must work to underlie the achievements of present-day Castleford. However, one of the agendas that emerges from community discussion on heritage is that it is the sense of community camaraderie – Castleford's heritage – that should be the basis on which change and growth will be undertaken. In this way, both Castleford's heritage is maintained, but also is allowed to change and grow, in so far as community networking and camaraderie is continued, but that Castleford as 'Roman town' and 'mining town' may continue to change and develop as new social, cultural and economic opportunities present themselves.

There are three interlinked consequences of the way heritage is remembered and commemorated in Castleford. Firstly, it acquaints children and new residents of Castleford with the life experiences and work skills of previous generations; while older residents engage with remembering their past experiences – collective memories are actively created and passed on. Secondly, these memories are then made meaningful in the context of celebrating community identity. Identity and cohesion is not only remembered but, most importantly, actually practised or performed during the festival and other heritage activities. The performance of community identity is achieved by the opportunities the festival represents in bringing the community together. This is achieved physically by providing opportunities for people to meet and network, but also in the very construction and celebration of community collective memories about what it means to be a resident of Castleford. Thirdly, these experiences are then used to frame and contextualize, and underline the inevitability, and indeed the desirability of, continued growth and change in Castleford. Thus, heritage as the performance of remembering, commemoration and of community cohesion becomes also the underpinning elements that allow and celebrate community change and growth. These processes are made all the more meaningful and significant as they are conducted in the context of the traumas and dislocations of the miners' strike and deindustrialization. The assertion of community identity, the process of teaching children about the work experiences and forms of solidarity of previous generations, and the attempts to underline the positives of change and development, are all active cultural and political assertions about the legitimacy of the Castleford community and its aspirations. Heritage is a discourse in which the historical, cultural and political legitimacy of interests and other groups are asserted and negotiated at local and national levels. In attempting to take control of the heritage discourse in and about Castleford, the community are asserting not only a local community identity but also making a statement about the political and economic legitimacy of the town and its residents.

Conclusion

In Castleford 'heritage' is revealed to be a complex cultural interaction between people, place and memory that both centres on and is the process of the maintenance and creation of community identity and cohesion. Tangible heritage sites and places are important aspects of heritage here, but are only part of the interlinked elements that define 'heritage'. Memories that are linked to fabric, as well as those that float free of physical symbolic anchors, are also important. Memories actively recalled include reminiscences about day-to-day life, family life, working experiences and industrial skills and knowledge amongst others and are vital elements in Castleford's heritage, but they too are only part of the story. The glue that links the tangible and intangible, and that makes heritage as physical site and/or intangible memory or cultural practice valuable and useful, are the everyday social interactions and experiences that define and maintain community cohesion. Mundane and quotidian events like shopping become significant because they are practices that daily 'preserve' the vital elements that give meaning to Castleford's heritage. Castleford's heritage is, in the only sense that really matters, its people and the community they create.

However, who and what this community is and what its aspirations are, may, from time to time, need to be reasserted, reconsidered, redefined or overthrown. In the aftermath of deindustrialization, the miners' strike, and in response to government initiatives on regeneration, the Castleford community found itself in a position where it was timely and useful to assess who they were and where they wanted to go as a collective entity. 'Heritage' was used as a focal point to assess and consider who and what the community was. What was drawn out from the community and labelled 'heritage' was part of a process of remembering those things that defined the community and made it 'special'. However, this is not simply a passive process of the recollection of memories – as Wertsch (2002) points out, remembering is also about meaning making. The Forum Project, festival, and other community activities are projects and events where aspects of Castleford's heritage – aspects and elements that make up 'community' – were identified, remembered, considered and negotiated. The festival and other projects were making 'heritage' not only in terms of providing events where experiences and memories of them were made to be remembered in the future, but also because they were events in which memories were recalled, their meanings and values negotiated and defined, and community agendas and aspirations were negotiated and legitimized. Heritage is therefore a process of active identity making and remaking, a useful cultural tool or discourse through which a community or other group or collective defines themselves. What is important, however, is that this is a process that is more about change than cultural stasis. It is a process not simply about the preservation or conservation of traditions, but is also a process in which cultural and social values are rewritten and redefined for the needs of the present. Castleford as a community embraces change, as many of those interviewed explicitly stated, and the visions of heritage on offer in Castleford identified the need to underpin community confidence in the changes currently facing residents. However, heritage as a cultural tool of remembering and meaning making will always be utilized for the needs of the present, and responds to the aspirations and desires of those defining heritage and doing the remembering. As such the past, with its different needs and aspirations, can never be 'preserved' with meanings and values unchanged. As Urry (1996) notes, the past will always be understood in the context of the present, but as 'heritage' the past becomes a cultural tool around which meaning is actively remade and consumed in and for the present.

The mutability of culture was an issue of concern identified by a number of Western commentators on the implementation of the 2003 UNESCO *Convention for the Safeguarding of the Intangible Cultural Heritage*, discussed in Chapter 3. These critics recognized that attempts to 'preserve' intangible cultural expression would result in the 'freezing' of cultural expression (see, for instance, Amsell 2004; Kirshenblatt-Gimblett 2004). As Kirshenblatt-Gimblett observes, the listing of cultural properties on lists like the World Heritage List tends to remove sites from their cultural context so that everything on the list becomes the context for everything else on the list (2004: 57). The idea that heritage preservation is about fossilization and the 'conserve as found' ethos, and that they are irrelevant to the preservation of intangible cultural expression, is based on the idea that the intangible is linked to 'living' traditions. As argued in Chapter 3, these assumptions are very revealing about Western perceptions of 'heritage' and the workings of the AHD. In effect, they assume the tangible is somehow 'dead' and paradoxically 'preservable'. However, Castleford reveals the interlinked nature of intangible and tangible heritage, and how the tensions between ideals of preservation and intangible cultural expression also matter for tangible heritage.

The cultural landscape of Castleford has changed dramatically over many residents' lives – some of those changes are lamented and others are celebrated. Memories and social relations alter and are interlinked to transformations in the landscape, but that does not necessarily mean that heritage is 'lost'. The market hall is still preserved in Castleford, but no longer as a market; it is now used for exhibitions and ceremonies in the festival and the Forum Project hopes to see it reused as a gallery space. The market hall is no longer preserved as a market, but its role as a place of community socializing is maintained. These new uses will leave their own marks on the market hall and, subsequently, its fabric will be changed and altered. Its most important value – the intangible cultural practices – although altered in many ways, are continued and in that sense the market hall is 'preserved' even though its fabric is altered. The continued use of the banners in festival and other events, if allowed by the museums, will eventually see wear and tear and repair work done on them – like the market hall, the value of the banners to the community lies in their use and use means change. Nothing can be, nor should be, 'conserved as found' otherwise it ceases to be heritage and to have ongoing cultural meaning. Only those things that can be used, and are subject to change, are heritage in any meaningful sense. The management and conservation practices that attempt to 'preserve as found' tangible heritage items and places are in fact a cultural process that creates new meanings for the tangible heritage under its care. As argued in Chapter 3, all heritage practices and uses are part of a wider process of meaning making. Some are undertaken at international level through the construction of the World Heritage List, some are undertaken at national level through the preservation, exhibition and promotion of selected 'heritage' places and items, and others, as at Castleford, are undertaken in a range of ways at community level.

8

'THE ISSUE IS CONTROL'

Indigenous politics and the
discourse of heritage

The previous chapters have revealed the ways in which 'heritage' as a discourse is a part of the social processes of meaning making. Heritage is a process of remembering that helps to underpin identity and the ways in which individuals and groups make sense of their experiences in the present. In this process, physical objects, places or sites, collective or individual memories and acts – such as the Castleford Festival, passing on family stories to children, learning to visit and 'read' certain places or landscapes, etc. – and other forms of intangible experience, all become focal points, or cultural tools, for heritage practices concerned with defining, re/creating, negotiating, proclaiming and preserving identity. The identity that is created may, depending on those defining the discourse, revolve around a sense of nation, class, gender, ethnicity, family or a range of other collective experiences . . . and some heritage discourses have more power and authority than others do. This simple observation, however, is important for understanding the consequences of the ability of various groups to have their discourse about heritage recognized within the authorized discourse. Heritage and the identities and understandings of both the past and the present it creates do not simply exist internally to the group or other collective that has created them – they do work, or have a consequence, in wider social, cultural, economic and political networks. They have a consequence for, and in, the day-to-day lives of individuals beyond the provision of a sense of self or collective identity.

This consequence became apparent in the last chapter, where the ability to define and provide cohesion to a community was shown to have significant consequences for the legitimacy granted to that community's aspirations and desires. The ability to recognize and understand the consequences of the work that heritage does in everyday life is compromised within the AHD. This is because the AHD naturalizes itself to such an extent that it cannot see that competing discourses either exist or, if they are perceived, that they have any legitimacy. The degree of its naturalization reduces the ability of the AHD to comprehend or understand that it has a consequence beyond what it may intend – the preservation of material 'heritage'. Nonetheless, the AHD, or more precisely certain agents in its establishment and dissemination, have been under sustained criticism precisely because of the work that the AHD does outside of the processes of preservation and conservation. Indigenous communities from around the world, and in particular communities from North America, Australia and New Zealand, Africa, Japan and Scandinavia, have been increasingly vocal in their criticism of the ways 'heritage' has been used to define their identities. Since the late 1960s and early 1970s, Indigenous peoples in post-colonial countries have been publicly agitating for the right to control their own heritage, and thus the cultural tools to define who they are and how the rest of the world sees them. This chapter examines the criticisms levelled at heritage practitioners by Indigenous peoples in order to explore more fully the consequences that heritage discourses have. The focus of the chapter is the adversarial nature of Indigenous criticism of the AHD, which illustrates the dissonant nature of heritage, but also the political work that heritage discourses do within identity politics. Central to the tensions between Indigenous peoples and heritage practitioners is the issue of control – who should control how heritage is defined and understood. This is not an abstract issue, as who controls the discourse also controls an important resource of political power. Further, the issues raised in this chapter, although discussed in terms of Indigenous heritage, are equally relevant to other subaltern expressions of heritage, and aim to illustrate that the dissonant aspects of any definition of heritage are not only integral to an understanding and theorization of heritage, but in understanding the political work 'heritage' does.

The history of Indigenous critique – or why the control of heritage matters

Indigenous peoples from around the world have perhaps been the most strident and vocal groups to criticize Western perceptions of heritage, and the way these perceptions have dominated international and national heritage management processes. This is because, as will become clear, Indigenous communities have a lot at stake in the way their heritage is defined, understood and managed. Although a range of heritage practitioners and institutions have been criticized by Indigenous communities and activists, archaeologists have been a central focus of much of their criticism. This is because the AHD identifies Indigenous heritage as primarily 'prehistory', and thus 'archaeological data'. I have argued elsewhere (Smith 2004) exactly why it is that archaeologists merited this critique, and how archaeological perceptions of Indigenous heritage have become naturalized within the practices of heritage management. It is, however, important to revisit briefly those arguments here. The late 1960s and 1970s was an important period in the history of Indigenous colonial resistance, as a number of important events and processes coincided in this period and made 'heritage' one of the important focal issues in Indigenous political and economic programmes of resistance. During this period, Indigenous peoples from around the world were increasingly finding more effective ways of making their demands for land, sovereignty and equity listened to in public arenas. Indigenous peoples have, since initial contact with Europeans, resisted the invasion of their lands, fought against colonial incursions and dispossession, and agitated for a range of political and economic rights. However, it was not until the late 1960s that these struggles fully entered public consciousness. This decade saw the conjunction of increasing public political awareness over a range of civil and environmental issues facilitated by increasing access to a diverse array of media outlets. A number of public demonstrations also facilitated the increase in public awareness of Indigenous civil and land rights issues. These included the publication of manifestoes such as Vine Deloria's *Custer Died for Your Sins* (1969) in the United States; the occupation of Alcatraz Island by the San Francisco Bay Area's Indians of All Tribes in 1969; the occupation of lands by the Gurindji in 1966 in Australia; and the 'Freedom Rides' led by the Aboriginal activist Charles Perkins, which toured rural Australia and drew public attention to racist practices of apartheid. They also included public demands for the reburial and repatriation of human remains and items of material culture. However, it was at the point when Indigenous political movements were gaining broad public recognition that archaeologists and other heritage practitioners delivered to themselves stewardship and control over heritage – including Indigenous heritage.

The cementing of archaeological knowledge and values in the AHD through legislative, policy and management practices also occurred at this crucial period. Archaeologists in the United States, Australia and New Zealand began lobbying for legislation to protect and manage 'archaeological' sites in those countries during the late 1960s and 1970s (Fung and Allen 1984; Zimmerman 1998; Smith 2004). At the same time, the Anglophone discipline of archaeology fervently embraced the various epistemological methodological and discursive trappings of the physical sciences. The development of what archaeologists refer to as 'processual theory' in the 1960s is significant, as it not only marked increasing assertions by the discipline that it is a 'science' producing scientific knowledge, it also had an important consequence for the management of heritage and the AHD in post-colonial countries. The assertion of scientific expertise and authority helped to legitimize the public claims of archaeologists as stewards over the past – particularly an Indigenous past that was seen as 'dead' or near extinction in received accounts of post-colonial history. The legislation enacted during the 1970s to protect Indigenous heritage, and the management practices they underpin, helped to cement the authority of archaeological science and expertise. It did so to such an extent that the discipline's allegiance to a scientistic discourse and epistemology is assured, despite the attempts of a range of critical debates from within the discipline to challenge it (see, for instance, Conkey and Spector 1984; Leone et al. 1987; Shanks and Tilley 1987; McGuire 1992; Hodder 1999; amongst others). Also, during the 1970s, the technical process referred to as cultural resource management in the United States, or cultural heritage management in Australia, or as arch-aeological heritage management in Europe, began to be identifiable and formalized. This process is underwritten both by protective heritage or cultural resource legislation, and by a range of national and international charters and conventions and other policy documents. Denis Byrne (1991) has argued that it is a process within which Western conceptualizations of heritage and the European conservation ethic, what I refer to as the AHD, is deeply embedded and naturalized. The export of the Western European model of heritage management around the world has been identified as part of the processes of Western colonization, and an expression of Western cultural imperialism, that has tended to result in the alienation of local communities from their cultural heritage (Byrne 1991; Ndoro and Pwiti 2001; Pagan-Jimenez 2004). Archaeologists tend to visibly dominate the management process, as they will be found working in government agencies, amenity societies and as private or freelance consultants undertaking site assessments, salvage or management and protective works.

As the visible face of the management process, and because archaeological expert knowledge and pronouncements about the Indigenous past and heri-tage have become embedded in the AHD, and in the legislative and technical processes of management that reproduce the AHD, archaeologists are explicit and legitimate targets for Indigenous criticism and activism. As Leonard Forsman (1997: 109) points out:

> archaeological sites may be the only pristine resource remaining from the aboriginal world that has not been encroached upon by non-Indians. Therefore, Indians see archaeology as a 'last stand' in their struggle to maintain their land base, identity, and sovereignty.

It is difficult, as he goes on to observe, to ask Indigenous peoples to sacrifice their beliefs and sense of identity to satisfy archaeological curiosity, when Indigenous people have been required to give and relinquish so much in colonial history (Forsman 1997: 109). A significant expression of Indigenous criticism occurred through and within demands for the return or repatriation of human skeletal remains, and of sacred or other significant aspects of their material culture held in museums and universities. However, calls for the return of material items and human remains, and the sustained criticism of archaeological knowledge and practices, cannot simply be viewed as specific conflicts between different cultural viewpoints, but are rather explicitly part of Indigenous negotiations about the legitimacy of their cultural and political claims to land and other resources. The ability to control the values and meanings given to heritage becomes vital in struggles for political and cultural recognition. However, the wider contexts within which these demands and criticisms reside are often obscured by the AHD. In their attempts to rebuff or challenge Indigenous calls for the repatriation and return of heritage items, archaeologists, museums and other heritage practitioners and institutions tend to invoke two specific elements of the AHD – firstly, that of the universal rights and values of scientific knowledge and practice, and secondly, Western property rights, which Lahn (1996) identifies as the 'finders keepers' principle. In this way, the conflict with Indigenous peoples is either generalized as a conflict between 'science and religion', or reduced to a specific issue of ownership over the past, which is invariably and rhetorically posed as the question: 'Who owns the past?' Neither characterization of the conflict is useful.

> Perhaps the best policy for the archaeologists would be to declare themselves a religion, with DNA fingerprints their sacramental totem ... If you say, 'Look, here is overwhelming evidence from carbon dating, from mitochondrial DNA, and from archaeological analyses of pottery, that X is the case' you will get nowhere. But if you say, 'It is a fundamental and unquestioned belief of my culture that X is the case' you will immediately hold a judge's attention.
> (Dawkins 1998)

By defining the debate, as the scientist Richard Dawkins does here, as a conflict between science and religion, the cultural values of science are immediately obscured and the debate is defined as one of 'truth' against 'faith' or 'reason' against 'irrationality'. This is important because it obscures the power and authority that 'rational', 'informed' or 'intellectual' knowledge about 'heritage' has and the role that it plays in defining identity and collective memory. Intellectual or expert knowledge about heritage becomes authorized and authoritative due to its appeals to universal applicability; and 'other' forms of knowledge about the nature and meaning of heritage become simply that – 'other' and marginal as the self-interested special pleadings of minority groups. This is also true of the characterization of the debate as one over 'ownership' – here, the debate is reduced to one of technical and legal issues of possession, or is so abstracted that combatants can declare or concede that no one can claim 'ownership' over something so ephemeral as 'the past'. Although these characterizations have dominated the responses of archaeologists, museums and other heritage practitioners and institutions to Indigenous criticisms, there has nonetheless been a significant base of support for Indigenous peoples and their aspirations within the discipline of archaeology and museum-based heritage practitioners. Codes of ethics acknowledging Indigenous rights of custodianship over their heritage have been published by organizations such as the World Archaeological Congress (1989), Australian Archaeological Association (1991), Museums Australia

(1999), Canadian Archaeological Association (1997), Society for American Archaeology (Lynott and Wylie 2000), and other documents and manifestos have been attempted to facilitate consultation between researchers, heritage managers and Indigenous communities (see, for instance, Davidson et al. 1995; Nicholas and Andrews 1997; Swidler et al. 1997; Trapeznik 1997, 2000; Dongoske et al. 2000; Goldstein 2000; Watkins et al. 2000; Zimmerman 2001; DCMS 2003; Smith and Wobst 2005). However, the ability of the various codes of ethics to open up effective and useful dialogue with Indigenous peoples has yet to be adequately gauged (Smith and Burke 2003) and, have as yet done little to change the power and authority of the AHD. As McNiven and Russell (2005) point out, the structural relationship between museums, archaeologists and other heritage practitioners and Indigenous peoples still remains in many ways a colonial one as the relations of power have not altered.

Power relations have not altered because the basic issue at stake is not recognized in the way the debates and conflicts tend to be characterized . . . and the basic issue in these conflicts is control. By this, I mean control over the meanings and values given to the past and control, ultimately, over the cultural tools important in memory and identity work – items or acts of heritage. As the Tasmanian Aboriginal activist Ros Langford (1983: 2) so powerfully pointed out to an audience of Australian archaeologists:

> The issue is control. You seek to say that as scientists you have a right to obtain and study information of our culture. You seek to say that because you are Australians you have a right to study and explore our heritage because it is a heritage to be shared by all Australians, white and black. From our point of view we say – you have come as invaders, you have tried to destroy our culture, you have built your fortunes upon the lands and bodies of our people and now, having said sorry, want a share in picking out the bones of what you regard as a dead past. We say that it is our past, our culture and heritage and forms part of our present life. As such it is ours to control and it is ours to share on our terms.

The issue of control over heritage is political because it is a struggle over power – not only because different interests will have different and usually unequal access to resources of power, but also because heritage is itself a political resource. As argued in Chapter 5, heritage places and processes can be, and are, used to legitimize and delegitimize claims to identity and thus claims to resources.

The experiences of marginalization and disenfranchisement have been shaped and defined by the way colonial governments have categorized and understood Indigenous peoples. The power that the cultural process that is heritage therefore has to define identity is keenly understood by and reflected in the historical and contemporary experiences of Indigenous peoples. Archaeology and anthropology, as is well documented, were disciplines whose knowledge and practices became embedded in the colonial process (see Cowlishaw 1987; Biolsi 1998; McNiven and Russell 2005). The nineteenth- and twentieth-century collection of human remains, religious and everyday artefacts by both archaeologists and anthropologists was part of racist research that relabelled Indigenous peoples as 'colonized' and 'primitives', objectified them as natural history specimens, and helped to justify and underpin a series of genocidal acts and government policies (see, for instance, Trigger 1980, 1989; Cowlishaw 1987; Attwood 1989; Jaimes 1992; McGuire 1992; Watkins 2003; McNiven and Russell 2005). Indigenous people have, since first contact with Europeans, been subjected to intense 'scientific' scrutiny by a range of academic disciplines and intellectuals. The study of Indigenous culture, social practices and material culture has produced continuous academic and public debate about the identity of Indigenous peoples (Langton 1993; Watkins 2003). Governments and their bureaucracies have used the knowledge obtained through this close observation to help them classify and define who is or is not 'indigenous', 'Native' or 'Aboriginal', and thus who has rights to certain resources and who becomes subjected to a range of 'special treatments' – which in the past included the removal of children, the segregation of populations onto reserves and so forth. As Michael Dodson (1994: 4), one time Aboriginal and Torres Strait Islander Social Justice Commissioner, observes: 'supposedly objective definitions [of identity] are ideological tools, designed to assist the state in applying its policies of control, domination and assimilation' (see also Deloria 1969, 1998; Jaimes 1992).

Both tangible and intangible heritage serve as resources of power in this process of surveillance as they become symbolic of identity claims. They are also important 'theatres of memory' where the processes of heritage are made meaningful and given expression. Subsequently, and as noted above, the ability of Indigenous interests to control symbolic heritage resources is politically important for demonstrating the legitimacy of cultural claims. However, the ability of governments and policy makers to also control symbolically important heritage, or vest that control in 'objective' experts through the heritage management process, is also an exercise in which the ability to grant or withhold legitimacy to Indigenous cultural claims may be regulated or governed by governments and their policy makers (Smith 2004). For instance, it is no coincidence that the main Christian churches in southern Africa were located near major cultural sites. As Ndoro and Pwiti (2001: 32) argue, this was a colonial tactic to suppress African cultural activities and expression. Heritage places and the associated processes of remembering and meaning making that occur at them are 'resources' in wider struggles over the political and cultural legitimacy given to Indigenous aspirations – in short they are resources of power (see also Cheung 2005).

Cultural differences and discursive barriers

Chapter 2 discussed how the political and dissonant struggles in which heritage issues and processes play a part are obscured by the nature of the AHD and its emphasis on the aesthetic, historical and scientific values of heritage. However, these issues can also be further obscured, as noted above, in the way certain dissonant claims and conflicts are characterized as issues of 'ownership' or as 'belief' against 'reason'. In this section, I want to examine how Indigenous conflicts over heritage are obfuscated in yet another way. This obfuscation occurs when the dissonant interest or discourse has fundamentally different ways of understanding and defining the nature and meaning of 'heritage'. The cultural differences between Indigenous and Western perceptions are significant in both escalating and complicating debate and conflict, but also in obfuscating the political nature of heritage. At one level, the politics of identity is obscured when heritage practitioners characterize conflict as only being about cultural difference. This is not to say that the cultural differences are not fundamentally important, but that these conflicts will also be about issues of control (see below). However, in order to understand the political and dissonant nature of heritage, and before examining the politics of the issue in more detail, it is first important to identify and understand, in broad terms at least, the cultural differences.

Needless to say there are substantive cultural differences between how Indigenous peoples and adherents to the Western AHD view Indigenous heritage — whether that be human remains, or religious or secular sites, places, artefacts or landscapes. It also scarcely needs saying that there is not a unified or single 'Indigenous' point of view or cultural tradition. My aim here is not to talk about specific cultural differences, as that is impossible — even in regions like Australia or North America, the cultural expressions, histories and traditions of different Indigenous communities are extremely diverse. Rather, my aim is to highlight some of the broad differences that tend to be expressed or arise in the Indigenous critique of heritage issues, and that have specifically added confusion and extra dimensions to the conflict. While there is a political urge to challenge archaeological pronouncements and knowledge about the past, because they tend to be privileged in the management process and in the interpretation of sites for the public, these challenges also occur because of fundamental cultural differences about the meaning and nature of the past. The dominance of non-Indigenous perceptions in the legal and heritage management process has been identified as actively and materially alienating communities from their cultural heritage (Fourmile 1989a, 1989b; Tsosie 1997; Anyon et al. 2000; Ndoro and Pwiti 2001; Cheung 2005). One of the ways that it does this, which is a significant aspect of cultural difference, is the tension over the perception of 'past' and 'present'. One of the crucial points of difference that Nicholas identifies is the Western tendency to separate the 'real world' from the 'supernatural world', the present from the past and people from nature (2005: 85, see also 2001). As he notes, these divisions do not exist in the worldviews of many Indigenous cultures and the 'separation of past and present . . . is not only illogical according to some members of Indigenous societies, but many also threaten the integrity of [Indigenous] worldview and beliefs' (2005: 85).

Another basic cultural difference is that many Indigenous communities simply cannot see the point of archaeologists or other researchers studying the past or studying things like human remains (Zimmerman 1989a: 212). The way curiosity about the past or aspects of it is felt, defined and expressed can be entirely different to the Western sense of curiosity and drive to know and understand the past. This can be exacerbated by the assumptions held by many heritage practitioners that the only way anyone can truly know about the past of Indigenous peoples is through archaeology. One of the Western AHD's normative beliefs is that archaeology is the only 'science' that has the ability to objectively reconstruct and explain the past in cultures without written histories or texts. However, many communities know their own history, which is often defined and conveyed through oral history and tradition, and may have little or no synergy with archaeological versions of the past. On the other hand, some communities do value archaeological input to augment what they know of their past – but often the archaeological or other expert view is simply that: the archaeological view and not necessarily embraced uncritically for its 'scientific validity' or its 'objectivity'. Not only is the expert view often perceived as culturally very different, but it may also be perceived by Indigenous peoples as constructed by and for the use of researchers and thus of little interest to communities. As Badger Bates requests in Australia, knowledge gained by researchers about the Indigenous past should be constructed with input from Indigenous peoples and not simply related to them as undisputable fact: 'Don't just study the old things . . . Just come and out and talk with the people, you know, and do the study with the people and for the people, not just for themselves (Aboriginal Ranger, National Parks and Wildlife Service, in SBS 1991).

Another significant tension here, as Deloria observes (cited in Zimmerman 1989a: 213), is the assumption by many Western experts of 'the past' that Indigenous peoples are not capable of preserving or understanding their own past. However, not only are there basic and extensive differences between Indigenous and Western understandings of the nature and meaning of the past, and those objects of heritage that symbolize that past (Zimmerman 1989b; Pullar 1994; Ucko 2001), but also about how that past can be quantified and communicated. Another significant tension emerges over the legitimacy of oral history or oral traditions, which are viable sources of information and knowledge in many Indigenous cultures (Anyon et al. 1997; Echo-Hawk 1997, 2000). However, this form of knowledge is viewed with distrust or suspicion within the AHD, given its tendency to privilege the tangible, and to use material evidence or the written word in evaluating the meaning and value of history and the past. To acknowledge the legitimacy of oral history is also to concede some of the privilege gained through the power/knowledge claims of expertise (Whiteley 2002). As Zimmerman (2000) notes, many archaeologists are simply reluctant to give up their control over the interpretation of the past. Yet failure to acknowledge the legitimacy of oral history, and developing and propagating histories and interpretations of the past different to those expressed in oral history, jeopardizes Indigenous cultural continuity (Nicholas 2005: 89).

The nature of 'time' is another significant conceptual hurdle. In the Western AHD things that are 'old' are seen as intrinsically valuable, mysterious and wondrous – they are the proper objects of heritage preservation and conservation. Any item that is very 'old' acquires a patina of reverence in the AHD. Further, the older an object, place or human remain is understood to be, the more it is perceived to be both scientifically valuable and of universal relevance. This may be an expression of the extent to which national narratives are linked to the AHD. Objects that predate the formation of nation states are often perceived primarily for their universal relevance to human history regardless of the current geo-political space in which they occur; while relatively younger sites are more easily perceived to be linked to specific cultural and/or national identities. Places, artefacts or human remains found in the estates of Indigenous peoples are likely to be understood firstly for their universal values – possibly again because of the lack of 'national' narratives that make sense within the AHD. In any case, a difficult issue for adherents of the AHD to comprehend is that for many Indigenous people the issue of depth of time simply does not apply (see Anawak 1989; Swain 1993; Brody 2001). The value of an item of heritage may neither be increased nor decreased by its age.

This issue is particularly pointed in debates over the repatriation of human remains. For instance, different conceptualizations of time have been significant in the repatriation conflict over the 9,000-year-old remains found at Kennewick in Washington State, and subsequently called Kennewick Man by some archaeologists, or the Ancient One by many American Indians. These remains are perceived by some archaeologists as being only significant to human history precisely due to their age, and that they are way too old to be linked to a single living community (for critical overviews of this debate, see Watkins 2000, 2004; Smith 2004; Smith and Zimmerman in press). However, the Confederated Tribes of the Umatilla Reservation, who have claimed the remains as those of an ancestor, see the issue of time as insignificant, and consider the fact that the remains were found in their tribal area as indicative of their cultural links and responsibilities to the remains (Minthorn 1996). For many Westerners human remains of those that are perceived to have died a long time ago, like at Kennewick, engender entirely different emotional and cultural responses than do the remains of those who have died relatively recently. The recently dead will often engender a strong range of emotional responses, while very ancient or 'old' remains may elicit primarily curiosity. The age of human remains does not necessarily temper, as it tends to do in the West, the intensity of the ancestral link that some Indigenous communities may have to the remains.

Another related issue is that of genealogical descent. In arguments over reburial, and the repatriation of human remains in particular, museums, archaeologists and other researchers have argued that Indigenous peoples must show some biological link to the remains (see, for instance, Buikstra 1981; Meighan 1984, 1992; Jones and Harris 1997; Owsley 1999; Jenkins 2003; for responses to this and for overviews of the repatriation debate, see also Layton 1989; Mihesuah 2000; Bray 2001; Fforde and Ormond Parker 2002). This is because in many Western cultures it is often necessary to trace some form of direct biological link to a population or individual to show kinship, and thus be able to claim their remains or associated material culture as part of your own heritage. In some, but not all, Indigenous cultures, identifying direct biological linkages may be irrelevant, and entirely different criteria are used for identifying ancestral/descendent links not only to human remains, but also to land and to cultural places and items of heritage value. As Deloria notes, it is traditions and not genetics that may hold communities together (cited in Gulliford 2000: 11).

Another issue that heritage practitioners must also deal with is the idea that heritage is something that must be actively conserved, and that items left in the landscape and apparently 'abandoned' must come under the stewardship and care of heritage professionals. Decay and erosion must be arrested in the Western conservation ethic – but this is not always considered appropriate in Indigenous cultures. In some cultures, such as the Zuni of North America, the decay and eventual destruction of some heritage items serves a cultural purpose. As one Zuni spokesperson is reported to have observed: 'Everything for ceremonial, religious and ritual purposes that my culture makes is meant to disintegrate . . . to go back into the ground. Conservation is a disservice to my culture' (Edward Ladd 1992, quoted in Sease 1998: 106). For other communities, the decay of heritage items may be viewed as part of a natural cycle whose interruption makes no sense. Nor does the 'discovery' of places and things that have been abandoned or forgotten necessarily mean that they no longer have value to the Indigenous communities they are associated with – their 'abandonment' and later 'discovery' by archaeologists or other researchers does not necessarily mean that their primary values are or should be 'archaeological' or other 'universal' values. Nor does material left or buried in the ground necessarily mean that it may become, as Gary White Deer observes, buried treasure to be claimed by its 'finders' (1997: 38).

The various cultural differences and expectations about the nature and meaning of the past and the way it is researched and knowledge disseminated

286

adds to the sense in which Indigenous interests and heritage experts tend to talk past one another. Dorothy Lippert (1997) observes that communication is a central issue between Indigenous peoples and archaeologists and other heritage 'experts'. The discursive barriers between these groups have been a significant hurdle in debates – a situation that many authors, both Indigenous and non-Indigenous, stress can only be constructively dealt with if communication is undertaken on both sides from the basis of relationships of trust and with critical awareness and honesty (Carter 1997; Zimmerman 2001, 2005; Greer et al. 2002; Smith et al. 2003b; Rigney and Worby 2005). The discursive barriers can also only begin to be overcome if, as I have argued elsewhere (Smith 2004), communication is also based on a critical understanding of the relations of power that may exist between archaeologists, other heritage 'experts' and Indigenous peoples. Understanding both the cultural and political consequences of how heritage is defined and used is critical in facilitating communication and negotiations between heritage practitioners and Indigenous groups, as it reveals why controlling the heritage process is so important to many Indigenous people.

There are many cultural differences that impede negotiations between Indigenous groups and heritage professionals; however, for many Indigenous communities the control of heritage is not only about defending belief systems, but is embedded in wider struggles to control identity and the cultural and political legitimacy that Indigenous people are afforded by governments and society. In this struggle, Indigenous adversarial discourses about heritage are about the ability to assert control over culture, and as such attempt to overturn the legacies of colonial domination and control.

Controlling heritage

Indigenous cultural identity is an important resource of power that has been used by and against Indigenous people. The control of cultural identity is important in the development of Indigenous politics. Indigenous material culture as a physical symbol of cultural identity also becomes an important political resource in this context. As Ros Langford (1983) pointed out, the control of Indigenous heritage is not only important in the negotiation of land claims and access to other resources, it is also important in the control and maintenance of community cohesion and identity, and in asserting a sense of self-sufficiency and self-worth. She notes that if control of heritage is not returned to Indigenous people, then the perception of Indigenous people as powerless victims is propagated: 'if we Aborigines cannot control our own heritage, *what the hell can we control?*' (1983: 4, emphasis in original). Control of heritage, and thus cultural identity and meaning making, is not only a vital resource in political negotiations, it is also a vital resource for Indigenous cultural expression, community continuity and cohesion:

Indigenous peoples throughout the world recognise that, at the core of the violation of our rights as peoples, lies the desecration of our sovereign right to control our lives, to live according to our own laws and determine our futures. And at the heart of the violation has been the denial of our control over our identity, and the symbols through which we make and remake our culture and ourselves . . . Recognition of a people's fundamental right to self-determination must include . . . the right to inherit the collective identity of one's people, and to transform that identity creatively according to the self-defined aspirations of one's people and one's own generation. It must include the freedom to live outside the cage created by other people's images and projections.

(Dodson 1994: 5)

Subsequently, the ability to control heritage plays at least three interlinked and important roles. The first is to define community identity; the second is to create and recreate new political identities from which to assert and negotiate with governments the legitimacy of a range of cultural and civil rights; and the third is to demonstrate control over a political resource. In the first instance, the ability to control heritage is important to Indigenous communities, as with any other community or collective, in maintaining or establishing community pride, cohesion and identity. However, this takes on an added urgency in many Indigenous communities because of the dislocation or disruptions to cultural knowledge and practices that have occurred through colonization, and the structural racism inherent in the bureaucracies of many white settler societies. Cultural revitalization has become a vital project in communities beset with substance abuse, third world health levels, high infant mortality rates, domestic violence, high incarceration rates and the other ravages that colonization, ghettoization and poverty bring. Demands for the repatriation of cultural artefacts and human remains, and the challenge to the assumption that the heritage management process adequately deals with Indigenous conceptualizations of the past and their heritage, have become integral in resurrecting or underlying community pride. As Alice Kelly, Mutti Mutti Elder from the Lake Mungo region of Australia, observes, the ability to possess and control heritage is about cultural dignity and pride – she explains here why her community were against the excavation of a newly discovered burial at Lake Mungo:

We will not have the ancient graves of our ancestors disturbed by Johnny-come-latelies who blew in on the tradewinds only two hundred years ago. [The new skull] came for a purpose: it was not an accident. It was to remind us of our ancestry and to give back our dignity that we had lost 200 years ago.

(Quoted in Gostin 1993: 63–4)

Here, a newly eroded burial becomes both symbolic of Aboriginal occupation of Australia, and a chance to remember and create new meanings about what it means to be a member of a particular community. As another elder notes:

> It should be Aboriginal people that are there looking after them kind of things. It is always white people that have something to do with it.
>
> (Alice Bugmy, elder, SBS 1993)

Aboriginal Australians, along with other Indigenous people, are often effectively legislated out of any effective say in the management of their heritage, and as heritage resources are collected and scattered in museum collections outside of community control Indigenous people lose access to the cultural tools important for remembering and meaning making. As Henrietta Fourmile (1989a: 4) observes:

> The net effect of the lack of our own cultural and historical resources and the difficulties of access to those that exist elsewhere is to foster our dependence on non-Aboriginal specialists in law, history, anthropology . . . and in Aboriginal affairs generally. They effectively become our brokers in transaction between Aboriginal communities and the various institutions and the public at large which have an interest in our affairs and thereby usurp our role as history tellers. This in turn causes much resentment.

Gordon Pullar (1994), when discussing the cultural revitalization on Kodiak Island, Alaska, observed the important role the repatriation process played within this. He noted that the repatriation of human remains was tightly linked to efforts to promote a strong sense of identity and self-esteem among the community's youth. As he goes on to argue, the state's ability to effectively claim 'ownership' of Indigenous ancestral remains through the heritage management process is a powerful symbolic statement, and if this ownership was uncontested then the community 'would have a very difficult time developing the self-esteem that would permit them to feel equal to all others in [the United States]' (Pullar 1994: 18). Not only is control over heritage vital in the re/creation and maintenance of community identity, it also becomes a vital component in challenging received colonial notions of Indigenous culture. This may be achieved in a range of ways, through the development and expression of pride in cultural identity, and the self-assurance that comes with the ability to control, and to demonstrate that control, over symbolically important aspects of both tangible and intangible heritage. It also becomes important if 'heritage' is also understood and conceptualized as an experience. If the central essence of heritage is, as I have been arguing throughout the previous chapters, what occurs at places of 'heritage' rather than simply the sites or places themselves – then control over heritage becomes fundamentally more significant, and has more material consequences than is usually allowed in understanding conflicts over heritage as being about symbolic identity politics. This is not to say that the possession of items of tangible heritage is not about symbolic identity politics – but that there are other dimensions and factors in operation as well.

The ability to control and define the experiences of being in place, and of remembering and meaning making, are central to defining identity, and asserting and making sense of an individual and community's place in the world and the social, political and cultural networks in which individuals and communities may reside. This ability is also central to embodying and asserting challenges to authorized and received perceptions of identity. One of the ways this is being done in many Indigenous cultures is to assert Indigenous control within the heritage management processes. In the United States, Stapp and Burney (2002) have traced the development of 'tribal cultural resource management', where tribal groups have developed programmes and strategies for managing their heritage in culturally appropriate and meaningful ways. Tribal groups have successfully lobbied state and federal governments to take on legal responsibilities for heritage management within their cultural territories, and some tribal programmes may employ non-Indian archaeologists – although these archaeologists will be answerable to Indian concerns and issues (Anyon and Ferguson 1995; Anyon et al. 1997, 2000; Dongoske and Anyon 1997; Watkins 2000). One of the things these programmes 'do', beyond the provision of culturally meaningful management processes and protocols, is represent a clear statement of control. While these programmes may have to work within the context of state and federal cultural resources laws, nonetheless the ability to employ, or not, archaeological or other 'experts' is a powerful statement and an expression of cultural sovereignty. In addition, many communities around the world have developed protocols and programmes to facilitate constructive and meaningful consultations and negotiations with archaeologists, other heritage practitioners and academic researchers, and have ensured that community needs and desires have been inserted into not only management, but also research programmes (see, for instance, Greer and Henry 1996; Ucko 2001; Clarke 2002; Smith et al. 2003a; Smith and Wobst 2005).

By controlling the moment of heritage, Indigenous communities have also developed strategies to foster understanding of their culture, experiences and identities in non-Indigenous populations. Significant campaigns and projects by a range of Indigenous communities across the world have, for instance, been undertaken to control the use of heritage places, and intangible heritage events, including such things as dance, song, knowledge about foods, bush skills and so forth, in cultural tourism (see, for instance, Finlayson 1996; Fourmile 1996; TAPC 2004; Beck et al. 2005). The increasing interest in Indigenous cultures as tourist destinations is well documented (Isaacson and

Ford 2005: 262), as are the ways in which Indigenous cultures have been exploited and bowdlerized in this process (Hollinshead 1992; Altman and Finlayson 2003). In asserting identity and challenging received and authorized ideas about that identity, the ability to control tourist experiences becomes significant. For instance, one white Australian tour operator, in discussing the importance of tourism for, in his words 'resurrecting Aboriginal culture', went on to observe:

> Bringing [tourists] to the area gives Aboriginal people the opportunity to show off their culture . . . and teaching the rest of the world about their culture and teaching younger Aboriginal people about their own cultural and resurrecting their culture. What is needed is to have the elders and the traditional cultural people from the area and have the younger people who are coming up to learn not only the culture but learn to interpret the culture in a way that is easy for tourists to understand. Not to change it, but to interpret it better . . . [goes on to talk about how useful it would be to get Aboriginal people dancing for the tourists]. . . Need to get younger or even older people who have a little bit of stamina and a little bit of rhythm and poise or something – that's what is needed to invigorate the Aboriginal people – need to get attractive people and teach them what they are supposed to do . . .
>
> (Interviewed 1999)

Although this tourist operator may have been genuine in his support for Aboriginal culture, his understanding of what constitutes 'proper' or 'acceptable' tourist experiences only propagates received colonial and racist notions of Aboriginal culture and people. The point here is that controlling the heritage experience or moment of heritage is integral to defining and articulating messages for both non-Indigenous audiences and Indigenous performers/audiences. As Tony Perkins observes, one of the important reasons his community is involved in ecotourism is 'to show that the culture is really alive . . . to get the message out that Yarrawarra [Aboriginal Corporation] and where it's based had real culture and real history that was very important to the Aboriginal people living here' (Beck et al. 2005: 231). There are numerous examples of Indigenous communities developing tourism programmes and businesses that are explicitly aimed at providing tourists with not only information but also, importantly, with experiences, which may facilitate the examination of received ideas about history and Indigenous identity and culture. The Tjapukai Aboriginal Cultural Park, Australia, for instance, is a dance theatre, which was formed by a 'cross-cultural group of entertainers' and which works in partnerships with local communities (TAPC 2004) and provides visitors with a powerful introduction to the cultures of northern Queensland. It does this through dance, the re-telling of oral history and cultural knowledge, and through traditional museum displays. The park's web page announces that it represents 'the first ever opportunity for tourist visitors to experience and interact with a 40,000-year-old culture that most Australians had relegated as belonging to social security handouts and fringe dwellers an exhibition space' (TAPC 2004). Heritage centres like this, and more traditional museums such as the Sámi Museum, Sidda in Finland and the National Museum of the American Indian in the United States, when working publicly in close partnership with Indigenous communities, offer venues where the heritage experience may be constructively changed to challenge colonial preconceptions. Not everyone of course will necessary listen to or comprehend the messages constructed by Indigenous communities. However, the performance of control has a material consequence at local and nation level in engendering pride and community cohesion and, as Abercrombie and Longhurst (1998) note, this meaning will diffuse out into the everyday lives of performers and audience. As Dodson again observes:

> Those Aboriginalities have been, and continue to be, a private source of spiritual sustenance in the face of others' attempts to control us. They are also a political project designed to challenge and subvert the authorised version of who and what we are.
>
> (1994: 10)

Interlinked with expressions of community cohesion and the challenging of received colonial notions of identity is the second role that the ability to control heritage achieves: the creation and recreation of new political identities through which to negotiate a range of cultural and civil rights and sovereignty issues. In the late 1960s and early 1970s, Indigenous political movements began to coalesce and assert themselves. In America, for instance, the organization that named itself the American Indian Movement, or AIM, attempted to represent broad American Indian interests (Means, with Wolf 1995; Smith and Warrior 1996; Deloria and Lytle 1998; Riding In 2000). In Australia, the Land Rights Movement developed in the early 1970s and gave direction to Aboriginal political activism (Millar 1986). Similar movements began in other countries and regions, for example New Zealand (Maaka and Fleras 2000) and Scandinavia (Ucko 2001). Central to movements like these were the assertion of a collective political identity. These identities, as Lowenthal (1998: 182) notes in relation to Australia, had not existed before colonization. There was, for instance, no consensual concept of a collective 'Australia' and Aboriginal people were, and continue to be today, culturally and linguistically diverse. Lowenthal goes on to state that, 'Aborigines became one people, consciously identified with their island continent, only when it ceased to be theirs, as an aftermath of British invasion and settlement' (1998: 182). The shared experiences of colonization, dispossession and racism – but also of resistance to them – have helped to foster another layer of Indigenous identity additional to community cultural identity. However, this is not simply a consequence of the shared experiences of dispossession and resistance; it is also part of an active and continuous process of resistance itself.

The ability to articulate the experiences of shared discrimination and resistance within an Indigenous (as opposed to indigenous) identity becomes significant for pursuing agendas at both national and international levels. For instance, the power and solidarity given to Aboriginal interests, under a collective politicized identity as 'Aboriginal people' or 'Indigenous Australians', has facilitated not only the lobbying of museums and universities to return heritage items, but also the brokering of codes of ethics that acknowledge the custodial rights of Indigenous Australians over their heritage (see, for instance, AAA 1991; Museums Australia 1999). It has also provided a platform from which to lobby state and national governments, including that of the United Kingdom. Due to the effective lobbying of Australian and other Indigenous peoples, the British government has recently begun addressing repatriation issues (DCMS 2003) – a significant event in a country very reticent to examine its colonial past (note, for example, the issue of the 'Elgin Marbles' and other cultural treasures). Other significant developments in the construction of a 'pan-Aboriginality' or an Indigenous Australian Identity were, firstly, the adoption in 1971 of the Aboriginal flag and later, in 1992, the Torres Strait Islander flag. These flags unite and represent the collective experiences of Indigenous Australians. The second development was the erection of the Aboriginal Tent Embassy on the lawns of Parliament House in Canberra, the nation's capital in 1972, a performance that represented the assertion of Aboriginal sovereignty, and challenged received ideas about the nature of the 'settlement' of Australian colonies.

The articulation of consensual identities not only draws attention to the shared colonial and so-called post-colonial experiences of Indigenous peoples, it is also as much a statement and performance about sovereignty, self-determination and political legitimacy as Western performances about national identities are. Indigenous peoples here are drawing on consensual understandings of their experiences within colonial histories to assert new identities as 'First Nation Peoples', in much the same way that the consensual view of history deployed in and by the AHD underpins Western national identities – only here the politics of the process are more stark, precisely because this tactic is being deployed outside authorized discourses. The identity politics played out by Indigenous peoples are no more or less politicized than the identity politics that underlie, for instance, the claim that the English country house is an icon of English national identity. As discussed in Chapter 4, the 1974 exhibition at the Victoria and Albert Museum – *The Destruction of the Country House, 1875–1975* – was an explicit, and successful, attempt to legitimize not only a way of life, but ultimately the very historical and contemporary social identity of the aristocracy and landed gentry in England. The identity politics that underlie the preservation of elite houses are, however, often far less obvious because of the extent to which they are conducted within and have become naturalized in and by the English AHD.

The project of constructing indigeneity is about challenging the very legitimacy of the colonial process; it is about the transfer of power from 'those who have it to those who never consented to its extinguishment'; and it is a process and a performance that forces public debate 'about who controls what, and why' (Makka and Fleras 2000: 95). The assertion of heritage in this construction is important, although not so much in terms of control over particular heritage places or events, but rather over the cultural process of heritage itself. One of the significant oppositional strategies and discourses that is brought to bear by those opposing Indigenous political aspirations and movements is the reconstruction of Indigenous identity as 'static' – and thus more controllable and subject to regulation and authentication via the pronouncements about what constitutes 'real' Indigenous identity by experts such as anthropologists, historians and archaeologists.

One of the key strategies here is the construction of the idea and discourse of 'tradition'. 'Tradition', particularly when applied to Indigenous culture, is often popularly constructed as something from an 'authentic' but distant past; it is static and unchanging. Indigenous culture has itself been essentialized, through not only colonial processes, but more recently through such things as the processes of cultural tourism and cultural heritage management, and is often defined as something essentially 'traditional' and thus 'unchanging'. Through the heritage management process not only material places and sites, but also the cultures associated with those places, become the subject of technical problems of conservation and preservation. It was argued in Chapter 3 that one of the things 'done' by the way 'heritage' is defined and then valued within the Western AHD is to obscure the ways in which cultural processes and meanings are regulated. One of the key principles in heritage management and conservation is the idea that the cultural significance, values and character of a place or monument should not be altered by the way it is managed and used. By claiming to manage material cultural heritage in such a way, and by simultaneously ignoring the mutability of cultural significance, what results is the 'preservation' and regulation of the cultural values and meanings associated with the heritage place itself. In effect, but without explicitly acknowledging it, the heritage management and conservation process is about the management or regulation of cultural meanings and values and, ultimately, the processes of remembering that make and remake meaning and value in the present. The ways in which this 'fossilization' of culture occurs is often obscured, as argued in Chapter 3, because the primary focus of the management and conservation gaze is the material culture and not on the cultural processes that occur at them and are affected by them. As cultural tools in the processes of remembering and meaning making, heritage places are, as demonstrated both above and in Chapter 7, intimately about negotiating cultural change. However, these cultural tools are managed in such a way as to privilege the idea of 'tradition' and thus stasis – they are conserved as originally found, or at least how colonial discourses defined them when they encountered them. This is also linked to the perception that heritage values are only to be found in 'authentic' material objects, and it is only their use in, or association with, cultural practices that authenticates culture and identity. In this way, Indigenous identity and cultural practices have themselves been subjected to, and regulated by, authorizing heritage discourses. Subsequently, and as noted in Chapter 2, unless Indigenous people are seen to be practising culture in a way that corresponds to received colonial views about what constitutes 'real' American Indians, Aborigines, Maoris and so forth, the practices and the identities associated with them are often not identified as legitimate or valid within the authorized heritage and other colonial discourses.

Thus the ability to control heritage is not only about being able to control community identity, it is also about the power to control political identity, and negotiating the ways in which communities may choose to align with other Indigenous communities at regional, national or international levels. It is also about controlling the processes of remembering and the negotiation of cultural change. This control is particularly vital in communities and populations that are attempting to assert self-determination, and who are attempting to negotiate and assert new ways of 'being' that deal with the traumas of colonial dispossession, and that challenge received perceptions about their history and culture. These aspirations also take on added significance when underpinning negotiations with governments and policy makers about the legitimacy of Indigenous claims to land and other economic resources. The power to lobby governments effectively will rest on how governments perceive the political legitimacy – and, in the case of Indigenous interests, the cultural legitimacy – of the demands and claims. The possibility of challenging authorized discourses and other accounts of Indigenous culture, history and experiences is fundamentally important in attempting to get governments to listen to the legitimacy of Indigenous claims. The capacity to control symbolically important heritage is a performative and political act in the negotiation of political legitimacy.

Subsequently, the third interlinked ability that the control of heritage facilitates is the demonstration of command over a political resource. The sense of 'politics' here does not simply lay in the role heritage plays in underpinning and negotiating the legitimacy of cultural and political claims and demands. It also lays in the observation that heritage is itself primarily a process that is fundamentally about the negotiation of cultural and social conflicts. In Indigenous identity politics, heritage is demonstrated to be about dissonance – about the assertion of certain Indigenous cultural values

over non-Indigenous, colonial or Western values, and/or about the negotiation and renegotiation of meaning as communities deal with past cultural
and political traumas. The heritage process is inherently dissonant, as a constitutive social process that, on the one hand, attempts to regulate cultural
expression while, on the other hand, attempts to work out, contest and/or
challenge the cultural and social meanings that will prevail in the present, it
becomes important within certain struggles. These struggles may occur at
family, local, community, national and international levels, but central to
them will be conflict over whose experiences and perspectives are valid and
whose are not. As such, the ability to control the process of meaning making
and remembering that is the fundamental element or substance of heritage
becomes vital, not only for Indigenous peoples, but also for a range of other
subaltern groups.

This brings us back to the repatriation issue. The repatriation of human
remains and cultural artefacts is, as noted above, not only about ensuring
that remains and items are treated in culturally appropriate ways, it is also
about the representational politics of controlling a political resource. The
retention of collections of Indigenous human remains and artefacts by
museums and universities, without the active consent of Indigenous peoples,
conveys a powerful symbolic message, however unintentional that may be,
about the legitimacy of colonial history and narratives. The repatriation of
remains is a symbolic event, or performance, that explicitly recognizes the
political legitimacy of Indigenous identity claims. As Nancy Fraser (2000)
argues, the 'politics of recognition' is an important area of political negotiation. The public recognition of culture, while it cannot remedy injustices in
and of itself, can, if properly conceived, aid the material processes and strategies needed to remedy injustices (2000: 2). As colonial history reveals, misrecognition may also produce real injuries and injustices. The return of
human remains and artefacts are not, as Appleton (2003) has asserted, empty
'feel good' gestures that do little to address material inequity. Repatriation is
itself a performance of heritage, where not only the control of cultural meaning making is returned to Indigenous communities, the identity of the
Indigenous peoples concerned is reasserted, legitimized and remembered. In
1992, the remains of a young woman who died in Australia more than
24,000 years ago were returned to the local Aboriginal community. The
return of the Lake Mungo Woman, as these remains are known, to community control was a very important symbolic act that acknowledged the
custodial rights of the local community, the legitimacy of their cultural
claims to the region in which she was found, and the legitimacy of their
knowledge about their own history and identity. The symbolism of this
return is all the more powerful because of what the archaeologists involved in
the return relinquished. These remains were very important in the history of
Australian archaeology, helping to change dramatically archaeological
understanding about the age and nature of the peopling of Australia – to a

very real extent the discoveries at Lake Mungo put Australian archaeology on the world archaeological map (see Lourandous 1997, for details about these discoveries). The remains were items of great scientific status, and closely associated with the career of at least one senior archaeologist. Further, within the context of archaeological discourses, the venerable age of the remains made them highly scientifically significant and of universal value. The idea that such very old remains could be linked to a living community is very difficult for many enmeshed within the Western AHD to appreciate or understand. Subsequently, their return to the community sends out a power-ful public message about the legitimacy of Aboriginal cultural knowledge, and the equitable place that Aboriginal culture and people *should*, although as yet do not, occupy in Australian society.

Conclusion

The capacity to control the heritage process – the experiences of place and the practices of remembering – that defines and gives meaning to construc-tions of identity is an integral element of the heritage process itself. Without control over this process, or a sense of active agency in it, individuals and communities become subjected to received notions and ideas about who they are or should be – control is vital if the heritage process and the identities it constructs are to have real personal and cultural meaning for those associated or engaged with particular heritage places. However, this control is also important because of the political and cultural power of 'heritage' to repre-sent and validate a sense of place, memory and identity. This chapter has examined the Indigenous criticism of the AHD to illustrate the political consequences of heritage discourses. One profound consequence that such discourses, and in particular the AHD, have is the power to legitimize or delegitimize identity claims, which themselves may be important in wider political negotiations over access to social, legal and economic resources. It has revealed how the dissonant nature of heritage is integral to any con-ceptualization of the heritage process – that heritage is ultimately about the negotiation of meaning and identity, often in opposition to received percep-tions of identity, and often in terms of dealing with traumatic past and present experiences. Moreover, it is a dissonant process in which meaning and identity are continually constructed and negotiated anew as political and cultural circumstances dictate.

Although the issues raised in this chapter are starkly exposed due to their placement outside of both the AHD and the Western worldview, they nonetheless have relevance to other expressions of heritage. The political work that heritage does in legitimizing and delegitimizing Indigenous cul-tural identity is a role that is fundamental to the heritage process generally. Both subaltern and authorized heritage discourses work in similar ways to grant or withhold power to other conceptualizations of identity and social and cultural experiences. These discourses compete with each other for authority and legitimacy, so that the meanings about the past and present they represent are validated, and this in turn will help to validate present social and cultural experiences. This process was also revealed in Chapters 6 and 7, where discourses about working class experiences competed with the AHD, in a process that was about negotiating and validating the experiences of people from working class communities in the present. Heritage itself becomes a resource of power in these and wider negotiations, because of its representational power, but also because it is a process of meaning making where the ability to challenge and change received 'expert' and authorized notions of history and identity can be worked out and enacted.

'Heritage' as an identifiable discourse garnered more public attention in the 1960s and 1970s, as subaltern identity politics become a specific public issue. Increasingly assertive Indigenous claims about their ability to control and assert their own identity coincided with the identification of material culture as 'heritage', and its regulation and management by a body of expertise and technical and legal processes. This confluence of events and processes had a significant political impact for Indigenous political and cultural claims and aspirations. However, this confluence did not simply impede and regulate Indigenous cultural and political aspirations, but also had similar implications for a range of other subaltern communities. Commentators on the history of heritage as a phenomena have noted that the discourse of 'heritage' is something that appears to have 'arrived' – or at least found a new intensity of expression – in Western contexts in the 1960s and 1970s (Chase and Shaw 1989; Hunter 1981; Lowenthal 1998; see also Chapter 1). Certainly, formal and technical processes of conservation and management become very clearly articulated in this period through legal instruments and national and international policy documents, conventions and charters. Meanwhile, globalization has seen an increase in the assertion of local and community identity claims that are expressed and disseminated through a broadening range of media. I am not suggesting a 'conspiracy' of social and cultural control, but rather heritage did become a useful discourse through which to make sense of, regulate and ultimately control the increasing public emergence of local and competing claims to a range of cultural, social, historical and other identities and experiences.

CONCLUSION

This book started with the argument that there is an 'authorized heritage discourse', which takes its cue from the grand narratives of Western national and elite class experiences, and reinforces ideas of innate cultural value tied to time depth, monumentality, expert knowledge and aesthetics. This is a strong characterization of a discourse, and one that tends to overlook the fact that the discourse can be, and often is, more nuanced and mutable over time and space than I have room to represent it. It is also a discourse that is open to contestation, not just from external groups but from within as well – as there are heritage experts who actively work to facilitate the broadening of the definition of heritage, and to develop inclusive practices that acknowledge the diversity of heritage experiences. However, the book does demonstrate the way in which the discursive field has been historically and institutionally constituted, and that this dominant heritage discourse works to exclude, despite the intentions of individual practitioners, non-expert views about the nature and meaning of 'heritage'. The examples explored in this volume show that the definitions of heritage that we adopt, and the language we use to frame conservation, preservation, interpretation and other management practices, have consequences – they matter in terms of practice. Any discourse, particularly when it is promoted by bodies of 'experts', state-sanctioned agencies and international bodies like ICOMOS and UNESCO, carries power. However, the power of the AHD also lies in the way it continually legitimizes the experiences and worldviews of dominant narratives about nation, class, culture and ethnicity – experiences and understandings about the world that traditionally find synergy with the institutions and bodies of expertise that use and promote the discourse. This is not to say that the AHD cannot be changed, but that without recognizing the ideological and political underpinnings of the discourse any attempts at change may be confined to particular events rather than represent a real systemic challenge.

The AHD is also powerful, not simply because of its institutional position, but also because of the cultural work it does in legitimizing certain experiences and identities – it is powerful because it is a form of 'heritage' itself. The existence of an AHD, whatever its particular nuances or variations across time and space, is part of the cultural and social process of heritage, and is itself constitutive of 'heritage'. It not only identifies those things, and sometimes events, that must nationally or internationally be valued and treasured as 'heritage', it itself is a process of heritage as I have been defining it in this book. The AHD is a process of mediating cultural change and of asserting, negotiating and affirming particular identities and values. It is a process wherein the narratives, values and cultural and social meanings that underpin certain identities – often national ones – are asserted, assessed and legitimized. The subjectivity of this discourse is obscured not only by its association with objective expertise, but because of its characterization of heritage as a tangible and immutable 'thing' – its identification of heritage as 'physical' renders the values and ideologies the discourse represents as tangible and self evident. However, the AHD is as much about mediating and legitimizing identity as are the competing heritage discourses identifiable within Indigenous communities (Chapter 8) or at Castleford (Chapter 7).

This book also started on the banks of a river and at a moment when I was considering the insights I had gained through working with Australian Indigenous people on heritage issues. Indigenous peoples have been extremely active and assertive in their opposition to received and other 'authorized' views of, and discourses about, their identities and heritage. The experiences of Indigenous peoples in asserting their heritage have much to offer in understanding the role of heritage in non-Indigenous or Western contexts. Stepping outside of the AHD, as one is vigorously encouraged to do when working with Indigenous peoples, serves as a useful counterpoint, and allows insights to emerge when considering the processes and experiences that underlie one's own cultural and social identity. The politics of identity are particularly pointed with Indigenous peoples, especially in postcolonial contexts, but the range of issues that I have identified in Chapter 8 (see also Smith 2004) are equally relevant to any other heritage context. Heritage is a subjective political negotiation of identity; however, the processes that underpin and link identity to places or events of 'heritage' are often lost or obscured by the nature of the AHD. One of the ways this is done is the way Western heritage discourses seek to legitimize themselves, and the identities they reflect and construct, through the naturalization of heritage as something that 'just is', which suggests that they are immutable and not open to challenge.

It has been the task of this book to step outside of the AHD and offer a reconsideration of heritage, not as a thing but as a cultural process – to examine not only what the AHD 'does', but what competing discourses about heritage also 'do' to get a sense of the cultural and social phenomena that is 'heritage'. To facilitate this examination, I have used a number of themes established in Chapter 2 – identity, intangibility, memory and remembering, performance, place and dissonance – to help capture a range of moments when the AHD is being utilized, or when it is mutating or being challenged. Individually or in concert, do these themes tell us anything that is useful about the nature and use of heritage?

The idea of 'identity' tends to be unproblematically linked with concepts of 'heritage', and while this link is not at all disputed the actual processes and activities that are enacted to forge links between heritage and identity are often not identified in the literature. This is because the idea or possibility that links to identity actually need to be actively forged, or continually remade and created, tend to be obscured by the dominant assumptions that tangible heritage 'just is', and that the identities they represent are defined by inherent qualities of the heritage site or object. However, if heritage has no inherent qualities what are the implications for the creation, maintenance or assertion of identity? Certainly, identity must be viewed as an active process of continual creation and recreation, where links and associations with the past, and subsequently the tangible heritage places or objects that represent that past, are continually remade and negotiated. The various chapters in this book capture a range of heritage moments, which reveal the active way in which links between places of heritage and identity are made and remade. This remaking is sometimes done within the AHD, or in opposition to it, or simply without reference to the AHD at all, but all are done as active and creative processes.

In Chapter 4, people visiting country houses, although not always consciously forging or creating identity, were nonetheless active in their pursuit of it. Country house visiting, despite being seen by many to simply represent a leisure activity or nice day out, was nonetheless a leisure choice that spoke to people's sense of identity. The identities constructed here were also multi-layered, with the houses speaking both to a sense of English nationalism and class hierarchies and status. Moreover, it was in the activity of the visit, rather than in the simple knowledge that these houses existed, that people were both finding and expressing a sense of who they were – and indeed who they wanted to be. The identities being constructed here were also exclusionary – the sense of identity that emerges in this chapter is one in which 'likeness' is being actively sought and constructed. All identity construction is to a certain extent exclusionary as it defines who you are not, as much as who you are. However, here the sense of who is excluded was being actively made and was central to the heritage experience.

As illustrated in Chapter 5, this sense of exclusion will always be inherently political. The various social and cultural identities, again actively constructed around the Riversleigh landscape, demonstrate that material forms of heritage, and the discourses about them, provide a legitimizing force for assertions of identity that at times vigorously seek to marginalize or delegitimize others. The ways identities are constructed and the sense of legitimacy given to them through associations with particular forms of 'heritage' will have consequences in wider social and cultural debates, and in struggles over certain resources – as occurred at Riversleigh. Both the identity performances association with Riversleigh and the English country house have repercussions within debates about such things as social and economic equity, multiculturalism and so forth. In particular, they have implications for the historical and cultural legitimacy of other groups and communities, either not associated with, or marginalized by, the master narratives drawn upon in the creation of the identities represented by these places.

The sense of active identity creation is also illustrated at the industrial museums (Chapter 6), at Castleford (Chapter 7) and in Indigenous communities (Chapter 8). Although identities here were often constructed in vigorous opposition to the AHD, it is important to note that the processes of celebrating and asserting identity were also used as platforms from which current social, economic and political experiences were examined and contextualized. Although there is a sense that identity was actively being recreated through the country house visit, there is also a sense of its regulation or governance by the way the sites were managed and interpreted for the visitors – and a sense that many visitors connived in that regulation. This self-regulation is marked by the lack of critical engagement many people had with the house they were visiting, and the absence of attempts to draw on their experiences to comment on other aspects of their lives. This absence is particularly marked in comparison to the way identities were not only constructed, but also then used by individuals and communities described in Part III of this book. Chapters 6–8 illustrate that the processes in which people engage to facilitate the expression and recreation or assertion of identities are often intertwined with, or become the basis of, critical commentary about their social, economic or political positions and experiences, and vice versa.

This point is particularly apposite at Castleford, where a process of active and self-conscious identity creation drew upon, and critically examined and contextualized, a range of community experiences. The self-conscious interlinking of past and present community experiences was itself part of a dynamic process of negotiation about where and how the community was changing and developing. The process of identity formation both grew out of and influenced the negotiation of community agendas and aspirations about regeneration and development. As such, heritage becomes a discourse about and through which identity claims are re/created and legitimized – it is not a static process but one in which identity is continually remade and expressed to meet the current and changing needs of individual, community or nation.

Memory and remembering are particularly useful concepts in understanding the processes of heritage, and in identifying the processes people draw upon to link identity with tangible and intangible places and events of heritage. In Chapters 4 and 5, it was the collective memories, often about nation, that tended to be drawn on and rehearsed and 'passed on' and these became emotionally legitimized and naturalized through their incorporation into people's sense of self and belonging. In Chapters 6 and 7, memories, and the processes of remembering, were revealed as vital in the ways in which people were constructing and reconstructing identity and feelings of kinship and belonging. Emotional remembering was important here too – passing on to friends and relations not just information about 'what happened when', but also feelings of comradeship, gratitude, injustice, kinship and belonging. The sense of historical gratitude and humility that emerged in Chapters 7 and 8 were about forging links with the past, but also about underpinning a sense of identity that recognized the changing nature of that identity, and the need and desirability of change. The lesson offered by the experiences of Indigenous people discussed in Chapter 8 is the need to control the processes of remembering. Without the ability to control how experiences are remembered and the meanings drawn from those remembrances, an individual or community's identity runs the risk of being governed or arbitrated by external forces. Control and the recognition that self-conscious self-expression is a legitimate form of identity construction is vital. A strong impression emerges in much of the heritage literature that a self-conscious sense of identity construction is somehow 'inauthentic' or subjective and thus invalid. What Chapters 6–8 illustrate, particularly in comparison to Chapters 4 and 5, however, is that self-conscious articulations and negotiations about the meaning of the past and the places of heritage are healthy and vital to community self-worth and development.

By incorporating ideas about memory and remembering into definitions of heritage, a more nuanced understanding of the emotional quality and power of the cultural process of heritage emerges. The idea that heritage is engaged with the construction and negotiation of meaning, in this case through remembering, reinforces the idea of heritage as an active process and not a passive subject of management. The act or performances of remembering help to bind groups together not only at national, but also at sub-national, community levels.

The theme of memory and remembering was also important for identifying the experiences that heritage as a process itself offered. Heritage not only engages with acts of remembering, but is also concerned with the creation of shared experiences and the memories of these. This issue emerged particularly in Chapters 4, 6 and 7, where the acts of visiting places of heritage (country houses or industrial museums) or participating in heritage events in Castleford became not just about past memories – or about the past – but were places and events situated in the present that created 'heritage'. In this case, the heritage being created was the memories about shared experiences – be those experiences of a simple leisure activity, passing on of and receiving family or other collective memories, or participating in a family or community event. Thus, collective memories, and the activity of remembering, are integral to any idea of heritage – heritage places are not just an aid to memory, but are about the creation of shared memories that work to help create and maintain bonds between family and community members. Above all, the theme of remembering alerts us to the idea that heritage is a culturally directed process of intense emotional power, that is both a personal and social act of making sense of, and understanding, the past and the present.

The idea of 'performance' and performativity has also been useful in challenging the idea that visitors to heritage sites and museums are passive receptors of the messages that site managers and curators create. As Chapters 4 and 6 reveal, visitors interact with those messages in a number of ways – they may reject them outright, engage with them critically or uncritically or regard them with ambivalence. Even when, as tended to happen at the country house sites, people uncritically embraced them, they were not necessarily doing so passively. The idea of performativity highlights the emotional and physical experience of heritage and stresses the idea of 'doing' – that heritage is not something that is necessarily possessed, or only possessed, but that a thing becomes heritage because it is used as heritage or because it is a place that facilitates the doing of heritage performances. Those performances may be the commemoration of collective national and class memories (Chapter 4), wherein such memories and their values and meanings are legitimized through their commemoration. They may be performances of certain behaviours that mark an individual as a particular member of a group, as in Chapter 5 for instance, where palaeontologists were shown acting out certain gendered performances to mark and legitimize their identities as not only palaeontologists, but as the cultural 'owners' of a particular resource (in this case, the Riversleigh fossil deposits and landscape). Performances of reminiscence and the passing on of memories, at industrial museums and at Castleford, were also used in underlining the importance of the meanings constructed through the activities of remembering and identity formation. Heritage performances at Castleford – particularly those associated with the festival – also marked out those commonplace areas of life worthy of celebration, which needed to be remembered as important in and to people's everyday lives. The performativity of heritage at Castleford also worked to recognize the importance of, and reinforce, community social networks – the festival itself often became a moment through which performers and audiences reflected on, reconsidered, negotiated or affirmed a range of community issues, relations and values. The performances of control (Chapters 7 and 8) were also important in asserting the meaning of identity and its value as a cultural and political statement of self-determination.

The point was made forcefully by residents of Castleford that nothing is really heritage unless it is being used – the value for any object or site comes from its use. This use takes on a performative edge because in moments of heritage that use may become exaggerated or marked out in some way to signal the importance of the act. In the country house performance, this may be marked by, for instance, adopting hushed tones in your conversation as you wander through the house. At Castleford, it may be marked by the use of things like the pit banners, maypole and the display of rag rugs and miners' equipment in the context of the yearly festival. Whatever the context, heritage activities take on a performative edge – or become a performance – as they mark out and define the things, processes or events that are important for underlying identity and shared memories and values.

The idea of performance has useful implications for how 'sense of place' is defined and used. The idea of place is another theme explored in this book, and the idea of place discussed in Chapter 2 brings us back to the materiality of heritage. However, it also reveals a tension between place, and the activities that go on at them, and offers a reconsideration of how place, site or artefact – the material – is important to a sense of heritage. If a place becomes important, or becomes 'heritage' because of the activities that occur at it, those performances may also become marked as important or as 'heritage' because of the place of their doing. An important inter-relation is identified between place and performance in several chapters of the book. Being at a country house or in the landscape of Riversleigh, for instance, was an active demonstration of the possession of the skills, taste, values – the cultural capital – to read and understand the semiotics of the place, and thus to be members of certain collectives. Being at Tolpuddle, the place where the Martyrs lived and were arrested, or being in museums containing mining artefacts or taking the underground tour of an ex-mine at the NCMM, helped to underline the sense of occasion and importance of the heritage activities – or performances – that were being undertaken between family members or by individuals. The sense of being at the places where these things happened was emotionally useful in underlining the memories and values being passed on to other family members or for individuals simply remembering and reaffirming their own identities and social values.

As Chapter 4 illustrated, the country houses had themselves an affect – their comforting atmosphere and ambiance helped to facilitate engagement with comfortable and comforting messages about nation and class identity. However, at Beamish, the fact that material was not in situ was not found to be a particular problem for visitors; material authenticity or authenticity of place was not a major issue here. Rather, what was important for many was whether or not Beamish gave people the opportunity to remember – to use material items (no matter their locational 'authenticity') to jog their memories, or as props and prompts in telling stories about their own or their parents' lives and experiences to other family members. What this tells us is that it is the utility of a place or artefact in invoking, signifying or otherwise connecting with people's wider social experiences, memories and knowledge that is important, and what determines if it becomes used as a place or object of heritage, rather than any innate quality. Thus, for a place or artefact to be heritage it needs to speak to present-day cultural, political and social needs – places or artefacts of heritage are 'heritage' because they are cultural tools in the heritage process. However, as a cultural tool of heritage, sites and artefacts can and do become integral to the heritage process, and can and do have their own affect, creating an important inter-relationship – the point being that this inter-relationship is created and actively maintained and not based on innate characteristics. The power of the affect material places and objects have also relies on the power given to them in heritage discourses, and the way they are *conceived* and valued as items of desire, status, or simply as possessing innate values and properties.

A sense of place was constructed at country houses, museums, Castleford and Riversleigh that facilitated and underpinned people's sense of belonging and identity, but the sense of place that was constructed derives from an active sense of experience with and in the place. The power of place derives not only from the values we associate with it, but from the emotional power of the experiences it represents and facilitates in creating. The symbolic power of place cannot be underestimated; the importance of the symbolism of owning or controlling places or objects was demonstrated in both Chapters 7 and 8. Chapter 8, in particular, illustrates the political and cultural importance not only of controlling the processes of remembering, but also the arenas and forums in which these occur. It is not only symbolically important to control the symbols of identity such as Indigenous human remains, or Roman artefacts and pit banners, but to control the use they are put to and the experiences they facilitate and frame. If part of the heritage process is to negotiate and experiment with changing social values, meaning and identity, the possibility of a place, or physical spaces, where that can be done in security needs to be understood.

The idea of dissonance also has utility in understanding the nature and process of heritage. The existence of the AHD and the work that it does promoting a consensus view of history (Chapters 1 and 3) ensures that there will always be excluded communities – and thus dissonant – accounts of heritage and heritage experiences. A sense of dissonance occurred in all the moments of heritage examined in this book, though at different levels of intensity. At Castleford and in many Indigenous communities, the sense of identity and heritage that were constructed tended to occur in opposition to, and certainly outside of, the dominant discourses – making them dissonant in varying ways. This sense of dissonance must acknowledge the differences in the persuasive and legitimizing power of different heritage discourses. At country houses, a seam of dissonance ran under the comfortable identities of nation and class that were being constructed – although many people were comfortable in the messages they constructed and took away about the houses, many also still wondered about the servants and what their lives might represent. This seam of dissonance also illustrates that no heritage discourse or moment of heritage is necessarily uniformly shared or homogeneously constructed; rather, there are always elements of dissent and challenge, and thus the possibility of change within it.

Meaning and identity are not static, but are continually negotiable or open to negotiation. At Riversleigh, heritage performances were utilized to legitimize and de-legitimize a range of interests in struggles over resources, and this was important in demonstrating that heritage is also a political process, and that heritage places or objects can become resources of power. Understanding the unequal deployment of resources of power in the heritage process is important for understanding why communities like Castleford, or those Indigenous communities in post-colonial contexts, are passionate in their assertion of their identities and sense of heritage. The dismissal, for instance, of the Castleford Heritage Trust as 'just a half dozen old ladies' (Drake personal communication), as has been done by officials in positions of power over that community, marks the extent to which the sense of community offered by the Trust and other residents is not only dissonant, but also why it matters. The ability of communities to assert their own sense of self-worth not only challenges established heritage discourses, but also destabilizes the narratives of nation and class that assume that experiences of people in communities like Castleford do not matter. The identity politics played out by Indigenous peoples, people in communities like Castleford, or by people managing or visiting country house sites or industrial museums, sit within and play a part in broader issues and debates about social and political equity. The very context of heritage issues, and the debates and social and cultural experiences that they feed into and subsequently help to legitimize and de-legitimize, means that all heritage is dissonant as all heritage is political and thus 'uncomfortable'.

The final theme I need to return to is that of intangibility. The idea of intangibility facilitated the removal of our gaze from the physical aspects of heritage that have tended to form the focus of the AHD. Subsequently, this has ensured that a range of other elements or aspects of heritage have revealed themselves. By de-privileging the physical aspects of heritage, the elements that link heritage with identity and social and cultural values and meanings have been illuminated. These elements include the importance of acts of remembering and memory making, the dissonant nature of heritage, and the political power that can be invested in heritage processes, sites and objects, as well as the performativity of heritage and ways in which this is used to signal and demarcate moments of identity and value creation or recreation and negotiation. All heritage is ultimately intangible – although I have returned full circle to this proposition, it is an understanding of heritage that is ultimately fruitful. It is fruitful as it challenges the materialist idea of heritage and the ideological baggage that goes with that, and yet also challenges the critiques of heritage that warn against its stultifying backward reactionary glances. Heritage is a cultural and social process; it is the experiences that may happen at sites or during the acting out of certain events; it is a process of remembering and memory making – of mediating cultural and social change, of negotiating and creating and recreating values, meanings, understandings and identity. Above all, heritage is an active, vibrant cultural process of creating bonds through shared experiences and acts of creation.

I am not claiming to offer a fully rounded or complete re-theorization of heritage. However, what I hope these insights and analysis achieve is to offer a more useful point of departure for understanding the nature and power of heritage in Western contexts. Much more research needs to be done in uncovering the moments and elements of 'heritage', and to explore the links between ideas of heritage and expressions of identity. It is important that further research be undertaken that aims to map out the consequences of 'heritage' and to understand the social, cultural and political work that it does, and the networks of meaning and practice it sits within. It is through understanding the use that places and processes of heritage are put to in the present, the way the present constructs it, the role that heritage plays and the consequences it has, that a useful sense of what heritage *is* and *does* can be achieved.

NOTES

2 HERITAGE AS A CULTURAL PROCESS

1 'Country' refers to the land or landscape that Aboriginal people associate themselves with, and it is the area of land from which is drawn a sense of place: that is, identity, sense of belonging and community. For further discussion of this, see Rose and Clarke (1997) and Head (2000a).

2 In Australia, as in the Americas, National Parks are areas where certain activities, particularly those associated with fishing and hunting, are normally prohibited. Indigenous peoples in these countries often hold 'special' rights to undertake 'traditional' hunting and fishing practices in parks, a situation that is often stridently contested by non-Indigenous hunters and fishing enthusiasts.

3 AUTHORIZING INSTITUTIONS OF HERITAGE

1 Emma Waterton, University of York, recorded this assertion in an interview with government employees.

4 THE 'MANORED' PAST

1 Exact figures for 2005 could not be determined, but see the following websites for details of houses open to the public: Historic Houses Association, http://www.hha.org.uk/; English Heritage, http://www.english-heritage.org.uk/; National Trust in England, http://www.nationaltrust.org.uk/main/. See also figures in Mandler (1997) and Barker (1999).

2 The introduction of interpretation planning at organizations such as English Heritage is a recent development aimed at challenging this genre.

3 For further details of these houses, consult: http://www.harewood.org/ for Harewood House; http://www.waddesdon.org.uk/ for Waddesdon Manor; http://www.nationaltrust.org.uk/main/ or http://www.nationaltrust.org.uk/main/ w-vh/w-visits/w-findaplace/w-nostellpriory.htm for Nostell Priory; http://www.english-heritage.org.uk/ for Belsay Hall, Brodsworth Hall and Audley End.

4 English Heritage (EH), although a government agency reporting to the Department for Culture, Media and Sport, also offers membership to the public who receive free entry to sites managed by EH and a subscription to their quarterly magazine, *Heritage Today*, on heritage issues.

5 FELLAS, FOSSILS AND COUNTRY

1 The Australian Bureau of Statistics, Year Book 2002, http://www.abs.gov.au/ reports that just under 15 per cent of the Australian population live in rural areas; in 1911, this percentage was much higher at 43 per cent, but still representing less than half of the population.

2 Paddy Pallin was the founder of a range of camping and outdoor activity stores.

3 The style of referencing or referring to questionnaire and interview data used in the rest of this book is not adopted in this chapter to ensure anonymity in a small community where debates over land management issues are still occurring.

4 Larrikin is an Australian term referring to an individual who possesses irreverent and self-deprecating humour, mocks authority and generally behaves in a comical fashion.

6 LABOUR HERITAGE

1 For further information about the three museums, consult: http:// www.beamish.org.uk/ for the North of England Open Air Museum, Beamish; http://www.ncm.org.uk/ for the National Coal Mining Museum; and http:// www.tolpuddlemartyrs.org.uk/ for the Tolpuddle Martyrs Museum.

2 See the Office for National Statistics' website and their description of the classification of ethnicity used in Britain: http://www.statistics.gov.uk/about/ Classifications/ns_ethnic_classification.asp. Categories used include 'White', 'Mixed', 'Asian-British', 'Black-British', etc.

7 THE SLATE WIPED CLEAN?

1 In 1984, the Government's National Coal Board announced its intention of closing 20 mines, with the loss of about 20,000 jobs, declaring that agreements reached after the 1974 miners' strike had become obsolete. This act was part of Margaret Thatcher's Conservative Government's attempt to reduce the power of the unions, the government having begun stockpiling coal for several months prior to this announcement in preparation for a lengthy battle with the powerful National Union of Mineworkers (NUM). On 12 March 1984, Arthur Scargill, president of the NUM, called a national strike against the pit closures. Thatcher was able to declare the strike illegal and mobilized the police to deal with picket lines to ensure strike breakers could be bussed into the mines. The strike ended on 3 March 1985, almost a year after it began. Many mines were closed thereafter, with the government arguing that less expensive coal could be imported from overseas. The strikers had spent almost a year on strike pay, many were in debt, and many lost their jobs. The loss of the strike, its economic consequences, the effect of pit closures and the attack on community solidarity as part of the government's attempts to demoralize striking miners have had a significant and long-term effect, especially in many northern communities in England who had depended on the coalmining industry (http://en.wikipedia.org/wiki/UK_ miners'_strike_(1984–1985)#History; see also Milne 2004; Hutton 2005, for further details).

2 Back-to-back housing refers to terraced buildings literally built back-to back – houses commonly sharing not only walls on either side, but back walls as well. They tended to be one room deep, often with three rooms built one above the other. They were built from the eighteenth century onwards in response to rapidly growing urban populations as workers moved into expanding industrial towns from rural areas. They were constructed in rows or within 'courts', and

blocks of houses often shared ablution facilities. Their cramped design became associated with overcrowding, disease and poverty. Although such housing did once occur in Castleford, most of the housing was terraced and possessed small yards. 'Back-to-back' is interchangeably used by some residents in Castleford to refer to both terraced housing and 'back-to-back' houses — the main difference between the two being the presence of a small back yard.

3 Interviews are referenced anonymously by the abbreviation 'Cas' followed by a field number and the year date. Transcripts of interviews are lodged with the Castleford Heritage Trust under this code.

4 The Heritage Lottery Fund (HLF), established by Parliament in 1994, is a body in the United Kingdom that gives and oversees grants for heritage projects at local, regional and national levels. The grant scheme is funded by money raised by the National Lottery. For further information, see http://www.hlf.org.uk/English/.

5 As Keith Emerick, Inspector for Ancient Monuments, English Heritage, notes (personal communication) his first involvement with the CHT was over the use of the bathhouse and the community wish to have it opened up and interpreted. Although he was not concerned about the conservation issues as such, he was aware that the community agendas were very likely to become lost, if not highjacked, within the ensuing technical concerns about conservation issues.

REFERENCES

AAA (Australian Archaeological Association) (1991) *Code of Ethics*, at: http://www.australianarchaeologicalassociation.com.au/codeofethics.html (accessed 15 September 2001).

Abercrombie, N. and Longhurst, B. (1998) *Audiences: A Sociological Theory of Performance and Imagination*, London: Sage.

Abroe, M.M. (1998) 'Observing the Civil War Centennial: Rhetoric, reality and the bounds of selective memory', *Cultural Resource Management*, 21(11): 22–25.

Ah Kit, J. (1995) 'Aboriginal aspirations for heritage conservation', *Historic Environment*, 11(2–3): 31–36.

Aikawa, N. (2004) 'An historical overview of the preparation of the UNESCO International Convention for the Safeguarding of the Intangible Heritage', *Museum International*, 56(1–2): 137–149.

Allen, G. and Cantell, T. (1978) 'Left to rot: What future for decaying historic buildings?', *Architects' Journal*, 22: 987–1002.

Allfrey, M. (1999) 'Brodsworth Hall', in G. Chitty and D. Baker (eds) *Managing Historic Sites and Buildings: Reconciling Presentation and Preservation*, London: Routledge.

Altman, J. and Finlayson, J. (2003) 'Aborigines, tourism, and sustainable development', *Journal of Tourism Studies*, 14(1): 78–91.

Amselle, J.L. (2004) 'Intangible heritage and contemporary African Art', *Museum International*, 56(1–2): 84–89.

Anawak, J. (1989) 'Inuit perceptions of the past', in R. Layton (ed.) *Who Needs the Past?*, London: Unwin Hyman.

Anderson, B. (1991) *Imagined Communities*, London: Verso.

Andreae, S. and Binney, M. (1978) *Tomorrow's Ruins?*, London: SAVE Britain's Heritage.

Andreae, S., Binney, M. and Griffiths, C. (1981) *Silent Mansions: More Country Houses at Risk*, London: SAVE Britain's Heritage.

Anon (2004) *Annual Visitor Numbers, 1999–2004*, unpublished report, Beamish: The North of England Open Air Museum.

Anon (2005) 'Visitor Research Trends – 1994 to 2004, Harewood House', unpublished report, Harewood: Harewood House.

Anyon, R. and Ferguson, T. (1995) 'Cultural resources management at the Pueblo of Zuni, New Mexico, USA', *Antiquity*, 69: 913–930.

Anyon, R., Ferguson, T.J., Jackson, L., Lane, L. and Vicenti, P. (1997) 'Native

American oral tradition and archaeology: Issues of structure, relevance and respect', in N. Swidler, K. E. Dongoske, R. Anyon and A. S. Downer (eds) *Native Americans and Archaeologists: Stepping Stones to Common Ground*, Walnut Creek, CA: AltaMira.

Anyon, R., Ferguson, T. and Welch, J. (2000) 'Heritage management by American Indian Tribes in the Southwestern United States', in F. McManamon and A. Hatton (eds) *Cultural Resource Management in Contemporary Society*, London: Routledge.

Apostolakis, A. (2003) 'The Convergence Process in Heritage Tourism', *Annals of Tourism Research*, 30(4): 796–812.

Appleton, J. (2003) 'No bones about it: Tech central station – where free markets meet technology', at: http//:www.techcentralstation.com (accessed 16 January 2004).

Archer, M. (1990) 'The muddled molar mystery of Riversleigh', *Australian Natural History*, 23(4): 334–335.

—— (1996) 'Miocene Madonna and Child', *Nature Australia*, Summer: 70–71.

Archer, M. and Hand, S.J. (1987) 'Evolutionary considerations', in L. Cronin (ed.) *Koala, Australia's Endearing Marsupial*, Sydney: Reed Books.

Archer, M., Godthelp, H., Hand, S.J. and Megirian, D. (1989) 'Fossil mammals of Riversleigh, Northwestern Queensland: Preliminary overview of bio-stratigraphy, correlation and environmental change', *Australian Zoologist*, 25(2): 29–65.

Archer, M., Hand, S.J. and Golthelp, H. (1988) 'Riversleigh – window on our ancient past', *Australian Geographic*, 9: 40–57.

Archer, M., Hand, S.J. and Golthelp, H. (1996) *Riversleigh: The Story of Animals in Ancient Rainforests of Inland Australia*, Kew, Victoria: Reed Books.

Archer, M., Hand, S.J., Golthelp, H. and Creaser, P. (1997) 'Correlation of the Cainozoic sediments of the Riversleigh World Heritage fossil property, Queensland, Australia', in J. P. Aguilar, S. Legendre and J. Michaux (eds) *École Pratique des Hautes Études*, Montpellier: Institut de Montpellier.

Arthur, J. (1999) 'The eighth day of creation', in R. Nile (ed.) *Imaginary Homelands*, St Lucia: University of Queensland Press.

Ascher, R. (1960) 'Archaeology and the public image', *American Antiquity*, 25(3): 402–403.

Ashton, P. (2005) 'Contested pasts and controversial presents', unpublished conference paper, People and their Pasts Conference, Ruskin College, Oxford, 16 September 2005.

Ashworth, G. and Tunbridge, J. (1996) *Dissonant Heritage: The Management of the Past as a Resource in Conflict*, Chichester: Wiley.

Aslet, C. (1982) *The Last Country Houses*, New Haven and London: Yale University Press.

Attenborough, D. (1991) 'Foreword', in M. Archer, S. J. Hand and H. Godthelp (eds) *Riversleigh: The Story of Animals in Ancient Rainforests of Inland Australia*, Kew: Reed Books.

Attwood, B. (1989) *The Making of the Aborigines*, North Sydney: Allen & Unwin Australia.

Australia ICOMOS (1979) *Charter for the Conservation of Places of Cultural Significance (Burra Charter)*.

—— (1999) *Charter for the Conservation of Places of Cultural Significance (Burra Charter)*.

—— (2005) 'Burra Charter website', at: http://www.icomos.org/australia/burra.html (accessed 12 December 2005).

Australian Museum (2002) 'Australia's thylacine: To clone or not to clone?', at: http://www.amonline.net.au/thylacine (accessed 12 November 2005).

Bagnall, G. (2003) 'Performance and performativity at heritage sites', *Museum and Society*, 1(2): 87–103.

Barker, E. (1999) 'Heritage and the country house', in E. Barker (ed.) *Contemporary Cultures of Display*, New Haven, CT: Yale University Press.

Barthel, D. (1996) *Historic Preservation: Collective Memory and Historical Identity*, Newark, NJ: Rutgers University Press.

Barthel-Bouchier, D. (2001) 'Authenticity and identity: Theme parking the Amanas', *International Sociology*, 16(2): 221–239.

Bartlett, R.H. (1993) *The Mabo Decision*, Sydney: Butterworths.

Bauman, Z. (1987) *Legislators and Interpreters*, Cambridge: Polity Press.

Beck, W., Murvey, D., Perkins, C. and Perkins, T. (2005) 'Aboriginal ecotourism and archaeology in coastal NSW, Australia: Yarrawarra Place Stories Project', in C. Smith and H. M. Wobst (eds) *Indigenous Archaeologies: Decolonizing Theory and Practice*, London: Routledge.

Beidler, P.D. (1999) 'Ted Turner et al. at Gettysburg; or, re-enactors in the attic', *Virginia Quarterly Review*, 75(3): 488–503.

Belfiore, E. (2002) 'Art as a means of alleviating social exclusion: Does it really work? A critique of instrumental cultural policies and social impact studies in the UK', *International Journal of Cultural Policy*, 8(1): 91–106.

Bender, B. (1992) 'Theorising landscapes, and the prehistoric landscapes of Stonehenge', *Man*, 27(4): 735–755.

—— (1998) *Stonehenge: Making Space*, Oxford: Berg.

—— (2002) 'Time and landscape', *Current Anthropology*, 43(5): 103–112.

Bennett, T. (1988) 'Museums and "the people" ', in R. Lumley (ed.) *The Museum Time Machine: Putting Cultures on Display*, London: Routledge.

—— (1995) *The Birth of the Museum: History, Theory, Politics*, London: Routledge.

Berking, H. (2003) ' "Ethnicity is everywhere": On globalisation and the transformation of cultural identity', *Current Sociology*, 51(3–4): 248–264.

Bhaskar, R.A. (1978) *A Realist Theory of Science*, Brighton: Harvester Press.

—— (1989) *Reclaiming Reality*, London: Verso.

Bickford, A. (1981) 'The patina of nostalgia', *Australian Archaeology*, 13: 7–13.

—— (1985) 'Disquiet in the warm parlour of the past: Material history and historical studies, Calthorpes House Museum, Canberra', *History and Cultural Resources Project: Part 2, Seminar Papers*, Canberra: Committee to review Australian Studies in Tertiary Education.

Billig, M. (1995) *Banal Nationalism*, London: Sage.

Binney, M. (1984) *Our Vanishing Heritage*, London: Arlington Books.

Binney, M. and Grenfell, L. (1980) *Drowning in VAT*, unpublished pamphlet, London: SAVE Britain's Heritage.

Binney, M. and Martin, R. (1982) *The Country House: To Be or Not To Be*, London: SAVE Britain's Heritage.

Binney, M. and Milne, E. (1982) *Vanishing Houses of England: A Pictorial Documentary of Lost Country Houses*, London: SAVE Britain's Heritage.

Biolsi, T. (1998) 'The anthropological construction of "Indians": Haviland Scudder Mekeel and the search for the primitive in Lakota Country', in T. Biolsi and L. J. Zimmerman (eds) *Indians and Anthropology: Vine Deloria Jr and the Critique of Anthropology*, Tucson, AZ: University of Arizona Press.

Birckhead, J., DeLacy, T. and Smith, L. (eds) (1992) *Aboriginal Involvement in Parks and Protected Areas*, Canberra: Aboriginal Studies Press.

Blake, J. (2001) *Developing a New Standard-setting Instrument for the Safeguarding of Intangible Cultural Heritage: Elements for Consideration*, Paris: UNESCO.

Boswell, D. and Evans, J. (eds) (1999) *Representing the Nation: A Reader, Histories, Heritage and Museums*, London: Routledge

Bourdieu, P. and Wacquant, L. (2000) 'NewLiberalSpeak: Notes on the new planetary vulgate', *Radical Philosophy*, at: http://www.radicalphilosophy.com (accessed 30 June 2005).

Bowdler, S. (1988) 'Repainting Australian rock art', *Antiquity*, 62: 517–523.

Boyd, B., Cotter, M., O'Connor, W. and Sattler, D. (1996) 'Cognitive ownership of heritage places: Social construction and cultural heritage management', in S. Ulm, I. Lilly and A. Ross (eds) *Archaeology and Material Culture Studies in Anthropology*, St Lucia: Anthropology Museum, University of Queensland.

Boyer, M.C. (1994) *The City of Collective Memory: Its Historical Imagery and Architectural Entertainments*, Cambridge, MA: Massachusetts Institute of Technology Press.

Bray, T. (2001) 'American archaeologists and Native Americans: A relationship under construction', in T. Bray (ed.) *The Future of the Past: Archaeologists, Native Americans, and Repatriation*, New York: Garland Publishing.

Brett, D. (1996) *The Construction of Heritage*, Cork: Cork University Press.

Brody, H. (2001) *The Other Side of Eden: Hunter Gathers, Farmers, and the Shaping of the World*, London: Faber and Faber.

Brower, B.C. (1999) 'The preserving machine: The "new" museum and working through trauma – *the Musee Memorial pour la Paix of Caen*', *History and Memory*, 11(1): 77–103.

Bruno, R. (1999) *Steelworker Alley: How Class Works in Youngstown*, Ithaca, NY: Cornell University Press.

Buikstra, J. (1981) 'A specialist in ancient cemetery studies', *Early Man*, 3(3): 26–27.

Bumbaru, D. (2003) 'Tangible and intangible: The obligation and desire to remember', at: http://www.international.icomos.org/victoriafalls2003/bumbaru_eng. htm (accessed 4 April 2003).

Burgman, M. and Burgman, V. (1998) *Green Bans, Red Union: Environmental Activism and the New South Wales Builders Labourers' Federation*, Sydney: University of New South Wales Press.

Burman, P. (1995) 'A question of ethics', in C. Communications (ed.) *The Conservation and Repair of Ecclesiastical Buildings*, London: Cathedral Communications.

Burton, A. (2003) 'When was Britain? Nostalgia for the nation at the end of the "American Century" ', *Journal of Modern History*, 75: 395–374.

Butler, J. (1993) *Bodies that Matter: On the Discursive Limits of 'Sex'*, New York: Routledge.

Butt, P. and Eagleson, R. (1993) *Mabo: What the High Court Said*, Sydney: Federation Press.

Byrne, D. (1991) 'Western hegemony in archaeological heritage management', *History and Anthropology*, 5: 269–276.

—— (2001) 'Landscapes of segregation', unpublished conference paper, Australian Institute of Aboriginal and Torres Stright Islander Studies, at: http://www. aiatsis.gov.au/rsrch/conf2001/PAPERS/BYRNE.pdf (accessed 12 December 2004).

—— (2003) 'Nervous landscapes: Race and pace in Australia', *Journal of Social Archaeology*, 3(2): 169–193.

Byrne, D., Brayshaw, H. and Ireland, T. (2001) *Social Significance: A Discussion Paper*, Sydney: Department of Environment and Conservation NSW.

Cameron, C. and Gatewood, J. (2000) 'Excursions into the unremembered past: What people want from visits to historical sites', *Public Historian*, 22(3): 107–127.

Cameron, C. and Gatewood, J. (2003) 'Seeking numinous experiences in the unremembered past', *Ethnology*, 42(1): 55–71.

Cameron, W.E. (1901) 'Geological observations in northwestern Queensland. Annual Report Queensland Department of Mines, 1900–1902', *Geological Survey Queensland Publications*, 159: 186–191.

Canadian Archaeological Association (1997) 'Statement of Principles for Ethical Conduct Pertaining to Aboriginal Peoples', at: http://www.canadianarchaeology. com/ethical.lasso (accessed 1 December 2005).

Cannadine, D. (1983) 'The context, performance and meaning of ritual: The British monarchy and the "invention of tradition", *c.* 1820–1977', in E. Hobsbawm and T. Ranger (eds) *The Invention of Tradition*, Cambridge: Cambridge University Press.

—— (1995) 'The first hundred years', in H. Newby (ed.) *The National Trust: The Next Hundred Years*, London: National Trust.

Carman, J. (1993) 'The P is silent . . . as in archaeology', *Archaeological Review From Cambridge*, 12(1): 37–53.

—— (1996) *Valuing Ancient Things: Archaeology and Law*, London: Leicester University Press.

—— (1998) 'Object values: Landscapes and their contents', in M. Jones and I. Rotherham (eds) *Landscapes – Perception, Recognition and Management: Reconciling the Impossible?*, Sheffield: Wildtrack Publishing.

—— (2002) *Archaeology and Heritage: An Introduction*, London: Continuum.

—— (2005) *Against Cultural Property: Archaeology, Heritage and Ownership*, London: Duckworth.

Carrier, P. (2005) *Holocaust Monuments and National Memory Cultures in France and Germany Since 1989*, New York: Berghahn Books.

Carter, C.E. (1997) 'Strait talk and trust', in N. Swidler, K. E. Dongoske, R. Anyon and A. S. Downer (eds) *Native Americans and Archaeologists: Stepping Stones to Common Ground*, Walnut Creek, CA: AltaMira.

Casey, E. (1996) 'How to get from space to place in a fairly short stretch of time: Phenomenological prolegomena', in S. Feld and K. Basso (eds) *Sense of Place*, Santa Fe, CA: School of American Research Press.

—— (1997) *The Fate of Place: A Philosophical History*, Berkeley, CA: University of California Press.

—— (2000) *Remembering: A Phenomenological Study*, Bloomington, IN: University of Indiana Press.

Castells, M. (2004) *The Power of Identity*, Oxford: Blackwell.

Catalyst (2002) 'Creation versus evolution', at: http://www.abc.net.au/catalyst/stories/s692487.htm (accessed 21 January 2006).

—— (2005) 'Intelligent design', at: http://www.abc.net.au/catalyst/stories/s1486827.htm (accessed 21 January 2006).

Chang, T., Milne, S., Fallon, D. and Pohlmann, C. (1996) 'Urban heritage tourism: The global–local nexus', *Annals of Tourism Research*, 23(2): 284–305.

Channel4 (2002) 'Time Team 2002: Castleford. Programme Transcript', at: http://www.channel4.com/history/timeteam/castleford_t.html (accessed 7 October 2005).

Charlesworth, S. (2000) *A Phenomenology of Working-class Experience*, Cambridge: Cambridge University Press.

Chase, M. and Shaw, C. (1989) 'The dimensions of nostalgia', in C. Shaw and M. Chase (eds) *The Imagined Past: History and Nostalgia*, Manchester: Manchester University Press.

Cheung, S.C.H. (2005) 'Rethinking Ainu heritage: A case study of an Ainu settlement in Hokkaido, Japan', *International Journal of Heritage Studies*, 11(3): 197–210.

Chippindale, C. (1985) 'English Heritage and the future of Stonehenge', *Antiquity*, 59: 132–137.

—— (1986) 'Stoned Henge: Events and issues at the summer solstice', *World Archaeology*, 18(1): 38–55.

Choay, F. (2001) *The Invention of the Historic Monument*, Cambridge: Cambridge University Press.

Chouliaraki, L. and Fairclough, N. (1999) *Discourse in Late Modernity: Rethinking Critical Discourse Analysis*, Edinburgh: Edinburgh University Press.

Claessen, H.J.M. (2002) 'Comments', *Current Anthropology*, 43(1): 148.

Clark, K. (ed.) (1999) *Conservation Plans in Action: Proceedings of the Oxford Conference*, London: English Heritage.

—— (2005) 'The bigger picture: Archaeology and values in long term cultural resource management', in C. Mathers, T. Darvill and B. J. Little (eds) *Heritage of Value, Archaeology of Renown: Reshaping Archaeological Assessment and Significance*, Gainesville, FL: University Press of Florida.

Clarke, A. (1993) 'Cultural resource management as archaeological housework: Confining women to the ghetto of management', in H. du Cros and L. Smith (eds) *Women in Archaeology: A Feminist Critique*, Canberra: Department of Prehistory, Research School of Pacific Studies, Australian National University.

—— (2002) 'The ideal and the real: Cultural and personal transformations of archaeological research on Groote Eylandt, northern Australia', *World Archaeology*, 34(2): 249–264.

Clayton, I. (ed.) (2005) *Castleford Heritage Trails: In the Footsteps of . . .*, Castleford: Castleford Heritage Trust.

Cleere, H. (ed.) (1984) *Approaches to the Archaeological Heritage*, Cambridge: Cambridge University Press.

—— (1996) 'The concept of "outstanding universal value" in the World Heritage Convention', *Conservation and Management of Archaeological Sites*, 1(4), 227–233.

—— (2001) 'The uneasy bedfellows: Universality and cultural heritage', in R. Layton, P. G. Stone and J. Thomas (eds) *Destruction and Conservation of Cultural Property*, London: Routledge.

Coleman, S. and Crang, M. (eds) (2002a) *Tourism: Between Place and Performance*, New York: Berghahn Books.

—— (2002b) 'Grounded tourists, travelling theory', in S. Coleman and M. Crang (eds) *Tourism: Between Place and Performance*, New York: Berghahn Books.

Colley, L. (1999) 'Britishness in the 21st Century, Millennium Lecture, 10 Downing Street website', at: http://www.number-10.gov.uk/output/Page3049.asp (accessed 6 June 2005).

Conkey, M. and Spector, J. (1984) 'Archaeology and the study of gender', *Advances in Archaeological Method and Theory*, 7: 1–38.

Connerton, P. (1991) *How Societies Remember*, Cambridge: Cambridge University Press.

Conway, M.A. (1997) 'The inventory of experience: Memory and identity', in J. W. Pennebaker, D. Paez and B. Rime (eds) *Collective Memory of Political Events: Social Psychological Perspectives*, Hillsdale, NJ: Lawrence Erlbaum Associates.

Cookson, N. (2000) *Archaeological Heritage Law*, Chichester: Barry Rose Law Publishers.

Corner, W. and Harvey, S. (ed.) (1991) *Enterprise and Heritage*, London: Routledge.

Cornforth, J. (1974) *Country Houses in Britain: Can They Survive?*, London: Country Life.

—— (1998) *The Country Houses of England, 1948–1998*, London: Constable.

Corsane, G. (2005) 'Issues in heritage, museums and galleries: A brief introduction', in G. Corsane (ed.) *Heritage, Museums and Galleries: An Introductory Reader*, London: Routledge.

Cotter, M., Boyd, B. and Gardiner, J. (eds) (2001) *Heritage Landscapes: Understanding Place and Communities*, Lismore, NSW: Southern Cross University Press.

Cowlishaw, G. (1987) 'Colour, culture and the Aboriginalists', *Man*, 22: 221–237.

Crang, M. (1996) 'Magic Kingdom or a magical quest for authenticity?', *Annals of Tourism Research*, 23(2): 415–431.

—— (2001) *Cultural Geography*, London: Routledge.

Creaser, P. (1990) 'Cradle of life: Riversleigh fossils reveal rainforest secrets', *Habitat Australia*, February: 24–28.

—— (1994) 'Australia's World Heritage fossil nomination', in D. O'Halloran, C. Green, M. Stanley and J. Knill (eds) *Geological and Landscape Conservation*, London: Geological Society.

Crouch, D. (2002) 'Surrounded by place: Embodied encounters', in S. Coleman and M. Crang (eds) *Tourism: Between Place and Performance*, New York: Berghahn Books.

—— (2003) 'Space, performing, and becoming: Tangles in the mundane', *Environment and Planning A*, 35: 1945–1960.

Crouch, D. and Parker, G. (2003) ' "Digging-up" utopia? Space, practice and landuse heritage', *Geoforum*, 34: 395–408.

Crouch, M. (1963) *Britain in Trust*, London: Constable Young Books.

Cruddas, J., Hiles, R. and Burns, C. (2004) *Beamish Housekeeping Manual*, Beamish: North of England Open Air Museum.

Curthoys, A. (1997) 'History and identity', in W. Hudson and G. Bolton (eds) *Creating Australia: Changing Australian History*, St Leonards, Sydney: Allen and Unwin.

—— (1999) 'Expulsion, exodus and exile in White Australian historical mythology', in R. Nile (ed.) *Imaginary Homelands*, St Lucia: University of Queensland Press.

Daniels, S. (1993) *Fields of Vision: Landscape Imagery and National Identity in England and the United States*, Princeton, NJ: Princeton University Press.

Darvill, T. (2005) 'Sorted for ease and whiz'?: Approaching value and importance in archaeological resource management', in C. Mathers, T. Darvill and B. J. Little (eds) *Heritage of Value, Archaeology of Renown: Reshaping Archaeological Assessment and Significance*, Gainesville, FL: University Press of Florida.

Davidson, I., Lovell-Jones, C. and Bancroft, R. (eds) (1995) *Archaeologists and Aborigines Working Together*, Armidale, NSW: University of New England Press.

Davis, P. (1999) *Ecomuseums: A Sense of Place*, London: Leicester University Press.

Davison, P. (2005) 'Museums and the re-shaping of memory', in G. Corsane (ed.) *Heritage, Museums and Galleries: An Introductory Reader*, London: Routledge.

Dawkins, R. (1998) 'Science and sensibility', Queen Elizabeth Hall Lecture, 24 March.

Department for Culture, Media and Sport (DCMS) (2003) *The Report of the Working Group on Human Remains*, London: Department for Culture, Media and Sport, Cultural Property Unit.

Deacon, H., Dondolo, L., Mrubata, M. and Prosalendis, S. (2004) *The Subtle Power of Intangible Heritage: Legal and Financial Instruments for Safeguarding Intangible Heritage*, Cape Town: Human Sciences Research Council.

Dean, M. (1999) *Governmentality: Power and Rule in Modern Society*, London: Sage.

Dean, M. and Hindess, B. (eds) (1998) *Governing Australia*, Cambridge: Cambridge University Press.

Debary, O. (2004) 'Deindustrialisation and museumification: From exhibited memory to forgotten history', *Annals of the American Academy of Political and Social Science*, 595(1): 122–133.

DeBlasio, D. (2001) 'The immigrant and the trolley park in Youngstown, Ohio, 1899–1956', *Rethinking History*, 5(1): 75–91.

Deckha, N. (2004) 'Beyond the country house: Historic conservation as aesthetic politics', *European Journal of Cultural Studies*, 7(4): 403–423.

Deeben, J. and Groenewoudt, B. (2005) 'Handling the unknown: The expanding role of predicative modelling in archaeological heritage management in the Netherlands', in C. Mathers, T. Darvill and B. J. Little (eds) *Heritage of Value, Archaeology of Renown: Reshaping Archaeological Assessment and Significance*, Gainesville, FL: University Press of Florida.

Department of the Environment and Heritage (DEH) (2005) *Australian Fossil Mammal Sites (Riversleigh/Naracoorte)*, Sydney: Dore.

Deloria, V. Jr. (1969) *Custer Died for Your Sins: An Indian Manifesto*, London: Macmillan.

—— (1992) 'Indians, archaeologists, and the future', *American Antiquity*, 57(4): 595–598.

—— (1998) 'Conclusion: Anthros, Indians, and planetary reality', in T. Biolsi and L. J. Zimmerman (eds) *Indians and Anthropologists: Vine Deloria Jr. and the Critique of Anthropology*, Tucson, AZ: University of Arizona Press.

Deloria, V. Jr. and Lytle, C.M. (1998) *The Nations Within: The Past and Future of American Indian Sovereignty*, Austin, TX: University of Texas Press.

Dening, G. (1994) *Mr Bligh's Bad Language: Passion, Power and Theatre on the Bounty*, Cambridge: Cambridge University Press.

Derry, L. and Malloy, M. (eds) (2003) *Archaeologists and Local Communities: Partners in Exploring the Past*, Washington, DC: Society for American Archaeology.

Department of the Environment, Sport and Territories (DEST) (1993) 'Nomination of Australian Fossil Sites', unpublished report, Canberra: Department of the Environment, Sport and Territories.

Deveraux, K. (1997) 'Looking at country from the heart', in D. Bird Rose and A. Clarke (eds) *Tracking Knowledge in Northern Australian Landscapes*, Darwin: North Australian Research Unit.

Diaz-Andreu, M. (under review) *World History of Archaeology in the Nineteenth Century: Nationalism, Imperialism and the Past*.

Diaz-Andreu, M. and Champion, T. (eds) (1996) *Nationalism and Archaeology in Europe*, London: UCL Press.

Diaz-Andreu, M., Lucy, S., Babic, S. and Edwards, D. (2005) *The Archaeology of Identity*, London: Routledge.

Dicks, B. (1997) 'The life and times of community – Spectacles of collective identity at the Rhondda Heritage Park', *Time and Society*, 6(2–3): 195–212.

—— (2000a) *Heritage, Place and Community*, Cardiff: University of Wales Press.

—— (2000b) 'Encoding and decoding the people', *European Journal of Communication*, 15(1): 61–78.

—— (2003) 'Heritage, governance and marketization: A case study from Wales', *Museum and Society*, 1(1): 30–44.

Diethorn, K. and Bacon, J. (2003) 'Domestic work portrayed: Philadelphia's restored Bishop William White House – a case study', in G. Dubrow and J. Goodman (eds) *Restoring Women's History Through Historic Preservation*, Baltimore, MD: Johns Hopkins University Press.

Dodson, M. (1994) 'The Wentworth Lecture – the end in the beginning: Re(de)finding Aboriginality', *Australian Aboriginal Studies*, 1: 2–13.

Domicelj, J. (1992) 'Foreword', in M.-K. P. and M. Walker (eds) *The Illustrated Burra Charter: Making Good Decisions About the Care of Important Places*, Sydney: Australia ICOMOS.

Donald Insall Associates (2000) 'Chatterley Whitfield Colliery: Conservation Statement', unpublished report, Chester: Stock on Trent City Council and English Heritage.

Dongoske, K.E. and Anyon, R. (1997) 'Federal archaeology: Tribes, diatribes, and traditions', in N. Swidler, K. E. Dongoske, R. Anyon and A. S. Downer (eds) *Native Americans and Archaeologists: Stepping Stones to Common Ground*, Walnut Creek, CA: AltaMira.

Dongoske, K.E., Aldenderfer, M. and Doehner, K. (eds) (2000) *Working Together: Native Americans and Archaeologists*, Washington DC: Society for American Archaeology.

Donnelly, J.F. (ed.) (2002) *Interpreting Historic House Museums*, Walnut Creek, CA: AltaMira.

Drake, A. (2004) 'The Castleford Heritage Project: A Personal View', Heritage Lottery Fund Conference, Dublin, Ireland, unpublished transcript of conference paper.

Dubrow, G. (2003) 'Restoring women's history through historic preservation: Recent

developments in scholarship and public historical practice', in G. Dubrow and
J. Goodman (eds) *Restoring Women's History Through Historic Preservation*, Baltimore,
MD: Johns Hopkins University Press.

Dubrow, G. and Goodman, J. (eds) (2003) *Restoring Women's History Through Historic
Preservation*, Baltimore, MD: Johns Hopkins University Press.

Earl, J. (2003) *Building Conservation*, Shaftesbury: Donhead.

East Hertfordshire (2005) 'Planning issues: Conservation areas and guidence notes,
principles of conservation and repair', at: http://www.eastherts.gov.uk/guidnote/
principles_of_conservation/full_document.htm (accessed 25 May 2005).

Echo-Hawk, W. (1997) 'Forging a new ancient history for Native America', in
N. Swidler, K. E. Dongoske, R. Anyon and A. S. Downer (eds) *Native Americans
and Archaeologists: Stepping Stones to Common Ground*, Walnut Creek, CA:
AltaMira.

Echo-Hawk, W. (2000) 'Ancient history in the New World: Integrating oral
traditions and the archaeological record', *American Antiquity*, 65(2): 267–290.

Edley, N. (2001) 'Analysing masculinity: Interpretive repertoires, ideological
dilemmas and subject positions', in M. Wetherell, S. Taylor and S. J. Yates (eds)
Discourse as Data: A Guide for Analysis, London: Sage.

Emerick, K. (2003) 'From Frozen Monuments to Fluid Landscapes: The Conservation
and Preservation of Ancient Monuments from 1882 to the Present', unpublished
PhD thesis, Department of Archaeology, York: University of York.

English Heritage (2000) *Power of Place: The Future of the Historic Environment*, London:
English Heritage.

Escobar, A. (2001) 'Culture sits in places: Reflections on globalism and subaltern
strategies of localisation', *Political Geography*, 20: 139–174.

Evans, M. (1991) 'Historical interpretation at Sovereign Hill', in J. Rickard and
P. Spearritt (eds) *Packaging the Past? Public Histories*, Melbourne: Melbourne
University Press.

Fairclough, G. (1993) *Discourse and Social Charge*, Cambridge: Polity Press.

—— (1999) 'Protecting the cultural landscape: National designation and local
character', in J. Grenville (ed.) *Managing the Historic Rural Landscape*, London:
Routledge.

Fairclough, G. and Rippon, S. (eds) (2002) *Europe's Cultural Landscape: Archaeologists
and the Management of Change*, Brussels: Europae Archaeologiae Concilium.

Fairclough, G., Lambrick, G. and McNab, A. (1999) *Yesterday's World, Tomorrow's
Landscape: The English Heritage Historic Landscape Project 1992–94*, London: English
Heritage.

Fairclough, N. (2000) *New Labour, New Language?*, London: Routledge.

—— (2001) 'The discourse of New Labour: Critical Discourse Analysis', in
M. Wetherell, S. Taylor and S. J. Yates (eds) *Discourse as Data: A Guide for Analysis*,
London: Sage.

—— (2003) *Analysing Discourse: Textual Analysis for Social Research*, London:
Routledge.

Fairclough, N., Graham, P., Lemke, J. and Wodak, R. (2004) 'Introduction', *Critical
Discourse Studies*, 1(1): 1–7.

Fairclough, N., Jessop, B. and Sayer, A. (2003) 'Critical realism and semiosis',
in J. Roberts (ed.) *Critical Realism, Discourse and Deconstruction*, London:
Routledge.

Fairweather, I. (2003) 'Showing off: Nostalgia and heritage in North-Central Namibia', *Journal of Southern African Studies*, 29(1): 279–296.

Falk, H. and Dierking, L.D. (1992) *The Museum Experience*, Washington, DC: Whalesback Books.

FATE (2005) 'Future of Australia's Threatened Ecosystems', at: http://www.fate.unsw.edu.au/index.htm (accessed 4 January 2005).

Fforde, C. (2004) *Collecting the Dead: Archaeology and the Reburial Issue*, London: Duckworth.

—— (2002) 'Collection, repatriation and identity', in C. Fforde, J. Hubert and P. Turnball (eds) *The Dead and Their Possessions: Repatriation in Principle, Policy, and Practice*, London: Routledge.

Fforde, C. and Ormond Parker, L. (2002) 'Repatriation developments in the UK', London: *European Network for Indigenous Australian Rights*.

Fforde, C., Hubert, J. and Turnbull, P. (eds) (2002) *The Dead and Their Possessions: Repatriation in Principle, Policy, and Practice*, London: Routledge.

Figlio, K. (2003) 'Getting to the beginning: Identification and concrete thinking in historical consciousness', in S. Radstone and K. Hodgkin (eds) *Regimes of Memory*, London: Routledge.

Finlayson, J. (1996) 'Aboriginal cultural tourism: Is there a sustainable future?', in L. Smith and A. Clarke (eds) *Issues in Management Archaeology*, St Lucia: Anthropology Museum, University of Queensland.

Fischer, F. (2003) *Reframing Public Policy: Discursive Politics and Deliberative Practices*, Oxford: Oxford University Press.

Fog Olwig, K. (2002) 'Response to Nas', *Current Anthropology*, 43(1): 145–146.

Forsman, L.A. (1997) 'Straddling the current: A view from the bridge over clear salt water', in N. Swidler, K. E. Dongoske, R. Anyon and A. S. Downer (eds) *Native Americans and Archaeologists: Stepping Stones to Common Ground*, Walnut Creek, CA: AltaMira.

Foucault, M. (1991) 'Governmentality', in G. Burchell, C. Gordon and P. Miller (eds) *The Foucault Effect*, London: Wheatsheaf Harvester.

Fourmile, H. (1989a) 'Aboriginal heritage legislation and self determination', *Australian Canadian Studies*, 7(1–2): 45–61.

—— (1989b) 'Who owns the past? Aborigines as captives of the archives', *Aboriginal History*, 13: 1–8.

—— (1996) 'Aboriginal identity and tourism: A changing relationship', in L. Smith and A. Clarke (eds) *Issues in Management Archaeology*, St Lucia: Anthropology Museum, University of Queensland.

Fraser, N. (2000) 'Rethinking recognition', *New Left Review*, at: http://www.newleftreview.net/NLR23707.shtml (accessed 12 November 2003).

Frijda, N.H. (1997) 'Commemorating', in J. W. Pennebaker and B. Rime (eds) *Collective Memory of Political Events: Social Psychological Perspectives*, Mahwah, NJ: Lawrence Erlbaum Associates.

Fung, C. and Allen, H. (1984) 'Perceptions of the past and New Zealand archaeology', *New Zealand Archaeological Association Newsletter*, 27(4): 209–220.

Gable, E. and Handler, R. (2003) 'After authenticity at an American heritage site', in S. M. Low and D. Lawrence- Zúñiga (eds) *The Anthology of Space and Place: Locating Culture*, Malden: Blackwell.

Gard'ner, J. (2004) 'Heritage protection and social inclusion: A case study from the

Bangladeshi community of East London', *International Journal of Heritage Studies*, 10(1): 75–92.

Gilroy, P. (1987) *There Ain't no Black in the Union Jack: The Cultural Politics of Race and Nation*, London: Routledge.

Goldstein, L. (2000) 'The potential for future relations between archaeologists and Native Americans', in M. Lynott and A. Wylie (eds) *Ethics in American Archaeology*, Washington, DC: Society for American Archaeology.

Goody, B. (1998) 'New Britain, new heritage: The consumption of a heritage culture', *International Journal of Heritage Studies*, 4(3–4): 197–205.

Gostin, O. (1993) *Accessing the Dreaming: Heritage, Conservation and Tourism at Lake Mungo National Park*, Underdale: Aboriginal Research Institute Publications, University of South Australia.

Graham, B. (2002) 'Heritage as knowledge: Capital or culture?' *Urban Studies*, 39(5–6): 1003–1017.

Graham, B., Ashworth, G. and Tunbridge, J. (2000) *A Geography of Heritage: Power, Culture and Economy*, London: Arnold.

—— (2005) 'The uses and abuses of heritage', in G. Corsane (ed.) *Heritage, Museums and Galleries: An Introductory Reader*, London: Routledge.

Graham, C. (2001) 'Blame it on Maureen O'Hara: Ireland and the Trope of Authenticity', *Cultural Studies*, 15(1): 58–75.

Grainge, P. (1999) 'Reclaiming heritage: Colourization, culture wars and the politics of nostalgia', *Cultural Studies*, 13(4): 621–638.

Greenspan, A. (2002) *Creating Colonial Williamsburg*, Washington, DC: Smithsonian Institution Press.

Greer, S. and Henry, R. (1996) 'The politics of heritage: The case of the Kuranda Skyrail', in J. Finlayson and A. Jackson-Nakano (eds) *Heritage and Native Title: Anthropological and Legal Perspectives*, Canberra: Institute of Aboriginal and Torres Straight Islander Studies.

Greer, S., Harrison, R. and McIntyre-Tamwoy, S. (2002) 'Community-based archaeology in Australia', *World Archaeology*, 34(2): 265–287.

Grenville, J. (ed.) (1999) *Managing the Historic Rural Landscape*, London: Routledge.

Grieve, N.F. (2005) 'The Urban Conservation Glossary', at: http://www.trp.dundee.ac.uk/research/glossary/glossary.html (accessed 15 December 2005).

Gulliford, A. (2000) *Sacred Objects and Sacred Places: Preserving Tribal Traditions*, Boulder, CO: University Press of Colorado.

Hajer, M. (1996) 'Discourse coalitions and the institutionalisation of practice: The case of acid rain in Britain', in F. Fischer and J. Forester (eds) *The Argumentative Turn in Policy Analysis and Planning*, Durham, NC: Duke University Press.

Halbwachs, M. ([1926] 1992) *On Collective Memory*, Chicago, IL: University of Chicago Press.

Halewood, C. and Hannam, K. (2001) 'Viking heritage tourism: Authenticity and commodification', *Annals of Tourism Research*, 28(3): 565–580.

Hall, C.M. and McArthur, S. (eds) (1996) *Heritage Management in New Zealand and Australia*, Auckland: Oxford University Press.

Hall, M. (1996) 'Heads and tales', *Representations*, 54(Spring): 104–123.

—— (2001) 'Cape Town's District Six and the archaeology of memory', in R. Layton, P. G. Stone and J. Thomas (eds) *Destruction and Conservation of Cultural Property*, London: Routledge.

Hall, S. (1999) 'Whose heritage? Un-settling "The Heritage", re-imaging the post-nation', *Third Text*, 49: 3–13.

—— (2001) 'Foucault: Power, knowledge and discourse', in M. Wetherell, S. Taylor and S. J. Yates (eds) *Discourse Theory and Practice: A Reader*, London: Sage.

Handler, R. (2003) 'Cultural property and culture theory', *Journal of Social Archaeology*, 3(3): 353–365.

Handler, R. and Gable, E. (1997) *The New History in an Old Museum: Creating the Past at Colonial Williamsburg*, Durham, NC: Duke University Press.

Handler, R. and Saxton, W. (1988) 'Dyssimulation: Reflexivity, narrative, and the quest for authenticity in "living history" ', *Cultural Anthropology*, 3(3): 242–260.

Harding, S. (1986) *The Science Question in Feminism*, Milton Keynes: Open University Press.

Harkin, M. (1995) 'Modernist anthropology and tourism of the authentic', *Annals of Tourism Research*, 22(3): 650–670.

Harley, J.B. (1988) 'Maps, knowledge, and power', in D. Cosgrove and S. Daniels (eds) *The Iconography of Landscape*, Cambridge: Cambridge University Press.

Harrison, J.D. (2005) 'Ideas of museums in the 1990s', in G. Corsane (ed.) *Heritage, Museums and Galleries: An Introductory Reader*, London: Routledge.

Harvey, D. (1996) *Justice, Nature and the Geography of Difference*, London: Blackwell.

Harvey, D.C. (2001) 'Heritage pasts and heritage presents: Temporality, meaning and the scope of heritage studies', *International Journal of Heritage Studies*, 7(4): 319–338.

Hayden, D. (1997) *The Power of Place*, Cambridge, MA: MIT Press.

Head, L. (2000a) *Second Nature: The History and Implications of Australia as Aboriginal Landscape*, New York: Syracuse University Press.

—— (2000b) *Cultural Landscapes and Environmental Change*, London: Arnold.

Heelas, P. (1996) 'Introduction: De-traditionalization and its rivals', in P. Heelas, S. Lash and P. Morris (eds) *De-traditionalization*, Oxford: Blackwell.

Heelas, P. Lash, S. and Morris, P. (eds) (1996) *De-traditionalization*, Oxford: Blackwell.

Hewison, R. (1981) *In Anger: British Culture and the Cold War, 1945–60'*, New York: Oxford University Press.

—— (1987) *The Heritage Industry: Britain in a Climate of Decline*, London: Methuen.

Hingley, R. (2000) *Roman Officers and English Gentlemen: The Imperial Origins of Roman Archaeology*, London: Routledge.

Hirst, J.B. (1989) 'The pioneer legend', in J. Carroll (ed.) *Intruders in the Bush: The Australian Quest for Identity*, Oxford: Oxford University Press.

Hiscock, P. and Hughes, P. (1984) 'A brief history of archaeological work in northwestern Queensland', *Queensland Archaeological Research*, 1: 117–119.

Hjemdahl, K.M. (2002) 'History as a cultural playground', *Ethnologia Europaea*, 32(2): 105–124.

Hobsbawm, E. (1983a) 'Introduction: Inventing traditions', in E. Hobsbawm and T. Ranger (eds), *The Invention of Tradition*, Cambridge: Cambridge University Press, pp. 1–15.

—— (1983b) 'Mass-producing traditions: Europe, 1870–1914', in E. Hobsbawm and T. Ranger (eds) *The Invention of Tradition*, Cambridge: Cambridge University Press.

REFERENCES

Hobsbawm, E. and Ranger, T. (eds) (1983) *The Invention of Tradition*, Cambridge: Cambridge University Press.

Hodder, I. (1999) *The Archaeological Process: An Introduction*, Oxford: Blackwell.

—— (2003) 'Sustainable time travel: Toward a global politics of the past', in S. Kane (ed.) *The Politics of Archaeology and Identity in a Global Context*, Boston, MA: Archaeological Institute of America.

Hodges, A. and Watson, S. (2000) 'Community-based heritage management: A case study and agenda for research', *International Journal of Heritage Studies*, 6(3), 231–243.

Hodgkin, K. and Radstone, S. (2003a) 'Transforming memory', in K. Hodgkin and S. Radstone (eds) *Contested Pasts: The Politics of Memory*, London: Routledge.

—— (2003b) 'Introduction: Contested pasts', in K. Hodgkin and S. Radstone (eds) *Contested Pasts: The Politics of Memory*, London: Routledge.

Holcomb, B. (1998) 'Gender and heritage interpretation', in D. Uzzell and R. Ballantyne (eds) *Contemporary Issues in Heritage and Environmental Interpretation*, London: Stationery Office.

Hollinshead, K. (1992) ' "White" gaze, "Red" people – shadow visions: The disidentification of "Indians" in cultural tourism', *Leisure Studies*, 11(1): 43–64.

—— (1997) 'Heritage tourism under post-modernity: Truth and the past', in C. Ryan (ed.) *The Tourist Experience: A New Introduction*, London: Cassell.

—— (1999) 'Surveillance of the world of tourism: Foucault and the eye-of-power', *Tourism Management*, 20: 7–23.

hooks, b. (2000) *Where We Stand: Class Matters*, New York: Routledge.

Hope, J. (1993) 'Double bind: Women in the cultural heritage business in NSW', in H. du Cros and L. Smith (eds) *Women in Archaeology: A Feminist Critique*, Canberra: Department of Prehistory, Research School of Pacific Studies, Australian National University.

Hopper-Greenhill, E. (1991) *Museum and Gallery Education*, Leicester: Leicester University Press.

Hubert, J. and Fforde, C. (2005) 'The reburial issue in the 21C', in G. Corsane (ed.) *Heritage, Museums and Galleries: An Introductory Reader*, London: Routledge.

Hufford, M. (ed) (1994) *Conserving Culture: A New Discourse on Heritage*, Urbana, IL: University of Illinois Press.

Hunter, J. and Ralston, I. (eds) (1993) *Archaeological Resource Management in the UK: An Introduction*, Stroud: Alan Sutton.

Hunter, M. (1981) 'The preconditions of preservation: A historical perspective', in D. Lowenthal and M. Binney (eds) *Our Past Before Us, Why Do We Save It?*, London: Temple Smith.

Hutton, G. (2005) *Coal not Dole: Memories of the 1984/85 Miners' Strike*, Catrine: Stenlake Publishing.

Huyssen, A. (2003) *Present Pasts, Urban Palimpsests and the Politics of Memory*, Stanford, CA: Stanford University Press.

ICOMOS (1964) *International Charter for the Conservation and Restoration of Monuments and Sites (Venice Charter)*.

—— (1982) *Historic Gardens (Florence Charter)*.

—— (1987) *Charter for the Conservation of Historic Towns and Urban Areas (Washington Charter)*.

—— (1990) *Convention on the Means of Prohibiting and Preventing the Illicit Import, Export and Transfer of Ownership of Cultural Property.*

—— (1994) *The Nara Document on Authenticity.*

—— (1996) *Charter on the Protection and Management of Underwater Cultural Heritage.*

—— (1999a) *Charter on the Built Vernacular Heritage.*

—— (1999b) *International Cultural Tourism Charter.*

Inglehart, R. and Baker, W. (2000) 'Modernisation, cultural change, and the persistance of traditional values', *American Sociological Review*, 65: 19–51.

Ingold, T. (1993) 'The temporality of the landscape', *World Archaeology*, 25(2): 152–174.

Isaacs, A. and Monk, J. (eds) (1987) *The Cambridge Illustrated Dictionary of British Heritage*, Cambridge: Cambridge University Press.

Isaacson, K. and Ford, S. (2005) 'Looking forward – looking back: Shaping a shared future', in C. Smith and H. M. Wobst (eds) *Indigenous Archaeologies: Decolonizing Theory and Practice*, London: Routledge.

Jaimes, M. (1992) 'Federal Indian identification policy: A usurpation of indigenous sovereignty in North America', in M. Jaimes (ed.) *The State of Native America: Genocide, Colonization and Resistance*, Boston, MA: South End Press.

Jenkins, J. (1994) *From Acorn to Oak Tree: The Growth of the National Trust, 1895–1994*, London: Macmillan.

Jenkins, T. (2003) 'Burying the evidence', *Spiked Culture*, at: http://www.spiked-online.com (accessed 4 June 2004).

John Carr and Associates (2000) *The Tolpuddle Martyrs: From Arrest, Through Hell, to Freedom*, London: Trades Union Congress.

Johnston, C. (1992) *What is Social Value?*, Canberra: Australian Government Publishing Service.

—— (1993) 'Gaps in the record: Finding women's places', in H. du Cros and L. Smith (eds) *Women in Archaeology: A Feminist Critique*, Canberra: Department of Prehistory, Research School of Pacific Studies, Australian National University.

Jokilehto, J. (1999) *A History of Architectural Conservation*, Amsterdam: Elsevier, Butterworth, Heinemann.

Jones, D. and Harris, R. (1997) 'Contending for the dead', *Nature*, 386: 15–16.

Jones, M. and Rotherham, I. D. (eds) (1998) *Landscapes – Perception, Recognition and Management: Reconciling the Impossible?* Sheffield: Wildtrack Publishing.

Jones, S. (2005) 'Making place, resisting displacement: Conflicting national and local identities in Scotland', in J. Littler and R. Naidoo (eds) *The Politics of Heritage: The Legacies of 'Race'*, London: Routledge.

Kammen, M. (1991) *Mystic Chords of Memory: The Transformation of Tradition in American Culture*, New York: Knof.

Kane, S. (2003) 'The politics of archaeology and identity in a global context', in S. Kane (ed.) *The Politics of Archaeology and Identity in a Global Context*, Boston, MA: Archaeological Institute of America.

Kawashima, N. (1999) 'Knowing the public: A review of museum marketing literature and research', *Museum Management and Curatorship*, 17(1): 21–39.

Keith, M. and Pile, S. (eds) (1993) *Place and the Politics of Identity*, London: Routledge.

Kerr, J.S. (1990) *The Conservation Plan*, Sydney: NSW National Trust.

King, T. (1998) *Cultural Resource Laws and Practice: An Introductory Guide*, Walnut Creek, CA: AltaMira.

—— (2002) *Thinking about Cultural Resource Management: Essays From the Edge*, Walnut Creek, CA: AltaMira.

King, T., Hickman, P. and Berg, G. (1977) *Anthropology in Historic Preservation: Caring for Culture's Clutter*, New York: Academic Press.

Kirshenblatt-Gimblett, B. (1998) *Destination Culture: Tourism, Museums and Heritage*, Berkeley, CA: University of California Press.

—— (2004) 'Intangible heritage as metacultural production', *Museum International*, 56(1–2): 52–64.

Klein, K.L. (2000) 'On the emergence of *memory* in historical discourse', *Representations*, 69: 127–150.

Knecht, M. and Niedermüller, P. (2002) 'The politics of cultural heritage: An urban approach', *Ethnologia Europea*, 32(2): 89–104.

Knell, S.J. (2003) 'The shape of things to come: Museums in the technological landscape', *Museum and Society*, 1(3): 132–146.

Kristiansen, K. (1984) 'Denmark', in H. Cleere (ed.) *Approaches to the Archaeological Heritage: A Comparative Study of World Cultural Resource Systems*, Cambridge: Cambridge University Press.

Kurin, R. (2002) 'Comments', *Current Anthropology*, 43(1): 144–145.

—— (2004) 'Safeguarding intangible cultural heritage in the 2003 UNESCO Convention: A critical appraisal', *Museum International*, 56(1–2): 66–76.

Lahn, J. (1996) 'Dressing up the dead: Archaeology, the Kow Swamp remains and some related problems with heritage management', in L. Smith and A. Clarke (eds) *Issues in Archaeological Management*, St Lucia: Tempus Publications, University of Queensland.

Lake, M. (1991) 'Historical homes', *Australian Historical Studies*, 24: 46–54.

—— (1992) 'The politics of respectability', in G. Whitlock and D. Carter (eds) *Images of Australia*, St Lucia: University of Queensland Press.

Langford, R. (1983) 'Our heritage – your playground', *Australian Archaeology*, 16: 1–6.

Langton, M. (1995) '*Well, I Heard it on the Radio and & Saw it on the Television . . .*', North Sydney: Australian Film Commission.

Lattas, A. (1992) 'Primitivism, nationalism and individualism in Australian popular culture' in B. Attwood and J. Arnold (eds), *Power, Knowledge and Aborigines*, Victoria: La Trobe University Press, pp. 45–58.

Layton, R. (1989) *Who Needs the Past? Indigenous Values and Archaeology*, London: Unwin Hyman.

Leone, M.P., Mullins, P.R., Creveling, M.C., Hurst, L., Jackson-Nash, B., Jones, L.D., Jopling-Kaiser, H., Logan, G.C. and Warner, M.S. (1995) 'Can an African-American historical archaeology be an alternative voice?', in I. Hodder, M. Shanks, A. Alexandri, V. Buchli, J. Carman, J. Last and G. Lucas (eds) *Interpreting Archaeology*, London: Routledge.

Leone, M.P., Potter, P.B., Jnr and Shackel, P.A. (1987) 'Toward a critical archaeology', *Current Anthropology*, 28(3): 283–302.

Lewis, B. (2003) *Up Sticks and a Job for Life: Voices from the Selby Coalfield*, Pontefract: Pontefract Press.

Light, D. (2000) 'Gazing on communism: Heritage tourism and post-communist identities in Germany, Hungary and Romania', *Tourism Geographies*, 2(2): 157–176.

Ling Wong, J. (1999) 'Multicultural interpretation and access to heritage', unpublished paper, Back Environment Network, England.

—— (2000) 'Visualising heritage participation by ethnic groups', unpublished paper, Back Environment Network, England.

Linkon, S. L. and Russo, J. (2002) *Steeltown USA: Work and Memory in Youngstown*, Lawrence, KS: University Press of Kansas.

Lipe, W.D. (1977) 'A conservation model for American archaeology', in M. B. Schiffer (ed.) *Advances in Archaeological Method and Theory*, Volume 5, New York: Academic Press.

Lippert, D. (1997) 'In front of the mirror: Native Americans and academic archaeology', in N. Swidler, K. E. Dongoske, R. Anyon and A. S. Downer (eds) *Native Americans and Archaeologists: Stepping Stones to Common Ground*, Walnut Creek, CA: AltaMira.

Littler, J. and Naidoo, R. (2004) 'White past, multicultural present: Heritage and national stories', in H. Brocklehurst and R. Phillips (eds) *History, Nationhood and the Question of Britain*, Basingstoke: Palgrave Macmillan.

—— (eds) (2005) *The Politics of Heritage: The Legacies of 'Race'*, London: Routledge.

Longhurst, B., Bagnall, G. and Savage, M. (2004) 'Audiences, museums and the English middle class', *Museum and Society*, 2(2): 104–124.

Lorimer, H. (2005) 'Cultural geography: The busyness of being "more-than-representational" ', *Progress in Human Geography*, 29(1): 83–94.

Lourandos, H. (1997) *Continent of Hunter-gatherers: New Perspectives in Australian Prehistory*, Cambridge: Cambridge University Press.

Low, S.M. and Lawrence-Zúñiga, D. (eds) (2003a) *The Anthology of Space and Place: Locating Culture*, Malden, MA: Blackwell.

—— (2003b) 'Locating culture', in S. M. Low and D. Lawrence- Zúñiga (eds) *The Anthology of Space and Place: Locating Culture*, Malden, MA: Blackwell.

Lowenthal, D. (1985) *The Past is a Foreign Country*, Cambridge: Cambridge University Press.

—— (1998) *The Heritage Crusade and the Spoils of History*, second edition, Cambridge: Cambridge University Press.

—— (1999) 'Review: The fall and rise of the stately home by P. Mandler', *Journal of Historical Geography*, 25(2): 294–246.

—— (2005) 'Natural and cultural heritage', *International Journal of Heritage Studies*, 11(1): 81–92.

Luly, J. and Valentine, P.S. (1998) *On the Outstanding Universal Value of the Australian Fossil Mammal Site (Riversleigh/Naracoorte) World Heritage Area*, Townsville: School of Tropical Environment Studies and Geography, James Cook University.

Lumley, R. (2005) 'The debate on heritage reviewed', in G. Corsane (ed.) *Heritage, Museums and Galleries: An Introductory Reader*, London: Routledge.

Luud, A., Liblik, V. and Sepp, M. (2003) 'Landscape evaluation in industrial areas', *Oil Shale*, 20(1): 25–32.

Lynott, M. and Wylie, A. (2000) 'Stewardship: The central principle of archaeological ethics', in M. Lynott and A. Wylie (eds) *Ethics in Archaeology*, Washington, DC: Society for American Archaeology.

Maaka, R. and Fleras, A. (2000) 'Engaging with indigeneity: Tino Rangatiratanga in Aotearoa', in D. Ivison, P. Patton and W. Sanders (eds) *Political Theory and the Rights of Indigenous Peoples*, Cambridge: Cambridge University Press.

Macalister, T. (2002) 'Selby closes with loss of 5,000 jobs', *Guardian Unlimited*, at: http://www.gardian.co.uk/recession/story/0,7369,756148,00.html (accessed 1 November 2005).

McBryde, I. (1993) 'Foreword: "In her right place . . ."? Women in archaeology, past and present', in H. du Cros and L. Smith (eds) *Women in Archaeology: A Feminist Critique*, Canberra: Department of Prehistory, Research School of Pacific Studies, Australian National University.

MacCannell, D. (1973) 'Staged authenticity: Arrangements of social space in tourist settings', *American Journal of Sociology*, 79(3): 589–603.

—— (1999) *The Tourist: A New Theory of the Leisure Class*, Berkeley, CA: University of California Press.

McCrone, D., Morris, A. and Kiely, R. (1995) *Scotland – The Brand: The Making of Scottish Heritage*, Edinburgh: Edinburgh University Press.

Macdonald, S. (1997) 'A people's story? Heritage, identity and authenticity', in C. Rojek and J. Urry (eds) *Touring Cultures: Transformations of Travel and Theory*, London: Routledge.

—— (2003) 'Museums, national, postnational and transcultural identities', *Museum and Society*, (1): 1–16.

Macdonald, S. and Shaw, C. (2004) 'Uncovering Ancient Egypt: The Petrie Museum and its public', in N. Merriman (ed.) *Public Archaeology*, London: Routledge.

McGimsey, C.R. (1972) *Public Archaeology*, New York: Seminar Press.

McGrath, A. (1997) 'Sexuality and Australian identities', in W. Hudson and G. Bolton (eds) *Creating Australia: Changing Australian History*, St Leonards, Sydney: Allen and Unwin.

McGuire, R.H. (1992) 'Archaeology and the first Americans', *American Antiquity*, 94(4): 816–832.

McIntosh, A. and Prentice, R. (1999) 'Affirming authenticity: Consuming cultural heritage', *Annals of Tourism Research*, 26(3): 589–612.

—— (2004) 'Tourist's appreciation of Maori culture in New Zealand', *Tourism Management*, 25(1): 1–15.

McLean, F. (2006) 'Introduction: Heritage and identity', *International Journal of Heritage Studies*, 12(1): 3–7.

McManamon, F. (1996) 'The Antiquities Act – setting basic preservation policies', *Cultural Resource Management*, 19(7): 18–23.

McNiven, I. and Russell, L. (2005) *Appropriated Pasts: Indigenous Peoples and the Colonial Culture of Archaeology*, Walnut Creek, CA: AltaMira.

Malcolm-Davies, J. (2004) 'Borrowed robes: The educational value of costumed interpretation at historic sites', *International Journal of Heritage Studies*, 10(3): 277–293.

Mandler, P. (1996) 'Nationalising the country house', in M. Hunter (ed.) *Preserving the Past: The Rise of Heritage in Modern Britain*, Stroud: Alan Sutton.

—— (1997) *The Fall and Rise of the Stately Home*, New Haven, CT: Yale University Press.

Manidis Roberts (consultants) (1998) 'Riversleigh Management Strategy', Exhibition Draft, unpublished Report to the Queensland Department of Environment, Brisbane.

Mansfield, N. (2004) 'Radical banners as sites of memory: The National Banner survey', in P. A. Pickering and A. Tyrrell (eds) *Contested Sites: Commemoration, Memorial and Popular Politics in Nineteenth Century Britain*, London: Ashgate.

Markwell, S., Bennett, M. and Ravenscroft, N. (1997) 'The changing market for heritage tourism: A case study of visitors to historic houses in England', *International Journal of Heritage Studies*, 3(2): 95–108.

Marston, G. (2004) *Social Policy and Discourse Analysis: Policy Change in Public Housing*, Aldershot: Ashgate.

Mason, R. (2004) 'Conflict and complement: An exploration of the discourses informing the concept of the socially inclusive museum in contemporary Britain', *International Journal of Heritage Studies*, 10(1): 49–73.

—— (2005) 'Museums, galleries and heritage: Sites of meaning-making and communication', in G. Corsane (ed.) *Heritage, Museums and Galleries: An Introductory Reader*, London: Routledge.

Massey, D. (1994) *Space, Place and Gender*, Cambridge: Polity Press.

Mathers, C., Darvill, T. and Little, B.J. (eds) (2005) *Heritage of Value, Archaeology of Renown: Reshaping Archaeological Assessment and Significance*, Gainesville, FL: University Press of Florida.

Meaney, N. (2001) 'Britishness and Australian identity', *Australian Historical Studies*, 116: 76–90.

Means, R. with Wolf, M. (1995) *Where White Men Fear to Tread: The Autobiography of Russell Means*, New York: St Martin's Griffin.

Meighan, C. (1984) 'Archaeology: Science or sacrilege?' in E. Green (ed.) *Ethics and Values in Archaeology*, New York: Free Press.

—— (1992) 'Some scholars' views on reburial', *American Antiquity*, 57(4): 704–710.

Mellor, M. and Stephenson, C. (2005) 'The Durham Miners' Gala and the spirit of community', *Community Development Journal*, 40(3): 343–351.

Menon, A.G.K. (2002) 'Conservation in India – a Search for Direction', at: http://www.architexturez.net/+/subject-listing/000058.html (accessed 25 May 2005).

Merriman, N. (1989) 'Museum visiting as a cultural phenomenon', in P. Vergo (ed.) *The New Museology*, London: Reaktion Books.

—— (1991) *Beyond the Glass Case*, Leicester: Leicester University Press.

—— (2004) 'Involving the public in museum archaeology', in N. Merriman (ed.) *Public Archaeology*, London: Routledge.

Meskell, L. (2001) 'Archaeologies of identity', in I. Hodder (ed.) *Archaeological Theory Today*, Cambridge: Polity Press.

—— (2002) 'The intersections of identity and politics in archaeology', *Annual Review of Anthropology*, 31: 279–301.

—— (2003) 'Pharaonic legacies: Postcolonialism, heritage and hyperreality', in S. Kane (ed.) *The Politics of Archaeology and Identity in a Global Context*, Boston, MA: Archaeological Institute of America.

Mihesuah, D. (2000) 'American Indians, anthropologists, pothunters, and repatriation: Ethical, religious, and political differences', in D. Mihesuah (ed.) *Repatriation Reader: Who Owns American Indian Remains?*, Lincoln, NE: University of Nebraska.

Miller, J. (1986) *Koori: A Will to Win*, Sydney: Angus and Robertson.

Milne, S. (2004) *The Enemy Within: Thatcher's Secret War Against the Miners*, London: Verso.

Minthorn, A. (1996) 'Human remains should be reburied', at: http://www.umatilla.nsn.us/kennman.html (accessed 16 January 2003).

Misztal, B.A. (2003) *Theories of Social Remembering*, Maidenhead: Open University Press.

—— (2004) 'The sacralisation of memory', *European Journal of Social Theory*, 7(1): 67–84.

Morris, A. (1877) *Manifesto of the Society for the Protection of Ancient Buildings*, London: Society for the Protection of Ancient Buildings.

MORI (2000) *Attitudes Towards the Heritage: Research Studies Conducted for English Heritage*, London: English Heritage.

Moser, S. (1995) 'Archaeology and its disciplinary culture: The professionalisation of Australian prehistoric archaeology', unpublished PhD thesis, University of Sydney.

Mowljarlai, D. and Peck, C. (1987) 'Ngarinyin cultural continuity: A project to teach the young people the culture, including the re-painting of Wandjina rock art sites', *Australian Aboriginal Studies*, 2: 71–73.

Mowljarlai, D., Vinnicombe, P., Ward, G.K. and Chippendale, C. (1988) 'Repainting of images on rock in Australia and the maintenance of Aboriginal culture', *Antiquity*, 62: 690–696.

Moyo, S.P.C. and Sumaili, T.W.C. (1985) *Sub-regional Seminar on Oral Traditions*, Lusaka: Division for Culture Research, Institute for African Studies, University of Zambia.

Munjeri, D. (2004) 'Tangible and intangible heritage: From difference to convergence', *Museum International*, 56(1–2): 12–20.

Murray, T. (1989) 'The history, philosophy and sociology of archaeology: The case of the Ancient Monuments Protection Act 1882', in V. Pinsky and A. Wylie (eds) *Critical Traditions in Contemporary Archaeology*, Cambridge: Cambridge University Press.

Murtagh, W.J. (1997) *Keeping Time: The History and Theory of Preservation in America*, New York: Wiley.

Museums Australia (1999) 'Policies: Continuous cultures ongoing responsibilities', at: http://www.museumsaustralia.org.au/structure/policies/ppno/ccor.htm (accessed 22 March 2004).

Nadel-Klein, J. (2003) *Fishing for Heritage: Modernity and Loss Along the Scottish Coast*, Oxford: Berg.

National Trust (2005) 'The charity', at: http://www.nationaltrust.org.uk/main/ w-trust/w-thecharity.htm (accessed 9 January 2006).

Nas, P. (2002) 'Masterpieces of oral and intangible culture: Reflections on the UNESCO World Heritage List', *Current Anthropology*, 43(1): 139–148.

Ndoro, W. and Pwiti, G. (2001) 'Heritage management in southern Africa: Local, national and international discourse', *Public Archaeology*, 2(1): 21–34.

Newman, A. (2005a) ' "Social exclusion zone" and "the feelgood factor" ', in G. Corsane (ed.) *Heritage, Museums and Galleries: An Introductory Reader*, London: Routledge.

—— (2005b) 'Understanding the social impact of museums, galleries and heritage though the concept of capital', in G. Corsane (ed.) *Heritage, Museums and Galleries: An Introductory Reader*, London: Routledge.

Newman, A. and Mclean, F. (1998) 'Heritage builds communities: The application of

331

heritage resources to the problems of social exclusion', *International Journal of Heritage Studies*, 4(4–3): 143–153.

—— (2004) 'Editorial', *International Journal of Heritage Studies*, 10(1): 5–10.

Nicholas, G.P. (2001) 'The past and future of indigenous archaeology: global challenges, North American perspectives, Australian prospects', *Australian Archaeology*, 52: 29–40.

—— (2005) 'The persistence of memory; the politics of desire: Archaeological impacts on Aboriginal peoples and their response', in C. Smith and H. M. Wobst (eds) *Indigenous Archaeologies: Decolonizing Theory and Practice*, London: Routledge.

Nicholas, G.P. and Andrews, T.D. (eds) (1997) *At a Crossroads: Archaeology and First Peoples in Canada*, Burnaby: Archaeology Press, Simon Fraser University.

Nora, P. (1989) 'Between memory and history: *Les Lieux de Memoire*', *Representations*, 26(Spring): 7–24.

Norfolk (Duke of Norfolk) (1987) 'Forward', in A. Isaacs and J. Monk (eds) *The Cambridge Illustrated Dictionary of British Heritage*, Cambridge: Cambridge University Press.

NWS (1993a) ' "Dinosaur Country" tag a boost for NW tourism', *North Western Star*, 17 September.

—— (1993b) 'Isa tardy marketing tourism', *North Western Star*, 28 April.

—— (1993c) 'Editorial: Moderate plans for centre', *North Western Star*, 10 June.

—— (1994a) 'Editorial: World Heritage equals bonanza', *North Western Star*, 20 December.

—— (1994b) 'Heritage listing welcome', *North Western Star*, 19 December.

—— (1994c) 'Disneyland, science theme for new tourist centre', *North Western Star*, 11 June.

—— (1995) 'Growth through fossil sharing', *North Western Star*, 1 June.

—— (1996) 'Editorial: Fossils will mean tourism future', *North Western Star*, 27 June.

—— (1997) 'Centre finalist in State awards', *North Western Star*, 24 June.

—— (1999) 'Fossil boon for Isa', *North Western Star*, 18 June.

ODPM (Office of the Deputy Prime Minister) (n.d.) 'Regeneration of former coal-field areas', at: http://www.odpm.gov.uk/stellent/groups/odpm_urbanpolicy/documents/pdf/odpm_urbpol_pdf_607983.pdf (accessed 6 November 2005).

Office of National Statistics (2004) *The National Statistics Socio-Economic Classification User Manual*, London: Her Majesty's Stationery Office.

Olick, J.K. (1999) 'Collective memory: The two cultures', *Sociological Theory*, 17(3): 333–348.

Oliver, B. and Reeves, A. (2003) 'Crossing disciplinary boundaries: Labour history and museum studies', *Labour History*, at: http://www.historycooperative.org/journals/lab/85/oliver.html (accessed 1 August 2005).

Olsen, B. (2001) 'Excavating the other: European archaeology in the age of globalisation', in K. Kobylinski (ed.) *Quo Vadis Archaeologia: Whither European Archaeology in the 21st Century?*, Warsaw: European Science Foundation.

Owsley, D. (1999) 'From Jamestown to Kennewick: An analogy based on early Americans', in R. Bonnichsen (ed.) *Who Were the First Americans? Proceedings of the 58th Annual Biology Colloquium, Oregon State University*, Covallis: Centre for the Study of the First Americans, Oregon State University.

Pagan-Jimenez, J. (2004) 'Is all archaeology at present a post-colonial one?

Constructivist answers from an eccentric point of view', *Journal of Social Archaeology*, 4(2): 200–213.

Pearce, D. (1989) *Conservation Today*, London: Routledge.

Pearce, S.M. (1992) *Museums, Objects and Collections: A Cultural Study*, Leicester: Leicester University Press.

—— (1998) *Collecting in Contemporary Practice*, London: Sage.

Pearson, M. and Shanks, M. (2001) *Theatre/Archaeology*, London: Routledge.

Pearson, M. and Sullivan, S. (1995) *Looking After Heritage Places*, Melbourne: Melbourne University Press.

Pendlebury, J., Townshend, T. and Gilroy, R. (2004) 'The conservation of the English cultural built heritage: A force for social inclusion?', *International Journal of Heritage Studies*, 10(1): 11–31.

Pennay, B. (1996) 'Reading the local historical environment', in L. Smith and A. Clarke (eds) *Issues in Management Archaeology*, St Lucia: Anthropology Museum, University of Queensland.

Pennebaker, J.W. and Banasik, B.L. (1997) 'On the creation and maintenance of collective memories: History as social psychology', in J. W. Pennebaker, D. Paez and B. Rime (eds) *Collective Memory of Political Events: Social Psychological Perspectives*, Hillsdale, NJ: Lawrence Erlbaum Associates.

Pevsner, N. ([1959] 1986) *The Buildings of England. Yorkshire: The West Riding*, Harmondsworth: Penguin Books.

Philip, J. and Mercer, D. (2002) 'Political pagodas and veiled resistance: Contested urban space in Burma', *Urban Studies*, 39(9): 1587–1610.

Pickering, P.A. (2004) 'The Chartist rites of passage: Commemorating Fergus O'Connor', in P. A. Pickering and A. Tyrrell (eds) *Contested Sites: Commemoration, Memorial and Popular Politics in Nineteenth Century Britain*, London: Ashgate.

Pickering, P.A. and Tyrrell, A. (2004) 'The public memorial of reform: Commemoration and contestation', in P.A. Pickering and A. Tyrrell (eds) *Contested Sites: Commemoration, Memorial and Popular Politics in Nineteenth-Century Britain*, London: Ashgate.

Pickles, A. (2003) 'Prologue', in B. Lewis (ed.) *Up Sticks and a Job for Life: Voices from the Selby Coalfield*, Pontefract: Pontefract Press.

Poirrer, P. (2003) 'Heritage and cultural policy in France under the Fifth Republic', *International Journal of Heritage Studies*, 9(2): 215–225.

Poria, Y., Butler, R. and Airey, D. (2001) 'Clarifying heritage tourism', *Annals of Tourism Research*, 28(4): 1047–1049.

—— (2003) 'The core of heritage tourism', *Annals of Tourism Research*, 30(1): 238–254.

Prentice, R. (1993) *Tourism and Heritage Attractions*, London: Routledge.

—— (1996) 'Managing implosion: The facilitation of insight through the provision of context', *Museum Management and Curatorship*, 15(2): 169–185.

—— (1998) 'Recollections of museum visits: A case study of remembered cultural attraction visiting on the Isle of Man', *Museum Management and Curatorship*, 17(1): 41–64.

—— (2001) 'Experiential cultural tourism: Museums and the marketing of the new romanticism of evoked authenticity', *Museum Management and Curatorship*, 19(1): 5–26.

—— (2005) 'Heritage: A key sector in the "new" tourism', in G. Corsane (ed.) *Heritage, Museums and Galleries: An Introductory Reader*, London: Routledge.

333

Prentice, R., Witt, S. and Hamer, C. (1998) 'Tourism as experience: The case of heritage parks', *Annals of Tourism Research*, 25(1): 1–24.

Pullar, G. (1994) 'The Qikertarmiut and the scientist: Fifty years of clashing world views', in T. Bray and T. Killion (eds) *Reckoning with the Dead: The Larson Bay Repatriation and the Smithsonian Institution*, Washington, DC: Smithsonian Institution.

Purvis, T. and Hunt, A. (1993) 'Discourse, ideology, discourse, ideology, discourse, ideology . . .', *British Journal of Sociology*, 44(3): 473–499.

Rains, A., Muskie, E. S., Widnall, W. B., Hoff, P. H., Tucker, R. R., Gray, G. and Henderson, L. G. (eds) ([1966] 1983) *With Heritage so Rich*, Washington, DC: Landmark Reprint Series, Preservation Press.

Read, P. (2000) *Belonging: Australians, Place and Aboriginal Ownership*, Cambridge: Cambridge University Press.

Reas, P. and Cosgrove, S. (1993) *Flogging a Dead Horse: Heritage, Culture and its Role in Post-Industrial Britain*, Manchester: Cornerhouse.

Reynolds, H. (1987) *The Law of the Land*, Ringwood, Victoria: Penguin Books.

—— (1989) *Dispossession: Black Australians and White Invaders*, Sydney: Allen and Unwin.

Richards, A.J. (1997) *Miners on Strike: Class Solidarity and Division in Britain*, London: Berg.

Richardson, T. and Jensen, O. (2003) 'Linking discourse and space: Towards a cultural sociology of space in analysing spatial policy discourses', *Urban Studies*, 40(1): 7–22.

Riding In, J. (2000) 'Repatriation: A Pawnee's perspective', in D. Mihesuah (ed.) *Repatriation Reader: Who Owns American Indian Remains?*, Lincoln, NE: University of Nabraska.

Rigney, D. and Worby, G. (2005) 'Towards an Indigenous research charter', in C. Smith and H. M. Wobst (eds) *Indigenous Archaeologies: Decolonizing Theory and Practice*, London: Routledge.

Rodman, M.C. (2003) 'Empowering place: Multilocality and multivocality', in S. M. Low and D. Lawrence- Zúñiga (eds) *The Anthology of Space and Place: Locating Culture*, Malden, MA: Blackwell.

Rose, D.B. (1996) *Nourishing Terrains: Australian Aboriginal Views of Landscape and Wilderness*, Canberra: Australian Heritage Commission.

Rose, D.B. and Clarke, A. (eds) (1997) *Tracking Knowledge in North Australian Landscapes*, Darwin: North Australia Research Unit.

Rose, N. (1993) 'Government, authority and expertise in advanced liberalism', *Economy and Society*, 22(3): 283–299.

Rose, N. and Miller, P. (1992) 'Political power beyond the State: Problematics of government', *British Journal of Sociology*, 43: 173–205.

Rosenzweig, R. and Thelen, D. (1998) *The Presence of the Past: Popular Uses of History in American Life*, New York: Columbia University Press.

Ross, M. (2004) 'Interpreting the new museology', *Museum and Society*, 2(2): 84–103.

Rouse, J. (1987) *Knowledge and Power*, Ithaca, NY: Cornell University, Press.

Rowan, Y. and Baram, U. (2004) *Marketing Heritage: Archaeology and the Consumption of the Past*, Walnut Creek, CA: AltaMira.

Ruskin, J. ([1849] 1899) *Seven Lamps of Architecture*, London: George Allen.

Russo, J. and Linkon, S.L. (2005) 'Introduction: What's new about new working-class studies?', in J. Russo and S. L. Linkon (eds) *New Working-class Studies*, Ithaca, NY: Cornell University Press.

Samuel, R. (1994) *Theatres of Memory. Volume 1: Past and Present in Contemporary Culture*, London: Verso.

Sandell, R. (2003) 'Social inclusion, the museum and the dynamics of sectorial change', *Museum and Society*, 1(1): 45–62.

SAVE (1984) 'Mr Lawson, You have Damned our Best Hopes for Britain's Historic Buildings', unpublished pamphlet, London: SAVE Britain's Heritage.

Sayer, A. (1992) *Method in Social Science: A Realist Approach*, second edition, London: Routledge.

SBS (1991) *Vox Populi – Lake Mungo*, Special Broadcasting Service, Australia, Broadcast 10 August, AIATSIS Film Archive Number LV1831.

——— (1993) *From Spirit to Spirit – Mungo Lady*, Special Broadcasting Service, Australia, Broadcast 28 October, AIATSIS Film Archive Number LV2663.

Schadla-Hall, T. (1984) 'Slightly looted: A review of the Jorvik Viking centre', *Museums Journal*, 84(2): 62–4.

——— (2004) 'The comforts of unreason: The importance and relevance of alternative archaeology', in N. Merriman (ed.) *Public Archaeology*, London: Routledge.

Schaffer, K. (1988) *Women and the Bush: Forces of Desire in the Australian Cultural Tradition*, Cambridge: Cambridge University Press.

Schnapp, A. (1984) 'France', in H. Cleere (ed.) *Approaches to the Archaeological Heritage: A Comparative Study of World Cultural Resource Systems*, Cambridge: Cambridge University Press.

Schofield, A.S. (1992) *'Old' Whitwood: From Domesday to VJ Day*, Castleford.

Schouten, F.F.J. (1995) 'Heritage as historical reality', in D. Herbert (ed.) *Heritage, Tourism and Society*, London: Pinter.

Schwarz, B. (2003) ' "Already the past": Memory and historical time', in S. Radstone and K. Hodgkin (eds) *Regimes of Memory*, London: Routledge.

Schwyzer, P. (1999) 'The scouring of the white horse: Archaeology, identity and heritage', *Representations*, 65: 42–62.

Sears, L.J. (2002) 'Comments', *Current Anthropology*, 43(1): 146–147.

Sease, C. (1998) 'Code of ethics for conservation', *International Journal of Cultural Property*, 7: 98–115.

Shackel, P. (2001) 'Public memory and the search for power in American historical archaeology', *American Anthropologist*, 103(3), 655–670.

Shanks, M. (1992) *Experiencing the Past*, London: Routledge.

——— (2004) 'Three rooms: Archaeology and performance', *Journal of Social Archaeology*, 4(2): 147–180.

Shanks, M. and Tilley, C. (1987) *Re-constructing Archaeology: Theory and Practice*, Cambridge: Cambridge University Press.

Silberman, N. (1995) 'Promised lands and chosen peoples: The politics and poetics of archaeological narrative', in P. L. and C. Fawcett Kohl (eds) *Nationalism, Politics and the Practice of Archaeology*, Cambridge: Cambridge University Press, pp. 249–262.

Skeates, R. (2000) *Debating the Archaeological Heritage*, London: Duckworth.

Slack, M. (1998) 'Aborigines, settlers and the native police: A reassessment of the frontier in far northwest Queensland', unpublished BA Honours thesis, University of New South Wales, Department of History.

Smardz Frost, K.H. (2004) 'Archaeology and public education in North America', in N. Merriman (ed.) *Public Archaeology*, London: Routledge.

Smith, C. and Burke, H. (2003) 'In the spirit of the code', in L. J. Zimmerman, K. D. Vitelli and J. Hollowell-Zimmer (eds) *Ethical Issues in Archaeology*, Walnut Creek, CA: AltaMira.

Smith, C. and Wobst, H.M. (eds) (2005) *Indigenous Archaeologies: Decolonizing Theory and Practice*, Routledge: London.

Smith, C. and Zimmerman, L. (eds) (in press) *Kennewick Man: Perspectives on the Ancient One*, Walnut Creek, CA: AltaMira.

Smith, L. (1993) 'Towards a theoretical overview for heritage management', *Archaeological Review from Cambridge*, 12: 55–75.

—— (1995) 'Cultural resource management and feminist expression in Australian archaeology', *Norwegian Archaeological Review*, 28(1): 55–63.

—— (1996) 'Significance concepts in Australian management archaeology', in L. Smith and A. Clarke (eds) *Issues in Management Archaeology*, St Lucia: Anthropology Museum, University of Queensland.

—— (1999) 'The last archaeologist? Material culture and contested identities', *Aboriginal Studies*, 2: 25–34.

—— (2004) *Archaeological Theory and the Politics of Cultural Heritage*, London: Routledge.

Smith, L., Clarke, A. and Allcock, A. (1992) 'Teaching cultural tourism – some comments from the classroom', *Australian Archaeology*, 34: 43–47.

Smith, L., Morgan, A. and van der Meer, A. (2003a) 'Community-driven research in cultural heritage management: The Waanyi Women's History Project', *International Journal of Heritage Studies*, 9(1): 65–80.

Smith, L., Morgan, A. and van der Meer, A. (2003b) 'The Waanyi Women's History Project: A community partnership project, Queensland, Australia', in L. Derry and M. Malloy (eds) *Archaeologists and Local Communities: Partners in Exploring the Past*, Washington, DC: Society for American Archaeology.

Smith, L. and van der Meer, A. (2001) 'Landscape and the negotiation of identity: A case study from Riversleigh, northwest Queensland', in M. Cotter, B. Boyd and J. Gardiner (eds) *Heritage Landscapes: Understanding Place and Communities*, Lismore: Southern Cross University Press.

Smith, P. and Warrior, R. (1996) *Like a Hurricane: The Indian Movement from Alcatraz to Wounded Knee*, New York: New Press.

Spearritt, P. (1991) 'Money, taste and industrial heritage: Conflicts between historical importance and cultural significance', *Australian Historical Studies*, 24: 33–45.

Stanton, C. (2005) 'Serving up culture: Heritage and its discontents at an industrial history site', *International Journal of Heritage Studies*, 11(5): 415–431.

Stapp, D.C. and Burney, M.S. (2002) *Tribal Cultural Resource Management*, Walnut Creek, CA: AltaMira.

Starn, R. (2002) 'Authenticity and historic preservation: Towards an authentic history', *History of the Human Sciences*, 15(1): 1–16.

Stenning, A. (2005) 'Re-placing work: Economic transformations and the shape of a community in post-socialist Poland', *Work, Employment and Society*, 19(2): 235–259.

Stone, L. (1991) 'The public and the private in the stately homes of England, 1500–1990', *Social Research*, 58(1): 227–251.

Strangleman, T. (1999) 'The nostalgia of organisations and the organisation of nostalgia: Past and present in the contemporary railway industry', *Sociology*, 33(4): 725–746.

—— (2005) 'Class memory: Autobiography and the art of forgetting', in J. Russo and S. L. Linkon (eds) *New Working-class Studies*, Ithica, NY: Cornell University Press.

Stratton, M. and Trinder, B. (2000) *Twentieth Centry Industrial Archaeology*, London: E. and F. N. Spon.

Sullivan, S. and Bowdler, S. (eds) (1984) *Site Surveys and Significance Assessments in Australian Archaeology*, Canberra: Department of Prehistory, Research School of Pacific Studies, Australian National University.

Summers, A. (1975) *Damned Whores and God's Police: The Colonisation of Women in Australia*, Ringwood, Victoria: Penguin Books.

Sutton, R.K. (ed.) (2001) *Rally on the High Ground: The National Park Service Symposium on the Civil War*, online book, Ft. Washington, PA: US National Park Service.

Swain, T. (1993) *A Place for Strangers: Towards a History of Australian Aboriginal Being*, Sydney: Cambridge University Press.

Swidler, N., Dongoske, K.E., Anyon, R. and Downer, A.S. (eds) (1997) *Native Americans and Archaeologists: Stepping Stones to Common Ground*, Walnut Creek, CA: AltaMira.

Tarran, M. (1997) 'People, country, and protection of culture and cultural properties', in D. Bird Rose and A. Clarke (eds) *Tracking knowledge in Northern Australian Landscapes*, Darwin: North Australia Research Unit.

Taylor, M. (2003) *The Canal and River Sections of the Aire and Calder Navigation*, Barnsley: Wharncliffe Books.

Taylor, S. (2001) 'Locating and conducting discourse analytic research', in M. Wetherell, S. Taylor and S. J. Yates (eds) *Discourse as Data: A Guide for Analysis*, London: Sage.

Teather, E. and Chow, C. (2003) 'Identity and place: The testament of designated heritage in Hong Kong', *International Journal of Heritage Studies*, 9(2): 93–115.

Thapar, B.K. (1984) 'India', in H. Cleere (ed.) *Approaches to the Archaeological Heritage: A Comparative Study of World Cultural Resource Systems*, Cambridge: Cambridge University Press.

Thoden van Velzen, D. (1996) 'The world of Tuscan tomb robbers: Living with the local community and the ancestors', *International Journal of Cultural Property*, 5: 111–126.

Thrift, N. (2003) 'Performance and . . .', *Environment and Planning A*, 35: 2019–2024.

—— (2004) 'Intensities of feeling: Towards a spatial politics of affect', *Geografiska Annaler*, 86(B): 57–78.

Tilley, C. (1989) 'Excavation as theatre', *Antiquity*, 63: 275–280.

Tinniswood, A. (1989) *A History of Country House Visiting: Five Centuries of Tourism and Taste*, Oxford: Blackwell.

—— (1998) *The Polite Tourist: A History of Country House Visiting*, London: National Trust.

Titchen, S. (1996) 'Changing perceptions and recognition of the environment from cultural and natural heritage to cultural landscapes', in J. Finlayson and A. Jackson-

Nakano (eds) *Heritage and Native Title: Anthropological and Legal Perspectives*, Canberra: Australian Institute of Aboriginal and Torres Straight Islander Studies.

Tjapukai Aboriginal Cultural Park (TAPC) (2004) http://www.tjapukai.com.au (accessed 1 December 2005).

Tolpuddle Martyrs Museum (2001) http://www.tolpuddlemartyrs.org.uk/mus_frms.html (accessed 21 September 2005).

Trapeznik, A. (1997) 'Heritage and public history in New Zealand', *Public History Review*, 5/6.

—— (ed.) (2000) *Common Ground? Heritage and Public Places in New Zealand*, Dunedin: University of Otago Press.

Trentmann, F. (1999) 'Review: Peter Mandler, The fall and rise of the stately home (1997)', *Social History*, 24(1): 95–98.

Tribe, J. (1997) 'The indiscipline of tourism', *Annals of Tourism Research*, 24(3): 638–657.

Trigger, B.G. (1980) 'Archaeology and the image of the American Indian', *American Antiquity*, 45(4): 662–676.

—— (1989) *A History of Archaeological Thought*, Cambridge: Cambridge University Press.

Tsosie, R. (1997) 'Indigenous rights and archaeology', in N. Swidler, K. E. Dongoske, R. Anyon and A. S. Downer (eds) *Native Americans and Archaeologists: Stepping Stones to Common Ground*, Walnut Creek, CA: AltaMira.

Tuan, Y.-F. (2003) *Space and Place: The Perspective of Experience*, Minnesota, MN: University of Minnesota Press.

Tunbridge, J.E. (1998) 'The question of heritage in European cultural conflict', in B. Graham (ed.) *Modern Europe: Place, Culture, Identity*, London: Arnold.

Turnbull, D. (2002) 'Performance and narrative, bodies and movement in the construction of places and objects, spaces and knowledges: The case of the Maltese megaliths', *Theory, Culture and Society*, 19(5–6): 125–143.

Tyrrell, A. and Walvin, J. (2004) 'Whose history is it? Memorialising Britain's involvement in slavery', in P. A. Pickering and A. Tyrrell (eds) *Contested Sites: Commemoration, Memorial and Popular Politics in 19C Britain*, London: Ashgate.

Ucko, P. (2001) ' "Heritage" and "Indigenous peoples" in the 21st century', *Public Archaeology*, 1: 227–238.

UNESCO (1954) *Convention on the Protection of Cultural Property in the Event of Armed Conflict with Regulations for the Execution of the Convention.*

—— (1970) *Convention on the Means of Prohibiting and Preventing the Illicit Import, Export and Transfer of Ownership of Cultural Property.*

—— (1972) *Convention Concerning the Protection of the World Cultural and Natural Heritage.*

—— (1997) *Operational Guidelines for the Implementation of the World Heritage Convention.*

—— (2001a) *Convention on the Protection of the Underwater Cultural Heritage.*

—— (2001b) *First Proclamation of Masterpieces of the Oral and Intangible Heritage of Humanity.*

—— (2001c) *Proclamation of Masterpieces of the Oral and Intangible Heritage of Humanity: Guide for the Presentation of Candidature Files.*

—— (2003a) *Culture{s}: Diversity and Alliance.*

—— (2003b) *Convention for the Safeguarding of the Intangible Cultural Heritage.*

—— (2005) 'About World Heritage: Brief history', at: http://whc.unesco.org/pg.cfm?cid=169 (accessed 26 January 2006).

Urry, J. (1990) *The Tourist Gaze*, London: Sage.

—— (1995) *Consuming Places*, London: Routledge.

—— (1996) 'How societies remember the past', in S. Macdonald and G. Fyfe (eds) *Theorising Museums*, Oxford: Blackwell.

Uzzell, D. and Ballantyne, R. (1998) 'Heritage that hurts: Interpretation in a postmodern world', in D. Uzzell and R. Ballantyne (eds) *Contemporary Issues in Heritage and Environmental Interpretation*, London: Stationery Office.

van der Meer, A. (1997) 'Widtheringyapa: A Predictive Model for the Archaeology of the Riversleigh Management Unit Lawn Hill National Park', unpublished BSc Honours thesis, University of New South Wales.

van Dijk, T.A. (1998) *Ideology: A Multidisciplinary Approach*, London: Sage.

van Leeuwen, T. (1999) 'Discourses of unemployment in New Labour Britain' in R. Wodak and C. Ludwig (eds) *Challenges in a Changing World: Issues in Critical Discourse Analysis*, Wien: Passagen Verlag, pp. 87–100.

van Leeuwen, T. and Wodak, R. (1999) 'Legitimizing immigration control: A discourse-historical analysis', *Discourse Studies*, 1(1): 83–118.

van Zanten, W. (2004) 'Constructing new terminology for intangible cultural heritage', *Museum International*, 56(1–2): 36–44.

Vergo, P. (ed.) (1989) *The New Museology*, London: Reaktion Books.

Waitt, G. (2000) 'Consuming heritage: Perceived historical authenticity', *Annals of Tourism Research*, 27(4): 835–862.

Waitt, G. and McGuirk, P. (1996) 'Marking time: Tourism and heritage representation at Millers Point, Sydney', *Australian Geographer*, 27(1): 11–29.

Wakefield District Multi Agency Information Group (2002) 'The Index of Multiple Deprivation 2000: Understanding What it Means for Wakefield', unpublished report.

Walsh, K. (1992) *The Representation of the Past: Museums and Heritage in the Post-modern World*, London: Routledge.

Walvin, J. (2000) *Britain's Slave Empire*, Stroud: Tempus Publishing.

Ward, R. (1958) *The Australian Legend*, Melbourne: Oxford University Press.

Waterton, E. (2005a) 'Whose sense of place? Reconciling archaeological perspectives with community values: Cultural landscapes in England', *International Journal of Heritage Studies*, 11(4): 309–326.

—— (2005b) 'The communicability of "heritage" without words: A discourse-analytical approach', unpublished paper, Theoretical Archaeological Group Conference, Glasgow.

Waterton, E., Smith, L. and Campbell, G. (2006) 'The utility of discourse analysis to heritage studies: The Burra Charter and social inclusion', *International Journal of Heritage Studies*, 12(4): 339–55.

Watkins, J. (2000) *Indigenous Archaeology: American Indian Values and Scientific Practice*, Walnut Creek, CA: AltaMira.

—— (2001) 'Yours, mine, or ours? Conflicts between archaeologists and ethnic groups', in T. Bray (ed.) *The Future of the Past: Archaeologists, Native Americans, and Repatriation*, New York: Garland Publishing.

—— (2003) 'Beyond the margin: American Indians, First Nations, and archaeology in North America', *American Antiquity*, 68(2): 273–285.

—— (2004) 'Becoming American or becoming Indian? NAGPRA, Kennewick and cultural affiliation', *Journal of Social Archaeology*, 4(1): 60–80.

—— (2005) 'The politics of American archaeology: Cultural resources, cultural affiliation and Kennewick', in C. Smith and H. M. Wobst (eds) *Indigenous Archaeologies: Decolonizing Theory and Practice*, London: Routledge.

Watkins, J., Goldstein, L., Vitelli, K. and Jenkins, L. (2000) 'Accountability: Responsibilities of archaeologists to other interest groups', in M. Lynott and A. Wylie (eds) *Ethics in American Archaeology*, Washington, DC: Society for American Archaeology.

Weideger, P. (1994) *Gilding the Acorn: Behind the Facade of the National Trust*, London: Simon and Schuster.

Weiner, A.L. (1992) *Inalienable Possessions: The Paradox of Keeping-While-Giving*, Berkeley, CA: University of California Press.

Welldon Finn, R. ([1937] 1948) *The English Heritage*, London: Macdonald and Company.

Wertsch, J.V. (2002) *Voices of Collective Remembering*, Cambridge: Cambridge University Press.

West, P. (2003) 'Uncovering and interpreting women's history at historic house museums', in G. Dubrow and J. B. Goodman (eds) *Restoring Women's History through Historic Preservation*, Baltimore, MD: Johns Hopkins University Press.

West, S. (1999) 'Social space and the English country house', in S. Tarlow and S. West (eds) *The Familiar Past? Archaeologies of Later Historical Britain*, London: Routledge.

Wetherell, M. (2001) 'Introduction', in M. Wetherell, S. Taylor and S. Yates (eds) *Discourse Theory and Practice*, London: Sage.

White, R. (1992) 'Inventing Australia', in G. Whitlock and D. Carter (eds) *Images of Australia*, St Lucia: University of Queensland Press.

—— (2001) 'Cooee across the strand: Australian travellers in London and the performance of national identity', *Australian Historical Studies*, 116: 109–127.

White Deer, G. (1997) 'Return of the sacred: Spirituality and the scientific imperative', in N. Swidler, K. E. Dongoske, R. Anyon and A. S. Downer (eds) *Native Americans and Archaeologists: Stepping Stones to Common Ground*, Walnut Creek, CA: AltaMira.

Whitehead, C. (2005) 'Visiting with suspicion: Recent perspectives on art museums', in G. Corsane (ed.) *Heritage, Museums and Galleries: An Introductory Reader*, London: Routledge.

Whiteley, P. (2002) 'Archaeology and oral tradition', *American Antiquity*, 67(3): 405–415.

Wilders, D.G. (1995) *History of Castleford*, Castleford: Briton Press.

—— (2003) *Hartleys: Brick by Brick, Pot by Pot*, Castleford: Castleford Press.

Willems, W. (2001) 'Archaeological heritage management and research', in K. Kobylinski (ed.) *Quo Vadis Archaeologia: Whither European Archaeology in the 21st Century?*, Warsaw: European Science Foundation.

Williamson, T. (1995) *Polite Landscapes: Gardens and Society in Eighteenth-century England*, Stroud: Sutton Publishing.

Wilson, R. (2001) 'Novelty and amusement? Visiting the Georgian country house', *Historian*, 70: 4–9.

World Archaeological Congress (WAC) (1989) *The Vermillion Accord on Human Remains*.

Worsley, L. (2004) 'Changing notions of authenticity: Presenting a castle over four centuries', *International Journal of Heritage Studies*, 10(2): 123–149.

Wright, P. (1985) *On Living in an Old Country*, London: Verso.

—— (1991) *A Journey Through Ruins – The Last Days of London*, London: Hutchinson Radius.

Wylie, A. (1992) 'On skepticism, philosophy and archaeological science', *Current Anthropology*, 33(2): 209–213.

Yoshida, K. (2004) 'The museum and the intangible cultural heritage', *Museum International*, 56(1–2): 108–112.

Young, J. (1989) 'The biography of a memorial icon: Nathan Rapoport's Warsaw Ghetto monument', *Representations*, 26(Spring): 69–106.

Zarmati, L. (1995) 'Popular archaeology, and the archaeologist as hero', in J. Balme and W. Beck (eds) *Gendered archaeology*, Canberra: Department of Prehistory, Research School of Pacific Studies, Australian National University.

Zimmerman, L.J. (1989a) 'Made radical by my own: An archaeologist learns to accept reburial', in R. Layton (ed.) *Conflict in the Archaeology of Living Traditions*, London: Unwin Hyman.

—— (1989b) 'Human bones as symbols of power: Aboriginal American belief systems toward bones and "grave-robbing" archaeologists', in R. Layton (ed.) *Conflict in the Archaeology of Living Traditions*, London: Unwin Hyman.

—— (1998) 'When data become people: Archaeological ethics, reburial, and the past as public heritage', *International Journal of Cultural Property*, 7(1): 69–86.

—— (2000) 'A new and different archaeology? With a postscript on the impact of the Kennewick dispute', in D. Mihesuah (ed.) *Repatriation Reader: Who Owns American Indian Remains?*, Lincoln, NK: University of Nebraska.

—— (2001) 'Usurping Native American voice', in T. Bray (ed.) *The Future of the Past: Archaeologists, Native Americans, and Repatriation*, New York: Garland Publishing.

—— (2005) 'First, be humble: Working with Indigenous peoples and other descendant communities', in C. Smith and H. M. Wobst (eds) *Indigenous Archaeologies: Decolonizing Theory and Practice*, London: Routledge.

INDEX

Note: page numbers in *italics* refer to illustrations

Abercrombie, N. 67, 68, 270, 292
Aboriginal people: appropriation of culture
    172–3; cultural place 297; flag 293;
    heritage management 289; landscape
    170–1, 174–8, 309[1]n1; *see also*
    Indigenous people
Aboriginal Tent Embassy 293
aesthetics 4, 90
Africa 282
Aikawa, N. 106
Alcatraz Island 278
Amanas religious community 125
American Indian Movement 292
Ancient Monuments Act (UK) 22, 25
Ancient Monuments and Archaeological
    Areas Act (UK) 25
Anderson, B. 63–4
anthropology 282
Antiquities Act 19
ANZAC Day 201
Appleton, J. 296
appropriation of culture 171–3, 188
archaeological heritage management 26, 279
archaeologists 277, 278, 279–80, 284
archaeology: anthropology 282; burials 288;
    Castleford 240, 255; heritage archaeology
    45; masculinity 180; sites 19, 72, 94
Archer, M. 165, 167, 180, 182–3
architecture 19, 94, 96
aristocracy 145–6, 148; criticised 120;
    England 116; English country houses 161;
    identity 294; trade unions 232; visitors
    137–8; *see also* deference
Armistice Day 69
Arthur, J. 169, 173, 177
Ashton, P. 201

Ashworth, G. 80–2
assimilation 150, 171, 234
Aswan High Dam 95
*Athens Charter for the Restoration of Historic
    Monuments* 21, 89
Attenborough, Sir D. 181
audience factors 44, 67–8, 70, 104–5; *see also*
    visitors
Audley End *115,* 128
Australia 24; appropriation 171–2;
    authorized heritage discourse 162–3, 173;
    coins 172; conservation 23–4; dance
    theatre 291–2; history 37; ICOMOS 102,
    103; Land Rights Movement 292–3;
    landscape 168–9; Midland Railway
    Workshops 250–1; myths 170, 171, 172,
    180; national identity 169, 171–2;
    National Parks 309[1]n2; National Trust
    24–5; Native Title Act 172, 191;
    naturalization of heritage 171–2; NSW
    Heritage Act 25; post-colonialism 27; *see
    also* Aboriginal people; Burra Charter;
    Riversleigh; Waanyi
Australian Archaeological Association 280
Australian Fossil Mammal Sites World
    Heritage Area 163
authenticity 90; emotion 67, 218; English
    country houses 124–5; experience 71,
    73–4; heritage 27–8, 40, 71; landscape
    169–70; museums 195; social history
    museums 236; tourism 124; UNESCO 94
authority 89, 105–6
authorized heritage discourse (AHD) 4–5,
    28, 29–34, 44, 48–9, 299–308; Australia
    162–3, 173; conservation 88; cultural
    change 192, 299–300; dissonance 88;

Related titles from Routledge

Archaeological Theory and the Politics of Cultural Heritage
Laurajane Smith

'Smith's stunning book will change the discipline.' – *Larry J. Zimmerman, University of Iowa*

This controversial book is a survey of how relationships between indigenous peoples and the archaeological establishment have got into difficulty and a crucial pointer to how to move forward from these problems.

With lucid appraisals of key debates such as NAGPRA, Kennewick and the repatriation of Tasmanian artefacts, Laurajane Smith dissects the nature and consequences of this clash of cultures. Smith explores how indigenous communities in the US and Australia have confronted the pre-eminence of archaeological theory and discourse in the way the material remains of their past are cared for and controlled, and how this has challenged traditional archaeological thought and practice.

Essential reading for all those concerned with developing a just and equal dialogue between the two parties, and the role of archaeology in the research and management of their heritage.

ISBN10: 0–415–31832–7 (hbk)
ISBN10: 0–415–31833–5 (pbk)

ISBN13: 978–0–415–31832–7 (hbk)
ISBN13: 978–0–415–31833–4 (pbk)

Available at all good bookshops
For ordering and further information please visit:
www.routledge.com